SHAMROCKS AMONG THE POPPIES

Musa Qal'eh 2006: A Bloody Siege… And The Failures Behind it

Lt Col (Retd) Derek A. Plews VR

Helion & Company

Helion & Company Limited
Unit 8 Amherst Business Centre
Budbrooke Road
Warwick
CV34 5WE
England
Tel. 01926 499 619
Email: info@helion.co.uk
Website: www.helion.co.uk
Twitter: @helionbooks
Visit our blog https://helionbooks.wordpress.com/

Published by Helion & Company 2025
Designed and typeset by Mach 3 Solutions (www.mach3solutions.co.uk)
Cover designed by Paul Hewitt, Battlefield Design (www.battlefield-design.co.uk)

Text © Lt Col (Retd) Derek A. Plews VR 2025
Images © as individually credited
Maps drawn by George Anderson © Helion & Company Limited 2025

Every reasonable effort has been made to trace copyright holders and to obtain their permission for the use of copyright material. The author and publisher apologize for any errors or omissions in this work, and would be grateful if notified of any corrections that should be incorporated in future reprints or editions of this book.

ISBN 978-1-804518-09-0

British Library Cataloguing-in-Publication Data.
A catalogue record for this book is available from the British Library.

All rights reserved. No part of this publication may be reproduced, stored in a retrieval system, or transmitted, in any form, or by any means, electronic, mechanical, photocopying, recording or otherwise, without the express written consent of Helion & Company Limited.

For details of other military history titles published by Helion & Company Limited contact the above address, or visit our website: http://www.helion.co.uk.

We always welcome receiving book proposals from prospective authors.

Contents

Musa Qala by Ranger Adam Dunlop		v
Foreword		vi
Glossary		viii
Author's note		xvi
Introduction		xviii
Part 1		21
1	The Road to Helmand…	23
	Cool Britannia and Blair's Global Britain	24
	The Global War on Terror	26
2	NATO – A Broken Lance	28
	New NATO Strategy – Same Old Problems	31
3	The Iraq Effect	37
	Party and Nation Split	38
	Shock and Awe…and Then What?	41
	Go First…Go Fast…Go Home…	43
	Bloody August	48
	Fallujah	51
4	A Twenty-first Century Version of the Great Game	60
	The NATO Plan for Afghanistan	61
	A Mission in Crisis	63
	Red Cards and Reluctance	63
Part 2		69
5	Intelligence Failure	71
	A Little Knowledge…	74
	All Change at the MOD	78
6	Hello Helmand	84
7	The Mission Begins	91
	Command…Control…Confusion…	92
	Opium Wars	94
	Protecting the Weak	98
	The Road to Sangin	104
	The Mirror Crack'd…	107
	Reinforcements	109

Part 3		117
8	The Taliban	119
Part 4		145
9	Musa Qal'eh – a Modern Rorke's Drift?	147
	A Rickety Afghan Town	150
10	Basra, Baghdad, Bastion…	154
	Band of Musa Muckers	159
	Operation Snakebite	164
	First Blood	170
	Taliban Rocket Man	174
11	The Birth of Easy Company	177
	The Griffins Depart	181
	Welcome to Musa Qal'eh	182
	Death Comes Calling	185
	Friendly Fire?	191
12	Ceasefire	204
	'You Stop Shooting at us, We'll Stop Shooting at you…'	205
	Extraction	213
Part 5		219
13	The Aftermath…	221
	The Psychological Effects of War	221
	The MOD's Approach to Post-operational Stress Management	223
14	Welcome Home	225
	'Mad, Bad, Sad' – Myth and Reality	228
	Ricky's Story	233
15	Things Can Only Get Better – but when?	238
	The Armed Forces Covenant – a Toothless Tiger?	240
	Other Barriers to Care	242
16	The Wheels of State Turn Slowly	246
Bibliography		250
Index		266

Musa Qala
by Warrior Poet

What is my fragile mind concealing?
Only to me the truth's revealing.
I see it in the mothers' eyes –
Oh, had their sons ta'en their advice.

We were sent, or volunteered,
Waved to fate our families feared.
Proud and brave we flew with honour,
Now I'm empty – hope a goner.

Back in the sand we stood there ready,
Faced with death, our hands held steady.
The enemy came in mournful numbers,
We sent them down to Allah's slumber.

Long days bled to endless nights,
The Irish stood and held the fight.
Relieved of a most glorious death,
We swore to fight till our last breath.

Carted home in trucks like cattle,
Battered bones from endless battle.
Thirty miles we had to drive,
So precious helis could survive.

Musa Qala - Fortress of Moses,
The infamous siege - betrayed, forgotten.
We held the walls, they turned away,
Another debt we're left to pay.

To the men we lost to that war,
I'll remember them for evermore.

Faugh a Ballagh

This poem was penned by Musa Qal'eh veteran, Ranger (later Lance Corporal) Adam Dunlop, under the *nom-de-plume* Warrior Poet. The work, in the words of a survivor reflecting on combat, loss and betrayal, as well as the raw emotion of a soldier's memory, is a personal act of remembrance and a tribute to the men who did not come home. Adam was just 18 years old when he deployed to Afghanistan in 2006, returning for a second operational tour in 2008. He has since been diagnosed with Post Traumatic Stress Disorder (PTSD), attributed to his military service, and finds writing to be therapeutic, allowing him to tell his truth about war, challenge the stigma of mental illness, and give a voice to those who live with the lasting effects of modern combat.

Foreword

Afghanistan defined soldiering in the British Army for a generation. The immersion in fire experienced by 3rd Battalion, The Parachute Regiment Battlegroup in Helmand in 2006 reverberated across that army. There was admiration and there was jealousy. Professional soldiers worthy of that name in garrisons in the UK and Germany, and on operations in Iraq or Cyprus or Northern Ireland, wanted nothing more than to be part of the effort. The fear of missing out was tangible. I felt it. I probably felt it more acutely than many. In 2006, as the story in this book unfolded, I was commanding B Company of 1st Battalion, The Royal Irish Regiment, and we were in fine shape. We had a tour in West Africa and six months in Iraq under our belts, and we were on the edge of completing an intense six-week live firing exercise in the Jamaican jungle; we could not have been more ready. Yet when the call for reinforcements for 3 Para arced across the Atlantic and into the Caribbean, the requirement was for a platoon of 30 and not for my company of 100. So, some went, and some did not, and an element of this story covers the effect of that uncomfortable dynamic.

The subsequent few years would see almost the entirety of the army experience Afghanistan, and to feel the intensity of combat, the fear, the anger, the exhilaration. So, while the collective concern over missing out was misplaced, Op Herrick IV was the first chapter, it was where the unexpected was encountered for the first time. Every six-month deployment of combat brigades and battlegroups thereafter saw increasingly well-tuned preparation, of men, of training, of equipment. In time, after much trial and error, the British Army and Royal Marines would increasingly get the 'inputs' right in Helmand and would gain and hold the upper hand over the Taliban. But by about 2012, the sands of time had largely run out. To paraphrase the words of the famous maxim, while we had all the watches, the Taliban did indeed have all the time.

In the beginning though, in 2006, the inputs were far from right, arguably because our assumptions were wrong. Clausewitz's maxim is as well-known as it is ignored:

> The first, the supreme, the most far-reaching act of judgment that the statesman and commander have to make is to establish by that test the kind of war on which they are embarking; neither mistaking it for, nor trying to turn it into, something that is alien to its nature.

That 16 Air Assault Brigade was first into Helmand perhaps was a sound mitigation of what might have been a strategic gamble leading to a wholesale disaster. If one wanted to hedge against the potential for a violent and visceral reaction in the Pashtun tribal heartlands, then employing Britain's Airborne Forces as the early entry force was a wise choice. That brigade, which I once had the privilege of commanding, was and is forged around a culture of readiness, resilience, old fashioned hard discipline, and the driving of the highest standards. To build those characteristics requires investment. It paid off on Op Herrick IV in 2006, just as it later paid off when 16 Brigade led the British evacuation effort out of Kabul International Airport in 2021. In both circumstances, the soldiers of the brigade had the resilience to withstand the shock.

The Royal Irish Regiment is the last Irish Infantry Regiment of the Line, being the product of a series of amalgamations that increased in frequency since the Second World War. Today's Regiment sets great store by its past and present association with Britain's Airborne Forces. In the

Second World War, 1st (Airborne) Battalion, The Royal Ulster Rifles was a part of 6th (Airborne) Division, landing by glider in Normandy on D-Day, and months later leaping the Rhine by the same method in one of the final major acts of the war. The Rifles parted ways with their airborne brothers-in-arms after a difficult deployment to Palestine in 1946. By 2006, after a half-century-plus hiatus, the Ulster Rifles' descendants – The Royal Irish Regiment – were back alongside airborne forces, having been drafted into the newly formed 16 Air Assault Brigade in 1999. Then, the regiment itself was in a new 'form' with the latest round of Infantry amalgamations only having created The Royal Irish Regiment in 1992. I recall very clearly the memory and the 'sense' of being part of a regiment at that particular time that had much to prove to itself, and – especially in this uncompromising brigade – also to others. Amongst the sweat, blood, terror, tears, and the undoubted cost of successive tours of Helmand it did prove itself, and it grew through an awkward adolescence into a state of quiet, collective self-confidence.

Derek Plews covers the geopolitical dynamic and the operational decision-making that led to the battle of Musa Qal'eh in 2006. He also covers the experience of those who returned from battle to a system that was not configured – culturally or organisationally – to attend to the needs of combat veterans who needed to be reintegrated into an army that did not yet really comprehend what 3 Para Battlegroup had experienced. Combat is exclusive, it produces a bond that none can appreciate who were not part of it. There is no real point in trying to *understand* what another soldier has endured in war, it can be approximated, or compared to one's own experience, but never fully understood. Some returnees can be reintegrated, some drift and then return, and some, most sadly, are lost forever. A leader – a Commanding Officer – can try to arrest this dynamic, but it has a force of its own. He can only do his best, and I can testify that the then CO of 1 R Irish did just that. In doing so, he was an example of compassion and dedication that I could only aspire to when I had the privilege of leading the 1 R Irish Battlegroup in Afghanistan in 2010 (with 3 Para alongside us on our northern flank). By that time the Army had evolved a much better, but still far from perfect, understanding of how to deal with the impact of war on minds and bodies. There is much more that might be done to support combat veterans, and this book highlights the particular issue of addressing this challenge in an Irish context.

The episode covered here is one of the most important, the most intense, and the bloodiest chapter in the story of the Regiment's long involvement in Afghanistan. The period in question is still sufficiently close, and the impact of the events sufficiently deep, to stir the emotions and to unsheathe sharp-edged opinions. I know, personally, most of the people named in this book, from the Generals through to the Rangers of the Royal Irish and the Toms of the Parachute Regiment. I know the exceptional 3 Para men who led the predominantly Irish contingent in Musa Qal'eh: my great friend Major Adam Jowett, and his inspirational Company Sergeant Major, Jo Scrivener. The respect and affection towards these exceptional leaders from their Irish charges is as deep today as it was in 2006. I also know many of the wider players who are not named. All of them – named and unnamed – are good and decent men, but they operated in a system and in an army that was not ready for what confronted them. They played the hand of cards that was dealt to them. Some had a better hand than others, and some may have played a poor hand better than others. Regardless, each of them deserves our respect for being in the arena. *Ad Unum Omnes, Faugh a Ballagh!, Utrinque Paratus.*[1]

Major General (Retd) Colin R. J. Weir, CB, DSO, MBE
Colonel of the Regiment
Royal Irish Regiment

---

1 *Ad Unum Omnes* – All Together, as One (motto of UK Airborne Forces); *Faugh a Ballagh* – Clear the Way (motto of The Royal Irish Regiment); *Utrinque Paratus* – Ready for Anything (motto of the Parachute Regiment).

Glossary

ACM	Anti-coalition Militia. A term used by NATO to describe armed groups opposed to the international coalition and the elected government of Afghanistan. It was intended to reflect what some considered to be the fractured nature of the opposition, believed to consist of a number of groups which included – but was not limited to – the Taliban.
ANA	Afghan National Army.
ANP	Afghan National Police.
Anchor OP	Anchor Observation Post. An OP that remains in place, providing overwatch, while other elements manoeuvre or relocate.
AOO	Area of Operations. A defined geographical area assigned by a superior commander to a subordinate within which he may conduct operations.
AOR	Area of Responsibility. A defined geographical area within which a military commander has authority to plan and conduct operations.
AQI	Al Qaeda in Iraq. A militant Sunni organisation, affiliated with Al Qaeda, originally led by Abu Musab al-Zarqawi, opposed to the US-led invasion and occupation of Iraq and the Shi'ite-dominated Iraqi government.
ARRC	Allied Rapid Reaction Corps. A NATO multi-national force designed to be able to deploy rapidly in response to a crisis. The ARRC is not a standing formation, meaning that it has no forces permanently assigned. However, the headquarters element, for which the UK is the framework nation, is a permanently established organisation, based near Gloucester, and has provided the command-and-control function for various NATO deployments, including Bosnia (1995–96), Kosovo (1999) and Afghanistan (2006–07 and 2011).
Battlegroup	An army formation, usually based on an infantry or armoured unit and commanded at Lieutenant Colonel level, which has been task-organised to perform a particular mission. It may include infantry, armour and artillery elements as well as other support such as Intelligence Surveillance and Target Acquisition resources.
Butler Review	Named after its chair, Baron Butler of Brockwell, and also known as the Review of Intelligence on Weapons of Mass Destruction, this was established in 2004 to examine the intelligence on Iraq's Weapons of Mass Destruction, which played a key part in the Government's decision to invade Iraq in 2003.
C2	Command and Control.
C-17	Also known as Globemaster, a large transport aircraft, manufactured by the US company, Boeing, operated by the RAF.
Card Alpha	A card that sets out the 'guidance for opening fire for service personnel authorised to carry arms and ammunition on duty'. These are the rules that apply during normal peacetime circumstances and are based on the law of self-defence.

Caubeen	Irish Gaelic for 'battered old hat', the distinctive headdress of the Royal Irish Regiment, worn with a green feather hackle fixed behind the harp and crown cap badge.
CDS	Chief of Defence Staff. The UK's senior military officer, whose role is to advise the Prime Minister and Defence Secretary on the application of military force, and to exercise the highest level of command over UK national forces on operations.
CENTCOM	US Central Command. Based in Tampa, Florida, but with a forward headquarters in the Gulf state of Qatar, this is a US combatant command whose Area of Responsibility includes the Middle East, Central Asia and parts of South Asia.
CFLCC	Coalition Forces Land Component Command. The US-led headquarters that oversaw the invasion of Iraq in 2003. It was replaced by CJTF7 in June 2003.
CIVPOP	Military abbreviation for Civilian Population.
CJO/DCJO	Chief and Deputy Chief of Joint Operations. The commander and deputy commander of PJHQ.
CJSOR	Combined Joint Statement of Requirement. A NATO term which refers to a list of personnel, equipment and other resources required for the conduct of a specific operation.
CJTF7	Combined Joint Task Force 7. An interim military formation that directed the US effort in Iraq between June 2003 and May 2004.
CJTF76	Combined Joint Task Force 76. A US-led formation, part of Combined Forces Command – Afghanistan, responsible for conducting counter-insurgency operations.
CO	Commanding Officer. Usually refers to the commander of a unit such as a battlegroup, battalion or regiment.
COMSEC	Communications Security. Measures to avoid passing information likely to be of benefit to the enemy via military or civilian communications networks.
COSSEC	Chiefs of Staff Secretariat. The team responsible for managing the UK Chiefs of Staff meetings, including preparing agendas, issuing invitations, coordinating advice and recording discussions and decisions.
CPA	Coalition Provisional Authority. A body established to act as a transitional government in Iraq in the immediate aftermath of the US-led invasion in 2003. The body was initially headed by retired senior US Army Lieutenant General, Jay Garner, who was replaced by US diplomat, Paul Bremer.
CSTC–A	Combined Security Transition Command – Afghanistan. A multi-national, US-led military command, whose mission was to train the Afghan National Security Forces.
DCDS(C)	Deputy Chief of Defence Staff (Commitments). A senior (3-Star) military officer whose role was to provide advice to the UK Chiefs of Staff and ministers on the planning for and conduct of military operations.
DFID	Department for International Development. A UK government department that was merged with the Foreign and Commonwealth Department to create the Foreign Commonwealth and Development Office.
DG OpPol	Director General Operational Policy. A senior civil servant at the UK Ministry of Defence, whose role was to synthesise policy and military advice to the Chiefs of Staff and ministers.

DIS	Defence Intelligence Service (now known as Defence Intelligence). Led by the Chief of Defence Intelligence, this organisation works with other UK intelligence agencies such as GCHQ, MI5, MI6, to provide intelligence products to support policy and decision-making within the MOD and the wider UK government.
DPAs	Defence Planning Assumptions. These set out the scale and types of operations likely to be undertaken by the UK military. They form the basis on which the Armed Forces are staffed, funded and equipped.
DZ	Drop Zone. An area of ground into which paratroops will land during airborne operations.
DZ Flash	A square cloth badge of various colours, signifying the parent unit of airborne soldiers. The badges are intended to ensure that troops and commanders are able to identify their unit's personnel in the chaos of a drop zone or landing zone. The 3 Para DZ Flash consists of a green square. The Royal Irish badge was a square, split diagonally, with green and black sections. It had originally been worn by the soldiers of 1st (Airborne) Battalion, Royal Ulster Rifles, as they air-landed by glider in Normandy on D Day, 1944.
FAC	Forward Air Controller. Highly-trained specialists who liaise with attack aircraft to call-in air support for troops on the ground. Also known as a JTAC or Joint Terminal Attack Controller.
ECBA	Enhanced Combat Body Armour. Basic body armour, containing Kevlar and ceramic plates, designed to provide frontal and rear protection of key organs from small-arms fire and shrapnel.
ECM	Electronic Counter Measures. In this instance, a suite of equipment designed to counter the threat from radio-controlled bombs by jamming the firing signals.
EFP	Explosively Formed Projectile or Penetrator, designed to disable armoured vehicles by creating a jet of molten copper, capable of punching through protective armour.
FAB	*Faugh a Ballagh!* – Irish Gaelic for Clear the Way, the motto of the Royal Irish Regiment.
FATAs	Federally Administered Tribal Areas. A semi-autonomous tribal region in north-western Pakistan, directly administered by the federal government from Islamabad.
FCO	Foreign and Commonwealth Office. Now called the Foreign, Commonwealth and Development Office. The UK's foreign policy and diplomacy department.
FOB	Forward Operating Base. In Helmand, Camp Bastion was the UK's logistics hub. The Main Operating Base was at Lashkar Gah, and troops were deployed to a number of Forward Operating Bases, such as FOB Robinson near Sangin, FOB Price near Gereshk, and to smaller Patrol Bases (PBs) and Checkpoints.
FOO	Forward Observation Officer. Usually an NCO or officer from the Royal Artillery, who accompanies a military force in order to direct artillery support for attack or defence.
FORGEN	Force Generation. The process used to build a military force for a specific operation, usually based on a statement of requirement derived from the Concept of Operations designed by the planners.

FSG	Fire Support Group. An ad hoc grouping, possibly including heavy machine guns, mortars, grenade-launchers and anti-tank/anti-structural munitions, organised to support manoeuvre elements. Not to be confused with FST (Fire Support Team), a modern term for Forward Observation Party, whose role is to direct artillery fire and close air support onto enemy positions.
GPMG	The UK's General Purpose Machine Gun, a belt-fed weapon of 7.62mm calibre with a cyclic rate of fire of 650–800 rounds per minute and an effective range of 800m in the light role. It can engage targets at up to 1,800m in the sustained fire role if the strike can be observed.
Hesco	Collapsible wire mesh containers with a fabric liner that could be filled with sand or soil and joined together to form a temporary wall or building, providing protection against small arms fire and explosions. A modern take on the gabions (defensive works consisting of wicker baskets filled with stones) that the Duke of Wellington's soldiers would have recognised.
HCDC	House of Commons Defence Committee. A cross-party committee whose role is to scrutinise the Ministry of Defence as part of the parliamentary oversight process. The committee, usually chaired by an MP from the party in government, conducts inquiries into various aspects of departmental activity and has the power to send for relevant persons, papers and records.
HLS	Helicopter Landing Site.
HMT	His Majesty's Treasury. The UK department of state responsible for economic and finance policy and maintaining control over public spending.
HUMINT	Human Intelligence. Intelligence gathered from human sources and interpersonal contacts.
HVT	High Value Target. Originally a US term defined as an individual the enemy can least afford to lose or that provides him with the greatest advantage.
ICG	Iraq Communications Group. A cross-departmental group, chaired by the Prime Minister's Official Spokesman, to coordinate messaging on Iraq for UK audiences.
ICOM	A radio scanner used to listen-in to enemy transmissions. UK forces used the ICOM R10 receiver for this purpose in Afghanistan. ICOM is a British company based in Herne Bay, Kent.
Iraq Ba'ath Party	Sometimes referred to as the pro-Iraqi Ba'ath movement or the Arab Socialist Ba'ath Party – Iraq Region, this was a political party which governed Iraq between 1968 and 2003, when it was banned by the US-led Coalition Provisional Authority (CPA). Between 1992 and 2003 the party was led by Saddam Hussein. There are other branches of the party throughout the Middle East.
Iraq Inquiry	Commissioned by UK Prime Minister, Gordon Brown, in 2009, this inquiry was charged with identifying lessons that could be learned from the Iraq conflict that began in 2003. The Report of the Inquiry's findings was published in July 2016.
ISO	International Shipping Organisation. An ISO container is a steel shipping container, built to ISO standards, which can be securely loaded onto the trailer of an articulated lorry or similar vehicle. These were a familiar sight in Afghanistan, having been used to transport equipment to the theatre by ship and road.
ISAF	International Security Assistance Force. An international force, mandated by the UN Security Council in the aftermath of the US-led invasion of Afghanistan in 2001, whose role was to assist Afghan authorities to maintain security and develop new national security forces.

ISTAR	Intelligence, Surveillance, Target Acquisition and Reconnaissance. The assets and activities used to gather and process information to support military operations. For example, a reconnaissance patrol could be described as an ISTAR activity.
JAM	*Jaish al Mahdi*, the Mahdi Army. An Iraqi Shi'ite militia created by firebrand cleric, Muqtada al-Sadr, in June 2003, principally to defend Sadr-supporting Shi'ite neighbourhoods.
JDAM	Joint Direct Attack Munition. This is a 'dumb' free-fall bomb, fitted with an inertial navigation system, coupled with a Global Positioning Satellite guidance pack that converts it into a 'smart' munition, improving its accuracy.
JIC	Joint Intelligence Committee. An inter-agency body, sitting within the UK Cabinet Office, responsible for intelligence assessment, coordination and oversight of the Secret Intelligence Service (MI6), Security Service (MI5), Government Communications Headquarters (GCHQ) and the Defence Intelligence Service (DIS).
JOC	Joint Operations Centre. A headquarters from where military activities may be planned, monitored and directed.
JTAC	See FAC above.
KAF	Kandahar Air Field.
KFOR	Kosovo Force. A NATO-led international peacekeeping force, mandated under UN Security Council Resolution 1244 of 10 June 1999.
KIA	Kabul International Airport or Killed in Action.
LAV	Generic name for a family of Light Armoured Vehicles, including reconnaissance and Infantry Fighting Vehicle variants.
LEWT	Light Electronic Warfare Team. A small team of signallers, intelligence specialists and interpreters who contributed to the intelligence picture by monitoring enemy radio transmissions and gathering information about enemy movements, plans and local commanders.
Link	Another term for the ammunition belts used by British machine guns such as the GPMG and Minimi. The link refers to metal connectors which join the individual rounds together to form belts. These belts fall apart as the weapon is fired hence they are sometimes known as disintegrating link.
LMG	Light Machine Gun. In the British Army in 2006 this referred to the Minimi L110A2, a belt-fed machine gun, in 5.56mm calibre, with a cyclic rate of fire of up to 1,000 rounds per minute and an effective range of 800m.
LZ	Landing Zone. In airborne operations, an area of ground unto which a force arriving by fixed or rotary wing aircraft will touch down.
MAMBA	Mobile Artillery Monitoring Battlefield Radar. A radar system used to locate enemy artillery or mortar positions by tracking the shells in flight and using the data to compute a point or origin and firing solution.
Maroon Mafia	A disparaging term for the UK's airborne forces, in reference to their maroon berets.
MERT	Medical Emergency Response Team. A multi-disciplinary team, usually consisting of a doctor, a specialist nurse and two paramedics, trained to deploy by helicopter (Chinook) to provide hospital-level trauma care for wounded personnel during the evacuation process. The teams also included a small infantry element to provide force protection. During the Afghanistan campaign the MERTs were credited with saving the lives of many seriously-injured personnel.

MFC	Mortar Fire Controller. Usually a two-man team that directs mortar fire. With appropriate training these teams can also call-in artillery fire and air support.
MES	Mazar e Sharif. The fifth-largest city in Afghanistan and the capital of Balkh province. Located in the north of the country.
MI5	Also known as the Security Service, this is the UK's domestic intelligence and counter-intelligence service.
MI6	Also known as the Secret Intelligence Service, this is the UK's foreign intelligence and counter-intelligence service.
MNC–I	Multi-National Corps – Iraq. A 3-Star command, subordinate to MNF–I, providing direct command and control of coalition forces throughout the Iraq AOO. For example, MND(SE) reported to MNC–I.
MND(CS)	Multi-National Division (Central South). The Polish-led multi-national division responsible for providing security in the south-central region of Iraq after the US-led invasion. Its AOR included the provinces of Al Qadisiyah, Karbala, Babil and Wasit.
MND(SE)	Multi-National Division (South East). The UK-led multi-national division responsible for providing security in the south-east of Iraq after the US-led invasion. Its AOR included the provinces of Basra, Al Muthanna, Maysan and Dhi Qar.
MNF–I	Multi-National Force – Iraq. The highest level of command of coalition forces in Iraq, a 4-Star headquarters which replaced CJTF7.
Mousehole charge	An explosive charge used to blow a hole in the wall of a building to allow entry or exit or to provide an internal link between two conjoined buildings.
MOD	UK Ministry of Defence.
NAC	North Atlantic Council. The high-level political decision-making body of NATO.
NATO	North Atlantic Treaty Organisation. International political and military alliance formed in the aftermath of the Second World War to stand as a bastion against potential Soviet Union expansion.
NVGs	Night Vision Goggles or Glasses. Devices that can intensify moon and starlight to allow the user to see in the dark.
OC	Officer Commanding. In the UK military this term is used to describe the commander of a sub-unit such a company, battery or squadron, usually in the rank of Major.
Operation Herrick	The computer-generated code name for UK operations in Afghanistan between 2002 and 2014.
Operation Telic	The computer-generated code-name for UK operations in Iraq between 2003 and 2011.
O Group	Orders Group. Usually a carefully-choreographed gathering at which a military commander issues orders to his/her subordinates. Can also be used as a collective term for a commander's heads of departments.
OPLAN	Operation Plan. A detailed plan for conducting a military operation.
ORBAT	Order of Battle. The individual units that make up a formation or the overall structure of the army.
OSINT	Open-Source Intelligence. Intelligence derived from publicly or commercially available sources such as newspapers, broadcasters, publications and social media platforms.

PCRU	Post Conflict Reconstruction Unit. The forerunner of the Stabilisation Unit, and the Office for Conflict, Stabilisation and Mediation, the PCRU was established by the UK's Department for International Development (now part of the Foreign Commonwealth and Development Office) to help to improve the UK's capacity to contribute to achieving a stable environment in countries emerging from conflicts.
PKM	Russian-made belt-fed general-purpose machine gun in 7.62mm calibre, with a cyclic rate of fire of 600–800 rounds per minute and an effective range of up to 1,500 metres. Similar to the UK's GPMG.
PJHQ	Permanent Joint Headquarters. A UK tri-Service military headquarters, based at Northwood, Middlesex, on the outskirts of London, from where the Chief of Joint Operations and staff exercise day-to-day command on military operations. Commanded at 3-Star level (Vice-Admiral, Lieutenant General, Air Marshal).
POTL	Post Operational Tour Leave (pronounced Pottle). Service personnel were awarded a period of additional leave on return from operations.
PRR	Personal Role Radio. Small radio transmitters/receivers issued to individual soldiers to enable battlefield communication over short distances (up to 500m).
PRT	Provincial Reconstruction Team. These joint civilian and military teams were created to support the Government of Afghanistan to deliver improved governance and economic development at provincial level.
Ranger	The term used for a private solder in the Royal Irish Regiment, similar to Fusilier or Rifleman. It originates from when the regiment was known as the Royal Irish Rangers.
RAP	Regimental Aid Post. A first-line medical facility where the unit Medical Officer and his small team dress wounds, conduct minor surgery, and stabilised patients before they were evacuated to hospital at Camp Bastion.
RC(S)	Regional Command (South). The international coalition split Afghanistan into a number of regional commands. Regional Command (South) was responsible for military operations in the provinces of Nimruz, Helmand, Kandahar, Zabol, Uruzgan and Dai Kundi.
RPG	Rocket-Propelled Grenade. Originally a Soviet-made man-portable anti-tank weapon consisting of a launcher and a shaped-charge warhead attached to a rocket motor. Anti-personnel fragmentation warheads are also available.
RQMS	Regimental Quartermaster Sergeant. In the UK military this is an appointment held by a Warrant Officer Class II. The senior non-commissioned assistant to the Quartermaster in a battalion or regiment.
R&R	Rest and Recuperation. A period of leave or down-time to allow military personnel to recover from the rigours of operations.
RV	Military term for rendezvous.
SACEUR	The Supreme Allied Commander Europe. The military leader of NATO, a US 4-Star General.
SBMR–I	Senior British Military Representative – Iraq. The UK's senior military figure within the coalition headquarters in Iraq, usually a 3-Star officer (Lieutenant General).
Shura	An Islamic term for collective decision-making by a representative council. In Afghanistan the British used the term for any meeting with local people.
SI	Seriously Ill. Sometimes used instead of the triage term T1.

SIGINT	Signals Intelligence. Intelligence derived from electronic signals from communications, radar and weapon systems.
SMA	Sher Mohammad Akhundzada. An Afghan warlord, opium trafficker and former governor of Helmand province.
SOF	Special Operations Forces. A collective term for US Special Forces teams, e.g. Delta Force, Rangers and SEALs.
T1, T2, T3, T4	The UK military triage system uses these terms to signify the degree of severity of injuries: T1 – life-threatening. T2 – walking wounded. T3 – all others. T4 is an informal term sometimes used to indicate that a casualty is deceased.
TACSAT	Tactical Satellite Communications System. A portable communications system that allows radio messages to be passed via low-orbiting satellites.
TFH	Task Force Helmand.
UAV	Unmanned Aerial Vehicle. For example, during Operation Herrick IV the UK battlegroup operated the Desert Hawk UAV, a small unarmed drone used for local surveillance, capable of streaming high-quality, real-time imagery to a ground station.
UN	United Nations. An international organisation, founded in 1945, committed to maintaining international peace and security.
UNAMI	United Nations Assistance Mission for Iraq. A UN organisation tasked to advise and assist the government of Iraq on political dialogue and national reconciliation as well as supporting political processes such as the conduct of elections, legal reforms, promoting human rights and coordinating the delivery of humanitarian aid.
UNSC	United Nations Security Council. The Security Council has primary responsibility for the maintenance of international peace and security. It issues Resolutions with which UN member states are obliged to comply and it has the power to impose sanctions or authorise the use of military force to maintain or restore peace and security.
VBIED	Vehicle-borne Improvised Explosive Device. Military term for car or vehicle bomb. SVBIED is the term for Suicide Vehicle-borne Improvised Explosive Device or suicide car bomb.
WMIK	Weapons Mount Installation Kit. Pronounced 'wimick' this is the name given to a rugged rough-terrain vehicle, based on the Land Rover Wolf chassis, fitted to carry a range of weapons including GPMG and .50in Heavy Machine Gun, or Grenade Machine Gun. Used for reconnaissance, long-range patrolling and protection of logistics convoys.
WMD	Weapons of Mass Destruction, usually defined as including nuclear, chemical and biological weapons.

Author's note

This book tells the story of the Siege of Musa Qal'eh in 2006, when soldiers of The Royal Irish Regiment – my regiment – together with a small number of paratroopers, signallers, gunners and others, found themselves cut off and fighting for their lives in a village in the north of Afghanistan's Helmand Province.

There are other accounts of the fighting at Musa Qal'eh that summer and autumn. I have read them all. They are very good. But, like much of the literature spawned by the campaign in Afghanistan, these tend to tell the story from the perspective of the leaders, not the led. It seemed to me that there was room for a different approach, one that painted word pictures from another point of view – to give the private soldiers (and non-commissioned officers) a voice. These were the men – some not long out of boyhood – who stood to arms at the makeshift fighting positions and sangars in the dead of night, frightened and far from home, waiting for the report of a rocket-propelled grenade or recoilless rifle that would herald yet another Taliban attack, perhaps the ninth or tenth that day. These were the soldiers who saw their mates being killed or horrendously wounded, but who never failed to take their place on the firing line in the face of the fiercest enemy onslaughts, their sleep, what little there was of it, constantly interrupted by nightmares, horrific visions of what they had seen and done that day. This is, above all, their story and it is right that – as far as possible – it should be told in their words.

This book would not have been possible without the support and cooperation of a wide range of people, including politicians, generals and senior policy officials who made, or helped to make, the decisions that pointed the way to Helmand Province, as well as former and serving members of The Royal Irish Regiment and others who were there at that time. I am deeply indebted to all who gave so generously of their time and their memories, including those few who spoke on condition of anonymity for various reasons. Thanks are also due to military artist, David Rowlands, for permission to use his painting depicting Royal Irish Regiment soldiers at Musa Qal'eh, and to Colonel of the Regiment, Major General (Retd) Colin Weir, for his support and encouragement and also for writing the foreword. I would also like to thank Regimental Secretary, Lieutenant Colonel (Retd) Andy Hart, Deputy Colonel of the Regiment, Colonel Darren Doherty, and Colonel (Retd) Stewarty Douglas.

I am particularly grateful to my editor Andy Miles, to Duncan Rogers, and this team at Helion & Company. Also deserving of special mention is former Corporal Danny Groves, who entrusted me with his personal journal in which he made a contemporaneous record of key events – as he saw them – during his time in Musa Qal'eh.

Although this account is concerned with events that, at the time of writing, had occurred less than 20 years previously, it is, nevertheless, heavily dependent on the recollections of those who were present at that time. Memory is a fickle cognitive function. This may be part of the reason why, in some cases, individual accounts do not always align. I have done my best to assure historical accuracy by cross-checking with other sources where possible. This is, of course, proof, if any were needed, that writing contemporary history can involve some of the same challenges as engaging with events that occurred hundreds or even thousands of years in the past.

War does physical and mental damage. Physical wounds are visible and can often heal relatively quickly. Mental trauma can be less obvious and some who experience it may never fully recover from its effects. I saw this for myself as I conducted interviews with the combatants. Many of those with whom I spoke had experienced varying degrees of mental stress over the years. Soldiers who were relatively happy to talk about the fighting, became much more guarded when it came to relating the mental problems that had followed. Some of this reluctance was due to concerns about the social stigma that surrounds mental illness. Some of it was down to worries about the negative impact these psychological issues might have on current civilian (or military) careers. It is for these reasons that many of the contributions included in the final section of the book are anonymous. I make no apology for this. In the pursuit of writing 'good history', I would have preferred to put names to these sources, I have concluded, however, that it is more important that the stories are told, even if the identities of those concerned must remain hidden. I know who they are, and I am content that their accounts are reliable.

Military history is littered with examples of courage in the face of adversity. The campaign in Afghanistan is no different. There was no shortage of valour at Musa Qal'eh in 2006, and it is surprising that none of this was recognised by the honours system. But it took a different sort of bravery for Ranger Ricky Armstrong to share the experiences that led to mental breakdown, attempted suicide, and his journey to what is now, hopefully, a better place. I experienced some of the same raw courage in Lieutenant (now Lieutenant Colonel) Paul Martin, as he relived the event in which he sustained serious, life-threatening injuries while leading his platoon as it fought off a particularly determined Taliban attack.

Finally, a word about ranks and appointments. Throughout the book I have used the ranks and appointments held by individuals at the time of the events being discussed. This means that some of those named have more than one rank and/or appointment. For example, Field Marshal Lord Walker of Aldringham also appears as General Sir Mike Walker, Chief of the General Staff in the run-up to the invasion of Iraq and later as Chief of the Defence Staff. General Sir Gordon Messenger, who retired as Vice Chief of Defence Staff, was Colonel Messenger when he led PJHQ's Preliminary Operations team in Helmand in 2005.

DAP
December 2024

Introduction

For 37 hellish days and nights, during the late summer and early autumn of 2006, infantry soldiers from the 1st Battalion, The Royal Irish Regiment, fought a life-or-death struggle against hordes of Taliban insurgents as they battled for possession of a dusty, tumbledown, mud-brick compound in the town of Musa Qal'eh in Afghanistan's Helmand Province.

Surrounded, cut off, massively outnumbered, and eventually down to their last few bullets and mortar rounds, this small band of British soldiers beat off repeated assaults by a well-armed, resolute enemy, who were determined to breach the walls and kill the garrison. The attacks came thick and fast, sometimes as many as eight or 10 in a day. There were many occasions when only the firepower of NATO fast jets with their 1,000lb bombs and depleted uranium-tipped cannon shells, kept the attackers from achieving their bloody goal.

Shamrocks Among the Poppies[1] is a new account of this latter-day Band of Brothers, told mainly through the voices of the men who were there. It is a soldiers-eye view of the horrific and intense fighting that took place in that part of northern Helmand as an under-resourced British Task Force tried to bolster the position of the fledgling Afghan national Government and a weak Provincial Governor.

To understand why this small group of Irish warriors found themselves fighting for their lives in a remote outpost in Afghanistan in 2006, the reader is invited to take a lengthy and winding journey along some of the key geopolitical highways and byways of the late twentieth and early twenty-first centuries. Although this background material is substantial and complex, perhaps tempting the reader to jump ahead to the 'action', the reasons for – and the decision-making behind – the British decision to reinvest in Afghanistan in 2006 are critical to a clear understanding of how and why the Siege of Musa Qal'eh took place.

The starting point for the events described in these pages is not, as many believe, the terrorist attack on New York's Twin Towers in September 2001, but several years earlier, in the aftermath of Labour's landslide election victory in 1997. A young, and so far untested UK Prime Minister, Tony Blair, emboldened by a massive parliamentary majority, sought to stand tall on the international stage in a bid to take the country back to the glory days, before the break-up the empire, when Britannia ruled the waves and foreign leaders listened when she spoke.

Blair's chosen route to global influence took him across the Atlantic, to Washington, where he befriended US President, Bill Clinton, and later his successor, George W. Bush, a hawkish right-winger whose political creed was a world away from the young Prime Minister's centrist instincts. Politics makes for strange bed-fellows, however, and Blair subordinated his own outlook to that of his new best friend in a bid to gain traction in the White House and at the Pentagon.

But political alliances like this transatlantic axis can come with a high price tag, especially for the junior partner. For the Prime Minister, and the British people, the cost would be crushing. Hundreds of British service personnel would perish and many more would be left to struggle on

---

1   The Shamrocks in the title refers to The Royal Irish Regiment's Tactical Recognition Flash, a shamrock on a black background, worn on the right sleeve and on helmet covers.

in the face of life-changing physical and mental injuries as Blair took the country to war five times in six years in his bid to march in lock-step with the Americans. Families would be left devastated by their losses. Young men and women who should have parented a new generation and lived to watch their children grow up, would instead die in the towns and villages of Kosovo, the jungles of Sierra Leone, or the desert dust of Basra and Helmand. For Blair himself, the decision to stand shoulder to shoulder with Bush would play a large part in losing him the trust of the British people and thus his premature departure from Downing Street. For some senior military leaders, previously glittering reputations would be left tarnished by their failure to demonstrate moral courage and speak truth unto power.

The book analyses how a combination of Blair's determination to support Bush, come what may, and the necessity to shore-up a failing North Atlantic Alliance, led to the decision to send British troops into the Helmand badlands before the UK had properly disengaged from Iraq. It explains how that decision was flawed as key advisors and their intelligence experts failed to accurately appreciate the situation on the ground in Helmand, either because they lacked sufficient information on which to base their analysis or because they deliberately chose to ignore the warning signs. It describes the consequences of those failures, in terms of how they impacted on the size of the force package – troops, aircraft, ammunition, equipment – that was made available for operations in Afghanistan, and how military planners in London sought to make up for manpower and equipment deficiencies by drawing lines on a map and expecting that in-theatre commanders would stay within them, irrespective of how the tactical picture developed. Whatever the reason, the image of Helmand that was painted for public and parliamentary consumption, ahead of the deployment, created a false impression of relative peace and stability. The reality was rather different and more deadly. By late 2005, Helmand was a powder keg with a burning fuse, lit by a powerful combination of age-old tribal jealousies, fanned by the lucrative opium trade, and a growing Taliban resurgence.

This was the situation that faced The Royal Irish Regiment soldiers and their comrades of 16 Air Assault Brigade as they arrived in Helmand Province in 2006. Dealing with it would eventually lead to penny-packets of troops – too few for the tasks they faced – being sent to defend a series of run-down compounds, dubbed Platoon Houses, at Musa Qal'eh, Sangin, and Now Zad, far to the north of the provincial capital of Lashkar Gah, in an attempt to sustain the position of a weak and frightened Governor, Engineer Muhammad Daoud.

The fighting in the towns of northern Helmand during the summer and autumn of 2006 was some of the most intense experienced by British troops since the Korean War in the early 1950s. At Musa Qal'eh, the garrison, consisting mostly of Royal Irish Regiment soldiers, but with others from the Parachute Regiment, the Royal Corps of Signals, Royal Artillery, RAF Regiment and the Intelligence Corps, lost three of its number to Taliban fire, with many more being wounded, some seriously. In the circumstances, it was miraculous that the toll of deaths and injuries was not much higher.

The men overcame many difficulties during their time in the compound. But one thing over which they could not prevail was the inability of their senior commanders to keep them properly supplied with food and ammunition, and ensure that their wounded could be evacuated to hospital. The Taliban had effectively locked down the District Centre, sewing vehicle routes with improvised explosive devices to make it too costly in terms of potential casualties, and too manpower-intensive, to resupply the outstation by road. That left only the too-small fleet of Chinook helicopters to carry food, water, ammunition and other war stores into the compounds and evacuate the wounded and dead. Eventually, politicians and senior soldiers concluded that even resupply from the air was too dangerous, calculating that the loss of one of the big twin-rotor aircraft would be too much for UK public opinion to bear. As a result, the situation at Musa Qal'eh became unsustainable, forcing commanders and local elders to strike a deal with the Taliban that allowed the garrison to leave the compound. But the circumstances of their ignominious departure, on the cargo beds of Afghan 'jingly trucks', driven by Taliban insurgents, left many of the troops with profound feelings of anger and shame.

It was originally intended that this account would conclude at a desert landing site as the men clambered on board Chinook helicopters for the short flight back to Camp Bastion. But as the soldiers talked about their experiences, it quickly became apparent that it could not end there. To tell the whole story, it was clear that the narrative needed to set out not only the life-or-death struggle within the walls of the Musa Qal'eh District Centre, but also the ongoing legacy of the fighting in terms of its long-term effects on the soldiers who were there.

Over the months and years following the fighting, the physical wounds would heal. But for some, the psychological damage did not. Today, many of the soldiers who fought at Musa Qal'eh continue to suffer from the trauma of their experiences, diagnosed with Post Traumatic Stress Disorder and other mental illnesses. Some found they were unable to keep on battling with their demons and chose to end their mental torture by their own hands.

The final chapters are a description of the true consequences of high-intensity combat in terms of its mental scars, and the trials faced by some of the veterans – men who had put everything on the line for their country – as they struggle with a range of psychological conditions, brought on by what they had endured in Helmand Province.

The UK's reinvestment in Afghanistan in 2006 was a badly-planned and critically under-resourced political and military gamble. As usual, it was the 'Poor Bloody Infantry' who paid the price – in blood and mental distress – for avoidable, poor decision-making in Downing Street and at the Ministry of Defence, and who go on paying for the nation's failure to ensure they could get the mental health care they needed and deserved. This is their story.

Part 1

1

The Road to Helmand...

The path that would lead the soldiers of The Royal Irish Regiment to southern Afghanistan in 2006 – a deployment known by the computer-generated code-name, Operation Herrick IV – did not begin at their base, within the imposing grey stone ramparts of the eighteenth century barracks known as Fort George, near the Scottish city of Inverness. Nor did it start, as many believe, 3,000 miles further west, in Lower Manhattan, the site of Osama bin Laden's sickening attack on the Twin Towers on 11 September 2001. The scenes of devastation in New York's financial district had, of course, played a part in pointing the way to Central Asia. As British Prime Minister, Tony Blair, explained that same evening, addressing the world's media in Downing Street, the assault represented not just a strike against the United States, but on the free, democratic world. In the face of this international terrorism, Britain would stand 'shoulder-to-shoulder with our American friends in this hour of tragedy'.[1] But the images of destruction that flashed across the world's television screens on that autumn day, represented just one stage on the road to Helmand. The real starting point had occurred five years earlier with Labour's 1997 landslide election victory, it's roots tightly wrapped around Blair's vision of Britain as a global leader.

Blair has admitted that before coming to power he knew little about contemporary foreign affairs – perhaps a strange statement from someone who seemed so keen to stand tall on the world stage.[2] Although the new occupant of 10 Downing Street was an enthusiastic student of international history, general elections, he had noted, were seldom decided on external events.[3] Consequently, he and his fellow-architects of the New Labour project, had spent little time dwelling on foreign policy, as their 1997 manifesto confirms. The document is long on proposals for dealing with domestic issues, but very short on global matters. Its pages contain considerable detail on improving education; tackling crime; creating prosperity for all, through strong economic growth; and a promise to 'save the NHS'. But when it comes to the country's place on the world stage, it is much less forthcoming. There are some generalisations about putting the UK at the centre of Europe; strong defence through NATO; arms control and retaining the Trident nuclear deterrent; banning land mines; and a plan to conduct a foreign policy-led Strategic Defence Review.[4]

Events in the Balkans in 1998 were to become the catalyst that energised Blair to look more purposefully at Britain's role as a member of the international community. Inter-ethnic conflict in the Federal Republic of Yugoslavia had led to Serbia turning its military forces on the Albanian Kosovars in an orgy of killing and ethnic cleansing. The international response was initially feeble and demonstrated serious weaknesses in NATO's ability to tackle a growing humanitarian catastrophe on the

---

1　Tony Blair, *Tony Blair – A Journey* (London: Arrow Books, 2010), p.352.
2　Blair, *A Journey*, p.224.
3　Blair, *A Journey*, p.224.
4　Labour Party Election Manifesto 1997, <http://www.labour-party.org.uk/manifestos/1997/1997-labour-manifesto.shtml>, accessed 2 November 2023.

edge of Europe. Key European member states, including Germany, France and Italy, considered the cost – in financial and political terms – of committing ground troops, and concluded that the 'juice was not worth the squeeze'. The potential bill outweighed the perceived benefit.

The crisis also revealed a reluctance by the US, arguably at that time the world's only real superpower, to show firm leadership. President Bill Clinton, feeling domestic heat over allegations of sexual impropriety involving White House intern, Monica Lewinsky, seemed reluctant to pick a new fight with his political opponents over a country that few Americans beyond the Washington Beltway had even heard of or would have been able to pinpoint on a map. In March 1999 the House of Representatives had voted 219–191 to support sending US troops to Kosovo – but only if there was a peace agreement. Later that month, Clinton addressed the American people to spell out the case for air strikes. But, as he admitted in his memoirs, he found the argument for deploying ground troops as peace *enforcers* unattractive. Such a move would, he believed, cost American lives without increasing the likelihood of victory, and it would be difficult to convince voters in Kentucky that the situation in Kosovo justified the expenditure of American blood and treasure.[5] Clinton was personally troubled by television reports from the region, and by what his own intelligence agencies were telling him. But he was not yet sufficiently concerned to risk causing himself more political grief by opening up the option of deploying 'boots on the ground'.

Blair was appalled by what he had seen during the opening weeks of the crisis. European and American leaders had put narrow, national self-interest ahead of the lives of thousands of Kosovars, and apparently lacked the moral courage to take the steps necessary to end the killings and the forced evictions. He concluded that the only way to make progress was by personally stepping up to the mark, taking a strong leadership position, and 'staking all on winning'.[6] That included putting his relationship with Clinton on the line.

In a ground-breaking speech on foreign policy, at the Economic Club of Chicago on 22 April 1999, as NATO bombs were raining down, with little strategic effect, on the Serbian army, he put military intervention front and centre in the protection of human rights, making it a cornerstone of his vision of 'a more just international community'. As the Kosovo campaign was illustrating, military force could be an imperfect weapon, but there were occasions when it was the only tool in the box sharp enough to deal with dictators who were deliberately deaf to the usual diplomatic processes.[7] Global problems required global solutions. But to be effective, these had to be delivered through strong, respected international organisations such as NATO and the UN.[8] Worryingly, as events in Kosovo were demonstrating all too clearly, at least one of these key enablers – the North Atlantic Alliance – was broken. The credibility of NATO was in the balance and that was a significant problem for Blair and his new doctrine of international community.

Cool Britannia and Blair's Global Britain

Political commentator, Andrew Rawnsley, has claimed that Blair wanted to be a leader in Europe.[9] After their first meeting, Bill Clinton felt he would be 'a good leader for the UK and all of Europe'.[10]

---

5   Bill Clinton, *My Life* (London: Hutchinson, 2004), pp.850–851.
6   Blair, *A Journey,* p.237.
7   Blair, *A Journey,* p.368.
8   Blair, *A Journey,* p.225.
9   Andrew Rawnsley, *Servants of the People, The Inside Story of New Labour* (London: Hamish Hamilton, 2000), p.75.
10 Clinton, *My Life,* p.756.

Both the well-connected journalist, and the American President were selling him short. Despite his claimed ignorance of foreign affairs, Blair sought a much bigger prize: he saw himself standing beside Clinton, Yeltsin and Jiang Zemin as a leader on the global stage. That objective has endured over the years and is visible today through the work of his Global Institute for Change, which seeks to influence the polices of foreign governments.[11]

Speaking in Manchester, just before Labour's landslide General Election victory in 1997, Blair had declared: 'Century upon century, it has been the destiny of Britain to lead other nations…That should not be a destiny that is part of our history. It should be part of our future…We are a leader of nations or we are nothing'.[12]

But there were problems with that aspiration. As the twentieth century drew to a close, Britain no longer carried the military, economic and political weight that it had once wielded to such great effect. In the post-war, post-colonial era, the country had lost its empire, and with it much of its ability to influence world leaders and global events. Successive governments had cut the defence budget, paring the armed forces down to a shadow of their former size. Britannia might be 'cool' under New Labour, but she no longer ruled the waves and her voice carried little of its previous resonance and authority.

Margaret Thatcher had regained some ground in 1982, thanks to her steadfastness in the face of Argentina's invasion of the Falkland Islands, and later for her part in helping to bring Soviet President, Mikhail Gorbachev, to the negotiating table, and an end to the Cold War. However, her successor, John Major, despite leading the Conservatives to an unlikely election victory in 1992, had become distracted by internecine warfare within the party, mostly over its position on Europe. As a result, by 1997, Britain held little sway in Brussels – or anywhere else.

Blair understood that reinventing Britain as a 'leader of nations' was a tall order. The country's rehabilitation on the world stage would require more than the steely will of its new Prime Minister. And it would not happen at all unless he was able to build strong personal relationships with some of the big beasts that inhabited the political jungle beyond the shores of the United Kingdom. Nevertheless, he was determined to stand tall alongside the Chiracs and the Schröders, the Berlusconis and the Putins, the Zu Rongis and the Vajpayees. But he knew that he would only be able to do that if he could perch on the shoulders of an even more powerful and influential figure. It was this objective that motivated him, early on in his premiership, to befriend Clinton, even though the American's 'colourful' off-screen life could have been damaging for his own premiership. The relationship was not always easy. There were serious road bumps along the way, including major disagreements over the use of ground forces in the Kosovo campaign.[13] But Blair stuck with Clinton through thick and thin.

It was this same need for influence that led him to choose to walk in lock-step with Clinton's successor, the arch-Republican, George Walker Bush, a man who should have been Blair's political nemesis – not just in the initial aftermath of 9/11, but throughout the Bush presidency. Pledging support for Bush and the American people after the New York attack was an act of 'realpolitik'. But in doing so, Blair was also demonstrating that he had taken to heart Margaret Thatcher's advice in 1997 when she had told him it was 'the duty of a British Prime Minister to get on with a US

---

11   Kiran Stacey, 'The complex and corporate rise of the Tony Blair Institute', *the Guardian,* 17 September 2023, <https://www.theguardian.com/politics/2023/sep/17/tony-blair-institute-rise>, accessed 22 February 2025.

12   Bernard Crick, 'Blair should beware the boiling up of little irritations', the *Guardian*, (29 September 2003), <https://www.theguardian.com/politics/2003/sep/29/labour.uk>, accessed 6 March 2023.

13   Andrew Rawnsley, 'How Kosovo Strained Blair's Special Relationship', the *Guardian*, (17 September 2000), <https://www.theguardian.com/politics/2000/sep/17/labour.labour1997to99>, accessed 7 March 2023.

President'.[14] The young Prime Minister saw his role as a bridge, spanning the Atlantic, ensuring that the link between Europe and the US was strong, productive and two-way. By playing that part, and by maintaining a strong personal relationship with the US presidency, he calculated that he would strengthen his own reputation and give himself a more influential voice in discussions with Paris, Berlin, and Brussels as well as with other capitals in Europe and more widely. By getting close to Bush, by proving himself to be a loyal, faithful and dependable ally, willing to provide vocal support and then back it up with action – including military force – when required, he believed he would also gain some sway in shaping how the White House and the Pentagon chose to act on global issues.[15] The strategy worked, at least in the early days. Of all the world leaders Bush could have called first on the day after the Twin Towers fell, it was Tony Blair who was at the top of the list.[16]

This pursuit of international influence, coupled with a genuine desire to try to 'do the right thing', would drive Blair's decisions to lead the UK into armed conflict five times in six years, including Iraq (1998 and 2003), Kosovo (1999), Sierra Leone (2000) and Afghanistan (2001). But that same single-minded focus, fanned by an unshakable belief in his own judgement, would exact a heavy price on him, and on the Armed Forces that were to do his bidding. For Blair, the cost included losing the trust of a large section of the British people as well as the support of his party and many of his Cabinet colleagues, leading to a premature exit from 10 Downing Street in 2007. For the military, hacked down in size and underfunded for decades by Labour and Conservative administrations alike, it would mean years of overstretch, facilitated by the 'can-do' attitude of some senior military leaders, who encouraged Downing Street to believe it could keep on trying to do too much with too few people and not enough of the right equipment.

Labour's 1998 Strategic Defence Review (SDR), overseen by George Robertson, had been full of big ideas, but completely under-resourced. As former Chief of the Defence Staff, General Lord Walker of Aldringham, told the Iraq Inquiry, the review had been underfunded 'by well into a billion pounds'.[17] Lieutenant General Sir Richard Sherriff, who had commanded Multi-National Division (South-East) in Basra in 2006, described the SDR as 'resources-driven…in which the infantry in particular had been significantly reduced'.[18] The review had set out a new Defence agenda, but the Treasury had refused to provide sufficient funds to deliver it properly; Blair did not feel able to overrule his Chancellor on the matter; and it was left to Thomas Atkins, and his air and naval equivalents, to pay the price in the deserts of Iraq and in Afghanistan.

The Global War on Terror

On 26 January 2006, the Defence Secretary, Dr. John Reid, announced the composition of the British force to be deployed to southern Afghanistan later that year. Speaking from the Despatch Box in the House of Commons he told his fellow parliamentarians, and, by extension, the nation and the world, that the troops would be going there to 'help to create and to maintain a framework

---

14 Con Coughlin, *American Ally – Tony Blair and the War on Terror* (London: Politico's Publishing, 2006), p.14.
15 Blair, *A Journey*, p.352.
16 George W. Bush, *Decision Points* (London: Virgin Books, 2010), p.140.
17 General Lord Walker of Aldringham, Evidence to the Iraq Inquiry, 1 February 2010, <https://webarchive.nationalarchives.gov.uk/ukgwa/20160512094012/http://www.iraqinquiry.org.uk/transcripts/oralevidence-bydate/100201.aspx#pm>, accessed 7 November 2023.
18 Lieutenant General Sir Richard Sheriff, Evidence to the Iraq Inquiry, 11 January 2010, <https://webarchive.nationalarchives.gov.uk/ukgwa/20160512094010/http://www.iraqinquiry.org.uk/transcripts/oralevidence-bydate/100111.aspx>, accessed 7 November 2023.

of security on which legitimate Afghan institutions can grow and thrive'.[19] The mission was critical to the UK's national interest, he argued. Britain and her allies could not risk Afghanistan again becoming a sanctuary for terrorists:

> We cannot ignore the opportunity to bring security to a fragile but vital part of the world, and we cannot go on accepting Afghan opium being the source of 90 percent of the heroin that is applied to the veins of the young people of this country. For all those reasons, it is in our interests, as the United Kingdom and as a responsible member of the international community, to act', he told a hushed Commons chamber.[20]

Reid's long-awaited announcement went down well in the House. His Tory shadow, Dr. Liam Fox, welcomed the move to deploy 3,500 soldiers of 16 Air Assault Brigade, and the Government's stated objective to prevent Afghanistan from collapsing into a security vacuum that could easily be filled by Al Qaeda or other terrorist groups. 'We have a duty to stand with our allies – nations large and small that have joined the war on terror', he said.[21] Invoking the imagery of New York's Twin Towers, turned to rubble by the attacks of 11 September, 2001, and the bombings on the London Underground and at Tavistock Square on 7 July 2005, Fox added: 'The slaughter in New York and London reminds us that our national security is best served by denying a breeding ground to those who are opposed to our way of life'.[22]

Reid's claim that Britain was going to Afghanistan to help to bring peace, stability and the rule of law to an ungoverned part of that country, seemed a laudable and entirely legitimate reason to commit troops. But it was not the only reason for sending British soldiers to fight and die in the blast-furnace that was Helmand Province in the summer of 2006. In addition to Tony Blair's growing political problems on the domestic front over his decision to take part in George Bush's invasion of Iraq, other drivers included deepening concerns in Whitehall about NATO's ability to successfully prosecute its new mission in Afghanistan, and thus demonstrate its credentials as a global force for good, a key plank of the Prime Minister's doctrine of 'international community'; Blair's near-messianic determination to continue to support his American ally in the Global War on Terror, come what may; and his growing desire, shared by some at the FCO and the MOD, to break free from the increasingly difficult and dangerous situation in the 'land of the two rivers'.[23]

---

19 Dr. John Reid MP, Secretary of State for Defence, Statement to the House of Commons on Afghanistan, *Hansard*, 26 January 2006, col 1529, <https://publications.parliament.uk/pa/cm200506/cmhansrd/vo060126/debtext/60126-10.htm>, accessed 7 November 2023.

20 Dr. John Reid MP, Secretary of State for Defence, Statement to the House of Commons on Afghanistan, *Hansard*, 26 January 2006, col 1529, <https://publications.parliament.uk/pa/cm200506/cmhansrd/vo060126/debtext/60126-10.htm>, accessed 7 November 2023.

21 Dr. John Reid MP, Secretary of State for Defence, Statement to the House of Commons on Afghanistan, *Hansard*, 26 January 2006, col 1529, <https://publications.parliament.uk/pa/cm200506/cmhansrd/vo060126/debtext/60126-10.htm>, accessed 7 November 2023.

22 Dr. Liam Fox, Shadow Defence Secretary, *Hansard*, 26 January 2006, col 1533, <https://publications.parliament.uk/pa/cm200506/cmhansrd/vo060126/debtext/60126-10.htm>, accessed 7 November 2023.

23 Refers to the Tigris and Euphrates rivers, an ancient term for Mesopotamia, modern Iraq.

2

NATO – A Broken Lance

The North Atlantic Treaty Organisation, or NATO, as it is more commonly known, was born on 4 April 1949, in Washington DC, with the signing of the North Atlantic Treaty, sometimes referred to as the Washington Treaty. The pact derived its authority from Article 51 of the United Nations Charter, which sets out the inherent right of independent states to individual or collective defence. It is the idea that 'an attack on one is an attack on all', enshrined in Article 5 of the Treaty, that sits at the heart of NATO's purpose, committing each member to share the risks, responsibilities and benefits of collective defence.[1]

In 1949, the main purpose of the Treaty was to build a mutual assistance pact among the 12 original signatories, designed to stand up to the threat that the Soviet Union would seek to extend its hegemony over Eastern Europe to other parts of the continent. The original drafters did their jobs well. The objectives and structures they set out stood up to the test of time, requiring no significant amendments (apart from some protocols to facilitate the accession of new members). Over the next four decades, until the dissolution of the Soviet Union in 1991, the alliance formed an effective bastion against Russian aggression, playing its part in maintaining the two potential protagonists in a state of near-peaceful equilibrium that some have called 'The Cold War Stand-off'. With the break-up of the Warsaw Pact, and the birth of a new era of improved East–West relations, characterised by the signing of a range of arms control agreements, and a general feeling that the likelihood of a 'hot' conflict between the two blocs was receding, many people on both sides of Churchill's 'Iron Curtain' began to consider how they could lever fiscal benefits from the brave new world that appeared to be developing. Discourse soon turned to the idea of a 'peace dividend', funded by reducing weapons stockpiles and military footprints, turning tanks and guns into ploughshares, savings that were, in many military minds, '…too sharply taken in the euphoria and relief that followed the end of the Cold War'.[2] In the West, the debate quickly moved to the relevance of NATO and the future of the alliance in a world where the original *raison d'etre* for such an organisation appeared to be fading away.

Although there were differing views on the future of European defence and NATO, both the then British Prime Minister, Margaret Thatcher, and the US President, George Bush Snr, were clear that the North Atlantic Alliance remained essential, even if the threat no longer seemed to emanate from the East. This new thinking can be divined in a somewhat prophetic speech made by Thatcher just seven months after the Berlin Wall had tumbled. At a meeting of the North Atlantic Council, at the Scottish seaside golf course at Turnberry, near Ayr, on 17 June 1990, she

---

1 Founding Treaty of the North Atlantic Treaty Organisation (NATO), <https://www.NATO.int/cps/en/NATOhq/topics_67656.htm#:~:text=The%20foundations%20of%20the%20North,Atlantic%20Treaty%20Organization%20%E2%80%93%20or%20NATO>, accessed 6 March 2023.
2 General Sir Mike Jackson, *Soldier* (London: Transworld Publishers, 2007), p.370.

had asked: 'Ought NATO to give more thought to possible threats to our security from other directions?' Thatcher went on:

> There is no guarantee that threats to our security will stop at some imaginary line across the mid-Atlantic… With the spread of sophisticated weapons and military technology to areas like the Middle East, potential threats to NATO territory may originate more from outside Europe. Against that background, it would be only prudent for NATO countries to retain a capacity to carry out multiple roles, with more flexible and versatile forces.[3]

In expressing this view, Thatcher was, in effect, firing the first salvo in a campaign that would see a modernising NATO shift from a heavy, single focus on Europe and the North Atlantic to a more expeditionary 'out of area' mindset. The same point was echoed more recently by NATO Secretary General, Jens Stoltenberg. In a speech in Riga, Latvia, on 30 November 2021, recalling the end of the Cold War, he said: 'People said either NATO has to go out of business or out of area. We went out of area'.[4]

The first manifestation of this new approach occurred in 1992 when the alliance decided to become involved, with mixed results, in Bosnia-Herzegovina, and continued in March 1999, when NATO launched a 78-day bombing campaign in a bid to stop the humanitarian catastrophe that was unfolding in Kosovo. By the turn of the century, however, with George Bush Jnr now inhabiting the White House, Vice President Dick Cheney at the Naval Observatory on Massachusetts Avenue, and Donald Rumsfeld at the Pentagon, many in the Washington administration were once again asking: 'What is NATO for?' The alliance was expanding: the original 12 nations had been joined by seven more, with five or six others sitting on the sidelines waiting for their opportunity to take the field. But Republican hawks – the so-called 'neocons' of whom Cheney was the chief cheer-leader, supported by Rumsfeld himself and his deputy, Paul Wolfowitz – remained sceptical about whether the European nations would ever be prepared to ante-up their fair share of the insurance premium to keep themselves and fellow members safe. There was a strong view on the western shores of the Atlantic that Europe was leaving the US to shoulder too much of the fiscal burden of collective defence. At the same time, politicians in European capitals were heard to ask if America would really be prepared to risk Washington to deter an attack on Paris. Few wanted to 'kill off' NATO, but there was a need, many thought, particularly after the perceived poor performances in the Balkans, to make serious efforts to transform it – to turn it into a 'quicker, more mobile, more precise and more effective' partner, even as it enlarged to complete the reunification of Europe and developed a new relationship with Russia.[5]

Having based much of his military intervention policy on having effective international organisations, such as NATO and the UN, through which to act, Blair was concerned that a weak, ineffective Atlantic alliance would become a single point of failure. When the world needed to take action, there would be no 'force for good' to do the heavy lifting. These worries first became evident during the Kosovo campaign. Member states, including the US, had been reluctant to take the necessary action to ensure success. European leaders, Chirac (France), Schroder (Germany) and Massimo D'Alema (Italy), were happy to call on the Serbs to cease their process of ethnic

---

3 Margaret Thatcher, *Margaret Thatcher – The Downing Street Years* (London: Harper Collins, 1993), p.812.
4 Jens Stoltenberg, Secretary General, NATO, Speech at Riga, 30 November 2021, <https://www.NATO.int/cps/en/NATOhq/opinions_189089.htm?selectedLocale=en>, accessed 6 March 2023.
5 Steven Erlanger, 'For NATO, Little is Sure Now but Growth', *The New York Times* (19 May 2002), <https://www.nytimes.com/2002/05/19/world/for-nato-little-is-sure-now-but-growth.html?searchResultPosition=>, accessed 6 March 2023.

cleansing, and to back up their words with an aerial bombing campaign. But the trio were clear from the beginning that the use of ground forces should be ruled out explicitly from any threat of military action.[6] Blair rightly felt this position was 'utterly hopeless' as a negotiating tactic. It encouraged the Serbian leader, Milosevic, to believe the Alliance was not really serious and that he could continue to do as he wished.[7]

However, President Clinton and his advisors believed the case for committing US ground forces to the crisis would be a 'hard sell' in Washington and among his voters.[8] The administration was struggling to find a convincing argument to explain the US national interest in getting involved in Kosovo. And despite the closeness of his relationship with the British Prime Minister, Clinton steadfastly refused to make the case to his domestic audience.

As the weeks went by, Blair's heavyweight lobbying of Clinton and his inner circle began to have an effect. There were signs that the President was beginning to think seriously about shifting his position.[9] In the end, however, and somewhat ironically, it was a combination of Blair's boldness and Russian intervention that saved NATO's blushes, along with those of Clinton and the US. But it had been a close-run thing. Blair's willingness to put himself out on a limb by signalling that he was prepared to commit troops on the ground, together with media whispers that Clinton was also beginning to lean in that direction, had convinced Russia that the risks to its strategic interests were too great to allow Serbian leader Slobodan Milosevic to continue.

George Robertson announced on 29 May that Britain would send an additional 12,000 troops to neighbouring Macedonia, as part of KFOR, although he expressly denied that the expansion was intended to prepare the way for NATO to fight its way into Kosovo.[10] In Parliament later that day, at Prime Minister's Questions, Blair was more forward-leaning. When asked by Liberal Democrat leader, Paddy Ashdown, to agree that NATO had given itself a means of widening the option for the use of ground forces, Blair replied: 'There is no doubt at all that it is a significant and a right move…It is important to ensure that we have sufficient ground forces – we will need them on any basis…'[11] This was a long way from a definite confirmation, but it was a strong, if deniable, hint that he was prepared to use the force offensively if required. Detecting a hardening of the Alliance's position, Boris Yeltsin sent former Russian Prime Minister, Viktor Chernomyrdin, to warn the Serbian that if his actions provoked a ground war he could not count on Moscow for help.[12] Milosevic backed down. On 10 June the Serbian army began to withdraw from Kosovo. The humanitarian crisis had been prevented from becoming a disaster.

The Kosovo affair had helped to establish Tony Blair as a serious and determined international player, but it also left deep scars. It had exposed 'severe limitations' within NATO on many levels.[13] As he had pointed out in his Chicago speech, if NATO had failed, other dictators would be encouraged to 'doubt our resolve'.[14] Not only had important members of the Alliance's political leadership demonstrated a serious lack of commitment to take effective action, the NATO

---

6 Blair, *A Journey*, p.230.
7 Blair, *A Journey*, p.230.
8 Rawnsley, *Servants of the People*, p.270.
9 Christopher Meyer, *DC Confidential* (London: Weidenfeld and Nicholson, 2005), p.103.
10 '12,000 more UK Troops for Kosovo', *BBC News* (26 May 1999), <http://news.bbc.co.uk/1/hi/uk_politics/353495.stm>, accessed 4 November 2023.
11 Tony Blair, Prime Minister's Questions, *Hansard*, (26 May 1999), <https://hansard.parliament.uk/Commons/1999-05-26/debates/3eaf839e-1b51-4fb2-94c5-f8b812a1acab/CommonsChamber>, accessed 4 November 2023.
12 Meyer, *DC Confidential,* p.103.
13 Blair, *A Journey*, p.236.
14 Blair, *A Journey*, p.273.

machine itself had been found wanting. A long and cumbersome process for approving targets to be bombed meant opportunities were missed. Blair was aghast at the failure of the communications function at NATO headquarters, which was just about capable of managing in peacetime, but completely ineffective in a crisis. His media advisor, Alastair Campbell, was despatched to Brussels to sort it out. The military commander of the NATO Alliance, the Supreme Allied Commander Europe (SACEUR), US General Wes Clark, had to be restrained from potentially causing a clash between NATO and Russian troops at Pristina airport.[15] [16] Blair was more positive about the alliance's civilian head, Secretary General Javier Solana, the experienced Spanish politician, who he described as 'first class'. But he also noted that Solana had allowed himself to become trapped between the differing views of his political masters.[17] Clinton had been fulsome in his praise of Solana and Wes Clark, noting that they had managed the campaign 'with skill and determination'.[18] Despite this, following the Pristina airport stand-off, Clark was short-toured to be followed by General Joseph Ralston, and by October, 1999, just four months after Serbian forces withdrew from Kosovo, Solana had been replaced early by Blair's nomination for the post, George Robertson.[19] [20] NATO was too important to the 'global Britain' project for it to be allowed to stumble along from one crisis to another. Blair wanted his own man in the driving seat to oversee a serious overhaul of the political and military wings of the Alliance and to develop a new purpose that would, he hoped, keep it relevant and capable in the face of changing threats to peace and security.

New NATO Strategy – Same Old Problems

While the Kosovo crisis was playing out on the boundaries of Europe, the North Atlantic Council met in Washington where the Heads of State of member-countries agreed a New Strategic Concept, designed to change the defensive nature of the alliance and to allow for intervention in a wider range of circumstances.[21] It was a step in the right direction. But despite Blair's efforts to tackle some of the systemic problems, and the weight of Robertson's sure hand on the Brussels tiller, the parlous state of the relationship between NATO and the US improved very little in the following years. It would come into sharp focus once more in the immediate aftermath of 9/11. In Brussels, Robertson sprang into action almost before the dust had settled on the rubble of the collapsed towers. He embarked at once on a major diplomatic offensive to persuade the 19 member states to enact the collective defence provision in the Washington Treaty. The North Atlantic Council (NAC), the alliance's governing body, met at 2000hrs that evening and by 2120hrs a resolution, invoking Article 5, had been passed.[22] This was the first time in its 52-year history that NATO had agreed to take action on the basis of an attack on one of its members, and, significantly, it would be

---

15 Blair, *A Journey*, p.243.
16 Jackson, *Soldier,* pp.272–273.
17 Blair, *A Journey*, p.236.
18 Clinton, *My Life,* p.858.
19 William Arkin, 'The General Unease With Wesley Clark*'*, *Los Angeles Times* (7 December 2003), <https://www.latimes.com/archives/la-xpm-2003-dec-07-op-arkin7-story.html>, accessed 8 November 2023.
20 Solana had been due to step down from the post at the end of 1999 but left ahead of schedule after the appointment of Robertson, taking up the post as Secretary General of the Western European Union, and later president of the European Defence Agency.
21 The NATO Alliance's Strategic Concept (1999), <https://www.NATO.int/cps/en/NATOhq/official_texts_27433.htm>, accessed 4 November 2023.
22 Coughlin, *American Ally*, p.156.

the Europeans going to the aid of the US, and not the other way round. Robertson later described the decision as 'a dramatic act of solidarity'.[23] But it was to be a forlorn gesture. The US declined to take up the offer, fearing that by accepting NATO assistance they might lose control of their response to the 9/11 attack.[24]

As veteran British defence and security correspondent, Con Coughlin, has noted, Bush was determined to wage the war on terror on his terms and not those of the UN, NATO or any other international institution.[25] In his book, *American Ally,* Coughlin claims some in the US feared a coalition would hamper efforts to achieve swift results.[26] Andrew Hoehn and Sara Harting believe the Bush administration refused the NATO offer because they worried it would delay their goal to destroy Al Qaeda's strongholds, kill or capture its leaders and end the Taliban rule in Afghanistan.[27] America's general approach was to pursue a coalition of committed countries, if possible, but to act alone if necessary.[28] Rumsfeld had famously declared that 'the mission determines the coalition, the coalition must not determine the mission'.[29] This was viewed as a 'slap in the face' for NATO, and Rumsfeld's heavy-handed 'you're with us or you're against us' attitude was a catalyst for a new round of scepticism about the longer-term future of the alliance.[30]

George Robertson would later admit that the US decision to ignore NATO in the wake of 9/11 'left some bruises behind'.[31] It also sparked a period of introspection among the Europeans about security matters in general, the future of the alliance in particular, and a noisy debate about the role of NATO in the post-9/11 world. There was little consensus in Europe about what action it should take to address the threat of international terrorism. In June 2002, Robertson declared: 'NATO is a defensive alliance, we remain a defensive alliance. We do not go out looking for problems to solve'.[32] But three months later, in September of that year, his narrative had changed to emphasise the need to refocus NATO's military capabilities on twenty-first century threats, including terrorism and the dangers of weapons of mass destruction (WMD).[33] The Secretary General was desperately seeking a way to demonstrate his organisation's relevance, not in the face

---

23   Coughlin, *American Ally,* p.156.
24   Apart from allowing some aircraft of the Geilenkirchen-based NATO AWACS component to patrol US skies. <https://www.NATO.int/cps/en/NATOhq/topics_48904.htm#:~:text=AWACS%20surveillance%20aircraft%20played%20an,take%20place%20across%20the%20Alliance>, accessed 10 March 2023.
25   Coughlin, *American Ally,* p.157.
26   Coughlin, *American Ally,* p.157.
27   Andrew R Hoehn and Sarah Harting, 'Risking NATO: Testing the Limits of the Alliance in Afghanistan', Rand Corporation, 2010, pp.5–12, <www.jstor.org/stable/10.7249/mg974.af.9>, accessed 1 March 2023.
28   Bob Woodward, *Plan of Attack* (London: Simon and Schuster UK Ltd, 2004), p.155.
29   'Transcript of Rumsfeld's Pentagon Press Conference', *The Washington Post* (18 October 2001), <https://www.washingtonpost.com/wp-rv/nation/specials/attacked/transcripts/rumsfeld_text101801.html>, accessed 5 March 2023.
30   Steven Erlanger, 'For NATO, Little Is Sure Now but Growth', *The New York Times* (19 May 2002), <https://www.nytimes.com/2002/05/19/world/for-nato-little-is-sure-now-but-growth.html>, accessed 21 June 2023.
31   Robert G. Kaiser and Keith B. Richburg, 'NATO Looking Ahead to a New Mission', *The Washington Post* (5 November 2002), <https://www.washingtonpost.com/archive/politics/2002/11/05/nato-looking-ahead-to-a-mission-makeover/84f6164d-22c2-4bc8-9f5d-2a7fa92793db/>, accessed 21 June 2023.
32   Lord Robertson, Secretary General of NATO, NATO HQ Press Conference transcript dated 6 June 2002. <https://www.nato.int/docu/speech/2002/s020606f.htm>, accessed 21 June 2024.
33   Lord Robertson, Opening Statement at Informal North Atlantic Council Defence Ministers Meeting, Warsaw, 24 September 2002, <https://www.nato.int/cps/en/natohq/opinions_19723.htm?selectedLocale=en>, accessed 21 June 2024.

of a conventional menace from a significant power such as Russia or China, but in dealing with the new scourge of international terrorism and WMD.

But even as Robertson sought to reconnect with the Americans, Donald Rumsfeld was about to deal another blow to the increasingly fragile transatlantic relationship. At NATO's Prague Summit in November 2002, the US tried to repair some of the divisions by reconfirming its own commitment to the alliance. At a joint press conference with the Czech President, Vaclav Havel, Bush said: 'Our country is committed to NATO. A strong and vibrant NATO is in the best interest of America, so we'll be active and good partners. And we expect the same from our NATO friends'.[34] Bush also used the occasion to call on the Europeans to support his action against Iraq. 'If the decision is made to use military force we will consult with our friends, and we hope our friends will join us'. It would be for individual countries to decide for themselves what part, if any, they would play. [35] At the same time, however, the 'big bang' enlargement of the alliance, agreed at the summit, in which seven new members were admitted, caused some in Washington to think NATO was now too large to ever achieve a quick consensus for action or to act as a cohesive and unified group.[36] For Bush and Rumsfeld, the proof of this assertion lay just around the corner.

In early 2003, as Bush and Blair sought UN Security Council cover for their planned invasion of Iraq, new fissures began to open up between Europe and the US. France and Germany sided with Russia to oppose military action against the Saddam Hussein regime.[37] The situation worsened, to become an existential crisis for NATO, when Turkey, fearful that an attack on Iraq could cause Saddam to lash out against his northern neighbour, demanded NATO protection under Article 4 of the Washington Treaty.[38] Specifically, they asked for airborne early warning aircraft and Patriot air defence missile batteries to be sent to their southern border to defend against potential Iraqi aggression. The perceived threat came in the form of Iraq's Scud long-range rockets which, it was believed, could be tipped with high explosives or possibly even chemical or biological warheads.

Again, France's Jacques Chirac and Germany's Gerhard Schroder, this time backed up by Belgium, stood in the way, aided and abetted by the North Atlantic Council's predilection for unanimity in decision-making. Sixteen of the 19 member states were in favour of agreeing to Turkey's request, recognising that this was prudent contingency planning. However, the northern European trio held firm, believing that by agreeing to despatch defensive aids to Turkey the NATO alliance would be signalling that it believed military action against Iraq was a foregone conclusion.[39] Turkey did, eventually, receive the support it sought, but only after the UN Security Council had voted down a resolution authorising military force against Iraq. However, by then the damage to NATO's transatlantic relationship had been done.

Rumsfeld had already angered Berlin and Paris when he told journalists in January 2003 that Germany and France were 'old Europe', contrasting them with the vitality of the 'new Europe', made up of a large section of NATO's, formerly-communist accession countries. 'You look at vast

---

34 Transcript of Press Conference with Pres Vaclav Havel and President George W Bush, NATO Summit, Prague, 20 November 2002, <https://www.nato.int/cps/en/natolive/opinions_19684.htm>, accessed 21 June 2024.
35 Transcript of Press Conference with Pres Vaclav Havel and President George W Bush, NATO Summit, Prague, 20 November 2002, <https://www.nato.int/cps/en/natolive/opinions_19684.htm>, accessed 21 June 2024.
36 Hoehn and Harting, 'Risking NATO', p.19.
37 Blair, *A Journey*, p.423.
38 NATO Support to Turkey: Background and Timeline, NATO website, <https://www.NATO.int/cps/en/NATOhq/topics_92555.htm>, accessed 7 March 2023.
39 'Split Shows EU Divisions Over Iraq', *Irish Times* (11 February 2003), <https://www.irishtimes.com/news/split-shows-eu-divisions-over-iraq-1.348464>, accessed 7 March 2023.

numbers of other countries in Europe. They're not with France and Germany. They're with the United States'.⁴⁰ Germany's Foreign Minister, Joschka Fischer, implied Rumsfeld's comments were irrational and nonsensical, declaring that 'one should deal with each other rationally and with common sense'. French Government spokesman, Jean-Francois Cope, pointed out that being old also meant being wise, implying that the US was young and foolish.⁴¹ Both comments belied the very real hurt felt in the two capitals.

Now the irascible Defence Secretary added insult to injury by accusing Germany of being in the same league as Cuba and Libya in failing to support the UK-American axis in its confrontation with Iraq. Speaking at a session of the US House Armed Services Committee, Rumsfeld, described by one commentator as 'a blackbelt in bureaucratic infighting' said: 'There are three or four countries that have said they won't do anything. I believe Libya, Cuba and Germany, are that ones that I have indicated won't help in any respect'. As one reporter noted, Rumsfeld could hardly have been more wounding.⁴² Responding, Fischer simply shrugged his shoulders and muttered: 'Well, that's Rumsfeld'.⁴³ German Defence Minister, Peter Stuck, was in a much more combative mood. Addressing the German parliament, he described Rumsfeld's outburst as 'beyond impertinent'. And he added: 'It isn't acceptable. It is out of order. It is even un-American, when you consider that fairness is practically an American virtue'.⁴⁴ It was left to the redoubtable Republican foreign policy sage, Henry Kissinger, to spell out the extent of the damage that had been done. 'The road to Iraq disarmament has produced the greatest crisis in the North Atlantic Alliance since its creation, five decades ago', he wrote in an article for *The Washington Post*, published on 10 February. ⁴⁵

The war of words over Iraq left deep wounds on both sides in the debate. Once again, US officials were left to ponder the utility of the alliance. Some voices in the Bush administration were once more driven to ask if 'foot-dragging' over helping a NATO ally to defend itself called into question NATO's very purpose. As George Robertson pointed out a few days later: 'We were in the international spotlight and seen to be in disarray'.⁴⁶ Others returned to the idea that their interests could be best served by reverting to the policy of building ad hoc coalitions of the willing for specific campaigns. But the arguments also signified another dangerous development – a sharp

---

40 'US: Rumsfeld's 'Old' and 'New' Europe Touches on Uneasy Divide', *Radio Free Europe* (24 January 2003), <https://www.rferl.org/a/1102012.html>, accessed 7 March 2023.
41 'US: Rumsfeld's 'Old' and 'New' Europe Touches on Uneasy Divide', *Radio Free Europe* (24 January 2003), <https://www.rferl.org/a/1102012.html>, accessed 7 March 2023.
42 Rupert Cornwell, 'Rumsfeld 'mends fences' by lumping Germany with Cuba and Libya in an axis of bad boys', *The Independent* (8 February 2003), <https://www.independent.co.uk/news/world/politics/rumsfeld-mends-fences-by-lumping-germany-with-cuba-and-libya-in-an-axis-of-bad-boys-118343.html>, accessed 7 March 2023.
43 Rupert Cornwell, 'Rumsfeld 'mends fences' by lumping Germany with Cuba and Libya in an axis of bad boys', *The Independent* (8 February 2003), <https://www.independent.co.uk/news/world/politics/rumsfeld-mends-fences-by-lumping-germany-with-cuba-and-libya-in-an-axis-of-bad-boys-118343.html>, accessed 7 March 2023.
44 Barry James, 'Iraq Debate Intensifies Within European Union and NATO', *The New York Times* (13 February 2003), <https://www.nytimes.com/2003/02/13/international/europe/iraq-debate-intensifies-within-european-union-and-nato.html>, accessed 5 March 2023.
45 Henry Kissinger, 'Role Reversal and Alliance Realities', *The Washington Post,* (10 February 2003), <https://www.washingtonpost.com/archive/opinions/2003/02/10/role-reversal-and-alliance-realities/eb4531b4-43aa-493d-b28e-c4a375c6b4df/>, accessed 5 March 2023.
46 Michael R. Gordon, 'NATO Chief Says Alliance Needs Security Role in Afghanistan', *The New York Times*, (21 February 2003*),* <https://www.nytimes.com/search?dropmab=false&endDate=2003-0505&query=NATO%20Chief%20Says%20Alliance%20Needs%20Security%20Role%20in%20Afghanistan&sort=best&startDate=2003-01-02>, accessed 3 March 2023.

division within the European Union with the UK, Spain and Italy along with Denmark, Portugal, Poland, Hungary and the Czech Republic all signing a letter distancing themselves from the German and French position. This prompted the elderly Valery Giscard d'Estaing, President of the Convention on the Future of Europe, to accuse EU leaders of falling short of their commitment, under the Maastricht Treaty, to seek agreement on foreign policy issues.[47]

Against this difficult backdrop, Robertson was determined to find a way of guiding NATO back into America's affections. The arguments over Iraq had severely strained the alliance, he admitted, but he insisted that the damage was not irreparable.[48] German Defence Minister, Peter Stuck, perhaps seeking to hold out an olive branch to the US after the bruising encounters at the UN, suggested that NATO should take on the international security mission in Afghanistan.[49] Robertson jumped at the idea, calculating that Afghanistan offered a potential route to redemption. He gambled that with the US military now heavily focused on Iraq, a NATO offer to take on the International Security Assistance Force (ISAF) in Kabul would be welcomed as a way of easing the pressure on the American military and allowing the US to concentrate its efforts on the Middle East. At the same time, it would help to demonstrate that the alliance could reach far beyond its traditional European focus, and that it was rising to the challenges posed by Islamic terrorism. In short, the move would show that the alliance was not hobbled by the painful debates over Iraq, but was once more seeking to reinvent itself to face the changing geopolitical landscape, and thus was again an important player on the world stage. Stuck took the idea to Kabul where he gained President Karzai's blessing.[50] Robertson, meanwhile, pitched the proposal directly to Bush during a trip to Washington towards the end of February 2003 and was gratified when Bush gave it a cautious 'thumbs up'. Reporting on the meeting, Michael R. Gordon, of the *New York Times*, quoted Bush officials as saying: 'There is a general feeling that this is an interesting idea. We gave him [Robertson] a positive reaction and said let's talk some more'.[51] The Pentagon, initially sceptical, was also coming on board, beginning to recognise that stabilising Afghanistan had become a long-term proposition and that they needed to find ways to share the responsibility and the burden, particularly if they were going to focus on other priorities such as unseating the Iraqi leader, Saddam Hussain.[52]

The move, which included an implicit proposal to expand the ISAF mandate beyond Kabul, to eventually encompass the whole of the country, was the subject of some debate within the NAC. The French were outspoken in their hesitancy to endorse the plan, perhaps, with some prescience, fearful of the alliance's ability to achieve success in such a complex out-of-area commitment. Some felt it would be necessary to reduce the NATO contribution in Bosnia in order to free up troops

---

47 'Split shows EU Divisions over Iraq', *Irish Times* (11 February 2003), <https://www.irishtimes.com/news/split-shows-eu-divisions-over-iraq-1.348464>, accessed 4 March 2023.
48 Michael R. Gordon, 'NATO Chief Says Alliance Needs Security Role in Afghanistan', *The New York Times* (21 February 2003), <https://www.nytimes.com/2003/02/21/world/threats-responses-afghan-security-nato-chief-says-alliance-needs-role.html?searchResultPosition=1>, accessed 3 March 2023.
49 Hoehn and Harting, 'A Greater Role for NATO in Iraq', *Rand Corporation*, 2010, <www.jstor.org/stable/10.7249/mg974.af.11>, accessed 3 March 2023.
50 Hoehn and Harting, 'A Greater Role for NATO in Iraq', *Rand Corporation*, 2010, <www.jstor.org/stable/10.7249/mg974.af.11>, accessed 3 March 2023.
51 Michael R. Gordon, 'NATO Chief Says Alliance Needs Role in Afghanistan', *The New York Times* (21 February 2003), <https://www.nytimes.com/2003/02/21/world/threats-responses-afghan-security-nato-chief-says-alliance-needs-role.html>, accessed 4 March 2023.
52 Michael R. Gordon, 'NATO Chief Says Alliance Needs Role in Afghanistan', *The New York Times* (21 February 2003), <https://www.nytimes.com/2003/02/21/world/threats-responses-afghan-security-nato-chief-says-alliance-needs-role.html>, accessed 4 March 2023.

for Afghanistan. Others saw it, more positively, as a precursor to a post-conflict role in Iraq and a suitable test of NATO's competence in such a mission. At the NATO Parliamentary Assembly on 26 May 2003, Robertson pointed out that all of NATO's governments had agreed, at the previous Prague Summit, that the alliance should be able to go wherever required to ensure their common security. By taking on the Afghanistan commitment they were putting that pledge into action. 'NATO is not the world's policeman', he said, 'but it is more than Europe's neighbourhood patrol'. Going to Afghanistan would demonstrate that the international community was committed to the long-term goal of rebuilding peace and stability there, and it would also show 'that Europe and North America still believe that pragmatic, multilateral cooperation through NATO remained the best way to meet their common security challenges'.[53] After much talking, and despite some misgivings, the French came on board with a 'peace-enforcing' role and the NATO Heads of State endorsed the plan. SACEUR, US General James Jones, noted the decision was a 'clear statement of transition from a 20th century defensive, bipolar world to the multipolar, flexible need for rapid response across a myriad of threats'.[54] Afghanistan formally requested NATO to assume command of ISAF and on 11 August 2003, Brussels picked up the gauntlet, taking over the leadership of the force, then centred on Kabul and its environs. This was a significant event in the history of the North Atlantic Alliance. It marked the first time its 50-plus year history that it had agreed to conduct non-Article 5 ground operations outside continental Europe. Bush, for his part, would take a step nearer to NATO and Europe, visiting the EU and NATO Headquarters in Brussels in early 2005 when he had warm words of thanks for the European and North Atlantic Alliance's contribution to Afghanistan.[55]

NATO was now committed to Afghanistan. The reputation – and future – of the alliance was, to a large extent, dependent on its ability to successfully sustain the stabilisation and nation-building effort, not just in the relatively benign areas to the north and west, but also in the more difficult Taliban strongholds to the south and east. In New York on 13 October, the UN passed Security Council Resolution 1510, authorising the expansion of the ISAF mandate, *as resources permitted*, to support the Afghan Transitional Authority and its successors in the maintenance of security in areas of Afghanistan outside Kabul. The UN hoped this would ensure that the Afghan authorities, UN personnel and other international civilians engaged in reconstruction and humanitarian work, could operate in a secure environment and, at the same time, provide security assistance for the performance of other tasks in support of the Bonn Agreement.[56]

---

53 'NATO Secretary General Addresses Parliamentary Assembly', 26 May 2003, NATO website, <https://www.NATO.int/docu/speech/2003/index.html>, accessed 7 March 2023.
54 Hoehn and Harting, 'A Greater Role for NATO in Afghanistan', p.27.
55 George W. Bush, *Speech to EU Leaders, Brussels, 22 February 2005*, <https://georgewbush-whitehouse.archives.gov/news/releases/2005/02/20050222-8.html>, accessed 8 March 2023.
56 UN Security Council Resolution 1510, 13 October 2003, <http://unscr.com/en/resolutions/doc/1510>, accessed 6 March 2023.

3

The Iraq Effect

As the military planners began to think seriously about how NATO would tackle expanding the International Security Assistance Force mission to the south of Afghanistan, events in Iraq spiralled into a crisis that would have serious consequences not just for the Iraqi people, but also for Britain and the US as the occupying powers, for the Bush-Blair axis, and for the campaign in Helmand.

Tony Blair has maintained that the initial proposal to go to Afghanistan came from the MOD.[1] However, the decision to send British troops to support the NATO mission there was actually the result of two separate but related factors – a direct request from Washington, and the Prime Minister's politically-motivated reluctance to put more resources into Iraq. Air Chief Marshal Sir Jock Stirrup, formerly Chief of the Air Staff, and a member of the Chiefs of Staff Committee, who took over from General Sir Mike Walker as CDS, recalled that the US wanted a partner to hold the ring in Afghanistan so they could focus on Iraq.[2] That view is supported by Blair's successor, Gordon Brown, who confirms that the original request to do more there came from the Americans.[3] This is also backed up by a senior Defence insider, who was convinced that the original proposal on Afghanistan came from Washington, and that 'Blair had more or less agreed with Bush that we would do it' before it was even mooted in the MOD. According to this source, when the proposal was first put forward, the Chiefs rightly complained about overstretch and resources. They really did not want to do it. This was relayed to Blair who was 'not impressed' and insisted on seeing CDS. The meeting took place in the PM's study, next to the Cabinet Room in Downing Street.[4] The details of the discussion must remain confidential, but the result, according to the insider, was that the Chiefs changed their collective mind and fell into step with the Prime Minister's thinking.[5] Martin Howard, who, as DG OpPol, was very close to the debate, but not a party to the Downing Street meeting, had a different perspective. The Chiefs, he believed, were ambivalent. Some favoured a shift to Afghanistan but they were unsure of which way to jump. Howard did not have a sense of there being any strong push from No. 10 to prioritise Afghanistan or to 'move on to a 'good war'.[6] One person who was strongly opposed to the idea was the then Defence Secretary, Geoff Hoon. He told the Iraq Inquiry that he disagreed with deploying troops

---

1   Tony Blair, Evidence to Iraq Inquiry, 29 January 2010, <https://webarchive.nationalarchives.gov.uk/ukgwa/20171123123302/http://www.iraqinquiry.org.uk/the-evidence/witness-transcripts/>, accessed 10 March 2023.
2   Air Chief Marshal Sir Jock Stirrup, CDS, Evidence to HCDC, 4 May 2011, EV130, Q604, <https://publications.parliament.uk/pa/cm201012/cmselect/cmdfence/554/554.pdf>, accessed 24 June 2024.
3   Brown, *My Life, Our Times*, p.271.
4   Private interview.
5   Private interview.
6   Martin Howard, former Director General of Operational Policy (DG OpPol), MOD, interview with author.

to Afghanistan until the Iraq commitment had diminished. 'I believed it was necessary to reduce our commitment in Iraq before taking on what was a NATO mission and I felt that, at the time, given our commitments in Iraq, it was probably better to allow other countries to participate in that particular mission until we were in a better position to do so'.[7] This reluctance, in the face of Blair's apparent enthusiasm, may have been a factor in Hoon's subsequent removal from Defence in May 2005. 'Blair was looking for someone who was a bit more can-do about Afghanistan, and he got that in the form of John Reid', said the insider.[8] Lord Walker said later that he advised Hoon to 'say no' if he was unhappy with taking on the additional task.[9] However, this may have been politically naïve on Walker's part. If the Chiefs were now on board, it would have been difficult – probably impossible – for the mild-mannered Hoon to have continued to object and remain as Secretary of State. Lieutenant General Sir Rob Fry recalled that there was a sense in the British Army that Iraq had not been a success, 'that it was a scruffy, indeterminate thing that was difficult to end… it saw Afghanistan as a redemptive mission'.[10] The Chiefs knew they were taking a considered risk in having to sustain two theatres at the same time.[11] Afghanistan certainly became 'more attractive to the Chiefs once they decided that they wanted to get out of Iraq'.[12]

Party and Nation Split

It is not an exaggeration to state that Blair's decision to take the country into partnership with the US for the invasion of Iraq split the country as well as the Labour Party. The move was deeply detested by many people throughout the UK and beyond, both before and after the fighting. This public opprobrium was made worse by the failure to secure the UN's authorisation for military force. Britain and the US have always maintained that a Security Council Resolution was unnecessary. There can be little doubt, however, that UN approval would have helped to legitimise the planned regime-change in the public eye, and perhaps eased some of the domestic and international tensions it created. Although there was some political and public support in the country for ousting Saddam, the prospect of war in Iraq was toxic within large sections of the Labour Party, particularly among those on the left, sparking a spate of damaging ministerial resignations. These included the former Foreign Secretary, Robin Cook (by then Leader of the House of Commons); International Development Secretary, Clare Short; Home Office Minister, John Denham; and Health Minister, Lord Hunt of Kingsheath. It was just as unpopular with wide tracts of British society, who showed their anger by staging mass demonstrations in London and elsewhere. In the capital, the organisers, the Stop the War Coalition, claimed more than 2,000,000 protestors had taken to the streets. The Metropolitan Police estimated the crowd to be closer to 750,000.[13] Either way, the protests were symptomatic of strong public antipathy.

---

7   Geoff Hoon, Evidence to Iraq Inquiry, page 202. <https://webarchive.nationalarchives.gov.uk/ukgwa/20171123123302/http://www.iraqinquiry.org.uk/the-evidence/witness-transcripts/>, accessed 5 March 2023.
8   Private interview.
9   General Lord Walker of Aldingham, Evidence to Iraq Inquiry, <https://webarchive.nationalarchives.gov.uk/ukgwa/20171123123302/http://www.iraqinquiry.org.uk/the-evidence/witness-transcripts/>, accessed 12 March 2023.
10 Theo Farrell, *Unwinnable: Britain's War in Afghanistan 2001-1014*, (London: Vintage, 2017), p.148.
11 Lieutenant General Sir Rob Fry, interview with author.
12 Lieutenant General Sir Rob Fry, interview with author.
13 'Million March Against Iraq War', *BBC News*, <http://news.bbc.co.uk/1/hi/uk/2765041.stm>, accessed 7 November 2023.

Writing later about the decision, and the subsequent military action, the British Prime Minister admitted that despite following his own doctrine and using military force to unseat a dictator who was harming his own people and destabilising the region, by supporting Bush on Iraq he had unified all sections of his party against himself, leaving him politically vulnerable.[14] It was this vulnerability, demonstrated, for example, in the fear of worsening the damaging rift within the parliamentary Labour Party, that had prompted Blair to withhold authority for the military to make obvious preparations for war until December 2002 – possibly beyond the last safe moment. For Lieutenant General Sir John Reith, then Chief of Joint Operations at the Permanent Joint Headquarters in Northwood, this manifested itself in 'a reluctance to do things that were in the public eye'. Reith had wanted to make vital arrangements such as hiring transport ships, calling up reservists and asking the Services to purchase necessary equipment (known as Urgent Operational Requirements or UORs) as early as October of that year, but had been prevented from doing so by the politicians.[15] Chief of the General Staff in the run-up to the invasion, General Sir Mike Walker, believed he needed six months to prepare the Army properly for the invasion, but the politics meant he was given only four.[16]

These problems were caused partly by Blair's wish to keep open his options for military action, but also, and perhaps more importantly, to prevent anti-war factions within Labour and elsewhere from having sufficient time to mobilise parliamentary support against an invasion. As General Mike Jackson explained: '…The government did not wish to send signals, as it was put to me, as if war was inevitable'.[17] This reluctance had the effect of increasing risk for the military. The Armed Forces, and particularly the Army, would not have sufficient time properly to equip and train themselves.[18] [19] The same fear had earlier prevented the Whitehall communications machine from mounting a timely public information campaign to explain to the British public the need for military action against Iraq. This, in turn, had led to the Government placing an overly-heavy reliance on a hastily-compiled dossier of intelligence-based evidence. Published in September 2002, the document included inflated claims about Saddam Hussein's ability and willingness to use weapons of mass destruction – statements that were later disproved by evidence, or lack of it, on the ground, and which were criticised by both the Butler Review and the Iraq Inquiry.[20]

Lord Butler's report concluded that: '…it was a serious weakness that the JIC's (Joint Intelligence Committee) warnings on the limitations of the intelligence underlying some of its judgements were not made sufficiently clear…'.[21] The Iraq Inquiry noted that: 'The assessed intelligence had *not* [author's emphasis] established beyond doubt [as claimed by Blair in his foreword to the

---

14 Blair, *A Journey*, p.511.
15 Lieutenant General Sir John Reith, Evidence to the Iraq Inquiry, 15 January 2010, <https://webarchive.nationalarchives.gov.uk/ukgwa/20171123123302/http://www.iraqinquiry.org.uk/the-evidence/witness-transcripts/>, accessed 27 October 2023.
16 General Lord Walker of Aldringham, Evidence to the Iraq Inquiry, 1 February 2010, <https://webarchive.nationalarchives.gov.uk/ukgwa/20160512094012/http://www.iraqinquiry.org.uk/transcripts/oralevidence-bydate/100201.aspx#pm>, accessed 7 November 2023.
17 General Sir Mike Jackson, Evidence to the Iraq Inquiry, 28 July 2010, <https://webarchive.nationalarchives.gov.uk/ukgwa/20160512093902/http://www.iraqinquiry.org.uk/transcripts/oralevidence-bydate/100728.aspx#pm>, accessed 12 November 2023.
18 General David Richards, *Taking Command* (London: Headline Publishing Group, 2014), p.182.
19 Jackson, *Soldier*, p.332.
20 The Butler Review, or more formally, The Review of Intelligence on Weapons of Mass Destruction, was instituted by Tony Blair in February 2004, to examine the intelligence on Iraq's WMDs which played a key part in the Government's decision to invade Iraq.
21 Butler Review, <https://www.butlerreview.org.uk/report/report.pdf>, accessed 27 October 2023.

dossier][22] either that Saddam Hussein had continued to produce chemical and biological weapons or that efforts to develop nuclear weapons continued'.[23] Alastair Campbell, the No. 10 Director of Communications, has maintained that the document was not intended to make the case for war. But this has been challenged by a senior member of the Defence Intelligence Staff. Writing to the Iraq Inquiry, Major General Michael Laurie, stated: 'Alastair Campbell said to the enquiry that the purpose of the dossier was not "to make the case for war". I had no doubt at that time this was exactly its purpose and these very words [to make the case for war] were used'.[24]

A second collection of 'evidence', later dubbed by the media 'the dodgy dossier', was published in February 2003, just ahead of the crucial parliamentary debate on the planned invasion. This began as a proposal from the Iraq Communications Group (ICG), chaired by Campbell, and it was designed 'to get our media to cover this issue of the extent to which Saddam Hussein was developing his programme of concealment and intimidation of the United Nations inspectors'.[25] It was placed in the Library of the House on 3 February, 2003, the same day that the Prime Minister was to make a statement to the Commons about his recent visit to the United States, where he had met with President Bush at his ranch at Crawford, Texas. Referring to the document in Parliament, Blair had said: 'In the dossier that we published last year, and again in the material that we put out over the weekend, it is very clear that a vast amount of concealment and deception is going on [by Saddam Hussein to prevent the weapons inspectors from doing their job in Iraq]'.[26] It turned out that much of the key information contained in the document had been lifted from an article by Iraqi-American academic, Ibrahim al Marashi, a research associate at the Centre for Non-proliferation Studies of the Monterey Institute of International Studies, which had been published in the Middle East Review of International Affairs in 2002. The originator accused the dossier of 'distorting the intent' behind his work, and of using the material without attribution and without permission. Robin Cook, the former Foreign Secretary, who was strongly against the invasion, described the work as 'a glorious, spectacular own goal'.[27] The Foreign Affairs Select Committee concluded that the document was almost wholly counter-productive. By producing it, the Government had undermined the credibility of their case for war and of the other documents which were part of that case.[28]

Despite Campbell's claims, and the views of the Select Committee, it is difficult to conclude that these documents, at the time of publication, played no part in smoothing the path to conflict. As opinion polling on the eve of war showed, despite considerable public disquiet, the British

---

22 'Full Text of Tony Blair's Foreword to the dossier on Iraq', the *Guardian*, (24 September 2002), <https://www.theguardian.com/world/2002/sep/24/iraq.speeches>, accessed 7 November 2023.

23 *Report of the Iraq Inquiry*, Executive Summary, <https://webarchive.nationalarchives.gov.uk/ukgwa/20171123122743/http:/www.iraqinquiry.org.uk/the-report/>, accessed 7 November 2023.

24 'Iraq dossier drawn up to make the case for war – intelligence Officer', the *Guardian* (12 May 2011), <https://www.theguardian.com/world/2011/may/12/iraq-dossier-case-for-war>, accessed 7 November 2023.

25 Ninth Report of the Commons Select Committee on Foreign Affairs, 3 July 2003, <https://publications.parliament.uk/pa/cm200203/cmselect/cmfaff/813/81308.htm>, accessed 7 November 2023.

26 Tony Blair, Statement to Parliament, *Hansard*, Column 22 (3 February 2003), <https://publications.parliament.uk/pa/cm200203/cmhansrd/vo030203/debtext/30203-05.htm#30203-05_spmin4>, accessed 21 June 2024.

27 Robin Cook MP, Evidence to Commons Select Committee on Foreign Affairs, 17 June 2003, Q10, <https://publications.parliament.uk/pa/cm200203/cmselect/cmfaff/813/30617a02.htm>, accessed 9 November 2023.

28 Ninth Report of the Commons Select Committee on Foreign Affairs, 3 July 2003, <https://publications.parliament.uk/pa/cm200203/cmselect/cmfaff/813/81308.htm>, accessed 7 November 2023.

people were in favour of action against Saddam by a margin of 53 percent to 39 percent.[29] It is likely that alongside Blair's own confident and persuasive performance as he opened the debate, the dossiers did just enough to persuade some waverers on both sides of the House. Even if the doubters in Parliament were not fully convinced that the 'evidence' they contained amounted to an unassailable case, the fact that they existed was sufficient to sway some of the undecided to walk through the 'aye' lobby. If challenged by constituents later, they could always point to the dossiers and Blair's speech and claim they had been misled.

At just after 1230hrs on the afternoon of Tuesday, 18 March, the Deputy Speaker, Sir Alan Haselhurst, called the Prime Minister to the Despatch Box. Tony Blair rose from his seat on the green leather-clad Government benches, took a pace forward, and proceeded to make the case for war. At 2214hrs the division bell rang and the MPs filed out of the chamber and into the lobbies to cast their votes before streaming back into the chamber to await the result. The tellers, Tony Lloyd and Douglas Hogg, approached the Speaker, walking solemnly along the front benches before bowing and reading out the outcome – the ayes to the right 412, the noes to the left 149. Despite predictions to the contrary, the Government amendment had been passed. MPs had voted for the UK to 'use all means necessary to ensure the disarmament of Iraq's weapons of mass destruction'.[30] The majority for war was helped by the fact that 146 Conservatives voted with the Government. However, 153 Labour MPs either voted against or abstained, demonstrating the depth of division the issue had caused.

Just two days later, on the evening of 19 March, the night sky over Baghdad was lit up by the detonations of free-fall bombs and cruise missiles as the air campaign that heralded the invasion of Iraq got under way. By 1 May, after one month, one week and four days, Baghdad had fallen to US forces, Bush was able to declare an end to major combat operations.

Shock and Awe…and Then What?

Despite the lightning speed with which the initial military victory was delivered, and the relatively small number of coalition losses – the UK's fatalities in that phase totalled 33 – the big guns of Labour's anti-war caucus had landed some shots of their own against the Prime Minister, holing him below the waterline. Now, with a General Election less than two years away, some factions within the party were beginning to think their electoral prospects would be better with Gordon Brown at the helm.[31] In order to shore-up the damage done to his domestic reputation, and prevent further political harm, Blair would have no option but to tread very lightly when it came to future decisions about the use of the British armed forces in Iraq. He would not have a free hand to do what he wished, being constrained by public opinion, by his growing political weakness, and by the sight of Gordon Brown looming ever larger in his rear-view mirror.

The combat phase of the US/UK-led invasion that began with a 'shock and awe' bombing blitz on the evening of 19 March 2003 and concluded, just 43 days later, with the formal capitulation of the Iraqi military, had been spectacularly successful. But while Saddam's military machine had been defeated with relative ease, winning the peace was to prove to be a much more intractable

---

29 Iraq Trends poll by YouGov, <https://ygo-assets-websites-editorial-emea.yougov.net/documents/YG-Archives-Pol-Trackers-Iraq-130313.pdf>, accessed 7 November 2023.
30 House of Commons Debate on Iraq, *Hansard*, 18 March 2003, Column 760, <https://hansard.parliament.uk/Commons/2003-03-18/debates/ddc70cf1-f37d-4936-bc03-d5a5ecb02d40/Iraq>, accessed on 8 November 2023.
31 Blair, *A Journey,* p.511.

problem for the 'liberators'. Much of the blame for this must rest with Donald Rumsfeld and his ideologically-driven refusal to take seriously the post-conflict phase, made worse by Bush's decision to shift responsibility for managing the aftermath of the fighting from the State Department, which had developed a good plan, to the Pentagon, which thought everything would be fine once Saddam had been removed.[32]

For a short time after the guns fell silent, it looked as if Rumsfeld and the Pentagon might be proved correct. Large swathes of the Iraqi people initially welcomed the fall of Saddam, evidenced by the obvious joy that accompanied the symbolic toppling of his statue at Baghdad's Firdos Square, on the banks of the Tigris, on 9 April. However, the lack of a proper, well-considered and adequately-resourced plan for managing the peace; Paul Bremer's gross error in disbanding the Iraqi army and too quickly 'de-Ba'athifying' the Iraqi state;[33] [34] and the Coalition Provisional Authority's abject failure to make speedy progress in helping the country to reinvent itself on democratic principles, created a political vacuum.[35] At the same time, unemployment rocketed upwards, basic services closed down, and food and fuel ran short, leading to serious and widespread looting and disorder. With few indigenous forces to control the mayhem, the coalition was forced into the role of policeman. In attempting to maintain some semblance of order, the military rapidly shifted, in Iraqi eyes, from liberators to oppressors. Into this deepening void marched Sunni insurgents, labelling themselves as Al Qaeda in Iraq (AQI), led by Abu Musab al-Zarqawi, and the militias of firebrand Shi'ite cleric, Muqtada al-Sadr, known as the *Jaish al Mahdi* (the Mahdi Army, often abbreviated to JAM), as well as the malign influence of neighbouring Iran. Over the following months the security situation deteriorated as attacks increased on coalition forces around Baghdad and in the south, and inter-ethnic violence between Sunni and Shia groupings became widespread. Lieutenant General Sir Rob Fry, who, as the Deputy Chief of Defence Staff (Commitments), was the man responsible for advising the Service Chiefs on the conduct of operations, told the Iraq Inquiry:

> We did not fully estimate the sense of alienation the Sunni population would feel…We ignored diplomatic warnings of a very violent reaction inside Iraq [to the presence of foreign soldiers], and other sources who suggested we would quickly be seen as occupiers and aliens.[36]

General Sir Mike Jackson, who had taken over from General Sir Mike Walker as head of the Army in February 2003, admitted that the military planners had misjudged how the situation would develop after the war-fighting phase had been completed. 'There was an assumption that there would be a tolerable security situation in Phase 4', he said.[37] The military expected to be dealing

---

32 Jackson, *Soldier*, p.334.
33 Paul Bremer was appointed by President Bush as Presidential Envoy to Iraq on May 9, 2003, and was head of the Coalition Provisional Authority, reporting initially to Secretary of Defence, Donald Rumsfeld.
34 De-Ba'athification was a policy of the Coalition Provisional Authority to remove members of Saddam Hussein's Ba'ath Party from state institutions including central and local government, the police and the army. The removal of the Ba'athists from key posts brought the state to a near-standstill with shortages of electricity, water, food, fuel and a corresponding dip in local security and increased criminality.
35 The Coalition Provisional Authority (CPA) was established in May 2003 and was supposed to replace the Iraqi Government until a new administration could be formed post-hostilities. It lasted from 21 April 2003 until 28 June 2004.
36 Lieutenant General Sir Rob Fry, Evidence to Iraq Inquiry, 16 December 2009, <https://webarchive.nationalarchives.gov.uk/ukgwa/20171123123302/http://www.iraqinquiry.org.uk/the-evidence/witness-transcripts/>, accessed 9 March 2023.
37 The military conceive operations in four phases. Phase 1 – Preparation. Phase 2 – Conduct. Phase 3

with 'predominantly humanitarian' issues rather than a security problem. But within two months, events demonstrated that the coalition was faced with the latter.[38]

Go First…Go Fast…Go Home…

On 12 June 2003, a PJHQ assessment identified 'a trend showing increasing dissatisfaction of the civil populace in the UK AOR (Area of Responsibility)'. This was causing the relationship between the British forces and local civilians to deteriorate. The report attributed the problem to a number of factors: a growing shortage of food; failure to ensure essential services such as water, electricity and security; a general increase in anti-Coalition rhetoric from Shia clerics; inaccurate public information and news reporting; and little progress in the political process.[39] A week later, on 19 June, Sir John Sawers, in his role as Blair's Special Representative, working closely with the CPA, reported a worsening security situation in Baghdad.[40] Five days after that, six soldiers of the Royal Military Police were killed by an angry mob, after being cornered in a police station in the town of Majar al-Kabir, in Maysan Province, north of Basra.

The security picture was looking increasingly bleak and the obvious short-term solution was to broaden the military footprint. With the fledgling indigenous forces not yet ready to take on such a role, the only feasible alternative was to increase the number of coalition troops.

For the British, however, that was not an attractive proposition. In the aftermath of the 1998 Strategic Defence Review, and the resulting real-terms budget reductions, the size of the UK Armed Forces had been scythed down from 216,100 in 1997 to 201,400 in 2006. Over the 16 years from 1990, the reduction totalled 113,400. The Army's numbers had reduced by 45,100 over the same period.[41] Partly in answer to the falling numbers, and the new emphasis on contingency operations arising out of the review, the Army had adopted an informal doctrinal mantra of 'go first, go fast, go home'. In line with that thinking, the then Chief of Defence Staff, Admiral Sir Mike Boyce, had made it clear in his orders authorising combat operations in Iraq – known as CDS's Directive – that the force should be reduced to medium scale (i.e. a single brigade, sitting under a divisional headquarters) amounting to around 5,000 personnel, within four months.[42] The American military had initially planned to follow a similar path. General Tommy Franks had issued orders on 16 April to withdraw the US war-fighting units within 60 days and to use the incoming US forces for only up to 120 days. This would have reduced the US military presence

---

    – Exploit. Phase 4 – Stabilise.
38 General Sir Mike Jackson, Evidence to Iraq Inquiry, 28 July 2010, <https://webarchive.nationalarchives.gov.uk/ukgwa/20171123123302/http://www.iraqinquiry.org.uk/the-evidence/witness-transcripts/>, accessed 9 March 2023.
39 *Report of Iraq Inquiry*, Vol VII, p.224, <https://assets.publishing.service.gov.uk/media/5a7f968fe5274a2e8ab4d16a/The_Report_of_the_Iraq_Inquiry_-_Volume_VII.pdf>, accessed 11 November 2023.
40 Sir John Sawers, UK Special Representative to Baghdad, *Iraq Inquiry Report*, Vol 7, Section 9.2, p.226, <https://webarchive.nationalarchives.gov.uk/ukgwa/20171123122743/http://www.iraqinquiry.org.uk/the-report/>, accessed 25 October 2023.
41 Office of National Statistics, *UK Defence Statistics 2007*, <https://webarchive.nationalarchives.gov.uk/ukgwa/20140116144924mp_/http://www.dasa.mod.uk/publications/UK-defence-statistics-compendium/2007/2007.pdf>, accessed 9 November 2023.
42 CDS Directive, Evidence to Iraq Inquiry, Vol VII, p.17, <https://assets.publishing.service.gov.uk/media/5a7f968fe5274a2e8ab4d16a/The_Report_of_the_Iraq_Inquiry_-_Volume_VII.pdf>, accessed 9 November 2023.

in the country from 175,000 to 30,000 by the beginning of August. This was later reversed by Franks' successor at CENTCOM, General John Abizaid, when it became apparent that the US drawdown needed to be more gradual.[43] [44]

In accordance with Admiral Boyce's direction, the British contribution had been quickly reduced from its peak of 46,000 during the war-fighting phase, to less than a quarter of that number a few months later. When, by mid-2003, there were growing indications that the security situation was worsening, with rising British casualties and signs that the local insurgents were importing improved roadside bomb technology – Explosively-Formed Projectiles (EFPs) – from Iran,[45] there was very little appetite to reverse the outflow. The drawdown continued, more or less as planned, despite the worsening security situation on the ground. A few days after the Majar al-Kabir massacre, on 27 June, US National Security Advisor, Condoleezza Rice, told the British Defence Secretary that the US was concerned the UK drawdown of forces in the south meant a lessening of Britain's commitment to the struggle in Iraq. Hoon denied that was the case, explaining that force levels were based on a security assessment of the situation on the ground and adding that increasing numbers at that time might be perceived as heavy-handed and thus destabilising.[46] The Defence Secretary's response was perhaps a little disingenuous. The UK remained strongly committed to a successful outcome in Iraq, but neither the MOD nor the Prime Minister was keen to use any more than the absolute minimum number of troops necessary to meet the security needs of their area of responsibility in the south. Defence wanted its troops back so that it could begin to address the damaging effects of overstretch and Blair was reluctant to add to his political woes by seeking to increase the military footprint.

The MOD had gone into the invasion knowing full well that it had been operating in excess of the Defence Planning Assumptions (DPAs) for a number of years. Following the first Gulf War in 1990–91, UK forces had been deployed in conflicts in Bosnia, Kosovo, Sierra Leone and Afghanistan. One of the many problems caused by this relatively high operational tempo was frequent breaches of the so-called 'harmony guidelines', which were designed to provide for troops to spend at least two out of every three years at home. These breaches affected the Army unevenly. The impact fell disproportionately on some key enablers such as engineers, medics and signals personnel, all crucial to supporting a military force on operations. Although small numbers of extra troops – individual infantry companies or battalions – were despatched to Iraq from time to time over the months following the end of combat operations, the MOD resisted making larger increases, as sought by the US, even as failing security was preventing the delivery of the reconstruction and development work necessary to stabilise the country, win the Iraqi hearts and minds

---

43 *The US Army in the Iraq War – Vol 1: Invasion-Insurgency-Civil War*, p 146, <https://apps.dtic.mil/sti/pdfs/AD1066345.pdf>, accessed 10 November 2023.
44 Lieutenant General Ricardo Sanchez, *Wiser in Battle – A Soldier's Story* (New York: Harper Collins, 2008), p.442.
45 EFP = Explosively-Formed Projectiles. These were improvised versions of the shaped warhead of the ubiquitous rocket-propelled grenades, using a concave copper bowl at the end of a metal pipe packed with explosives. The copper bowl becomes molten when the explosive charge is detonated, and is capable of penetrating modern armour at a distance of several yards. The insurgents in southern Iraq used these in 'daisy chains', planting two or more devices in series by the roadside to explode simultaneously as a convoy passed. The attack could be initiated either by command wire or by a detonator buried in the road. In Basra, the driver of a British Challenger II main battle tank lost a leg when the vehicle was penetrated by one of these devices.
46 Discussion, Hoon – Rice, *Iraq Inquiry Report*, Vol VII, p.2230, <https://assets.publishing.service.gov.uk/media/5a7f968fe5274a2e8ab4d16a/The_Report_of_the_Iraq_Inquiry_-_Volume_VII.pdf>, accessed 10 November 2023.

and thus achieve mission success. Blair felt constrained by ongoing public disquiet about his decision to go to Iraq in the first place. In April, in a letter to Bush, he noted that there was '…a residue of discord…' over Iraq. 'People who disagreed…are desperate to be proved right. Every difficulty is magnified; every step forward ignored; every setback hailed as failure'.[47] Under these circumstances, and with no sign of the weapons of mass destruction on which the case for war had largely been based, it would have been difficult for the Prime Minister to sanction a significant reinforcement of the UK force. Such a move would undoubtedly have provoked a public outcry. Stoked by a critical and unconvinced media, this might even have led to further resignations among Cabinet colleagues and MPs, and thus to a political crisis.

At a meeting between Admiral Boyce (CDS) and CENTCOM Commander, General Tommy Franks, in mid-April, 2003, there had been a discussion about the possible deployment of the Allied Rapid Reaction Corps (ARRC) Headquarters as a follow-on for the US Combined Joint Task Force 7 (CJTF7). Under this proposal, the ARRC HQ would take over tactical command of all coalition forces in Iraq. The ARRC was – and is – a standing, rapidly-deployable headquarters, designed to provide command and control for a corps-sized military force (i.e. three or more fighting divisions and all their supporting arms and services). The UK is the framework nation and provides a sizeable proportion of the permanent staff, the remainder coming from other NATO member states.

On 17 April, Defence Secretary Hoon's Senior Private Secretary, civil servant, Peter Watkins, wrote, on behalf of his boss, to Sir David Manning, Blair's Foreign Affairs Advisor, to set out the MOD's view on the proposal. It was not at all enthusiastic. Taking on the additional responsibility would stretch UK resources to the limit and beyond. It would have a negative impact on Britain's ability to manage its own Area of Responsibility (AOR) in the south. Recovering from such an effort would be a major challenge and it would be some time – years – before the UK armed forces could return to the steady-state capability which the existing Defence Planning Assumptions mandated. For good measure, Watkins added: '…we could not enter into such a commitment without having absolute certainty about who would replace us and when'.[48] These were very strong words and were intended to leave the recipient – ultimately, the Prime Minister – in no doubt that the MOD thought this was a very bad idea and wanted no part of it. The same points would, presumably, have been true in relation to any deployment to Afghanistan.

In May 2003, Sir David Manning, went on a fact-finding visit to Iraq. While he was there, he crossed paths with the then Assistant Chief of the General Staff, Major General David Richards, who had been despatched by the Defence Secretary to gain 'ground truth'. Richards had been to Baghdad and saw that basic law and order was breaking down. Ordinary Iraqis were beginning to believe that their lives were as bad or worse than under Saddam. Richards felt, with some justification, that Baghdad was the coalition's centre of gravity, and therefore the highest priority. But the American troops seemed to have little idea of how to manage Phase 4. They insisted on patrolling in armoured vehicles, wearing dark glasses, which prevented eye-contact and thus made it hard to build trust with the locals.[49] The British experience in Northern Ireland,

---

47 Tony Blair, *Iraq Inquiry Report*, Vol VII, p.350, <https://assets.publishing.service.gov.uk/media/5a7f968fe5274a2e8ab4d16a/The_Report_of_the_Iraq_Inquiry_-_Volume_VII.pdf>, accessed 10 November 2023.

48 Letter, Watkins to Manning, 'Iraq: Possible Role for the ARRC', Evidence to Iraq Enquiry, <https://webarchive.nationalarchives.gov.uk/ukgwa/20171123123237/http://www.iraqinquiry.org.uk//media/244376/2003-04-17-letter-watkins-to-manning-iraq-possibl-e-role-for-the-arrc.pdf>, accessed 21 June 2024.

49 Richards, *Taking Command*, pp.187–188.

Bosnia and Kosovo, suggested a different, less hard-faced, non-confrontational approach was required. In discussions with Bremer, Manning and Sawers, Richards proposed that the British should deploy elements of 16 Air Assault Brigade (then in Basra with little to do) to Baghdad, to work with the US military to begin to rebuild the Iraqi police force. The diplomats liked the idea, as did senior US officers. But neither the commander of 16 Air Assault Brigade, Brigadier Jacko Page, nor PJHQ, was enthusiastic. They had a plan for getting the Brigade back to the UK as soon as possible and they did not want that disrupted by a diversion to Baghdad, even for just a few weeks.[50] Undeterred, Richards flew back to London to brief the Chiefs of Staff, while Manning set out the proposal to the Prime Minister. Meanwhile, in a bilateral meeting with Rumsfeld, Geoff Hoon said the UK would be happy to help with the security situation in Baghdad if needed. It could provide advisors.[51]

However, when the Chiefs met, on 22 May, to consider the suggestion, although Sawers, who was in London at the time, and Lieutenant General Tony Pigott, then Deputy Chief of Defence Staff (Commitments), spoke in favour, the Chiefs were not keen and raised numerous objections. These included concerns about the command and control arrangements and the difficulty that would arise in keeping the troops supplied when they would be far from their established national logistics chain, which had been designed to support a force based in the south of the country. They also noted that the US military did not think the deployment was essential.[52] The MOD subsequently wrote to Downing Street to explain why they felt the proposal lacked military merit. The Chiefs judged that the deployment was likely to have only a marginal effect and would carry significant risks of UK forces getting tied down in Baghdad 'and of an adverse impact on our exemplary approach in the south'.[53] Replying on behalf of the Prime Minister, Manning told Hoon's office that the Prime Minister accepted the advice but noted that the reference to the US military's view was at odds with what Bremer had told Sawers, Richards and Manning during the visit.[54] It should be understood that throughout this period, Sawers was struggling to achieve influence with the CPA.[55] It is possible that he considered that a significant injection of UK troops in support of the US in Baghdad might give him increased traction with Bremer.

Whatever motivated Manning and Sawers in their strong support for Richards' suggestion, it was not sufficient to persuade Blair to question the MOD's advice. If the Prime Minister had wanted to send troops north, he could have asked Defence to reconsider its view. That would have sent a strong message to the Chiefs and Hoon, and would likely have been sufficient to change the advice. Alternatively, he could have overruled the MOD and demanded that the troops be despatched. He did not, despite Manning's firm advice that he regarded most of Defence's

---

50   Richards, *Taking Command*, p.190.
51   Bi-lateral, Hoon – Rumsfeld, *Report of Iraq Inquiry*, Vol VII, p.200, https://assets.publishing.service.gov.uk/media/5a7f968fe5274a2e8ab4d16a/The_Report_of_the_Iraq_Inquiry_-_Volume_VII.pdf, accessed 11 November 2023.
52   Richards, *Taking Command*, p.193.
53   Letter, Watkins to Manning, *Report of Iraq Inquiry*, Section 9.2, p.209, <https://webarchive.nationalarchives.gov.uk/ukgwa/20171123122743/http://www.iraqinquiry.org.uk/the-report/>, accessed 10 November 2023.
54   Letter, Manning to Watkins (SPS/Defence Secretary), 27 May 2003, Evidence to Iraq Inquiry, <https://webarchive.nationalarchives.gov.uk/ukgwa/20171123123237/http://www.iraqinquiry.org.uk//media/231128/2003-05-27-letter-manning-to-watkins-security-in-baghdad.pdf>, accessed 10 November 2023.
55   *Report of Iraq Inquiry*, Vol VII, p.226, <https://assets.publishing.service.gov.uk/media/5a7f968fe5274a2e8ab4d16a/The_Report_of_the_Iraq_Inquiry_-_Volume_VII.pdf>, accessed 10 November 2023.

arguments as 'spurious'.⁵⁶ Manning later suggested to Richards that his letter contained 'the biggest bollocking by the Prime Minister in writing he had ever seen'.⁵⁷ The subsequent publication of Manning's note by the Iraq Inquiry shows that this is not the case. The contents of the document suggest it was no more than a raised Prime Ministerial eyebrow.⁵⁸ It can be concluded, therefore, that, even when faced with robust advice from his influential foreign affairs advisor, Blair had strong political reasons for not wishing to use his Prime Ministerial clout to change the decision and that these were closely tied to his growing political weakness and falling public popularity, associated with the Iraq campaign.

Despite the clear lack of military and political enthusiasm for sending the ARRC HQ to Iraq, demonstrated by the Chiefs in April, the MOD's Strategic Planning Group for Iraq (Operation Telic SPG) returned to the issue on 9 June 2003.⁵⁹ A briefing paper for the Chiefs of Staff noted that the ARRC remained a candidate, in US minds, to take over from CJTF7.

However, the SPG also pointed out what it considered to be a significant difficulty with such a move. The headquarters would not be effective unless it deployed with near to its full complement of staff and support. This would require NATO approval, as a significant proportion of the personnel came from nations other than the UK. Achieving this was likely to take some time, although the planned UN Security Council Resolution 1483 – which would clarify the US and UK responsibilities as occupying powers and authorise member states to assist – would be helpful. If the Chiefs were minded to comply, a political decision 'in principle' was required immediately in order to inform a final committal decision by 1 August, or to allow the US to make alternative arrangements. The Chiefs discussed the paper on 11 June and concluded that it was not possible to take a decision until there was clarity from the US about the future command and control arrangements.⁶⁰

The UK assumed command of Multi-National Division (South-East) (MND(SE)) in July, expanding its remit to two additional provinces, Dhi Qar and Muthanna. At about the same time, John Sawers noted in a telegram to London that the UK forces in the south were stretched thinly, having to provide security for four provinces. He added: 'We will have less than 10,000 troops to cover Basra and Maysan and to provide a reserve for any problems in the other two provinces'.⁶¹ While accepting that it was not his job to recommend how many troops were required to deliver the mission, he expected the task facing the force to become more difficult over the coming months and that '… we would be better off putting extra capability in place now than risking being exposed by events'. Blair suggested the UK numbers could be bolstered by foreign troops,

---

56 *Report of Iraq Inquiry*, Vol VII, p.209, <https://assets.publishing.service.gov.uk/media/5a7f968fe5274a2e8ab4d16a/The_Report_of_the_Iraq_Inquiry_-_Volume_VII.pdf>, accessed 10 November 2023.
57 Richards, *Taking Command,* p.194.
58 Letter, Manning to Watkins, 27 May 2003, 'Security in Baghdad', *Report of Iraq Inquiry*, p.209, <https://assets.publishing.service.gov.uk/media/5a7f968fe5274a2e8ab4d16a/The_Report_of_the_Iraq_Inquiry_-_Volume_VII.pdf>, accessed 11 November 2023.
59 Operation Telic was the computer-generated code-name for the invasion and subsequent occupation of Iraq.
60 Chiefs of Staff Committee Discussion, 11 June 2003, *Report of Iraq Inquiry*, Vol VII, p.222, <https://assets.publishing.service.gov.uk/media/5a7f968fe5274a2e8ab4d16a/The_Report_of_the_Iraq_Inquiry_-_Volume_VII.pdf>, accessed 10 November 2023.
61 Telegram 64, Sawers to FCO London, 3 July 2003, 'Personal: Iraq: Follow up to the Bush/Blair VTC', including Manuscript Comments Manning and Blair, *Report of Iraq Inquiry*, Vol VII, p.237. <https://assets.publishing.service.gov.uk/media/5a7f968fe5274a2e8ab4d16a/The_Report_of_the_Iraq_Inquiry_-_Volume_VII.pdf>, accessed 11 November 2023.

due to arrive over the coming months.[62] Here again, the British Prime Minister demonstrates a reluctance to increase UK troop numbers in the face of strong diplomatic advice about the requirement to do so.

The MOD's view was that the problems in Iraq were largely down to a lack of progress on rebuilding local infrastructure and institutions rather than too few troops. Outlining the conclusion of a Force Level Review on 28 July, Chief of Joint Operations, Lieutenant General Sir John Reith, told the Chiefs that the military was facing further calls on its resources. These included protection for key sites to support the reconstruction effort; Security Sector Reform activities (i.e. training Iraqi police and military); security for the UK Embassy Compound in Baghdad and the potential creation of a consulate in Basra; filling gaps in the CPA structure; and riverine and border patrols to combat smuggling. He concluded that a nominal uplift in manpower was required, amounting to an additional infantry company (four platoons); an out-of-theatre reserve (one infantry company) that could be based in Cyprus and deployed to Iraq quickly if required; and some additional specialist capabilities, including Arabic speakers. This small increase, amounting to around 160 personnel, of whom fewer than half would be in-theatre, was subsequently agreed by MOD ministers and reported to Downing Street.[63]

Bloody August

August 2003 was a bad month in Iraq. On Tuesday the 19th, a massive bomb detonated in a cement lorry, all but destroying the Canal Hotel in central Baghdad, the headquarters of the UN. The blast killed 22 people, including Secretary General, Kofi Annan's Special Representative in the country, Sergio Viera de Mello, and led to the withdrawal of all non-essential personnel from its Assistance Mission (UNAMI). Later, the British Embassy in Baghdad reported that there had been 237 significant security incidents across the country, over a 10-day period from the 17th.[64] On 23 August, three Royal Military Police soldiers died and a fourth was seriously wounded in a gun attack on a vehicle convoy in Basra. Four days later, another soldier was fatally wounded in an incident at Ali Al Sharqi in Maysan Province, 60km north-west of Al Amarah.[65] Five days after that, a large car bomb exploded outside the Imam Ali mosque in the city of Najaf. The device caused dozens of fatalities, including Shia religious leader, Mohammed Baqer al-Hakim. Detonated as worshipers streamed out of the building after Friday prayers, it had been intended to cause maximum carnage. The mosque was the site of Iraq's holiest Shia shrine and it was clear that the attack was carried out by Sunni extremists, calculated to inflame inter-communal violence.[66]

---

62 Telegram 64, Sawers to FCO London, 3 July 2003, 'Personal: Iraq: Follow up to the Bush/Blair VTC', including Manuscript Comments Manning and Blair *Report of Iraq Inquiry*, Vol VII, p.237, <https://assets.publishing.service.gov.uk/media/5a7f968fe5274a2e8ab4d16a/The_Report_of_the_Iraq_Inquiry_-_Volume_VII.pdf>, accessed 11 November 2023.

63 Lieutenant General Sir John Reith, Paper for Chiefs of Staff Committee, dated 28 July 2003, *Report of Iraq Inquiry*, https://webarchive.nationalarchives.gov.uk/ukgwa/20171123122743/http://www.iraqinquiry.org.uk/the-report/>, accessed 11 November 2023.

64 *Report of the Iraq Inquiry*, Vol VII, Section 9.2, p.259, <https://webarchive.nationalarchives.gov.uk/ukgwa/20171123122743/http://www.iraqinquiry.org.uk/the-report/>, accessed 11 November 2023.

65 Ministry of Defence, *British Fatalities, Operations in Iraq*, <https://www.gov.uk/government/fields-of-operation/Iraq>, accessed 11 November 2023.

66 '75 killed in mosque blast', the *Guardian*, (29 August 2003), <https://www.theguardian.com/world/2003/aug/29/iraq.usa>, accessed 11 November 2023.

The security situation in the country was clearly on a downward spiral. In Basra, the upsurge in violence prompted an emergency Force Level Review. Following a meeting with the Prime Minister and others, which took place on 2 September, Hoon's Private Secretary wrote to Downing Street with the news that the Defence Secretary was planning an immediate deployment of two further infantry battalions – 2nd Battalion, Light Infantry and 1st Battalion, Royal Green Jackets. In addition, a brigade headquarters, a third infantry battalion and engineer resources were being put on reduced notice to deploy.[67] Briefing material for the meeting revealed tension between Defence, FCO and DFID. The MOD considered that the other departments were leaning too heavily on military forces to deliver reconstruction and development – issues that were more properly the responsibility of the Foreign and International Development Secretaries and the CPA. 'The military can patch up utilities but it has neither the number, capability nor money to overhaul the country's infrastructure', the briefing note had pointed out. Hoon's Private Secretary advised his boss not to agree to a 'major, symbolic deployment' over and above what was already being offered.[68]

The reinforcement was announced to Parliament by the Defence Secretary on 8 September during Defence Oral Questions, a monthly event, known in the MOD as 'Top Day'.[69] In doing so, Hoon chose to explain the move as, in part, a response to the 'increasing demands resulting from the accelerated reconstruction programme' in the south.[70] Revealing a significant force uplift in this way was unusual. Under normal parliamentary procedure, important announcements such as this were expected to be made by means of a Ministerial Oral Statement, the title of which is printed on the daily Order Paper for all MPs and members of the Parliamentary Press Gallery (the political correspondents of the main domestic and foreign media outlets) to see. Under this procedure, the relevant Secretary of State or departmental minister makes a 10-minute statement at the Despatch Box and is then questioned on the detail by his Opposition 'shadow' minister, and other MPs. The question-and-answer session, which is generally restricted to the matter at hand, usually lasts for about an hour, but can be extended at the Speaker's discretion, depending on the number of members who indicate that they wish to ask a question. This process is designed to ensure that members are given a proper opportunity to scrutinise announcements and to hold the departmental minister to account. By revealing the force uplift at a busy, monthly oral questions, with MPs of all parties lining up to ask routine questions about all aspects of his departmental responsibilities, Hoon and Blair appear to have been seeking to limit parliamentary scrutiny of the announcement, down-playing its significance, and, hopefully, reducing media interest. This point was not lost on Conservative MP for Bracknell, Mr Andrew Mackay, who took the Defence Secretary to task. 'In my 20 years in the House I have never known a Secretary of State for Defence not give an oral statement to the House when so many troops have been deployed'.[71] The same

---

67 Letter Williams to Rycroft, 4 September 2003, *Report of Iraq Inquiry*, Vol VII, p.268, <https://assets.publishing.service.gov.uk/media/5a7f968fe5274a2e8ab4d16a/The_Report_of_the_Iraq_Inquiry_-_Volume_VII.pdf>, accessed 11 November 2023.

68 Minute, AD Iraq – APS/SofS, 2 September 2003, 'Post-Najaf; Meeting with the Prime Minister', *Report of Iraq Inquiry*, Vol VII, p.263, <https://assets.publishing.service.gov.uk/media/5a7f968fe5274a2e8ab4d16a/The_Report_of_the_Iraq_Inquiry_-_Volume_VII.pdf>, accessed 12 November 2023.

69 Top Day refers to the fact that Defence questions were at the top of the Order Paper that day and thus would be answered orally while questions below them, to other departments, were answered in writing.

70 Geoff Hoon, Secretary of State for Defence, Statement on Iraq, *Hansard*, 8 September 2004, Col 4, <https://hansard.parliament.uk/Commons/2003-09-08/debates/ab05aa2a-0b9e-4d9f-b201-02015f23e7d1/Iraq>, accessed 11 November 2023.

71 Andrew Mackay MP (Bracknell), *Hansard*, 8 September 2004, Col 4, <https://hansard.parliament.uk/Commons/2003-09-08/debates/ab05aa2a-0b9e-4d9f-b201-02015f23e7d1/Iraq>, accessed 11 November 2023.

point was echoed by the Tory Defence spokesman, Mr Bernard Jenkin.[72] By allowing the decision to be made in the MOD, and fronted in Parliament by the Defence Secretary, Blair could distance himself from it, and claim, with justification, that it was a military necessity.

By the middle of September, there were signs that the situation on the ground was stabilising again and General Sir Mike Jackson was able to report from a theatre visit that there was no requirement for a third additional battalion to be sent. The current threat came from numerous sources including organised crime, former regime loyalists and international terrorism. To counter these, Jackson counselled moving the focus of intelligence-gathering assets away from the search for WMD and towards counter-terrorism.[73]

A month later, the Defence Chiefs considered another paper, setting out options for the deployment of the ARRC HQ. The note described three potential courses of action: a moderate role in Afghanistan from August 2004; a more extensive role in Afghanistan, also from August 2004; or taking over as the Coalition HQ in Iraq (replacing CJTF7) from March 2005. All of these would have significant personnel impacts across the Army. This paper appears to have been deliberately written in a way that was designed to encourage the Chiefs to set a course away from Iraq and towards Afghanistan. The author, Lieutenant General Fry, pointed out that while Iraq offered the potential for the most challenging and high-profile employment of the headquarters, it remained unlikely, when push came to shove, that the Americans would be prepared to relinquish command of US forces to a British or NATO HQ. He also raised the spectre of the headquarters being deployed simply as a 'stop-gap between US commands, rather than as part of a wider strategic shift…'.[74]

Given the US military's known reluctance to place its troops under the command of another nation, it was not unreasonable for Fry to make this point. However, it had been the Americans who had first raised the possibility of the headquarters going to Iraq. They remained keen to plan for the relief of CJTF7, and the ARRC HQ was, in many ways, the ideal candidate to take on the role. It was, as General Mike Jackson, a former commander, has said, 'the jewel in the NATO command and control crown'.[75] It was well-trained, experienced, highly-regarded, and a known quantity to the US military, with a number of their own personnel holding key positions within its structure. It had performed well in its most recent operational mission in Kosovo and it was designed to deploy quickly and reach full operating capability within a short period of time, which would help to ensure a smooth transition with the least disruption. It is seldom advisable, as Abraham Lincoln is reputed to have said, to 'change horses in midstream', but if such a manoeuvre was considered necessary, the ARRC was an obvious choice. There would have been little to gain, and lots to lose, in terms of maintaining the operational tempo of the campaign, by using it in a

---

72 Bernard Jenkin, Shadow Defence Secretary, *Hansard*, 8 September 2004, Col 5, <https://hansard.parliament.uk/Commons/2003-09-08/debates/ab05aa2a-0b9e-4d9f-b201-02015f23e7d1/Iraq>, accessed 11 November 2023.

73 General Sir Mike Jackson, *Report of the Iraq Inquiry*, <https://assets.publishing.service.gov.uk/media/5a7f968fe5274a2e8ab4d16a/The_Report_of_the_Iraq_Inquiry_-_Volume_VII.pdf>, accessed 11 November 2023.

74 Minute DCDS(C) – COSSEC, 13 October 2003, 'HQ ARRC – options for deployment', *Report of Iraq Inquiry*, Vol VII, pp.283–284, <https://assets.publishing.service.gov.uk/media/5a7f968fe5274a2e8ab4d16a/The_Report_of_the_Iraq_Inquiry_-_Volume_VII.pdf>, accessed 14 November 2023.

75 General Sir Mike Jackson, Evidence to Iraq Inquiry, p.51, <https://webarchive.nationalarchives.gov.uk/ukgwa/20160512093902/http://www.iraqinquiry.org.uk/transcripts/oralevidence-bydate/100728.aspx#pm>, accessed 14 November 2023.

'stop-gap' role. Fry's advice may, therefore, have been tempered by wider considerations such as Downing Street reluctance.

In late November, with the JIC reporting signs that Al Qaeda leaders were looking for opportunities to play a greater role in Iraq, the US Joint Chiefs, switched tactics. They now asked if the UK would be prepared to send the ARRC HQ to Afghanistan.[76] Coming hard on the heels of Lieutenant General Fry's paper, putting a possible Afghanistan mission ahead of a deployment to Iraq, it is difficult to avoid the conclusion that senior Defence figures on both sides of the Atlantic had been conspiring to find a course of action that would be attractive to US and UK political and military leaders. US commanders, no doubt steered by their British counterparts, and in view of the earlier reluctance, appear to have concluded they could not rely on Blair to reinforce Iraq. If additional troops were required there – and they were – they would have to be American. With the Brits apparently beginning to focus on a new NATO mission in Afghanistan, perhaps there was a deal to be done that allowed the US to reduce its commitment there and switch resource to Iraq. In other words, the UK was now being invited to burden-share across the two theatres.

Foreign Office officials were initially supportive of the request. They pointed out that sending the headquarters to Iraq risked allowing the US to reduce its military commitment there and would add political risk for the UK. 'Our chance of success will be no better (or worse) than the Americans…We are unlikely to want to be put in such an exposed position for another two years'.[77] Edward Oakden, the FCO's Director of International Security, and Sir Peter Ricketts, the UK Permanent Representative to NATO, agreed. In Oakden's opinion, there was a strong view within Defence, including the Chief of the General Staff, that there was 'no attractive prospect' of using the ARRC in Iraq.[78] That being so, the UK now seemed to be leaning towards seeking to deploy it in Afghanistan – 'both to do the real job that needs doing on the ground there, and because that is the way to maintain UK leadership in NATO'.[79] But before that could happen, there would be another twist in the road.

Fallujah

On New Year's Day, 2004, Sir Jeremy Greenstock, the highly-experienced former UK Ambassador to the UN and Blair's new Special Representative for Iraq within the Coalition Provisional Authority, who had taken over from John Sawers, was reporting to London that 'this theatre is a

---

76 Minute, Thompson – Ehrman and Private Secretary (FCO), 20 November 2003, 'Possible Deployment of the ARRC to Afghanistan/Iraq', *Report of Iraq Inquiry*, Vol VII, p.298, <https://assets.publishing.service.gov.uk/media/5a7f968fe5274a2e8ab4d16a/The_Report_of_the_Iraq_Inquiry_-_Volume_VII.pdf>, accessed 21 June 2024.

77 Minute, Thompson to Ehrman and Private Secretary (FCO), 20 November 2003, 'Possible Deployment of the ARRC to Afghanistan/Iraq', *Report of Iraq Inquiry*, Vol VII, p.298, <https://assets.publishing.service.gov.uk/media/5a7f968fe5274a2e8ab4d16a/The_Report_of_the_Iraq_Inquiry_-_Volume_VII.pdf>, accessed 21 June 2024.

78 Email, Oakden to Ehrman and Adams, 20 November 2003, 'ARRC and Afghanistan', *Report of Iraq Inquiry*, Vol VII, p.299, <https://assets.publishing.service.gov.uk/media/5a7f968fe5274a2e8ab4d16a/The_Report_of_the_Iraq_Inquiry_-_Volume_VII.pdf>, accessed 8 March 2023.

79 Minute, Sawers to Private Secretary (Foreign Secretary), 27 November 2003, 'Deployment of the ARRC', evidence to Iraq Inquiry, p.305, <https://assets.publishing.service.gov.uk/media/5a7f968fe5274a2e8ab4d16a/The_Report_of_the_Iraq_Inquiry_-_Volume_VII.pdf>, accessed 8 March 2023.

security crisis'.[80] Two weeks later, Defence Secretary Hoon wrote to the Prime Minister, setting out plans for managing defence capability over the next 12 months. The letter did not make for pleasant reading in Downing Street nor, for that matter, in the MOD. It pointed out that the armed forces had been busier in the past three years than at any time since the Second World War and that capacity for activity until mid-2005 had been fixed by past decisions. In effect, the Defence cupboard was bare, with over 30 percent of resources committed to current operations. That position was not sustainable in the long term and there was a requirement to reduce effort in some areas in order to increase it elsewhere. In Hoon's assessment, strategic success in Iraq was the priority. There were four obvious conclusions: the UK needed to be careful about taking on anything new; there was little available for contingencies; they were going to have to accept some risk elsewhere – in Northern Ireland or Afghanistan – in order to get the armed forces back into balance; and they should hold the ARRC poised for roles in either Iraq or Afghanistan.[81]

Responding to the Defence Secretary's note, Jack Straw at the FCO also wrote to Blair, pointing out that, in his opinion, a substantial NATO role in Iraq was unlikely in the coming two years. That being so, he did not see a requirement to hold back the ARRC for Iraq. The risk in doing so would be to encourage the US to argue for significantly reducing their contribution in terms of military manpower. Overall, he favoured investing more in Afghanistan and deploying the ARRC to that country when the conditions were right, 'to ensure we deliver strategic success there…'.[82] The Foreign Office was now leading the charge towards shifting the policy focus from Iraq towards Afghanistan. Hoon's letter had proposed a 'sitting on the fence' approach, making no strong recommendation one way or the other. In contrast, however, Straw, at that time a key Blair ally, was making a serious bid to switch the strategic weight away from Iraq, which was growing increasingly unpopular at home. The matter was left unresolved at the start of the year. By the spring, however, events in Iraq would bring the spotlight back onto the NATO headquarters and the UK troop contribution there.

The city of Fallujah, on the banks of the River Euphrates, is a key population centre in what is known as the Sunni Triangle, an area stretching from Baghdad in the east to Tikrit, the birthplace of Saddam Hussein, in the north, and from there down to Ramadi in the west. This is a densely-populated region, where Saddam had enjoyed strong support, and where the Sunni branch of Islam holds sway. By the start of 2004, the city had become one of the most volatile areas of the country, with frequent attacks being carried out against coalition forces.

On 31 March, a soft-skinned SUV carrying lightly-armed US civilian security contractors, working for the Blackwater private military company, was ambushed by insurgents as it moved along one of the city's main thoroughfares. The contractors had been providing security for a convoy of catering trucks, and had been warned not to use the route through the centre of the city.[83] Using rocket launchers and automatic weapons, the attackers disabled the vehicles and in

---

80 Telegram, Greenstock to FCO, 011657ZJan04, Evidence to Iraq Inquiry, <https://webarchive.national-archives.gov.uk/ukgwa/20171123123237/http://www.iraqinquiry.org.uk//media/225184/2004-01-01-telegram-337-iraqrep-to-fco-iraq-six-final-months-of-occupation.pdf>, accessed 8 March 2023.
81 Letter, Hoon to Blair, '2004: Managing UK Defence Capability', 12 January 2004, Evidence to Iraq Inquiry, <https://webarchive.nationalarchives.gov.uk/ukgwa/20170203171757/http://www.iraqinquiry.org.uk/search/?query=&searchRefine=0&fm=0&fy=0&tm=0&ty=0&da=&dr=&dc=1&ft=1&sortByDate=true&page=22>, accessed 12 November 2023.
82 Letter, Straw to Blair, '2004: Managing UK Defence Capacity', dated 20 January 2004, Evidence to Iraq Inquiry, <https://webarchive.nationalarchives.gov.uk/ukgwa/20171123122901/http://www.iraqinquiry.org.uk/media/212193/2004-01-20-minute-straw-to-blair-2004-managing-uk-defence-capacity.pdf>, accessed 12 November 2023.
83 Sanchez, *Wiser In Battle*, p.330.

the ensuing gunfight the occupants were killed. Their bodies were then doused with petrol and burned, some of the remains being hung from a nearby bridge. The horrific scenes were captured on camera and quickly streamed around the globe.

In the immediate aftermath, Brigadier General Mark Kimmitt, Deputy Director of Operations, CJTF7, promised to hunt down the perpetrators.[84] Four days later, and under political pressure from Washington to respond, troops of the US 1st Marine Division, newly arrived in the area, and with little time to plan, launched Operation Vigilant Resolve. This heavily-kinetic attack was designed to arrest the killers of the Blackwater personnel; eliminate the city as a safe haven for Sunni insurgents; remove all weapons caches from the city; and establish long-term stability and security.[85] Over the following days the marines fought the insurgents with an intensity not seen by the Corps since the Battle of Hue during the Viet Cong's Tet Offensive in 1968. The assault, supported by the use of 'fast air' (F-16s), Cobra attack helicopters and AC-130 Spectre gunships, as well as the Marines' organic mortars and artillery, caused significant damage and destruction to buildings and infrastructure.

The insurgents, through a clever information campaign, aided by the Qatar-based Arabic television channel, Al Jazeera, made it look, to the rest of Iraq and the outside world, as if the US forces were destroying the city with no consideration for civilian losses. Video and stills imagery of wounded women and children supported the insurgents' narrative that emphasised the Americans' apparent indiscriminate use of force.[86] Lieutenant General Ricardo Sanchez, commanding CJTF7, wrote later: 'When the images of destruction were broadcast…most Sunnis felt Fallujah was an attack on their very existence…'[87] Already inflamed by what they were seeing on television and on the internet, when tribal leaders issued a call to arms, Sunnis began to attack coalition forces throughout the Triangle, while Shia insurgents, loyal to Muqtada al-Sadr, went on the offensive in Baghdad, Najaf, Karbala and Kut.

The explosion of violence prompted one of Blair's Private Secretaries to record: 'We are now fighting on two fronts for the first time. Overall, this is the most serious challenge we have yet faced'.[88] By the middle of April, the US military authorities in Baghdad made a formal request for the UK to send additional troops. This time the 'shopping list' was extensive. In addition to a Corps HQ to take over command of MND(SE) and neighbouring MND(CS), presumably to allow CJTF7 to concentrate on the situation further north, the request included an armoured infantry battlegroup as a short-term mobile theatre reserve; an expansion of the MND(SE) boundaries to backfill for Spanish troops who had been withdrawn by their Government; and further resources to protect the main supply routes from Kuwait and Umm Qasr port, to the south of Basra.

Once again, there was a reluctance to consider sending the ARRC HQ. The initial military advice to Hoon repeated the political requirement to seek NATO approval for such a deployment, and a clear concern about increasing the UK military's exposure to the consequences of future US action

---

84 'Iraqi ambush of Americans made a mockery of 'Mission Accomplished'', *Reuters* (16 March 2023), <https://www.reuters.com/world/middle-east/iraqi-ambush-americans-made-mockery-mission-accomplished-2023-03-16/#:~:text=%22Falluja%20is%20the%20cemetery%20of,Michael%20Teague%20and%20Scott%20Helvenston>, accessed 14 November 2023.
85 Sanchez, *Wiser in Battle*, p.332.
86 'Lessons from the First Battle of Fallujah: An Urban Warfare Project Case Study', *Modern War Institute West Point*, <https://mwi.westpoint.edu/lessons-from-the-first-battle-of-fallujah-an-urban-warfare-project-case-study/>, accessed 14 November 2023.
87 Sanchez, *Wiser in Battle,* p.350.
88 Record of briefing ahead of discussion between Blair and Bush, *Iraq Inquiry Report*, Vol VII, p.345. <https://assets.publishing.service.gov.uk/media/5a7f968fe5274a2e8ab4d16a/The_Report_of_the_Iraq_Inquiry_-_Volume_VII.pdf>, accessed 21 June 2024.

in Fallujah or elsewhere. However, in his memoir, *Leading from the Front,* the then Commander ARRC, Lieutenant General Sir Richard Dannatt, recounts a telephone call from ACGS, Major General David Richards, giving him a 'heads up' that the Chiefs had considered six options for reinforcing Iraq, four of which involved the deployment of his headquarters. Dannatt immediately called in his national contingent commanders, explained the situation, and asked them to sound out – informally – their individual governments. Thirteen of the 17 reported that their political masters would agree to a deployment to Iraq if a formal request was made. In Dannatt's view, that meant the ARRC would be able to deploy as a functioning, capable headquarters if required. Despite the advice being put forward by the MOD planners, there was apparently no real problem with sending the ARRC as far as a large majority of the individual troop-contributing nations were concerned. [89] Across Whitehall, at the Foreign Office, Jack Straw once again pointed out that deploying to Iraq would preclude the headquarters from being used in Afghanistan, probably until well into 2006, complicating the prospects of delivering the Government's objectives there. Straw accepted, however, that the decision-makers might have to recognise that Iraq was the higher priority.[90]

The Prime Minister's Private Secretary, Matthew Rycroft, wrote to the MOD on 26 April. First, he directed that any decisions about the American request should be 'clearly military-led'. He then went on to set out Blair's initial views on the matter. He did not endorse – or even refer to – the whole list of requests, limiting his comments to expanding MND(SE) to take up the slack caused by the withdrawal of the Spanish contingent, if militarily sensible, and not ruling out deploying the ARRC in the longer term. He did not wish to be rushed into a decision.[91] In reply, the MOD said the Defence Secretary and the Chiefs did not believe that deploying the ARRC should be actively considered for the time being. Further consideration should be given to widening the MND(SE) boundaries to take in the provinces of Najaf and Qadisiyah, but only if the FCO and DFID stepped up 'to ensure that acceptable arrangements are in place on the CPA (and post-CPA) side'.[92] In effect, Defence was saying that it was reluctant to accept additional responsibility on the ground unless the Foreign Office and the International Development department committed their people and financial resources to help with reconstruction and development. Defence could not be responsible for providing security *and* rebuilding infrastructure.

As April rolled into May, no decision had been reached, although the MOD was in discussions with the Pentagon and CENTCOM about the issue. On 4 May, Sir Nigel Sheinwald, minuted the Prime Minister, seeking 'an informal steer' about the US request in advance of talks between Chiefs and the US military.[93] Blair's response is not recorded, but it can, perhaps, be inferred. In

---

89   General Sir Richard Dannatt, *Leading From the Front – The Autobiography* (London: Transworld Publishers, 2010), pp.222–223.
90   Letter Owen to Rycroft, 22 April 2004, 'Iraq: US approaches for additional UK forces in Iraq', *Report of Iraq Inquiry*, Vol VII, p.355, <https://assets.publishing.service.gov.uk/media/5a7f968fe5274a2e8ab4d16a/The_Report_of_the_Iraq_Inquiry_-_Volume_VII.pdf>, accessed 21 June 2024.
91   Letter, Rycroft to Baker, 'Iraq: US Approaches for additional UK forces', *Report of Iraq Inquiry*, Vol VII, pp.360–361, <https://assets.publishing.service.gov.uk/media/5a7f968fe5274a2e8ab4d16a/The_Report_of_the_Iraq_Inquiry_-_Volume_VII.pdf>, accessed 21 June 2024.
92   Letter Baker to Rycroft, 29 April 2004, 'Iraq: UK Response to US Approaches', *Report of Iraq Inquiry,* Vol VII, p.364, <https://webarchive.nationalarchives.gov.uk/ukgwa/20171123123237/http://www.iraqinquiry.org.uk//media/212093/2004-04-29-letter-baker-to-rycroft-iraq-uk-response-to-us-approaches.pdf>, accessed 21 June 2024.
93   Minute, Sheinwald to Blair, 2 May 2004, 'US Request for More British Troops', *Report of Iraq Inquiry*, p.367. <https://assets.publishing.service.gov.uk/media/5a7f968fe5274a2e8ab4d16a/The_Report_of_the_Iraq_Inquiry_-_Volume_VII.pdf>, accessed 21 June 2024.

his note, Sheinwald reported the personal view of Lieutenant General Fry, that the force package was becoming necessary 'to underwrite our strategic success'. However, on 12 May, Fry prepared a paper for CDS and the MOD's Permanent Secretary, Sir Kevin Tebbit, considering the consequences and risks of strategic failure in Iraq. In this document he took a more nuanced line, suggesting that agreeing to the US requests, even in full, would not guarantee the achievement of steady-state criteria (i.e. the criteria the UK would use to judge success on the ground). Nor could he say, categorically, that refusal to do so would seriously impede progress or damage relationships within the coalition.[94] What had happened to cause Fry to amend his position in the space of eight days? One possible answer is that Blair had indicated that he did not favour making such a significant increase in troop numbers in Iraq and Fry was simply acting upon that steer.

The following day, Hoon, Walker and Fry attended a meeting in Downing Street, called by Blair, to consider the security situation in Iraq. When asked about the US request, CDS told the Prime Minister that such a substantial reinforcement would take the armed forces well beyond current planning assumptions. In plain language, it would add further to the overstretch problem. He undertook to provide a formal response the following week. Interestingly, Walker went on to explain that the Chiefs would be basing their views on three strategic yardsticks: solidarity with the coalition; increased influence over the coalition campaign; and enhanced control in handling the Shia population in the south.[95] The use of these handrails is instructive in terms of how the MOD perceived the issue. All of the tests that would inform the Chiefs' decision and advice were political. The one factor that does not appear to form part of the decision-making process is military necessity. Walker seems to be hinting that the only real driver for agreeing to the US request was to support political rather than military outcomes. Given the emphasis CDS had placed on overstretch in the armed forces, it appears the Chiefs were now setting out to make it difficult for the Prime Minister to approve the US request in order to ease their overstretch conundrum. If there was no military necessity, it would be more challenging to justify the deployments in Parliament or with the public. Alternatively, if they had already been 'steered' that the PM was not keen to have to announce a significant reinforcement, the Chiefs may have been attempting to make it easier for him to decline in order to save him political pain.

At the end of the discussion, Blair asked the MOD for '…their best proposals for enhancing Iraqi security capability across the whole country…'.[96] The Chiefs considered the matter on 19 May and agreed that the best military option was the deployment of the ARRC HQ to command MND(CS) and MND(SE), which would have freed-up CJTF7 to concentrate on the problems in central Iraq, and an additional brigade to replace US forces in Najaf and Qadisiyah, releasing American resources to move further north. There were, however, some real doubts about whether such a reinforcement could be delivered and sustained. A few days later, Hoon's office wrote to Downing Street setting out the Chiefs' advice and adding that in view of the impact of such a large

---

94 Minute, DCDS(C) to PSO/CDS, 12 May 2004, 'Strategic Failure in Iraq – Consequences and Risks', *Report of Iraq Inquiry*, Vol VII, p.371, <https://assets.publishing.service.gov.uk/media/5a7f968fe5274a2e8ab4d16a/The_Report_of_the_Iraq_Inquiry_-_Volume_VII.pdf>, accessed 21 June 2024.

95 Letter, Bowen to Baker, 13 May 2004, 'Iraq: Security', *Report of Iraq Inquiry*, Vol VII, p.372. <https://assets.publishing.service.gov.uk/media/5a7f968fe5274a2e8ab4d16a/The_Report_of_the_Iraq_Inquiry_-_Volume_VII.pdf>, accessed 21 June 2024.

96 Letter, Bowen to Baker, 13 May 2004, 'Iraq: Security', *Report of the Iraq Inquiry*, Vol VII, p.372, <https://assets.publishing.service.gov.uk/media/5a7f968fe5274a2e8ab4d16a/The_Report_of_the_Iraq_Inquiry_-_Volume_VII.pdf>, accessed 21 June 2024.

additional commitment, the deployment should be staged. The ARRC HQ should go as soon as possible: the Brigade should be put on notice to move but held back until 'absolutely necessary'.[97]

On receipt of the advice, Blair called a further meeting for 27 May but he only agreed to a small uplift for MND(SE), which was separate from the US request and followed renewed unrest in the south after a major firefight on 14 May, involving British troops and insurgents near Al Amarah, later known as the Battle of Danny Boy.[98] Before the meeting broke up, the Prime Minister emphasised that the UK must do what was necessary for the success of the overall mission. Operational military judgements must take precedence over political considerations. This could be interpreted as Blair telling the MOD that political factors related to the coalition (as Walker had outlined above), were not sufficient – on their own – to justify a significant reinforcement. However, a more cynical reading of this might be that Blair, with an eye to the future, wanted the record to show that political difficulties were not driving decisions.

A further discussion was scheduled for 3 June. However, before that meeting took place, the MOD's Permanent Secretary, Sir Kevin Tebbit, wrote to Defence Secretary Hoon, pointing out that the Chiefs' advice might have been misinterpreted. They had not set out what they thought was necessary, he claimed. They had merely told ministers what would be possible if there was the political will to comply with the US request.[99] This seems misleading. The Chiefs had been asked to provide their 'best proposals for enhancing Iraqi security'. They had been quite clear that they were setting out the 'best military option'. If they had intended to simply provide an appraisal of the art of the possible, it is more likely that they would have described a range of options with pros and cons against each, and then selected their preferred course of action. The Prime Minister had asked them a specific question and they were addressing that with their advice. Tebbit's intervention needs to be viewed against a contextual backdrop in which he was trying to manage major budget pressures arising from the unrealistic assumptions set out in SDR98. He did not wish to encourage the Treasury to think Defence was happy to accept a further significant commitment, even if the operational costs were to be borne by the Reserve. If the military kept stretching the elastic band and it did not snap, it would make it more difficult for him to argue that he needed a better financial settlement that recognised the actual demands being placed on his department.

The 3 June meeting happened as scheduled. A note of the discussion revealed a subtle change in the MOD's language, possibly as a result of Tebbit's intervention. Hoon and Walker explained that no more troops were required to support the UK's efforts within the MND(SE) AOR. However, if, for other (political) reasons (solidarity with the US, increased influence in Iraq, increased likelihood of achieving strategic goals in Iraq), it was decided to go ahead, 'the optimal

---

97 Letter, Naworynsky to Rycroft, 25 May 2004, 'Iraq: options for a UK military contribution to the wider South', *Report of Iraq Inquiry*, Vol VII, p.378, <https://assets.publishing.service.gov.uk/media/5a7f968fe5274a2e8ab4d16a/The_Report_of_the_Iraq_Inquiry_-_Volume_VII.pdf>, accessed 21 June 2024.

98 Danny Boy was the code-name for a British checkpoint on the outskirts of Al Amarah. Insurgents ambushed the position, being manned by elements of the Argyle and Sutherland Highlanders. They called for help from 1st Battalion, Princess of Wales' Royal Regiment, who were also ambushed as they made their way to the scene. The ensuing three-hour firefight became one of the fiercest engagements involving British troops in the whole of the Iraq campaign, with the fighting often at close quarters, and at bayonet point. Twenty-three insurgents were killed. There were no British fatalities although some were wounded. The battle sparked a major controversy over unfounded allegations that some of the insurgents who had been taken prisoner by the British were murdered or tortured.

99 Minute, Tebbit to Hoon, 28 May 2004, 'Iraq: UK military presence', *Report of Iraq Inquiry*, Vol VII, p.380. <https://assets.publishing.service.gov.uk/media/5a7f968fe5274a2e8ab4d16a/The_Report_of_the_Iraq_Inquiry_-_Volume_VII.pdf>, accessed 21 June 2024.

military solution would be to provide both the ARRC, as a three-star HQ to command both MND(SE) and MND(CS), and a brigade of troops'. There then followed a full discussion (not recorded in the No. 10 minute), after which Blair concluded that there would be no decision and that the issue should be kept under advisement for the time being.[100] By specifically stating that the British already had sufficient troops to manage the situation in their Area of Responsibility in the south and that the only reasons for agreeing to the US request were political, the Chiefs had now given the Prime Minister a way of avoiding a difficult decision. He took it, kicking the can further down the road.

The Defence Secretary visited Iraq later in the month and took the opportunity to discuss the American request with the Senior British Military Representative in Iraq (SBMRI), Lieutenant General John McColl. Perhaps unsurprisingly, given that McColl was the second-in-command at what was now known as Multi National Force–Iraq or MNF–I, he was supportive of the call for additional British troops.[101] He pointed out that the US forces were 'suffering'. A UK deployment would allow the British to conduct operations in MND(CS) from a UK perspective. If the additional resources were not provided there would be a higher level of risk to troops throughout Iraq and a further risk to the strategic mission. However, he described the continuing suggestion that more troops equalled greater influence on the US as 'embarrassing'. The number of British military personnel currently in senior positions within MNF-I and MNC-I (and hence the influence wielded), was already 'disproportionate to our overall troop deployment and financial contributions'.[102]

Meanwhile, back in London, the Cabinet Office decided to enter the debate on 14 June, when it circulated a paper intended to provide background ahead of a further discussion at the next ministerial meeting. This set out three options, slightly amended from those put forward earlier by the MOD: do nothing; deploy the ARRC with a brigade on standby; and simultaneous deployment of the ARRC and a brigade. The Cabinet Office suggested that since the US had not been putting pressure on the UK for a decision, a positive response was 'desirable but not critical'. This is supported by the then CDS, General Sir Mike Walker, who did not recall 'there being a very strong US requirement for us to provide more resources, although they would have been very happy if we had'.[103] These views are open to challenge. As General Sir Richard Dannatt has pointed out, the original US request had been couched in 'their usual, polite and non-pressurising way' but this did not mean it was not a serious ask.[104] The ARRC was a competent, worked-up Combined Joint Corps headquarters. There was nothing quite like it in the US inventory. The Combined Joint Force Land Component Command (CJFLCC) headquarters that had overseen the combat phase of the invasion had been custom-built for the task. Combined Joint Task Force 7, its successor, had been based on V Corps headquarters, but required significant augmentation to

---

100 Letter, Rycroft to Baker, 'Iraq: Prime Minister's meeting 3 June', dated 3 June 2004, *Report of Iraq Inquiry*, Vol VII, p.384. <https://assets.publishing.service.gov.uk/media/5a7f968fe5274a2e8ab4d16a/The_Report_of_the_Iraq_Inquiry_-_Volume_VII.pdf>, accessed 21 June 2024.
101 On 15 May 2004, CJTF7 was split in two. A new four-star command was created, known as Multi National Force – Iraq (MNF-I), under the command of General Ricardo Sanchez (who remained a three-star officer in the rank of Lieutenant General) and a subordinate Multi National Corps – Iraq (MNC-I), under another three-star officer, Lieutenant General Tom Metz. British Lieutenant General John McColl became the second-in-command of MNF-I and was also the Senior British Military Representative, Iraq (SBMRI).
102 Discussion, Hoon – McColl, 14 June 2004, Report of Iraq Inquiry, p.387, <https://assets.publishing.service.gov.uk/media/5a7f968fe5274a2e8ab4d16a/The_Report_of_the_Iraq_Inquiry_-_Volume_VII.pdf>, accessed 21 June 2024.
103 Field Marshal Lord Walker of Aldringham, interview with author.
104 Dannatt, *Leading from the Front*, p.223.

make it fit for purpose. The ARRC would come practically 'ready-made' for the task. In addition, during Hoon's discussion with Lieutenant General McColl, the Deputy Force Commander had pointed out that General Abizaid (CENTCOM) had recently commented that 'he had already asked for HQ ARRC six times'.[105] This is clear evidence that the Americans did, indeed, see the use of the headquarters as important but were, perhaps, being diplomatic in how they asked for it. Despite this, given the closeness of the military and political relationships between the UK and the US at that time, it seems unlikely that the basis of the request had been misinterpreted.

The Prime Ministerial group met again on 15 June, after which Blair's Private Secretary noted that although the UK should not close the door to the possibility of sending troops, the option should be kept open until the NATO Summit in Istanbul, planned for 28–29 June. Probably influenced by the Cabinet Office view, the minute added: '…there is no pressing military reason to send them, nor were we coming under much pressure from the US to do so. We should not raise US expectations by talking to them about the details of how the reinforcement might take place'.[106] It seems clear from this that, by this point, Blair had largely made up his mind that he would not sanction a significant reinforcement of the Iraq theatre. This conclusion is supported by the reference to the Istanbul Summit, given what was about to happen at that gathering. Retaining an option to deploy the ARRC to Iraq was no more than a nod to the reality on the ground. If the security situation had worsened significantly, the matter might have been reconsidered. That did not happen. Instead, the MOD's Director General Operational Policy (DG OpPol), Martin Howard, wrote to Hoon on 18 June, seeking a final political decision on the deployment. Howard did not recommend a particular option: the outcome of the earlier meeting in Downing Street had made that redundant. He simply restated the three possibilities for the employment of the ARRC and asked the Defence Secretary to agree that if ministers decided against Iraq, there were sound military and political reasons for committing the ARRC to Afghanistan in mid-2006 – a move that would 'chime well with plans for strategic hand-off in Iraq around mid-06'.[107]

An additional factor that may also have played a part in Blair's decision on the ARRC was the need to persuade NATO to establish a training mission in Iraq. The UK and US had concluded that security was the main problem. However, the solution needed to have an Iraqi face. It could not be delivered directly by the British and American military because they did not enjoy the consent of the Iraqi people. The answer, therefore, had to be to speed up the so-called 'Iraqi-isation' of the security apparatus. This meant putting greater effort into training indigenous police and military personnel, which in turn required additional resources to be channelled towards these activities. The coalition had enough on its plate dealing with the ongoing violence. It needed another partner to support the Security Sector Reform agenda. NATO had hinted that it might be prepared to play a part in this work, although French president, Chirac, remained unconvinced.[108] In a video conference with President Bush on 22 June, the Prime

---

105 Letter, Naworynsky – Owen, *Meeting between the Secretary of State for Defence and Senior British Military Representative – Iraq*, 17 June 2004, Report of Iraq Inquiry, Vol VII, p.387. <https://assets.publishing.service.gov.uk/media/5a7f968fe5274a2e8ab4d16a/The_Report_of_the_Iraq_Inquiry_-_Volume_VII.pdf>, accessed 21 June 2024.
106 Letter, Rycroft – Baker, 'Iraq: Prime Minister's Meeting, 15 June', *Report of the Iraq Inquiry*, Vol VII, p.388, <https://assets.publishing.service.gov.uk/media/5a7f968fe5274a2e8ab4d16a/The_Report_of_the_Iraq_Inquiry_-_Volume_VII.pdf>, accessed 21 June 2024.
107 Minute, Howard to PS/SofS (MOD), 'HQ ARRC Deployment Options', 18 June 2004, *Report of Iraq Inquiry*, Vol VII, p.390, <https://assets.publishing.service.gov.uk/media/5a7f968fe5274a2e8ab4d16a/The_Report_of_the_Iraq_Inquiry_-_Volume_VII.pdf>, accessed 21 June 2024.
108 'Bush Doesn't See NATO Sending in Troops for Iraq', *New York Times* (11 June 2004), <https://www.

Minister suggested that the forthcoming NATO Summit in Istanbul should be the vehicle to get NATO agreement.[109] By offering to use the ARRC to support the NATO mission in Afghanistan, Blair was perhaps seeking to smooth the way for the Alliance to agree to take on much of the training of the Iraqi police and military as well as avoiding the domestic fall-out from sending more British troops to Iraq.

In advance of the summit, the interim Iraqi Prime Minister, Ilyad Allawi, wrote to the NATO Secretary General, formally requesting NATO support.[110] On 28 June, in the Istanbul Summit Communique, the NATO Heads of State announced they had decided to offer assistance to the Government of Iraq with the training of its security forces. At the same time, the Alliance confirmed that it was expanding its mission in Afghanistan.[111] The following day, Tony Blair revealed that the ARRC Headquarters would be deploying there in 2006 as part of the NATO mission.[112] At Rheindahlen, in Germany, the ARRC planners put away their maps of Iraq and brought out a new set covering Afghanistan.

Blair had successfully navigated his way through a difficult and dangerous minefield. The Prime Minister had calculated that by assuming a greater role in Afghanistan, a theatre that continued to enjoy 'broad legitimacy', he would face less public resistance at home.[113] As General Dannatt, pointed out, the decision was 'a perfectly reasonable strategic gesture for the junior partner to make to the senior partner'. In essence, Britain was saying: 'We will take more of the burden in Afghanistan so you can take more of the burden in Iraq'.[114] Desmond Bowen believed the offer was warmly welcomed by the US military, who had already reduced their troop-strength in Afghanistan in favour of Iraq.[115] Blair's gesture would not free America from having to support the Afghanistan mission: there would still be significant US resources in that theatre, pursuing the counter-terrorist campaign, Operation Enduring Freedom. But it would mean Washington would have to find fewer additional troops to support the NATO mission as it moved south. More importantly, however, he had solved two difficult conundrums at a single stroke: he had avoided the political meltdown at home that would surely have followed any decision significantly to reinforce failure in Iraq, and, at the same time, achieved a pirouette back to Afghanistan, giving NATO a fighting chance of making a success of its new mission there, and thus upholding the reputation of the Alliance as a military force.

---

nytimes.com/2004/06/11/world/reach-war-summit-politics-bush-doesn-t-see-NATO-sending-troops-for-iraq.html?searchResultPosition=59>, accessed 18 November 2023.
109 'Record of video conference between Blair and Bush, 22 June 2004', *Report of Iraq Inquiry*, <https://webarchive.nationalarchives.gov.uk/ukgwa/20170831105402/http://www.iraqinquiry.org.uk/media/247918/the-report-of-the-iraq-inquiry_section-92.pdf>, accessed 18 November 2023.
110 NATO's Assistance to Iraq, <https://www.NATO.int/cps/en/NATOhq/topics_51978.htm?selectedLocale=en>, accessed 18 November 2023.
111 NATO Istanbul Summit Communique, 28 June 2004, <https://www.nato.int/cps/en/natohq/official_texts_21026.htm?selectedLocale=en>, accessed 21 June 2024.
112 *Report of Iraq Inquiry*, Vol VII, p.395, <https://assets.publishing.service.gov.uk/media/5a7f968fe5274a2e8ab4d16a/The_Report_of_the_Iraq_Inquiry_-_Volume_VII.pdf>, accessed 21 June 2024.
113 William Maley, *Rescuing Afghanistan* (London: Hurst, 2006), p.10.
114 General Lord Dannatt, evidence to the Iraq Inquiry, 28 July 2010, p.82, <https://webarchive.nationalarchives.gov.uk/ukgwa/20171123123302/http://www.iraqinquiry.org.uk/the-evidence/witness-transcripts/>, accessed 9 March 2023.
115 Desmond Bowen, interview with author.

4

A Twenty-first Century Version of the Great Game

As has been established above, the British decision to lean-in on Afghanistan was largely a way of side-stepping greater involvement in Iraq, potentially hastening the British pull-out from that theatre. But there were other geopolitical imperatives that helped to drive the move. Chief among these was a desire to keep in check Russian and Chinese influence in the wider South Asia region. This would have been at the front of Foreign Secretary, Jack Straw's mind when he pushed for the ARRC to be held back for use in Afghanistan.

As former UK National Security Advisor, Lord Mark Sedwill, had told a House of Lords committee in 2000, an unstable Afghanistan, as well as posing a direct threat to the security of the UK, could also unsettle an historically volatile region.[1] In this modern-day version of the so-called Great Game of the nineteenth century, such volatility, it was thought, could play to the benefit of Russia and China, the latter sharing a short land border, and importing significant quantities of minerals, including copper, that were vital to its manufacturing industries.[2]

But the move towards South Asia was also a matter of strategic necessity. By deciding to shift their focus to Iraq in 2002, the Americans and British had thrown away an opportunity to achieve a decisive outcome, leaving Afghanistan to fester and creating a strategic deficit. Having left the country with neither the resources nor the ambition to do anything significant, it had been allowed to drift. Re-engagement was 'the right thing to do in both moral and strategic terms'.[3] This view is supported by William Maley, an Australian academic who has written widely on Afghanistan. Maley noted that a fundamental mistake had been made by the Americans in 2002. With the Taliban dislocated and disempowered as a result of their military defeat, there was a genuine window of opportunity to expand ISAF and, with it, to create security, impose the rule of law and ensure that the writ of the Afghan government ran throughout the nation. However, as Maley argues, this would have been dependent on US airlift capability, which, with Washington's sights set firmly on Iraq, was not forthcoming.[4]

---

1 Lord Sedwill, former National Security Advisor, Evidence to House of Lords Select Committee on International Relations and Defence Inquiry, 'The UK and Afghanistan, transcript of evidence', 21 October 2020, <https://committees.parliament.uk/oralevidence/1102/pdf/>, accessed 13 March 2023.
2 Sherard Cowper-Coles, *Cables from Kabul* (London: Harper Press, 2011), p.77.
3 Lieutenant General Sir Rob Fry, interview with author.
4 Maley, *Rescuing Afghanistan*, p.65.

Following Blair's announcement in Istanbul, Geoff Hoon revealed at the NATO Ministerial Summit in Nice, in February, 2005, that the UK would be repositioning its forces from north to south, although there was no specific reference to Helmand at that time.[5]

The decision to switch fire to Afghanistan before the UK's drawdown in Iraq had been completed – and that would not happen until 2009 – was destined to have serious and damaging implications for the force that would be sent to Helmand in 2006. The Chiefs' agreement to take on the Afghan task was, at least to some extent, predicated on a continuing reduction in the military footprint in Iraq. As the security situation there deteriorated, the drawdown process had to be slowed and thus the availability of troops and equipment for other tasks was also reduced. Although this was balanced a little by the ending of the Northern Ireland commitment, Operation Banner, in effect, the equation on which the Chiefs had based their calculation to go to Afghanistan was now out of kilter. This, in turn, meant that a rigidly-enforced limit was imposed on the Helmand deployment. There were also wider implications for the Army, in terms of its engineers, logisticians and medics, and for some key RAF resources, particularly its support helicopters and their air and ground crews. Naval and air force personnel would find themselves filling various land-based appointments in both theatres as the manning stretch began to bite. As Dannatt declared, the overlapping operations in Iraq and Afghanistan represented 'the perfect storm', with the Army 'running hot' as it tried to deliver in both theatres. The demands on Defence were greater than its ability to provide for the needs of the individuals who were at the heart of operations. The increased tempo of operations, and the resulting reduction in intervals between deployments, had created a growing risk.[6]

The NATO Plan for Afghanistan

The plan for Afghanistan, conceived between Allied Joint Force Command at Brunssum in The Netherlands, and SHAPE, the Supreme Headquarters, Allied Powers in Europe, on the outskirts of Mons, in Belgium, was straightforward, at least on paper. NATO would expand its presence beyond Kabul on a step-by-step basis, moving counter-clockwise from north to east as conditions allowed.

In December 2003 the NAC authorised SACEUR to initiate the programme by taking over command of the German-run Provincial Reconstruction Team (PRT) in Kunduz,[7] while the eight remaining PRTs would continue under the control of the US-led counter-terrorist campaign, Operation Enduring Freedom. In June 2004, Allied leaders approved plans to establish four further PRTs in the north at Mazar-e-Sharif, Meymaneh, Feyzabad and Baghlan to complete Stage 1. The British contribution to this was a small number of staff officers at the ISAF headquarters, a former Afghan Army Officers' Club in Kabul, and a single infantry battalion, which was split between providing a security presence in the capital and supporting redevelopment in Mazar-e-Sharif or MES as it was known to the troops.

In his memoir, *A Journey,* Tony Blair claimed that by the autumn of 2004, although progress had been slow, Afghanistan seemed to be moving in the right direction, and was 'on the path

---

5   Lord Reid, evidence to HCDC, 8 Feb 2011, EV88, Q401, <https://publications.parliament.uk/pa/cm201012/cmselect/cmdfence/554/554.pdf>, accessed 9 March 2023.
6   Dannatt, *Leading from the Front,* pp.236–237.
7   PRTs were joint military-civilian organisations designed to operate in semi-permissive environments to support indigenous authorities to deliver security, stability and economic and social development as a means of helping to ensure that the authority of the Kabul Government was spread throughout the country.

to becoming a better state…'.[8] In many ways, that statement was accurate. Stage 1 of the ISAF expansion process had been completed successfully. Some stabilisation and development work had begun in the northern provinces, and presidential elections had taken place, free from significant disruption by the insurgents. Hamid Karzai was able to cast off his temporary cloak of office and don a new one of democratic legitimacy by being elected President with 55.4 percent of the votes cast. New state institutions had been created and the country seemed to be on its way to a better future.

On 10 February 2005, Stage 2 was set in motion, involving a move to the west, with PRTs in Herat and Farah, and later, in Chagcharan (Ghor province) and Qal'eh-e-Naw (Badghis province). A parliamentary election was scheduled for later that year, which would hopefully result in a democratically accountable government. But the progress made up to 2004, and the expected success of the second phase in the west, represented the easy part of NATO's task. The northern and western provinces were far from the traditional Taliban heartlands. Security there had been reasonably good following the banishment of the Taliban in 2001, particularly in the north, where the Northern Alliance remained strong. As a result, the PRTs had been able to get out on the ground, engage with local leaders, and start the process of economic and social development, including small improvements to the justice system and the rule of law. However, anyone with even a basic understanding of Afghanistan should have been able to foresee that the real test of NATO's ability and resolve would come when it sought to expand its writ to Helmand, Kandahar, Nimruz, Uruzgan and Zabul, and later when it moved to the east. Here, in the traditional and spiritual home of the Taliban, in close proximity to the porous, almost non-existent border with Pakistan's lawless Federally Administered Tribal Areas (FATAs), from where they could draw recruits and supplies, the challenge was bound to be much greater. The Taliban were certain to respond vigorously to any incursion onto their 'vital ground'.

The decision to commit the ARRC Headquarters to Afghanistan was significant in a number of respects. For the UK, it marked a clear line in the sand in terms of the country's foreign policy priorities and objectives. Whether intended or not, it signalled a shift away from Iraq. It was increasingly clear that the occupation forces were causing many of the security problems on the ground, and that the quicker the country could be handed back to Iraqi control the sooner much of the violence would cease, and the troops could come home. It also sent a powerful message to Afghanistan, its near neighbours, Iran, Pakistan and China, and the wider international community, that the West was serious about returning to the important task of ensuring there would be no safe haven there for terrorist groups – work that had been largely paused since 2002. The ARRC was not a panacea for all the problems associated with Afghanistan. In fact, in some ways its use was as much symbolic as it was physical. No one, least of all those in uniform, believed a single corps headquarters, could make the difference between success and failure. However, by agreeing to deploy its premier command and control asset, the alliance leadership was demonstrating just how important it regarded the job it had taken on, and why it was vital that its troop-contributing nations were prepared to step up to the plate and provide the resources necessary for success.

The effectiveness of the NATO mission would not be judged by purely military outcomes. The most important performance indicators would be the delivery of economic and social progress. In the north and west, far from the Taliban heartlands, these closely-related objectives had been relatively easy to accomplish. In the southern provinces, where lawlessness, brigandry, banditry and narcotics trafficking were embedded as a way of life, the challenge would be much greater. Here, it would be the military's task to take on the forces of religious conservatism; drugs warlords and

---

8   Blair, *A Journey,* p.362.

their private militias, who had much to lose in an economy no longer dominated by opium; and the Taliban, who were showing signs of recovering from the mauling they had received two years earlier. It was clear to the NATO planners that however good the ARRC was at providing effective command and control, it would be powerless to influence the desired outcomes in the south unless it had sufficient combat troops to do its bidding.

A Mission in Crisis

Despite the good work done in 2003 and 2004 to expand the ISAF footprint north and west of Kabul, by early 2005 there was a view in Britain and elsewhere that the campaign in Afghanistan was stagnating. Blair's successor, Gordon Brown, feeling under no obligation to defend his predecessor's record, was clear that the period between the end of 2001 and 2005 was 'wasted years [in Afghanistan] while the British and US focused on Iraq'.[9] Chief of the General Staff, General Sir Mike Jackson, with typical bluntness was certain 'the war in Iraq had… taken eyes off the Afghan ball'.[10] Michael Clark, a former Director General of the respected Defence think-tank, the Royal United Services Institute, went further, suggesting that by 2006 the allies were facing mission failure.[11] Lieutenant General Sir Rob Fry, agreed, concluding that by 2004, despite Tony Blair's up-beat assessment of progress, the military campaign had become 'moribund'.[12]

In Whitehall, there was growing concern that the NATO mission would be doomed unless a way could be found to bring the nation-building and counter-terrorist missions – at that point being pursued separately – under a single, unified command, and to deliver and demonstrate success in the south. As long as the American-led Operation Enduring Freedom was being pursued within a separate chain of command, which seemed unwilling to take the needs of nation-building into account, it was unlikely that an important NATO Line of Operation, which involved reaching out to the Afghan people and persuading them to support the Kabul Government, could ever be successful. It would be difficult, many argued, to persuade a shop owner in Kandahar Province to support the Government when the forces associated with that government were routinely bombing his town back to the stone-age in pursuit of the Taliban or Al Qaeda. With this in mind, it was agreed that when the NATO headquarters was fully functional, it would assume responsibility for coordinating both Operation Enduring Freedom and the nation-building effort. Desmond Bowen, Policy Director at the MOD from 2004 to 2006, is clear that the UK hoped a single, robust commander such as Lieutenant General Sir David Richards, might be able to reconcile these competing objectives in a way that allowed both to succeed or at the very least to ensure that one took proper account of the other.[13]

---

9   Brown, *My Life*, p.271.
10 Jackson, *Soldier*, p.364.
11 Professor Michael Clark, former Director General of RUSI, 'Afghanistan and the UK's Illusion of Strategy', <https://rusi.org/explore-our-research/publications/commentary/afghanistan-and-uks-illusion-strategy>, accessed 13 March 2023.
12 Lieutenant General Sir Rob Fry, Evidence to Iraq Inquiry, 16 December 2009, <https://webarchive.nationalarchives.gov.uk/ukgwa/20171123123302/http://www.iraqinquiry.org.uk/the-evidence/witness-transcripts/>, accessed 9 March 2023.
13 Desmond Bowen, interview with author.

Red Cards and Reluctance

In describing the NATO mission as 'moribund' General Fry may have been guilty of exaggerating to make a point. In 2004, although clearly not on its last legs, ISAF's expansion was certainly beginning to show signs of 'running out of steam' – just as the Taliban were making a comeback in the south of the country. At least part of the reason for the NATO malaise lay in what some member-nations were beginning to describe as an unfair distribution of military effort. Too many nations were content to stand back and allow a small group of willing countries to do much of the heavy lifting. It had long been argued that NATO has lacked the political cohesion and the military capabilities to respond effectively to modern threats. At the Prague Summit, in November 2002, Secretary General, George Robertson, had talked bullishly about the alliance's then-emerging ability, through its new NATO Reaction Force (NRF) concept, to 'bring together the best military capabilities of Europe and North America to fight together against common threats such as international terrorism'.[14] These were fine words, no doubt earnestly expressed. However, successive deployments, from the Balkans to Afghanistan, demonstrated that the alliance had often struggled to match the rhetoric and lofty ambitions with practical and effective action.

A recurring weakness, when it came to its military endeavours, had been the struggle to generate the required numbers of troops and equipment for some of the more challenging missions. While many nations had been prepared to provide personnel to undertake low-risk peacekeeping activities, fewer were quite so forward-leaning when it came to supporting operations with a heightened risk of high-intensity combat, which generally involved death or injury. For a combination of historical and political reasons, some member-nations feared the domestic implications of sustaining casualties or projecting force or both – either in their own backyard or further afield. In addition, force generation and deployments for some of the more hard-edged operations had often been frustrated by the system known as 'national caveats'.[15] These are 'red cards' which allow individual nations to stipulate exactly how their soldiers may be employed, and importantly, in the case of Afghanistan in 2006, exactly where they could and could not go. The caveats were kept confidential, lest those applying them might be embarrassed by any perceived lack of commitment. They were, however, made clear to planners and commanders of deployments, and could often be seen in the form of a 'caveats spreadsheet' in the CJ3 and CJ5 staff cells in NATO's operational and tactical headquarters.[16] Despite the understandable reluctance to discuss them outside the operational bubble, some of the limitations have found their way into the public domain. It is believed, for example, that the German mandate for participation in ISAF prohibited involvement in operations under Operation Enduring Freedom. As a result, reconnaissance photographs taken by German aircraft could not

---

14 Lord Robertson, Speech, NATO Summit, Prague, 20 November 2002, https://www.NATO.int/docu/speech/2002/s021120a.htm, accessed 9 March 2023.
15 The use of national caveats is provided for in Article V of the Washington Treaty (1949) which states: 'The Parties agree that an armed attack against one or more of them…shall be considered an attack against them all and consequently they agree that, if such an armed attack occurs, each of them, in exercise of the right of individual or collective self-defence recognised by Article 51 of the Charter of the United Nations, will assist the Party or Parties so attacked by taking forthwith, individually and in concert with the other Parties, *such action as it deems necessary*, including the use of armed force, to restore and maintain the security of the North Atlantic area'.
16 Within NATO at that time, military staff branches were numbered from 1 to 9. In the ARRC, which is a combined (multi-national) and joint (multi-service) headquarters, the staff cells have the prefix CJ for Combined Joint. CJ3 is the Operations cell, responsible for overseeing the 'here and now'. CJ5 is the Plans cell, responsible for developing future activities.

be shared if there was a risk that they might be used as part of the counter-terrorism efforts. At least one nation may have stipulated that its troops could not be deployed at night. Another ally was reported to have refused to allow Afghans to board their helicopters, regardless of whether they were members of the Afghan National Army, or if they were wounded and requiring casualty evacuation. Because of caveats imposed in an earlier deployment, the Canadian Battalion, known by its shortened form as CANBAT, was referred to in some circles as 'CANTBAT'. In 2006, as expansion resumed, the French contingent refused, for some time, to deploy beyond Kabul, and its soldiers were forbidden by their own Government from reinforcing NATO troops elsewhere in the country, although this restriction was later relaxed.[17] As he stood down as SACEUR in 2009, US General John Craddock blamed caveats for bringing 'increased risk to every service member deployed in Afghanistan …increased risk to mission success…' and said they were 'detrimental to effective command and control and unity of effort'.[18] There is little doubt that these caveats, together with a certain reluctance by some member states to put their troops in harm's way in the southern provinces, played a significant part in Britain's decision to deploy its soldiers into Helmand in a combat role in 2006, and to keep them there until 2014.

Under interrogation by members of the House of Commons Defence Committee, General Fry revealed that when the allies first began to think about 'reinvesting' in Afghanistan, in early 2004, there was 'no appetite that it was possible to discern, anywhere in NATO', to take on the Stage 3 task.[19] For the MOD this was clear, empirical evidence of the mission's morbidity, and immediately set alarm bells ringing. The Spanish sought a 'secret' meeting with MOD officials which turned out to be an opportunity to lobby for support to avoid them going to the south. 'Really, they would have preferred to stay well clear of Afghanistan, but if they did have to go somewhere they certainly did not want to go to the South', said a Defence official.[20] They eventually went to Herat in the west.

If NATO was only able to secure and stabilise half of the country there was a danger that a block of ungoverned space would be created around the area known as the Pashtun Belt, which included Helmand, Kandahar, Uruzgan and Pakistan's border provinces of Baluchistan and Waziristan. If that was allowed to happen, it would represent a complete failure of one of the key strands of the US and UK's strategic intent – to prevent Afghanistan from again becoming a safe haven for terrorists. The UK was also concerned at the prospect of NATO being seen to have capitulated after completing only half of the mission and 'the most benign half' at that.[21] Such an outcome was unthinkable from a British perspective. It risked the reputation of the alliance, placed a huge question-mark over its 'efficacy and its future role',[22] and would have left Blair's doctrine of International Community in tatters, bereft of an effective means of projecting military force in support of humanitarian objectives when required. It was these concerns that would drive the

---

17 Stephen M. Saideman, and David P. Auerswald. 'Comparing Caveats: Understanding the Sources of National Restrictions upon NATO's Mission in Afghanistan'. *International Studies Quarterly*, vol. 56, no. 1, 2012, pp.67–84. *JSTOR*, <http://www.jstor.org/stable/41409823>, accessed 10 Mar. 2023.
18 Arnaud de Borchgrave, UPI, *Commentary: NATO Caveats,* 10 July 2009, <https://www.upi.com/Emerging_Threats/2009/07/10/Commentary-NATO-caveats/UPI-47311247244125/>, accessed 12 March 2023.
19 Lieutenant General Sir Rob Fry, Evidence to HCDC, 8 February 2011, EV86, Q397, <https://publications.parliament.uk/pa/cm201012/cmselect/cmdfence/554/554.pdf>, accessed 12 March 2023.
20 Desmond Bowen, interview with author.
21 Lieutenant General Sir Rob Fry, Evidence to HCDC, 8 February 2011, EV87, Q397, <https://publications.parliament.uk/pa/cm201012/cmselect/cmdfence/554/554.pdf>, accessed 12 March 2023.
22 Lieutenant General Sir Rob Fry, Evidence to HCDC, 8 February 2011, EV87, Q397, <https://publications.parliament.uk/pa/cm201012/cmselect/cmdfence/554/554.pdf>, accessed 12 March 2023.

UK decision to play a leading part in the expansion plan and, at the same time, seek to revivify the NATO campaign. As Fry pointed out, had Britain not demonstrated leadership and agreed to take on Helmand, the consequences might have been terminal for the alliance. 'There is a chance that NATO would never have gone into the South of Afghanistan... We would also have created, de facto, the very ungoverned ground that we went there in the first instance to deny'.[23] That could not be allowed to happen and, it was decided, the best way to avoid it was for Britain to lead by example. There was also an honestly-held view in MOD Main Building that by taking on a leading role in the expansion to the south, the Brits could inject a much-needed shot of adrenalin directly into the main artery of the NATO mission.

But this had not been part of the plan back in 2004. As Lord Walker explained, the original decision to deploy the ARRC had been based on the fact that it, together with a single battlegroup already assigned to Afghanistan, would represent the UK's main contribution to the mission.[24]

By April 2005, after a great deal of debate behind closed doors in Brussels, London, The Hague, and in Ottawa, it had been agreed that the UK would lead in Helmand and it was expected, but not yet finally settled, that the Canadians would go to Kandahar and the Dutch to Uruzgan.[25] The UK-Netherlands-Canada coalition was stitched together by the military with no reference to policy officials or ministers until it had been agreed. According to Martin Howard, Fry, an outwardly bluff but inwardly very sophisticated and able Royal Marine, used his contacts to build a military consensus and then presented it as a 'done deal' for the politicians to rubber-stamp.[26] This was not intended to be a criticism, and there was no suggestion of any underhandedness. Howard was simply demonstrating his old boss's determination to 'get the job done'. Fry is happy to take the credit:

> We drove the relationship and the commitment. It was just common sense. The Canadians had been there before and we were aware that the Canadian military and political leadership were looking to make a contribution. The Dutch were old and trusted allies and people we had been very proximate to for a long time. So, we simply convened a few meetings to get the whole thing agreed. But there were no cosy chats over brandy and cigars, as one account has suggested.[27]

Helmand has become synonymous with British endeavour – and loss – in the campaign in Afghanistan. But although General Sir Mike Jackson has suggested the deployment there was presented to the Chiefs as a *fait accompli*, linked to the Prime Minister's enthusiasm to take on counter-narcotics, other evidence shows that going there was anything but a foregone conclusion. In an article for a RUSI publication in 2011, General Fry and the MOD's former Policy Director, Desmond Bowen, two men who were intimately involved in the policy-making at the time, were clear that Kandahar was the UK's first choice.[28] Kandahar was seen as being more critical to overall success than Helmand. It was in the Pashtun heartland, the place where the

---

23 Lieutenant General Sir Rob Fry, Evidence to HCDC, 8 February 2011, EV86, Q397, <https://publications.parliament.uk/pa/cm201012/cmselect/cmdfence/554/554.pdf>, accessed 15 March 2023.
24 Field Marshal Lord Walker of Aldringham, interview with author.
25 Lord Reid, Evidence to HCDC, 8 Feb 2011, EV88, Q407, <https://publications.parliament.uk/pa/cm201012/cmselect/cmdfence/554/554.pdf>, accessed 15 March 2023.
26 Martin Howard, former DG Op Pol, MOD, interview with author.
27 Lieutenant General Sir Rob Fry, interview with author.
28 Lieutenant General Sir Rob Fry and Desmond Bowen, *UK National Strategy and Helmand*, in Michael Clark (ed) The Afghan Papers: Committing Britain to War in Helmand, 2005-06, Routledge, p.71, <https://doi.org/10.4324/9780203096284>, 15 March 2023.

Taliban had made their last stand in 2001, and where they could be challenged directly. It was also a natural centre of gravity for British interests in South Asia. If Kandahar city and province could be brought under the authority of the Kabul Government, it would act as a powerful example for other parts of the country.[29] But the Canadians also wanted Kandahar, not only for some of the same reasons outlined above, but because they had already invested their own blood and treasure there in 2002. They were familiar with the ground and they were up for the challenge, Bill Graham, Minister of National Defence, told the Ottawa parliament on 12 October 2005.[30] Rob Fry put it in a slightly different light: 'The Canadian military was in search of redemption, having had a fairly long period of undistinguished activity and…Kandahar was seen by them as something they would like to do'.[31] Nick Beadle, a former senior civil servant and one of Defence Secretary, Des Browne's Private Secretaries, has claimed that Britain ended up with Helmand because 'we failed to persuade the US to back us against the Canadians'.[32] But in reality, Britain backed down because it wanted Ottawa locked-in to the mission and the price was agreeing that Canada could take on Kandahar.[33] 'It was a negotiation', recalled Fry. 'We were very keen to have them in. If the price of achieving that was Kandahar, that was a bargain in my view. It was not my decision, but it seemed to me to be a reasonable position. I don't think we would have done Kandahar any better or any worse than the Canadians'.[34] Fry detected some irritation that the UK had not been given what many considered to be the most important province, but felt that position was 'purblind and inward-looking' and that 'the important thing was that the NATO mission was a success, not whether the UK got the plum province'.[35]

The NATO plan for Stage 3, known as OPLAN 10302 (Revise 1), was published in an unclassified form on 8 December 2005 to facilitate discussions with the UN, the Afghan authorities and other international bodies.[36] This version of the document does not include the intelligence assessment that would have helped to shape the military approach. It does, however, note that the security environment would be 'more challenging' than that experienced in stages one and two. Although the public edition of the OPLAN said little about the enemy, it was clear that security operations were likely to range from 'local force protection in a permissive environment' to 'decisive, proactive military ground and air manoeuvre' (in other words, serious combat, with ground troops being supported by fast jets and helicopters), and that 'a robust approach would be necessary to maintain the initiative'.[37] Taking account of this, the planners quickly assessed that the military forces supporting the PRTs in the southern provinces would need to be able not only to keep the peace but, if necessary, to fight to create the security 'bubbles' that were a vital condition for delivering stabilisation and development. It was becoming clear to all that Stage 3 was going to

---

29   Prof. Michael Clark, *The Afghan Papers*, pp.14–15.
30   Report of Standing Committee on National Defence, *Canadian Forces in Afghanistan,* June 2007, <https://www.ourcommons.ca/Content/Committee/391/NDDN/Reports/RP3034719/nddnrp01/nddnrp01-e.pdf>, accessed 15 March 2023.
31   Lieutenant General Sir Rob Fry, interview with author.
32   Nick Beadle, Afghanistan and the Context of Iraq, in Michael Clarke, (2012) (ed). *The Afghan Papers: Committing Britain to War in Helmand, 2005–06* (1st ed.). Routledge. <https://doi.org/10.4324/9780203096284,> accessed 16 March 2023.
33   Prof Michael Clark, *The Afghan Papers*, p.15.
34   Lieutenant General Sir Rob Fry, interview with author.
35   Lieutenant General Sir Rob Fry, interview with author.
36   NATO SACEUR OPLAN 10302 (Revise 1), unclassified version, circulated under NATO International Military Staff document IMSM-0912-2005, dated 8 December 2005.
37   NATO SACEUR OPLAN 10302 (Revise 1), unclassified version, circulated under NATO International Military Staff document IMSM-0912-2005, dated 8 December 2005.

be different from the relatively straightforward 'peacekeeping' that had characterised Stages 1 and 2, and that the force laydown needed to reflect that reality.

The planning process identified the scale of resources that would be required and this, in turn, became the Combined Joint Statement of Requirement (CJSOR), NATO-speak for the size and shape of the force in terms of personnel, equipment and other resources. The CJSOR was designed to inform the force generation (FORGEN) process. This involved passing the Statement of Requirement to member-countries for them to decide which elements of the force they were able – and prepared – to provide. There then followed a conference of the contributing nations at which the NATO headquarters team attempted to arm-twist the country representatives to fill the gaps in the manning and equipment tables. If the process had work as intended, it should have resulted in all the requirements being met, although some nations might have attached national caveats to their contributions. It quickly became apparent, however, that despite the UK military's example, backed up by the Dutch and the Canadians, there was still a noted lack of enthusiasm among member-countries to get involved in the more difficult southern provinces. By late January 2006, only three months before the troops were due to deploy, the force generation process had still not been concluded, held up, despite Fry's coalition-building activities, by the Dutch Government's prevarications over whether or not to take on the lead role in Uruzgan. In a bid to force the Dutch to make a decision, the new Defence Secretary, Dr John Reid, deliberately delayed announcing details of the UK contribution until the Dutch parliament formally endorsed the deployment. Only on 26 January 2006 did Reid finally set out details of the UK force package and indicate that the first boots would hit the ground the following April. This delay would have profound implications for the force when it arrived.

The CJSOR for the initial deployment, like those for previous NATO operations, would never be met in full. As Des Browne, Reid's successor, told the House of Commons Defence Committee on 8 May 2007: 'Nobody in our department [the MOD] has any knowledge of any NATO CJSOR for any operation ever being fully fulfilled'.[38]

---

38 Des Browne, Evidence to HCDC, 8 May 2007, Q332, EV69, <https://publications.parliament.uk/pa/cm200607/cmselect/cmdfence/408/408.pdf>, accessed 24 June 2024.

Part 2

'By intelligence we mean every sort of information about the enemy and his country – the basis, in short, of our own plans and operations'.

Carl von Clausewitz
On War[1]

---

1   Carl von Clausewitz (trans. Michael Howard and Peter Paret), *On War* (London: Alfred A. Knopf, 1993), p.136.

5

Intelligence Failure

In one memorable episode of the British comedy series, *Fawlty Towers*, Manuel, the Spanish waiter, played brilliantly by Andrew Sachs, declares, in heavily accented tones, 'I know nothing'. The UK's decision to take responsibility for the security of Helmand Province in 2006 might be said to have been almost as badly informed. Major General Andrew Mackay, who commanded a brigade in Helmand in 2007 put it rather more starkly. In his view, the upper echelons of government, political, civil and military, went into Helmand 'with their eyes shut and their fingers crossed'.[1]

When the decision was made to take the lead in the province, the British military's intelligence picture in relation to the southern part of the country was undeniably poor. With no British troops and little local information-gathering infrastructure there, Defence's ability to build an accurate representation of the situation, what the Army calls the 'ground truth', was seriously limited. And yet, without a robust appreciation of what they were facing, senior political and military leaders not only decided to go ahead and invest in Helmand, they did so whilst imposing strict, non-negotiable limits on the size and scale of the deployment, both in terms of the number of troops and the types and quantities of equipment that they were prepared to make available.

The Helmand Task Force was initially limited to 3,250 personnel, an entirely contrived figure, rather than one that had been carefully crafted for the mission at hand. It was based partly on what could be spared from the Iraq campaign, but mostly on what the politicians were prepared to bear. The military planners at PJHQ and in the MOD believed the force was 'as large as we could get it' in the circumstances. They relied on firepower in the form of fast jets, attack helicopters and artillery to make up for the manpower deficit, but even getting approval for the vital hardware had been a struggle. Few of those who had been involved in the cross-departmental bartering process that had resulted in the final tally were under any illusion that they had come up with the perfect solution. But by the summer of 2005, when go-no-go decisions were needed in order to ensure the NATO timetable could be met, there was no time to go back over the arguments and no willingness, at senior levels, to reopen the debate. The clock was ticking on the ARRC deployment and Stage 3 expansion and it was felt that if the UK was not able to commit, the opportunity to stabilise the south would be lost, the overall NATO mission would fail, and the North Atlantic Alliance would be exposed as a paper tiger. That was not an edifying prospect for senior military officers at the Ministry of Defence, nor for the Prime Minister.

Accurate intelligence is a vital component of military planning and operations as well as diplomacy. As the Chinese philosopher, Sun Tzu said: 'If you know the enemy and know yourself, you need not fear the result of a hundred battles. If you know yourself but not the enemy, for every

---

1 'They Went Into Helmand With Eyes Shut and Fingers Crossed', *The Times* (9 June 2010). <https://www.thetimes.co.uk/article/they-went-into-helmand-with-eyes-shut-and-fingers-crossed-jvbhc2mr07p>, accessed 3 March 2023.

victory gained you will also suffer a defeat....'.[2] Recognising the validity of that statement, the first question in the British Army's 'Seven Questions' tactical combat estimate, a planning and decision-making support tool, taught to officer cadets and junior NCOs, is: 'What is the enemy doing and why?' If that question cannot be answered with a reasonable degree of certainty, then the rest of the process, and the resulting plan or decision, is likely to be compromised, at least to some degree. At the operational and strategic levels, a different, more complex approach is used, but the process remains focused on the enemy and the terrain – human and physical – on which operations are to be conducted. In a counter-insurgency or stabilisation scenario, such as the British faced in Helmand, planners would also want to know about the civilian population, including how locals were likely to react to the presence of the force; which groups would be pro, neutral and anti; and who the key local influencers were and how best to engage with them.

Of course, in the real world, the intelligence picture is hardly ever as complete or as comprehensive as commanders would like it to be. Military officers are taught to operate within this uncertainty. In the absence of detailed data, planners can and do make assumptions using their experience, knowledge and judgement, informed by an understanding of the adversary's doctrine, tactics and previous behaviours. In effect, they try to work out what they do not know from what they do. But in general terms, the better the intelligence picture, the more effective the plan or decision will be. The intelligence estimate, informed by reconnaissance and other activities and supported by an array of technological aids, will usually have a heavy influence on decisions regarding the size of the force, the types and quantities of equipment it will require; where it will be based; where it will and will not operate; what it will do and how it will do it. If the intelligence is limited or the quality is poor, the assumptions that it supports may well turn out to be unreliable or wrong.

Martin Howard, a former Deputy Chief of Defence Intelligence, is clear that the intelligence picture in 2004–5, was 'not really good enough'.[3] He is not alone in reaching that conclusion. Air Marshal Sir Stuart Peach, the then Chief of Joint Operations at PJHQ, paraphrasing Donald Rumsfeld, told the HCDC, that 'we knew what we knew'.[4] General Sir Peter Wall, Chief of the General Staff and, when the deployment was being planned, Deputy Chief of Joint Operations, admitted to the same Committee that there had been 'a failure of intelligence' before the move to Helmand.[5] General Sir Mike Walker, CDS, described the province as 'an empty hole…an ungoverned space' about which Defence 'did not have a clear picture'.[6] Only Walker's successor as CDS, Air Chief Marshal Sir Jock Stirrup, who had come into post in April 2006, just ahead of the arrival of British troops in Helmand, expressed a different view. 'We don't know much, but we know it's not the north. We know it is real bandit country', he apparently told a meeting of the Chiefs of Staff Committee. In evidence to the HCDC, he said later: 'It is not true that we didn't realise how difficult it was going to be, but clearly, we were pretty hazy about the extent and nature of the challenge. We recognised that we would have something of a break-in battle, develop the intelligence base, and then see where the mission went….'.[7] As events were to demonstrate, it was regrettable

---

2 Sun Tzu, *The Art of War*, (Oxford: Oxford University Press, 1971), p.82.
3 Martin Howard, interview with author.
4 Air Marshal Sir Stuart Peach, Chief of Joint Operations, Evidence to HCDC, 10 November 2010, EV35, Q135, <https://publications.parliament.uk/pa/cm201012/cmselect/cmdfence/554/554.pdf>, accessed 14 March 2023.
5 General Sir Peter Wall, Deputy Chief of Joint Operations, Evidence to HCDC 11 May 2011, EV144, Q672, <https://publications.parliament.uk/pa/cm201012/cmselect/cmdfence/554/554.pdf>, accessed 15 March 2023.
6 Elliott, *High Command,* p.139.
7 Air Chief Marshal Sir Jock Stirrup, CDS, Evidence to HCDC, 4 May 2011, EV130, Q599, <https://

that his fellow Chiefs did not take the views of the then Chief of the Air Staff more seriously as they agreed the manning and equipment package for the mission.

Knowing that information was scarce, the various intelligence agencies, including the Defence Intelligence Service (DIS), and the FCO-linked Secret Intelligence Service (SIS or MI6) began to work to improve the picture – no easy task. As Air Marshal Peach pointed out, Helmand was a complex province with an even more complex tribal dynamic.[8] A former Chief of Defence Intelligence and deputy chair of the UK Joint Intelligence Committee (the JIC), he was well-placed to make that assessment. Helmand was undoubtedly a difficult place in which to make use of the traditional tools of intelligence-gathering, such as signals intelligence (SIGINT) or human intelligence (HUMINT). In the case of the former, there were few 'signals' – radio and mobile phone traffic – to intercept. The use of the internet was not well-developed, particularly outside the big population centres (although Antonio Giustozzi suggests that by 2005 some Taliban commanders inside Afghanistan seemed to be equipped with laptops).[9] HUMINT required a presence on the ground, to develop, nurture and exploit information sources.

But a poor intelligence picture is not the same as a non-existent one. The reality is that although information relating to Helmand was not as plentiful as most people would have wished, the province was not quite the 'intelligence desert' that some have suggested. The British had been there in 2001 and 2002, and some officers believed they had a reasonable appreciation of the tribes, the warlords, the criminal gangs and the Taliban – or least a good enough understanding to know there was going to be trouble. As Brigadier Ed Butler, who had fought Al Qaeda and the Taliban there immediately following the 2001 invasion, pointed out:

> We knew about the tribal mix, the narco-criminals and the warlords. We also knew that the Taliban were going to respond to our presence. Pashtuns don't like foreigners, whether they are from a different tribe, a different district, or a different country. And the UK carried considerable historical baggage when it came to southern Afghanistan. By the time we got there, the Taliban had been running a very effective Information Operations campaign, aimed at influencing the Helmandi people against us.[10]

In one report a Taliban commander was quoted as saying: 'Our fathers and forefathers are scratching at the lids of their coffins to come out and throw out the infidels'.[11] In another, the Quetta Shura made it known that they intended to attack the British force in Helmand as soon as it arrived.[12, 13] Despite this understanding, it proved impossible for Butler to convince the senior decision-makers to act on the available knowledge, particularly when it came to the size of the force and the likely missions and tasks it was going to face. A number of possible factors may have accounted for this. The first was that many people, including some in key positions in Whitehall, were convinced – or at least wanted to believe – that the Taliban had been defeated in 2002 and no longer represented a significant threat. Secondly, although there was open-source intelligence

---

publications.parliament.uk/pa/cm201012/cmselect/cmdfence/554/554.pdf>, accessed 15 March 2023.
8 Air Chief Marshal Sir Stuart Peach, CJO, Evidence to HCDC, 10 November 2010, EV35, Q135, <https://publications.parliament.uk/pa/cm201012/cmselect/cmdfence/554/554.pdf>, accessed 13 March 2023.
9 Antonio Giustozzi, *Koran, Kalashnikov and Laptop*, p.13.
10 Brigadier Ed Butler, interview with author, 16 March 2023.
11 Brigadier Ed Butler, Evidence to HCDC, 15 March 2011, EV105, Q477, https://publications.parliament.uk/pa/cm201012/cmselect/cmdfence/554/554.pdf.
12 The Quetta Shura was, de facto, the Taliban's governing body and central command authority, based, as the title suggests, in the city of Quetta, just across the border in Pakistan.
13 Brigadier Ed Butler, *Setting Ourselves Up for a Fall in Afghanistan*, p.47.

(OSINT) to suggest that the Taliban were resurgent, the absence of significant militant activity against coalition forces in Helmand may have led the military and politicians into a false sense of security. The third reason is that whatever the intelligence said, the politicians and Chiefs had made commitments, based on the availability of resources, and there were no acceptable alternative options. For Butler, this position demonstrated 'varying degrees of self-denial and self-deception by senior British policy-makers'.[14]

A Little Knowledge…

With the British military and diplomatic footprint spread lightly there, particularly during the initial decision-making and pre-deployment phases (mid-2004 – mid-2005), any intelligence assessment was, of necessity, reliant, to a large extent, on US reporting. The Americans were more than willing to share what little information they had with the UK as co-members of the 'Five Eyes' alliance, which also comprised Australia, New Zealand and Canada.[15] This included information generated by the US PRT, at Lashkar Gah, and some American airborne and special forces operators. 173rd Airborne Brigade had elements of its 74th Long Range Surveillance Detachment, operating out of FOB Price, near Gereshk, together with personnel of 5th Special Forces Group Operational Detachment Alpha. The PRT was restricted to its base and the local environs and had little idea of what was happening in the wider province. The SOF team was hunkered-down, 'attaching themselves to the local culture and… doing nothing that might alienate the local population or the Taliban'.[16] Intelligence from these sources was limited, but the British were welcome to what there was. As Lieutenant General Ben Freakley pointed out: 'The British planning team had full access. Brigadier-General David Fraser, the Canadian officer commanding Regional Command (South), was completely open with them'.[17]

A small team from A Squadron, 22nd Special Air Service Regiment (22 SAS), was deployed in mid-2005 to inform the planning. They produced a detailed report which went to PJHQ. However, for some reason it was not made available to 16 Air Assault Brigade during its planning activities and the Brigade Commander had to resort to using his contacts at Hereford, the home of the Special Air Service Regiment, to gain access to it.[18] The content of the report remains highly-classified. However, in discussions with special forces colleagues Butler was told, in no uncertain terms, that although the situation on the ground appeared relatively benign, that could change very quickly once British boots hit the Helmand dirt.

'If you want an insurgency send in British troops' he was told by a senior SAS officer.[19] These reports also made it clear that the Taliban were present in far greater numbers than Government departments in London believed.[20]

As detailed planning for the deployment was stepped up in late 2005, PJHQ despatched a Preliminary Operations (Prelim Ops) team to the theatre. This small, multi-agency group was led by Royal Marine Colonel, Gordon Messenger, the Chief of Staff of the Joint Force Headquarters

---

14 Brigadier Ed Butler, *Setting Ourselves Up for a Fall in Afghanistan,* p.47
15 Lieutenant General Ben Freakley, former Commanding General, CJTF76, interview with author.
16 Lieutenant General Sir Rob Fry, Evidence to HCDC, 8 February 2011, EV87, Q.401, https://publications.parliament.uk/pa/cm201012/cmselect/cmdfence/554/554.pdf.
17 Lieutenant General Ben Freakley, interview with author.
18 Brigadier Ed Butler, interview with author.
19 Brigadier Ed Butler, interview with author.
20 Brigadier Ed Butler, *Setting Ourselves up for a Fall in Afghanistan,* p.47.

(JFHQ), a high-readiness, deployable, headquarters, commanded at 1-Star level (Brigadier), which was part of the PJHQ construct. Messenger was an experienced and highly-regarded officer who had commanded 40 Commando during the complex amphibious assault into the Al Faw Peninsula in southern Iraq, and in an action against Iraqi armour at Abu al Khasib, during the early days of the 2003 invasion, for which he was awarded the Distinguished Service Order (DSO). He would lead 3 Commando Brigade in Helmand on Op Herrick IX (November 2008 to April 2009), gaining a bar to his DSO. Promoted to full General in 2016, he completed his service as Vice Chief of the Defence Staff (VCDS) in 2019. Having been intimately involved in the early planning for the deployment, during the spring and summer of 2005, Messenger was the obvious choice to head up the group, which consisted of four or five members of the Joint Force Headquarters, a number of attached ranks, and civilian stabilisation and development specialists.

Messenger's mission was to set the conditions for the arrival of 16 Air Assault Brigade, and he had four key tasks. The first was to work with the civilian stabilisation experts and others, using military planning principles, to create what would later become known as The Joint UK Helmand Plan. This document set out, in some detail, how the UK would achieve its objectives for the province, taking account of the NATO OPLAN. Next, they were to improve the intelligence picture. This activity took place under Operation Malaya, named in homage to the successful British counter-insurgency operation in South-East Asia in the 1950s, and was the responsibility of a team of Territorial Army (now Army Reserve) special forces soldiers from 23rd Special Air Service Regiment (23 SAS). Based with the US SOF at FOB Price, the part-time SAS men would seek out 'ground truth' by travelling around the province, usually in lightly-armoured Snatch Land Rovers, engaging with local people and elders. The third element was to oversee the construction of basic infrastructure at Camp Bastion to provide basing facilities for 16 Air Assault Brigade as it arrived. Bastion would quickly develop from a couple of ISO shipping containers and a Temporary Landing Strip, to something approaching a major international airport, a complex akin in scale to London Heathrow, sitting on real estate comparable in size to the town of Reading. A large engineer element had been provided to undertake this work. The final task was to support the transition from what Messenger described as 'a hard-pressed, economy of scale US PRT' to a new, better-resourced UK equivalent that was intended to be a flagship for the stabilisation and development effort.[21]

Messenger and his team produced the Joint UK Plan for Helmand in early December 2005, and then flew back to the UK to present it to a Cabinet Office group chaired by senior civil servant, Margaret Aldred, the Deputy Head of the Foreign and Defence Policy Secretariat. The document remains classified but a redacted version was obtained by the author via a Freedom of Information Act request. In 12 pages it set out, in some detail, the high-level approach that should be adopted in the province, and supported this with a 21-page annex covering key outputs and a further 12 pages of risk analysis.[22]

The presentation was well-received by the Cabinet Office audience, who were generally receptive to the proposals for delivering economic development. These were based on the 'ink spot' approach that had been used to such positive effect in Malaya, half a century earlier. However, one element that sparked controversy was the strongly-stated view that, given the high level of dependence on the opium trade, the absence of any other significant form of industry, and the general lawlessness there, the UK's objectives for Helmand could not be achieved within the three years that had been

---

21   General Sir Gordon Messenger, interview with author.
22   The Joint UK Plan for Helmand: Final Report (redacted) pdf, dated 12 December 2005, provided to the author by the Foreign, Commonwealth and Development Office on 12 January 2024 in response to an FOI Act Request.

mandated and for which funding had been agreed. The team came under considerable pressure to contain the plan within the original time frame. This made no sense to the military nor to the development experts on the team. As Messenger later explained: 'If you just want to be disruptive and create chaos, you can do what you want in three years. But if you want to deliver a more rounded outcome, you have to accept that you are in there for longer. Hopefully, the military element reduces over time'.[23]

The security situation in Helmand at this time seemed relatively stable, at least on the surface. There were shooting and bombing incidents, but these were infrequent and dispersed, and the military and civilian personnel who were required to travel around the countryside, were initially content to do so in soft-skinned or lightly-armoured vehicles. The first British Serviceperson to visit Now Zad – a town that a few months later would become one of the most dangerous spots in the province – was a female Royal Navy Lieutenant attached to an Information Operations team, who was conducting a survey on the views of local women.[24]

Nevertheless, there was an underlying atmosphere that reeked of danger. Local people cited security, or lack of it, as their most important concern. They preferred not to leave their homes after dark, felt unsafe, and were no longer keen to pursue leisure activities like picnics or day trips to Kajaki or the Kala-e-Bost monument, an eleventh-century arch, originally part of a mosque, which appeared as an illustration on the 100 Afghani bank note.[25] Lashkar Gah felt relatively safe, but the outlying districts were a different story. Over the previous six months, security was perceived to have deteriorated as insurgents had stepped up the targeting of Government officials and coalition forces. Threats against Provincial Council candidates, schools and teachers increased. There were incidents involving US PRT members every few weeks.[26] Having witnessed the effects of IED attacks on American armoured Hummers, there were growing concerns about the blast-worthiness of the Pinzgauer trucks and Snatch Land Rovers that made up the bulk of the British vehicle fleet. Messenger sent back several reports on this to PJHQ, together with photographs showing what a US Humvee looked like when it had been in contact with one of these devices.[27] He also noted that the insurgents were using areas of sanctuary. They were capable of making good use of terrain – an indicator that they were tactically aware – and there was collusion with narcotics traffickers.[28] Major General Freakley described the area as 'largely low-threat' at the beginning of 2006. He had travelled extensively in the province, by road, in soft-skinned Humvees, accompanied by a small protection team in a lightly-armed, two-vehicle convoy. At that time, in his view, the main issue in Helmand was criminality associated with narcotics production. However, on the province's southern border with Pakistan, in the Bahram Chah district, there were a quarter of a million displaced persons, providing a ready source of Taliban recruits and representing a significant threat if motivated to act.[29] Further support was available in the madrassas and villages of the tribal areas of nearby Pakistan.[30] These points, taken together, supported the idea of a growing resurgence of the Taliban. Alarm bells should have been ringing in Whitehall and at PJHQ in Northwood. There was plenty of potential for things to go bad, but few of those making the high-level decisions had foreseen just how kinetic the situation would become.

---

23 General Sir Gordon Messenger, interview with author.
24 General Sir Gordon Messenger, interview with author.
25 UK Joint Plan for Helmand, p.5.
26 UK Joint Plan for Helmand, p.5
27 General Sir Gordon Messenger, interview with author.
28 UK Joint Plan for Helmand, p.5.
29 UK Joint Plan for Helmand, p.5.
30 Madrassas = Islamic religious schools.

Despite Butler's personal knowledge from his previous service there, PJHQ's understanding of tribal dynamics in the province, which was partly responsible for informing the MOD's perception of the situation, was not well-developed during the planning stage. Nor was there any real appreciation of the depth of the cultural antipathy of the Pashtuns towards foreigners, or the often-malign influence of local warlords, and how that impacted on tribal loyalties. These were all important elements of the human terrain analysis that should have informed the early planning process. Another huge gap in understanding was in relation to the Taliban themselves. There was a view, shared by many military and civilian actors at the time, that the Taliban had been defeated in 2001–2002 and did not, therefore, constitute a significant threat to stability and security. Indeed, in some circles, there was a reluctance to use the term 'Taliban' to describe the insurgents, some preferring to replace it with 'Anti-coalition Militias' (ACM), in an attempt to reflect what was believed, not always correctly, to be the fragmented, disorganised nature of the threat against coalition forces.

In March 2005, American Major General Eric Olson, then the Commanding General of Task Force 76, involved in counter-terrorism operations, described the Taliban as 'a force in decline'.[31] A month earlier, the *New Science Monitor* reported that 'there may only be 800 Taliban fighters left'.[32] As late as March 2006, Afghan and American officials still maintained that the Taliban were no longer able to fight large battles.[33] By 2003, however, it should have been clear, to anyone who took the trouble to look, that the Taliban had begun to regroup and to reassert themselves in the southern provinces. They had already started developing new roots inside Afghanistan and their spread, throughout the southern half of the country, took place, step by step, over the next four years'.[34] By 2004, they had launched recruiting drives and established new strongholds in parts of Uruzgan and Kandahar. Two years later they had practically eliminated the Government presence in most of southern and central Helmand, and were spreading west into Farah.[35] Over three days in January 2006, the Taliban launched bombing attacks across the south of the country. On 14 January a suicide car bomb struck a joint US/Afghan military convoy on a main road in southern Helmand, wounding one US soldier. The following day, a Canadian diplomat died in a suicide car bomb attack in the Spin Boldak area of Kandahar, and on 16 January 26 civilians were killed in two separate bombing attacks in the same province. The next day, Taliban commander, Mullah Dadullah, announced that 'hundreds of Taliban mujahedin are ready for suicide attacks, only awaiting orders from the leadership'.[36] Although this statement may have been more propaganda than reality, taken together with the other evidence it pointed to the fact that the Taliban were back in the south, and that the security situation there, never great, was becoming worse by the day.

This information came from open-source reporting (OSINT) and was available to anyone interested in assessing the situation at that time. The MOD appears to have made little use of this form of intelligence, perhaps because it conflicted with their preferred narrative.

---

31 Tim McGurk, 'The Taliban on the Run', *Time Magazine* (28 March 2005), <https://time.com/archive/6671860/the-taliban-on-the-run/>, accessed 23 March 2023.
32 Scott Baldauf and Ashraf Khan, 'New Guns, New Drive for Taliban', *New Science Monitor* (26 September 2005), <https://www.csmonitor.com/2005/0926/p01s03-wosc.html>, accessed 23 March 2023.
33 Carlotta Gall, 'Taliban Continue to Sow Fear', *New York Times* (1 March 2006), <https://www.nytimes.com/2006/03/01/world/asia/taliban-continue-to-sow-fear.html?searchResultPosition=1>, accessed 23 March 2023.
34 Antonio Giustozzi, *Koran, Kalashnikov and Laptop*, p.2.
35 Antonio Giustozzi, *Koran, Kalashnikov and Laptop*, p.5.
36 'Afghanistan: A Chronology Of Suicide Attacks Since 2001', *Radio Free Europe* website, 17 January 2006, <https://www.rferl.org/a/1064789.html>, accessed 15 March 2023.

When challenged by the HCDC on the potential threat in Helmand, Minister for the Armed Forces, Adam Ingram, played down the risk. He told the Committee on 7 March 2006, that while there were indicators of a Taliban presence on the ground it was 'not an overwhelming presence and the threat could be overstated'.[37] The MOD later described the capabilities of the Taliban and Al Qaeda in the south as 'limited', stating that the actual number of Taliban there 'could amount to over 1,000'.[38] In the face of Ingram's apparent *sangfroid*, it is unsurprising that the developing situation in southern Afghanistan seems to have had no significant bearing on the British thinking and planning. Despite the mounting evidence that security was deteriorating, there appears to have been no 'Question 4 moment'.[39] British planners either failed to ask themselves 'what has changed?' Or they did address the question but concluded that their assumptions remained valid. Alternatively, they may have recognised that their plan had been overtaken by events, but it was too late to make any significant changes. It was probably a combination of these last two factors that led to the final decisions. As Messenger has admitted: 'We did not really anticipate the backlash that came from the deployment of 16 Air Assault Brigade'.[40] The mission was taking on a life of its own. Momentum was building and few were prepared to muddy the water by asking difficult or unhelpful questions. As Post Conflict Reconstruction Unit lead, Mark Etherington put it: 'There was a real sense of the clock ticking, that the minister was jolly keen to get into Helmand – don't bring me bad news, bring me good news'.[41] General Sir Mike Jackson was clear that: 'We had made commitments…they are not the sort of thing you back away from'.[42] When Brigadier Andrew Kennett, Chief J5 (the senior planner) at PJHQ, questioned the likely Afghan reaction to the arrival of the force, Major General Peter Wall told him that the plans were the plans and there would not be no back-tracking.[43]

All Change at the MOD

Meanwhile, in MOD Headquarters, Iraq was continuing to demand the lion's share of senior attention and there was a significant change-over of key personalities involved in the decision-making process. This combination of events may have been responsible for taking eyes off the developing situation in Afghanistan. On 5 May 2005, Geoff Hoon, the long-serving, sensible, and reassuringly capable Defence Secretary, was replaced by Dr. John Reid, a staunch Blair loyalist and trouble-shooter who had previously been Minister for the Armed Forces and overseen the Labour Government's first Strategic Defence Review in 1998. In April 2006, General Sir Mike Walker,

---

37 Adam Ingram, Minister for the Armed Forces, Evidence to HCDC, 7 March 2006.
38 HCDC Report, *The UK Deployment to Afghanistan*, 6 April 2006, p.17, <https://publications.parliament.uk/pa/cm200506/cmselect/cmdfence/558/558.pdf>, accessed 15 March 2023.
39 Question 4 is the final part of the Mission Analysis stage in mission planning. At the end of the analysis the planners are supposed to consider if anything has changed that might have an impact on their deductions. Clearly, in this case, the security situation in Helmand had changed and this should have caused the planners to revisit their assumptions.
40 General Sir Gordon Messenger, interview with author.
41 Deborah Haynes, Anthony Loyd, Sam Kiley, Tom Coughlin, 'Officers' mess: military chiefs blamed for blundering into Helmand with 'eyes shut and fingers crossed'', *The Times*, 9 June 2010, <https://www.thetimes.com/article/officers-mess-military-chiefs-blamed-for-blundering-into-helmand-with-eyes-shut-and-fingers-crossed-gs9sdn8zn35>, accessed 20 March 2023.
42 Jack Fairweather, *The Good War – Why We Couldn't Win the War or the Peace in Afghanistan* (London: Jonathan Cape, 2014), p.153.
43 Fairweather, *The Good War*, p.148.

the Chief of the Defence Staff who had agreed to the original deployment, and led much of the high-level planning, retired. He was replaced by Air Chief Marshal Sir Jock Stirrup. Stirrup had been a very successful fast-jet pilot and a star student at the Higher Command and Staff Course, but some have questioned his qualification, as an aviator, to advise the Prime Minister and the Defence Secretary on the intricacies of two concurrent land campaigns. This may, on the face of it, seem to be a reasonable criticism, but it should be remembered that Stirrup was being backstopped by plenty of land experience, including the Chief of the General Staff (General Sir Mike Jackson, until August 2006, when he was replaced by the equally-capable General Sir Richard Dannatt); the Deputy Chief of Joint Operations (Major General Peter Wall); and, until January 2006, the Deputy Chief of Defence (Commitments), Lieutenant General Sir Rob Fry, who was replaced by Vice Admiral Charles Style.

It is a military truism that commanders always want more resources than they have been allocated. However, in a province that is nearly three times the size of Wales, a force of 3,500 – of whom only about 650 were combat troops, the others being supporting personnel – must surely have appeared, to any reasonably competent military planner, to be on the light side. General Jackson explained that the balance of judgement was for a relatively small force but backed up with significant combat support, notably Harrier ground-attack jets, artillery, and, for the first time in British service, the Apache AH-1 attack helicopter, equipped with the Longbow fire control radar.[44] Jackson would later admit that the size of the original deployment concerned him. 'I niggled away at the amount of combat power we were putting in at the beginning… I am content to say that the original plan and force levels were just about in balance. I would have wanted more [fighting troops]'.[45] Butler would tell Chief of Defence Staff, Stirrup, during a visit to the theatre, that the task required a division-sized deployment, a point Stirrup dismissed at the time.[46] Of course, with the UK still heavily engaged in Iraq, such a force would have been impossible to deliver. By 2010, however, after four years of relative failure, the UK force levels in Afghanistan reached a peak of about 10,000 – not far off Butler's assessment. In addition, the US had poured an additional 9,000 marines into Helmand and had taken over a significant proportion of the UK's original operating area.[47]

According to Lieutenant General Rob Fry, it was PJHQ's initial recommendation (presumably informed by the special forces reconnaissance, ahead of the deployment of the Preliminary Operations team), rather than Butler's gut feeling, based on his previous experience in the province, that had most influenced the MOD's thinking when it came to setting the scale of the British deployment in the spring of 2006. The PJHQ team estimated that a force of 'about 3,000' would be sufficient to achieve the mission. This was later revised up to 3,250 and then 3,500 when it was discovered that the initial calculation had omitted to include the Attack Helicopters and the RAF transport fleet personnel. In addition, roughly 900 UK personnel would deploy as part of the ARRC Headquarters, based in Kabul. Overall, it was expected that the UK contribution would peak at 5,700 and then fall back to a steady-state number of 4,700 (including the ARRC HQ).[48]

---

44 Jackson, *Soldier*, p.365.
45 General Sir Mike Jackson, evidence to HCDC, 15 March 2011, EV114, Q521, <https://publications.parliament.uk/pa/cm201012/cmselect/cmdfence/554/554.pdf>, accessed 20 March 2023.
46 Brigadier Ed Butler, interview with author.
47 Rajiv Chandrasekaran, 'Afghanistan, how the US army battled it out with the British', the *Guardian*, (3 July 2012), <https://www.theguardian.com/world/2012/jul/03/us-army-battles-british-afghanistan>, accessed 21 March 2023.
48 HCDC Report, *The UK Deployment to Afghanistan,* 6 April 2006, p.10, <https://publications.parliament.uk/pa/cm200506/cmselect/cmdfence/1211/1211.pdf>, accessed 21 March 2023.

Air Marshal Sir Glenn Torpy,[49] Chief of Joint Operations at PJHQ during the planning phase, accepted the initial assessment and passed it up to the Chiefs who rubber-stamped it, turning it into agreed Defence policy. There then followed a tough negotiation with the Treasury and others before the 3,500 figure and supporting equipment was agreed, in the summer of 2005. This was despite strong representations from Butler, who was convinced that the force laydown was insufficient to get the job done. By October of that year, with seven months to go before his troops began to arrive in the theatre, he was still attempting to have the figure revised upwards. In a note to PJHQ he pointed out: 'The force limit…will restrict our ability to maintain the initiative and tempo and deliver capability pan-RC(S).[50] It will affect concurrency and may mean we become fixed by the logistics laydown and force flow into theatre'.[51] These would turn out the be prescient words, but at the time they fell on deaf ears.

There were three principal factors that ensured the initial troop laydown was capped at 3,500. The first of these was to do with spending limits on Defence that were imposed by the Treasury. Although Tony Blair had repeatedly said the military could have whatever they wanted, that message clearly did not percolate next door to his Downing Street neighbour, the Chancellor, nor to the Treasury officials who were in day-to-day contact with the MOD. The cost of the Helmand deployment was to be met from the Reserve, which is controlled by HMT. Anyone who has ever worked in a Whitehall department knows that Treasury officials guard all calls on the Reserve as if the money is coming from their own personal bank accounts. Brown has denied that the Treasury sought to impose a cap on troop numbers or spending, although he admits that both he and his Chief Secretary to the Treasury, soon to be Defence Secretary, Des Browne, were sceptical about what they saw as the open-ended nature of the commitment.[52] However, that denial is not credible. The idea that the Treasury would have written a blank cheque for the deployment is inconceivable. They would certainly have sought to limit numbers as a cost-control measure and there would have been a hard-fought debate about every line of the budget. In the end, total expenditure was fixed at £1.5bn over three years, of which £100m was allocated for development.

As Lieutenant General Rob Fry explained, it was impossible to escape the long hand of the Treasury.[53] Air Marshal Glenn Torpy admitted that it took 'quite a lot of convincing' of the Treasury to ensure that the Harriers deployed'.[54] General Dannatt blamed politicians in general for not making sufficient funds available. 'Parsimonious wishful thinking… allowed politicians to send their citizens to war while refusing to provide the money necessary to ensure the success of the deployment'.[55] And he added: 'The oratory of our politicians with regard to financial support for our commitments abroad was heavily nuanced'.[56] In his book about military leadership in Iraq and Afghanistan, retired Major General Chris Elliott, recounts the scene at the Cabinet meeting when the details of the deployment were discussed and agreed, in January 2006. John Reid set out the plan and Blair then sought views around the table. When it became clear that the Cabinet was

---

49 Torpy was promoted to Air Chief Marshal and became Chief of the Air Staff in April 2006.
50 RC(S) = Regional Command (South), the regional headquarters for the whole of the southern part of the country, based in Kandahar, under the command of Canadian Brigadier-General David Fraser.
51 Brigadier Ed Butler, 'Setting Ourselves Up For a Fall in Afghanistan', *RUSI Journal* Vol 160, Issue 1, 2015, pp.46–57, p.49.
52 Brown, *My Life, Our Times,* pp.271–272.
53 Lieutenant General Sir Rob Fry, interview with author.
54 Air Marshal Sir Glenn Torpy, Evidence to Iraq Inquiry, 18 January 2011, p.97, https://webarchive.nationalarchives.gov.uk/ukgwa/20171123123053/http://www.iraqinquiry.org.uk/the-evidence/witnesses/t/air-chief-marshal-sir-glenn-torpy/. Accessed 2 April 2023.
55 Dannatt, *Leading from the Front,* p.292.
56 Dannatt, *Leading from the Front,* p.330.

in favour, Gordon Brown gathered up his papers, stood up and left, muttering darkly: 'Well that means I shall have to find the money from other programmes'.[57] Matt Kavanagh, a former advisor both to Chancellor Brown and Defence Secretary, Des Browne, suggested that the force package was based on what Reid and Blair thought they could get through Cabinet without a row.[58]

Secondly, 3,500 was the number it was felt would be manageable in view of the commitments in the Middle East. Air Marshal Torpy, told the Iraq Inquiry that the force structure was built around an acknowledgement that the UK had to continue to deliver certain capabilities in Iraq. 'We had shaped the force structure in Afghanistan to make it manageable across both theatres. We had constrained the size of it. We were sizing the initial force into Afghanistan to minimise the risk that things got delayed in Iraq'.[59] General Dannatt put it in opposite terms. He blamed the decision to go to Afghanistan for restricting what the Army was able to do in Iraq. 'We had no choice but to reduce our force in Iraq in order to increase our numbers in Afghanistan, regardless of whether the conditions on the ground in Iraq justified it or not'.[60] As the military and officials were working out the numbers, there was an assumption that force levels in Iraq would draw down more sharply than they did.[61] Even so, when, on 12 September, 2005, John Reid asked General Sir Mike Walker for an assurance that the Afghan deployment could be delivered, even if the situation in Iraq refused to comply with the Chiefs' earlier assumptions, Walker wrote: 'The short answer is yes, but to provide further reassurance…we have taken advice from the Chief of Joint Operations. He is clear that our plans in Afghanistan are deliverable, even if events slow down our Iraq disengagement'.[62] With retirement in sight, there was little risk for Walker in providing this 'get out of jail free' card, and Reid would use it to good effect before the HCDC and the Iraq Inquiry.

Thirdly, a force of about 3,000–3,500 was what the PJHQ reconnaissance in 2005 had suggested was necessary to carry out the mission as it was originally envisaged – that is, to provide a secure environment in Bastion, Lashkar Gah and Gereshk, in which the PRT, working with the Government of Afghanistan, could begin to deliver economic development. There is a problem with this number, however. It is possible that in arriving at the total, PJHQ was guilty of telling the MOD what it thought the Chiefs and Ministers wanted to hear. As Lieutenant General Sir Rob Fry, a former Chief of Staff at PJHQ acknowledged:

> I am sufficiently jaundiced to think that they [PJHQ] probably set the bill at what they thought we could afford. It was a bit of reverse engineering. To some extent, you've got to try and hit the market with what you think it is going to be interested in. But never to the extent that you are going to be compromising the mission by under-resourcing it at the outset.[63]

---

57 Christopher L. Elliott, *High Command – British Military Leadership in the Iraq and Afghanistan Wars* (London: C. Hurst and Co, 2015), p.138.
58 Matt Kavanagh, Ministerial Decision-Making in the Run-Up to the Helmand Deployment, *RUSI Journal*, Vol 157, Issue 2, <https://www.rusi.org/explore-our-research/publications/rusi-journal/ministerial-decision-making-run-helmand-deployment>, accessed 2 April 2023.
59 Air Marshal Sir Glenn Torpy, Evidence to Iraq Inquiry, 18 January 2011, p.90, <https://webarchive.nationalarchives.gov.uk/ukgwa/20171123123053/http://www.iraqinquiry.org.uk/the-evidence/witnesses/t/air-chief-marshal-sir-glenn-torpy/>, accessed 2 April 2023.
60 Dannatt, *Leading from the Front*, p.292.
61 Jackson, *Soldier*, p.365.
62 Dr John Reid, evidence to the Iraq Inquiry, p.59, <https://webarchive.nationalarchives.gov.uk/ukgwa/20171123123054/http://www.iraqinquiry.org.uk/the-evidence/witnesses/r/rt-hon-dr-john-reid/>, accessed 2 April 2023.
63 Lieutenant General Sir Rob Fry, interview with author.

General Messenger added:

> Iraq was still very much the priority. It was a hard-fought battle by Rob Fry and others to secure the investment in Helmand at that time. Everyone recognised that 3,250 was an entirely contrived figure that was partially to do with what it was felt could be spared from the Iraq effort, and about 90 percent a politically-bartered number… [64]

In this case, it seems that in attempting to balance the needs of both theatres, and come up with a plan that would meet the tests of military coherence and political appetite, PJHQ may have leaned too far towards the latter. Frank Ledwidge goes further: 'There is no evidence that senior British commanders ever took to heart the most serious of duties – advising and challenging. The approach by senior generals reflected more of what might be called a 'Yes PM' culture than the required application of professional critical thought, let alone a will routinely to challenge their masters'.[65] Major General Andrew Mackay agreed: 'We allowed ourselves to be politicised and to be too acquiescent in rolling over to political bidding', he told *The Times* newspaper in 2010.[66] With the historian's gift of 20-20 hindsight, there is little doubt that the Chiefs made an error of judgement in agreeing to take on the Afghanistan mission while the UK military still had its hand in the mangle in Iraq. It was a gamble. They wagered that they could get out of Iraq more rapidly than turned out to be the case. And they topped that up with a side-bet that 3,500 troops would suffice in Afghanistan, at least in the short-term. In both cases they lost their stakes… and perhaps, history may judge, their reputations.

On 26 January 2006, the Defence Secretary, Dr John Reid, announced details of the forthcoming deployment. The UK's contribution to the Helmand Task Force would include the Headquarters of 16 Air Assault Brigade and an airborne infantry battlegroup based on 3rd Battalion, The Parachute Regiment (3 Para). The force would also comprise eight Apache attack helicopters and four Lynx light utility helicopters of 9 Regiment, Army Air Corps, while 27 Squadron Royal Air Force would provide six Chinook support helicopters. Other capabilities included Scimitar and Spartan light armoured vehicles from the Household Cavalry Regiment; a battery of 105mm Light Guns from 7th (Parachute) Regiment, Royal Horse Artillery (7RHA); a battery of Desert Hawk unmanned aerial vehicles from 32 Regiment Royal Artillery; 13 Air Assault Regiment and 29 Regiment Royal Logistics Corps; 7 Battalion Royal Electrical and Mechanical Engineers; and 16 Close Support Medical Regiment. There would also be four additional RAF C-130 Hercules transport aircraft. Reid described this as 'a substantial package' and 'one that the Chiefs of Staff have agreed is necessary in order to maximise our chances and minimise our danger'.

The total number of troops in Afghanistan – those already there, those at the new ISAF headquarters, the Helmand Task Force, and the temporary surge of engineering capability – would fluctuate over the following few months, peaking briefly at some 5,700, before reducing, as planned, to fewer than 4,700 as the engineers who were to build Camp Bastion returned to the UK. The Harrier force would also withdraw in June. At that point, the UK boots on the ground would comprise those needed to command ISAF, some 300 troops engaged in support and training tasks

---

64 General Sir Gordon Messenger, interview with author.
65 Frank Ledwidge, *Losing Small Wars– British Military Failure in Iraq and Afghanistan* (New Haven and London, Yale University Press 2012), pp.122–123.
66 'They Went Into Helmand With Eyes Shut and Fingers Crossed', *The Times* (9 June 2010), <https://www.thetimes.com/article/they-went-into-helmand-with-eyes-shut-and-fingers-crossed-jvbhc2mr07p>, accessed 23 March 2023.

in Kabul, and the Helmand Taskforce.[67] One composite platoon of Royal Irish Regiment soldiers, Ranger Platoon, had already been blistered on to 3 Para to make up for significant under-manning in the rifle companies. Two further Royal Irish platoons – Somme and Barossa – would join later as reinforcements.

---

67 Dr. John Reid, Statement on Afghanistan, 26 January 2006, Hansard, Col 1530-1532, <https://publications.parliament.uk/pa/cm200506/cmhansrd/vo060126/debtext/60126-10.htm#60126-10_spmin0>, accessed 24 March 2023.

6

Hello Helmand

Helmand is Afghanistan's largest province by area, covering some 58,500 square kilometres with a population of around 1.4 million. That means it is almost three times the size of Wales but with a third of the people. It has a border – of sorts – with the Pakistan province of Baluchistan to the south, Kandahar and Uruzgan to the east, Nimroz and Farah to the west, and Ghor and Di Kundi to the north. Its topography consists of desert in the south and hills to the north which eventually become part of the Hindu Kush mountain range. Running through the centre of the province is the Helmand River and its green, fertile valley. Flying low and fast by Chinook helicopter between Lashkar Gah and Camp Bastion, the first-time visitor is invariably surprised by how suddenly the cultivated strip ends and the desert begins. One minute you are flying just above compounds, green fields, trees and canals, the next, seemingly at the flick of a switch, you are over brown, featureless sand and rock.

Along the river are the main population centres, which include, from north to south, the districts of Musa Qal'eh, Now Zad, Kajaki, Washer, Gereshk, Sangin, Nahr-e Saraj, Nad Ali, the provincial capital, Lashkar Gah, Garmsir, Reg-e-Khan, Neshin and Dishu. In the south, up against the Pakistan border, is the hill-district of Bahram Chah. The main east–west road is Highway 1, a circular route that winds its way right around the country, joining Helmand with Kandahar and with Nimruz and Farah. A north-south road, Highway 611 follows the course of the river, linking Lashkar Gah and Sangin. There are other minor roads and tracks connecting the main towns and villages, many of which become impassable during periods of heavy rainfall. The central area of the province to the west of the river is largely desert, the *Dasht-e-Margo* or Desert of Death. The British main operating and logistics base, known as Camp Bastion, was built from scratch in the desert, north-west of Lashkar Gah, consisting initially of a gravel landing strip, an operations centre, headquarters buildings, accommodation and medical facilities.

The people of Helmand are a warrior race of ethnic Pashtuns, practising an ultra-conservative form of Islam. It is every Pashtun's duty to defend his tribe's *Zan, Zar, Zameen* – women, gold, land.[1] A large majority – as much as 80 or 90 percent across the country as a whole – adhere to the Sunni form of Islam. The remainder are Shia. A tribal society, the population is divided into a complex mix of clans, of which the main groupings are the Durrani and the Ghilzai. Each of these is then divided into subgroups. For example, the Durrani confederation includes the Polpalzai, Barakzai, Alizai, Noorzai, Ishakzai, Schakzai and Alizai. These then break down further into numerous subgroups. These tribal affiliations are important. For most Helmandis, their loyalty is first and foremost to their tribe. If you ask a local where he is from, he is likely to answer with the name of his tribe or his village. He might mention his province, but it is unlikely that he will say he is an Afghan.

---

[1] James Fergusson, *Taliban* (London: Transworld Publishers, 2010), p.41.

The green zone is fed by the Helmand River, which rises in the mountains of Wardak and flows south for over 1,000 kilometres, before emptying into the Helmand Marshes on the Afghanistan-Iran border. The water is distributed to farmland on either riverbank via a complicated irrigation system, built with US aid money in the 1970s. A series of canals and channels, controlled by sluices, spread the water supply across the zone, making the Helmand River Valley one of the most fertile and productive parts of the country – the Afghanistan food-bank. Large numbers of cows, sheep, goats and chickens are raised in the fields and compounds. Donkeys and camels are used for labour and transport, and crops include tobacco, cotton, wheat, potatoes…and opium poppies. In the towns and villages, artisan workers, operating with few modern tools, produce an astonishing array of goods, ranging from farming implements to domestic essentials. In peaceful times, the bazaars in the main towns sold food, clothes, ironmongery and, incongruously, mobile telephones and sim cards, linked to the local Roshan and other mobile networks. British aid workers often remarked that they could get a better phone signal in Lashkar Gah than in some parts of the UK, although the satellite towers on which the networks depended, were vulnerable to Taliban mischief. Electricity is an important, if sometimes unreliable, commodity across the province. Provided by the Kajaki Dam hydro generating station in the north, it is distributed via a network of overhead power lines, which are susceptible to damage or attack. The Kajaki complex was another international aid project, sponsored by the US. The dam itself was built in the 1950s and the installation of the generating plant was completed in 1975. Despite the relatively primitive feel of the place, and, from 2006 onwards, the growing dangers of roadside bombs and mines, the roads and tracks were often busy with a surreal combination of modern, but often battered, pick-ups and cars, donkey-hauled carts, and large numbers of motorcycles. A small civilian airfield at Bost, near Lashkar Gah, provided access to domestic flights, linking Helmand with other parts of the country and beyond.

Notwithstanding the agriculture and basic manufacturing activities, the economy of Helmand, like much of Afghanistan at the time, was largely based on the illicit proceeds of opium production. And in the same way that narcotics leads to serious criminality in the West, Afghanistan too suffered from the effects of the drug trade. It has been estimated that 90 percent of the heroin on British streets originates in Afghanistan, and much of the country's production of the raw opium on which heroin is based, comes from Helmand. This trade spawned dangerous collectives of growers, buyers and distributers, often controlled by powerful local warlords, with their private armies, doling out their own brand of justice – almost a state within a state. As Gretchen Peters has pointed out, if Helmand was a separate country, it would have been the world's leading opium producer, with the rest of Afghanistan in second place.[2]

The main language in Helmand is Pashtu, but from time to time, Dari, a dialect of the Persian Farsi, can also be heard. Society is governed by the honour code of Pashtunwali, which pre-dates Islam, and consists of a number of tenets, such as *melmastia* (hospitality), *badal* (justice or revenge), and *nanawatai* (sanctuary). These creeds form the basis of the Pashtun way of life and are as strong today as they were when Second Lieutenant Winston Churchill accompanied the Malakand Field Force to fight wayward Pathans (another term for Pashtuns) during the Tirah Expedition in 1897–98. Pashtuns are warriors and are expected to defend their land, family and property against invaders.[3] Writing about his experiences, Churchill noted: 'The Pathan tribes are always engaged in private or public war. Every man is a warrior, a politician and a theologian. Every large house

---

2   Gretchen Peters, *Seeds of Terror – How Drugs, Thugs and Crime are Reshaping the Afghan War* (Oxford: One World Publications, 2009), p.5.
3   Yasmeen Aftab Ali, 'Understanding Pashtunwali'*, The Nation* (6 August 2013), <https://www.nation.com.pk/06-Aug-2013/understanding-pashtunwali>, accessed 22 March 2023.

is a real feudal fortress…Every family cultivates its vendetta, every clan, its feud. Nothing is ever forgotten and very few debts are left unpaid'.[4] Not much of that description had changed when the soldiers of 16 Air Assault Brigade arrived in Helmand in April 2006.

During the mid to late twentieth century, Afghanistan was a functioning if fragile monarchy, led by the King, Muhammad Zahir Shah. With state finances in disarray, the King was unseated in a coup, led by his cousin, Muhammad Daoud, in 1973, which heralded a period of Marxist rule. A further coup, this time against the communist regime, in 1978, brought about the Soviet intervention, which underpinned the regimes of Babrak Kamal and then Dr. Najibullah. However, when the Russians finally withdrew from the country in 1992, Afghanistan descended into civil war, sparked when Gulbuddin Hekmmatyar's *Hezb-e Islami* group, supported by Pakistan's notorious Inter-Services Intelligence (ISI), attempted to seize power. This resulted in conflict involving a number of armed bands, led by former Mujeheddin fighters such as Ahmad Shah Massoud, Burhanuddin Rabbani, Naqib Alikozai, Ismail Khan and Abdul Rashid Dostum. The Taliban, under Mullah Omar, took advantage of the chaos to seize control of the country, entering Kabul in triumph on 27 September 1996 – just as they would do once again, in August 2021, after repeating their march on the capital. The Taliban were themselves unseated in 2002, following the US-led response to the 9/11 attacks, replaced by Hamid Karzai's Western-backed Government. However, between 2002 and 2004, the writ of the Government was largely restricted to Kabul. In other parts of the country, much of the power was in the hands of the local warlords with their private militias.

Wary of their power, and seeking to avoid further conflict, Karzai sought to bring some of the warlords into the Government. This proved to be a double-edged sword. It meant these regional 'strongmen' were partially legitimised by being seen to be part of the Kabul administration. But it was also destabilising as they sought to favour their tribal friends, allies and relatives at the expense of everyone else.[5] In Helmand, the man with the power and influence was Sher Muhammad Akhundzada, or SMA as he was known to the British, a member of the Alizai tribe, and a particularly nasty piece of work. The nephew of an earlier provincial kingpin, Nasim Akhundzada, who had been a well-known narco-criminal during and immediately after the Russian invasion, SMA ran the province as his own private fiefdom and was widely believed to have been heavily involved of the opium trade.[6] Already a feared and dominant figure, Karzai had appointed him as the Provincial Governor, perhaps hoping that high office would help to clip his wings. In fact, it had the opposite effect, strengthening his position by allowing him to appoint tribal friends and relatives to key positions within the police and the regional government, creating the potential for instability and trouble later on.[7]

When British diplomats and development officials began to consider the province's 'human terrain' they quickly decided that SMA was one of the least appealing aspects of local society. There was a strong whiff of criminality about him. He was seriously disliked – even detested – by those tribes and leaders who did not benefit from his favour, and his alleged involvement in drugs and other dodgy activities made it very difficult for the British to contemplate working with him. How, they wondered, could they be seen to be cooperating with a man who was neck-deep in many of the activities they were trying to counter? Supporting this Governor was likely to drive away many of the tribal elders they needed to bring on-side if they were to have any hope of achieving their development goals.

---

4   Winston S Churchill, *My Early Life*, (London: Eland, 1930), p.10.
5   Giustozzi, *Koran, Kalashnikov and Laptop,* p.17.
6   Cowper-Coles, *Cables from Kabul,* p.80.
7   Giustozzi, *Koran, Kalashnikov and Laptop,* p.17.

There was an obvious absurdity about the UK, as the G8 lead nation on counter-narcotics, working with the man who, many believed, was right at the centre of the opium web in the province. It simply would not pass the *Daily Mail* test nor the local tribal leaders' 'sniff test'. The FCO concluded that SMA must go, and launched a lobbying campaign in Kabul to persuade Karzai to remove him. On one level, the diplomats had a good point. SMA was certainly a most unsavoury character, and some of his bad behaviour probably drove a good many locals into the arms of the Taliban. As Giustozzi has written, the Taliban attributed their success in gaining recruits in Helmand in 2006 to the excesses of SMA and his militias as well as his refusal to mend his ways.[8] Jack Fairweather claims that British diplomats in Kabul, believing SMA would undermine the UK mission from the outset, launched a crusade to have him sacked. Karzai was strongly opposed to removing Akhundzada, but finally agreed after the FCO claimed a large drugs haul had been discovered in his compound. The raid that uncovered the stash may have been a set-up by the FCO and SIS. Akhundzada had told the head of the US PRT, Jim Hogsburg, about the drugs, which he claimed to have seized and was about to burn. Hogsburg had inspected the haul before reporting it up his chain of command to the US Embassy in Kabul. It has been suggested that when this information was passed on to the FCO, they, or MI6, arranged for members of the Afghan counter-narcotics force – Task Force 333 – trained and supervised by UK special forces, to raid the compound and 'uncover' the cache.[9] Faced with this evidence, Karzai finally caved-in to British pressure and removed Akhundzada as Governor, replacing him, in early December, 2005, with Engineer Muhammad Daoud. It was a decision he regretted almost immediately. 'We removed Akhundzada on the allegation of drug-running, and delivered the province to drug runners, the Taliban, to terrorists, to a threefold increase of drugs and poppy cultivation', Karzai told a British newspaper.[10]

On another level, it could be argued that by the single act of getting rid of SMA, the FCO and the SIS made a significant contribution to the failure of the British mission in Helmand during the spring and summer of 2006. Akhundzada might have been a nasty piece of work. He might have given off an unpleasant odour. He might have alienated some of the tribes. But if Colonel Messenger and his Prelim Ops team found a relatively benign security environment in the provincial capital when they visited Helmand in late 2005, that was largely down to SMA and his militia, who had been holding the province in a vice-like grip, keeping the tribes in check, and acting as a powerful buffer against Taliban incursion, particularly south of Highway 1. As Messenger put it: 'There was a very strong tribal, SMA-based dynamic which was part of the fragility and also part of the stability of the place'.[11]

The British should have held their collective nose and kept SMA in post, at least until they were in a position to deliver security themselves. Frank Ledwidge pulled no punches when he noted: 'Removing SMA was the key act that created the chaos'.[12] Evicting SMA from the Governor's Palace simply shifted him beyond the influence of Kabul just when he was needed to control the Taliban.[13] Jean Mackenzie, of the Institute for War Reporting Agency, who lived and worked in the province, and understood the tribal dynamics as well as anyone, was highly critical of the

---

8 Giustozzi, *Koran, Kalashnikov and Laptop,* p.60.
9 Fairweather, *The Good War,* pp.162–163.
10 Damien McElroy, 'Afghan governor turned 3000 men over to Taliban', *The Daily Telegraph* (20 November 2009), <https://www.telegraph.co.uk/news/worldnews/asia/afghanistan/6615329/Afghan-governor-turned-3000-men-over-to-Taliban.html>, accessed 23 March 2023.
11 General Gordon Messenger, interview with author.
12 Ledwidge, *Losing Small Wars,* p.67.
13 Fairweather, p.163.

decision to have him removed. 'The British should not have tried to impose their views without knowing what was going on. SMA was unsavoury but effective. When he went, his men were left with loads of arms and nothing to do'. It was a recruiting field day for the Taliban.[14] Akhundzada admitted that he had encouraged his followers to take up Taliban offers of jobs and cash. In an interview with *Daily Telegraph* journalist, Damien McElroy, he explained: 'When I was no longer Governor the Government stopped paying for the people who supported me. I sent 3,000 of them off to the Taliban because I could not afford to support them'.[15] Two-times military commander in Afghanistan, General Dan McNeil, described SMA as 'a simple-minded tyrant' but agreed that he was effective as Governor because he was able to 'keep the bad guys at bay'. McNeil believed his removal had been 'a huge mistake'. He told *The Washington Post*: 'SMA was dirty but he kept stability because people were afraid of him'. [16]

A former Policy Director at the MOD, Desmond Bowen, who watched the situation play out from Whitehall, but was not, at that time, directly involved in the decision-making process, was highly critical of the move:

> It was a really bad piece of prissy DFID, FCO, MI6 work… Akhundzada was a really nasty piece of work, and no doubt he was a bad guy. Unfortunately, he was also the man who was keeping things stable in Helmand. Karzai did not want to get rid of him and it took an awful lot to persuade him to act.[17]

From where Brig Ed Butler was sitting, at his headquarters in Merville Barracks, Colchester, Essex, the FCO appeared to have made their move to unseat SMA without any thought for the wider consequences of the action. 'There was a disconnect between the Foreign Office and the military. No-one asked me if getting rid of SMA was going to be a problem'.[18]

The FCO's decision compounded another difficulty that Butler was wrestling with as the days ticked down to deployment. His preferred plan for 16 Air Assault Brigade was based on the idea that the majority of the force would be flown into Kandahar, where it could concentrate, acclimatise, prepare and achieve Initial Operating Capability (as a minimum),[19] while the Royal Engineers completed the task of building Camp Bastion. This would have been the logical and doctrinally pure approach, he had argued.[20] Once the whole force had arrived, and with Bastion ready to accept its new occupants, Butler's troops would be moved forward *en masse* into Helmand, supported by artillery, air and attack helicopters, and begin their work to create security around

---

14 Fairweather, p.163.
15 Damien McElroy, 'Afghan governor turned 3000 men over to Taliban', *The Daily Telegraph* (20 November 2009), <https://www.telegraph.co.uk/news/worldnews/asia/afghanistan/6615329/Afghan-governor-turned-3000-men-over-to-Taliban.html>, accessed 22 March 2023.
16 'The Afghan Papers – a secret history of the war', *The Washington Post*, (9 December 2019), <https://www.washingtonpost.com/graphics/2019/investigations/afghanistan-papers/afghanistan-war-corruption-government/>, accessed 3 April 2023.
17 Desmond Bowen, interview with author.
18 Brigadier Ed Butler, interview with author.
19 In deliberate deployments, military forces rarely hit the ground ready to fight. They reach operating capability in stages, undergoing acclimatisation, theatre-specific training etc. The first of these stages is known Initial Operating Capability (IOC), which means some elements of the force may be ready to conduct operations. Full Operating Capability (FOC) is achieved when all force elements have been deployed, have completed in-theatre preparations, and are ready in all respects to commence operations.
20 Brigadier Ed Butler, interview with author.

Lashkar Gah, Gereshk and Bastion.[21] Doing it this way would have allowed the British military to establish itself in its Area of Operations while many of the Taliban's local supporters were busy helping with the poppy harvest. But John Reid and the PJHQ 'movers' (transport and movement staff, or logisticians) scuppered that approach. Reid decided to put his foot on the ball, delaying the final 'go' decision in an effort to put pressure on the Dutch to commit to Uruzgan.[22] The Dutch, seeing much of the same intelligence reports as the British, had recognised that security in the south was beginning to unravel and their politicians began to get cold feet over the deployment.

This 'political pause', as Butler has described it, was not all bad news.[23] [24] A plus was that the delay provided 16 Air Assault Brigade with more, much-needed, time to prepare. On the debit side, however, it meant that rather than deploying in January, as originally planned, the force would not now begin to arrive in Helmand until April. Reid's decision, which was, in some ways understandable, inadvertently changed the deployment from the Afghan winter, when insurgency activity was usually reduced, to the spring, when the poppies had been tapped, the opium resin collected and Taliban's local foot soldiers were once again available for fighting. Meanwhile, the PJHQ transport planners, having to balance the needs of the Iraq and Afghanistan theatres with limited airlift capacity, decided that once the political go-ahead had been given, and the Temporary Landing Site and accommodation at Camp Bastion had been completed, the Brigade would be flown directly into Helmand at intervals, by Company Group. Under this plan, the in-load would take much longer than Butler had originally calculated. Capability would be 'dribbled' in as opposed to arriving as a joined-up fighting force, and the final elements would not reach Bastion until July. This represented a considerable problem for the Brigade Commander. He had wanted to have all of his combat power available from the beginning so he could get onto the front foot if the Taliban caused trouble. Instead, the PJHQ plan meant force ratios would favour the enemy at the start of the deployment, leaving him with no option but to react to Taliban aggression rather than taking his preferred proactive approach. The collective effect of these decisions was that 16 Air Assault Brigade would be arriving just as the traditional fighting season was getting under way, and without the benefit of SMA's fighters to help to keep the Taliban at arm's length. This left Governor Daoud vulnerable and meant that Butler and his force would have to face a growing Taliban threat 'right from the get-go'.[25]

Butler and others, like Desmond Bowen, felt the FCO decision on SMA was taken without proper consideration of the potential unintended consequences for the military side of the mission, or for the new Governor, Engineer Daoud. It was not that removing SMA was the wrong thing to do, but that more thought should have been given to the timing of when the axe would fall. 'SMA was the most powerful warlord in Helmand and he was keeping the lid on things. We should have left him in place until our military footprint was properly established and we had sufficient force elements in place to provide a security blanket. Once that had been achieved, he could have been removed and replaced by Daoud', Butler explained.[26] By doing it the other way around, the FCO inadvertently undermined the new Governor, and the Helmand Task Force, from the start.

---

21 Brigadier Ed Butler, interview with author.
22 Lord Reid, evidence to HCDC, 8 February 2011, EV86, Q409, <https://publications.parliament.uk/pa/cm201012/cmselect/cmdfence/554/554.pdf>, accessed 23 March 2023.
23 Brigadier Ed Butler, evidence to HCDC 15 March 2011, p EV103, Q472, <https://publications.parliament.uk/pa/cm201012/cmselect/cmdfence/554/554.pdf>, accessed 23 March 2023.
24 The Prelim Ops team was authorised to deploy early to oversee the development of facilities at Camp Bastion.
25 Giustozzi, *Koran, Kalashnikov and Laptop,* p.62.
26 Brigadier Ed Butler, interview with author.

In some ways, Daoud appeared, at first sight, to be a good choice to replace SMA. He was 'clean', with no known links to the opium trade, and had a reputation for being a good administrator. He was not thought to be susceptible to corruption, and he also understood development, having worked closely with the aid community in Kabul. The fact that he was not a tribal leader was considered to be a plus.[27] In reality, however, he was no match for the man he had replaced. He had no power-base in Helmand. He had no militia (he would later seek to create one). Although he was from Helmand, he had no real influence with the tribes. In a society that respected power, even if it was sometimes wielded from the muzzle of a Kalashnikov, he was the wrong man for the job and his critical weaknesses, which would soon become apparent, were among the key reasons why Task Force Helmand (TFH) found itself fighting pitched battles in Sangin, Musa Qal'eh and Now Zad when it should have been concentrating on providing security for the PRT at Lashkar Gah, Gereshk and Bastion.

---

27 Fairweather, pp.160–161.

7

The Mission Begins

When intelligence is scarce or incomplete, military risk is increased. This, in turn, calls for a greater focus on risk management and mitigation measures. These can include imposing limitations on how operations are executed, in time and space, or, in some cases, through the application of overwhelming force, aimed at completely overmatching the likely enemy threat, to bring about a favourable decision as quickly as possible. For the British, still heavily engaged in Iraq, the latter was not an option. Instead, with such a small number of troops available, the PJHQ planners intended to use tight geographical boundaries as one of their key risk management tools. They sought to ease political concerns by explaining that military activities would be focused on a small area in and around the provincial capital. The scheme of manoeuvre called for gradual, conditions-based expansion of stabilisation and development activity, starting in and around Lashkar Gah and Gereshk. Only when success had been achieved in those areas would it be possible to consider moving to other parts of the province. By that time, providing the drawdown in Iraq continued as planned, there might be more troops available to help with the security line of operation.

But this is not borne out in 16 Air Assault Brigade's mission, set out in the Joint Commander's Directive, which was: 'To conduct security and stabilisation operations within Helmand and the wider Regional Command (South), jointly with the Afghan Government, Other Government Departments and coalition partners, in order to support the Government of Afghanistan and its development objectives'.[1] If that mission statement is unpacked, it offers up a number of important points that would have shaped Butler's planning, and also the decisions he would make once deployed. The primary purpose was to conduct security and stabilisation operations. Security comes first. That makes sense because without security, there can be no stabilisation. The DFID teams could not do their job unless they could move around the area in relative safety, and the threat to development projects, as a result of insurgent activity, could be minimised. Second, the Brigade Area of Operations (AOO) was not restricted to the Lashkar Gah – Gereshk – Bastion triangle (later known as the Afghan Development Zone), but was clearly intended to cover the whole of Helmand, and, significantly, the wider RC(S) area, which included all of southern Afghanistan. This meant that Butler's small force of combat troops – no more than about 650 – might need to operate not just in a single province but right across the south, possibly in support of the US-led Operation Enduring Freedom. Butler would have been required to take that into consideration when deciding how to use his resources. Next comes what the military describe as the unifying statement – the 'why' or the purpose that should govern everything else. In this case operations were to be conducted *in order to support the Government of Afghanistan and its development objectives.* This means that Butler was, at all times, to have regard to the needs of the Government and its representative in Helmand, Governor Engineer Muhammad Daoud, as far as they related to the

---

1 Brigadier Ed Butler, *Setting Ourselves Up For A Fall in Afghanistan,* p.50.

development objectives. These were to do with security, improving the economy, justice, the rule of law, anti-corruption and counter-narcotics.

The mission statement was, no doubt, crafted with flexibility in mind. But what it achieved in flexibility it lost in focus and meant the Brigade would be faced with trying to be all things to all men. PJHQ's original intent, once the force had arrived in Helmand, and taking account of the limited resources, was to restrict military activities to the so-called 'lozenge' (later known as the Helmand Development Zone), the areas around the provincial capital, Lashkar Gah and Gereshk. This was designed to satisfy two important factors. The first of these was a recognition that the relatively small force should not attempt to 'boil the ocean' by trying to secure a geographic area that was beyond its ability to manage. Instead, it was to stay within a rigidly-defined space, avoid spreading itself too thinly, and, thus, reduce the chances of it being over-matched by the enemy. The second was the demands of the classic Templar 'ink spot' approach that had proved successful in Malaya in the 1950s. The PRT and its supporting military were to start small, demonstrate success, use that to win consent, and then utilise the resulting momentum to expand security and development to a wider area, similar to the way an ink spot spreads out on blotting paper. In other words, the mission was to be based on slow, gradual progress. Expansion would be dictated by conditions and available manpower. Butler admits that if circumstances had allowed him to follow that approach, the forces at his disposal might have been sufficient for the task. 'If we had been able to stick to the Lashkar Gah–Gereshk–Bastion triangle and simply acted as a guard force at those three locations, then 650 bayonets might have been enough'.[2] But the PJHQ concept of operations was flawed, underpinned by two false assumptions: that the AOO was essentially benign, and that the enemy would abide by the British plan. As events were to prove, PJHQ's approach represented the triumph of hope over reality and failed to apply the military truism: the enemy always gets a vote. Like Butler, Lt Col Stuart Tootal, Commanding Officer of the 3 Para Battlegroup,[3] had expected that his unit, together with its supporting arms and services (artillery, engineers, aviation, logisticians, medics) would all arrive in theatre at the same time. However, PJHQ had a different idea. A Company, together with Tootal's small tactical headquarters (TAC) would fly in at the beginning of April and the others would arrive at intervals over the following months. The two men challenged the decision. They needed all their combat power available as soon as possible, even if that meant the troops were a little less comfortable. The soldiers could cope with 'expeditionary' conditions. In the end, the movers found a way to speed up the inflow, pushing the other company groups into theatre in May, but some of his artillery and light armour would still not arrive in Helmand until July.[4]

Command…Control…Confusion…

Command and Control, often shortened to C2, is the term the military uses to describe the process of leading, directing and managing a force. Command and control, are exercised through a series of links – the chain of command – which runs from the individual soldier on the ground, upwards through the section, platoon, company, unit commanders and from there via brigade, division and

---

2   Brigadier Ed Butler, interview with author.
3   A battlegroup is a unit, usually based on an infantry battalion or an armoured regiment, that is task-organised for a specific mission. It is designed to be a self-contained fighting unit with its own infantry, armour, and supporting arms and services. A battlegroup can be further broken down into company groups.
4   Colonel Stuart Tootal, *Danger Close – Commanding 3 Para in Afghanistan* (London: John Murray, 2009), p.46.

(sometimes) corps[5] to PJHQ, and then to the Ministry of Defence, and the Defence Secretary. In the UK, although the monarch is the Commander in Chief, the power to direct military effort is vested, by Royal prerogative, in the Defence Secretary whose authority comes, in turn, from common law (Acts of Parliament). The Chief of the Defence Staff (CDS) commands the military on operations on behalf of the Secretary of State, and, together with the three Service Chiefs, is responsible for providing military advice to the Defence Secretary and the Prime Minister. CDS and the Service chiefs advise, ministers decide, and the consequences of those decisions in the form of strategic direction – orders – flows down the chain of command. The judgements on which the use of military force is based are made in London, either in the MOD or across Whitehall in Downing Street, informed by an array of sources. But the day-to-day command of forces 'in the field' is done by the Permanent Joint Headquarters, based at Northwood, a leafy north-west London suburb, at that time situated deep underground in a Cold War era bunker.[6] It was from there that the Chief of Joint Operations (CJO), a three-star military officer (Vice Admiral, Lieutenant General, or Air Marshal) and a sizeable tri-service staff, planned and directed military operations around the globe.[7]

The normal UK chain of command was complicated enough. But Task Force Helmand was actually answerable, variously, to three separate superiors. In addition to the national chain, the force also reported to Canadian Brigadier-General David Frazer, who was commanding a multi-national brigade in Regional Command (South) from his base in Kandahar. Frazer reported to US Major General Ben Freakley, in charge of Combined Joint Task Force 76, (CJTF76) part of Operation Enduring Freedom, and engaged in counter-terrorist operations throughout Afghanistan. Freakley, in turn, reported to Lieutenant General Karl Eikenberry, at Combined Security Transition Command – Afghanistan (CSTC–A), at Bagram Airbase, under US Central Command, which was based in Tampa, Florida, but with a forward headquarters in Doha, Qatar, in the Persian Gulf. In addition, from 4 May 2006, TFH would come under the International Security Assistance Force (ISAF) based in Kabul, where British Lieutenant General David Richards, had assumed command. Richards did not report directly to London, but up the NATO chain via Joint Forces Command at Brunssum in the Netherlands, to Brussels. It is easy to see, in this complicated web, how TFH could find itself being pulled in several different directions at the same time. On 31 July 2006, ISAF assumed command of both the NATO nation-building mission and the US counter-terrorism mission, easing the situation slightly.

The UK had contrived to make things even more complex. Brigadier Ed Butler, as commander of 16 Air Assault Brigade, should have been the man in charge of Task Force Helmand from the start. But with a 1-Star already in command in RC(S) it was felt at PJHQ that it would be wrong to have a British brigadier reporting to a Canadian of equal rank. To solve this perceived conundrum, it was decided that Butler would be the UK National Contingent Commander, but he would not command Task Force Helmand, at least initially. That job was given to newly-badged

---

5   The UK does not have a sufficiently large army to require a Corps level of command. However, the UK acts as the lead nation for the NATO Allied Rapid Reaction Corps (ARRC) headquarters, which can command multi-national forces up to corps level on operations. This was the case in Afghanistan after 4 May 2006.
6   The 1982 Falklands Conflict was conducted from the bunker, then part of the headquarters of the Navy's Commander-in-Chief Fleet. In 2010 PJHQ subsequently moved to new above-ground accommodation on the Northwood site.
7   The star system is an American way, adopted by NATO, of identifying senior military rank across the three services. It spans from 1-Star to 5-Star and includes Brigadier, Major General, Lieutenant General, General and Field Marshal (and their navy, air force and civilian equivalents). In the UK the Service Chiefs, the Vice Chief and CDS are all 4-Star officers with CDS in a position of *primus inter pares* (first among equals).

full Colonel, Charlie Knaggs, an affable Irish Guards officer, who had just relinquished command of his regiment. As General Sir Mike Jackson commented, this was 'not a solution that would ever have been recognised at staff college'.[8] Butler considered resigning over the matter. He had been looking forward to the challenge of leading his brigade on operations, and the decision to remove him from that position was a devastating blow. He resolved to 'crack-on', however, deciding that his resignation would damage him, be a betrayal of his soldiers, and not solve the problem. But it continued to rankle, and he continued to believe that the system was making a mistake by putting Knaggs into the command role when, as a first-tour Colonel, he lacked experience, and had not been involved in all the detailed planning beforehand. He also felt that if a Colonel was the preferred solution, it had to be a senior Colonel who had been selected to command a Type A Brigade, that is, an armoured or mechanised fighting formation rather than one of the regional administrative groupings.[9]

Lieutenant Colonel Stuart Tootal described it as 'a confusing command relationship'. In essence, it meant he had three bosses – Knaggs, Fraser and Butler.[10] It was difficult for Knaggs too. He had to answer to Fraser but also try to keep Butler happy. He had been 'parachuted' into the position from which his immediate national boss felt he had been usurped. He had not been part of the 'beat-up' process to prepare the Brigade for deployment. He was not a member of the 'maroon mafia'; and, for most of the soldiers under command, he was a completely unknown quantity. In short, he had been left to sink or swim. He sank. In his autobiography, Richards notes on 10 June that 'the UK Colonel in Helmand is not proving up to the job and needs his span of command reduced'.[11] This means Richards thought Knaggs was over-faced with the scale of the job of running the Task Force. A few weeks later Richards made up his mind to move the Guards officer sideways and restore Butler to command of TFH. But he was clear that it was Butler's responsibility to make the relationship with Frazer – who would be his immediate boss – work. 'I reassured him [Fraser] that if there was any hint of Ed failing to do what David ordered, I would have him sacked'.[12]

Opium Wars

British soldiers were never going to be welcome in Helmand. That fact would have been crystal-clear to anyone who had taken the trouble to read any nineteenth century military history before making the decision to send them there. Leaving aside the growing Taliban threat, the British Task Force that began arriving in the province in April 2006, was always going to face an uphill struggle to win hearts and minds. That was because Helmandis had been culturally programmed to regard the British in particular, and any foreigner in general, as feared invaders to be repelled at the point of a gun.

A task that was challenging enough to begin with, became even more difficult when the UK's political leadership, and those in charge at NATO HQ in Brussels, decided to talk-up the counter-narcotics element of the mission. Right from the beginning of the War on Terror, Tony Blair had turned to an anti-drugs narrative to help to justify, and build popular support for, Britain's involvement in Afghanistan. It would be difficult for his opponents to argue against military action that

---

8   Brigadier Ed Butler, *Setting Ourselves Up For A Fall in Afghanistan*, p.54.
9   Brigadier Ed Butler, interview with author.
10   Tootal, *Danger Close*, p.29.
11   Richards, *Taking Command*, p.224.
12   Richards, *Taking Command*, p.240.

was partly a response to 9/11 and also designed to strike a blow against the drugs menace that was ruining countless lives at home. Addressing a recalled House of Commons, on 8 October 2001, the day after British and US bomb and cruise missile attacks began on terrorist camps and Taliban installations in Afghanistan, he invoked the curse of narcotics as part of the argument for military action. 'We know the Taliban are largely funded by the drugs trade and that 90 percent of the heroin on British streets originates in Afghanistan', he said. 'So, this military action we are undertaking is not for a just cause alone. It is to protect our country, our people, our economy, our way of life. It is not a struggle remote from our everyday British concerns; it touches them intimately'.[13] Four years later, as he announced the 16 Air Assault Brigade deployment, Defence Secretary, John Reid, reprised the Blair script when he told Parliament:

> …we cannot go on accepting Afghan opium being the source of ninety percent of the heroin which is applied to the veins of the young people of our country. Stability [in Afghanistan] depends on… rooting out corruption and finding real alternatives to the harvesting of opium.[14]

The published version of the NATO OPLAN states that 'given the threats to stability arising from the drugs trade, ISAF will also support Afghan government counter-narcotics efforts…'[15] At a joint press conference with Afghan President, Hamid Karzai, on 11 May 2005, NATO Secretary General, Jaap De Hoop Scheffer, made it clear that the primary responsibility for drug eradication lay with the Afghan government, and that the UK was the G8 lead nation on counter-narcotics. But he explained that ISAF personnel would be 'assisting wherever that's possible'. 'Whatever we are able to do we will do', he told a journalist.[16] These statements, and others like them, uttered, in good faith, in London and in Brussels, were gifts to the Taliban's extremely effective propaganda machine. British and NATO officials could rightly claim that these remarks did not mean that their troops would be directly involved in eradicating poppies. However, a poorly-educated, probably illiterate, poppy farmer in Helmand's Sangin Valley was unlikely to see the subtle difference between a force that was 'supporting' or 'assisting' in the eradication of opium and one taking a more direct, hands-on, role.

In a society where literacy was not widespread Helmand had a strong tradition of oral history. Pashtun children learned about their religion, culture and tribal histories at their fathers' knees. One of the favourite stories is about how Afghan warriors defeated the British at the Battle of Maiwand, just across the border in Kandahar Province, in July 1880. Songs are sung and poems are recited about the great victory, which was still celebrated throughout the country each year. Exploiting the local antipathy towards foreigners, the Taliban had been running an effective information campaign against the British ever since the deployment had been announced. Taliban recruiters were out in the Helmand countryside telling farmers that the British were coming to burn their poppy harvests, destroying a critical element of their livelihoods. Colonel Gordon Messenger found it '…difficult to convince people that we weren't coming in to eradicate poppy. That's what they thought, everywhere I went. They envisaged helicopters and lines of troops destroying their

---

13 Tony Blair Statement to the House of Commons, 8 October 2001, *Hansard*, col 814, https://publications.parliament.uk/pa/cm200102/cmhansrd/vo011008/debtext/11008-01.htm, accessed 23 March 2023.
14 Dr John Reid, Statement to the House of Commons, 26 January 2006, *Hansard,* Col 1529, accessed 23 March 2023.
15 NATO OPLAN10302 (Revise 1) dated 8 December 2005, p.3.
16 Jaap De Hoop Scheffer, NATO Secretary General, joint press conference with Hamid Karzai, 11 May 2005, <https://www.NATO.int/cps/en/NATOhq/opinions_21766.htm?selectedLocale=en>,accessed 27 March 2023.

crops'.[17] The Taliban propagandists had clearly done their job well. But Messenger should not have been surprised at the attitude he found among the local people. He had been present at – and addressed – shuras with members of the Provincial Council and the Mullahs' Council when it was made clear that the British would be assisting the Government of Afghanistan with its counter-narcotics operations. A telegram from the US Embassy in Kabul to the State Department, dated 24 March 2006, reported on the meetings, which took place five days earlier. The PRT team included Colonel Messenger, Lieutenant Colonel Henry Worsley (incoming PRT Commander), Nick Kay, the FCO Regional Coordinator, and Susan Crombie, FCO Political Officer, assigned to the PRT. The telegram notes that Colonel Messenger told the meeting: 'No UK military personnel will be eradicating poppy; however, part of the UK mission is to support the government in its counter-narcotics efforts'.[18] For most Helmandis – indeed most British people – that statement might have seemed like splitting hairs. The British would not actually destroy poppy, but they would be supporting the Government of Afghanistan to do so. For a farmer in Helmand there was little difference. The British were the enemy.

Illicit opium production was unquestionably the central plank of the economy of Helmand Province, as it was for the country as a whole at that time. According to the UN's Office On Drugs and Crime's (UNODC) Afghanistan Opium Survey, 2005, published in November of that year, 2,000,000 people across the country were involved in opiate production – nearly 10 percent of the entire population. The export value of the opium and opium products was estimated at $2.7bn or 52 percent of the country's GDP. In the national production league, Helmand was at the top of the table, with a total of 26,500 hectares of land sown with poppy – 25 percent of Afghanistan's total output and double the amount grown in neighbouring Kandahar (12,989ha). Nationwide, 356,000 families were involved in poppy cultivation that year. Compared to the value of wheat ($550 per ha), Poppy was worth substantially more at $5,400 per ha or $138 per kg.[19] It is clear from these statistics that opium was big business for Afghanistan and why those involved in the drug trade might react badly to anyone who threatened to get in the way of the money that was feeding their children and paying off their debts.

Afghan farmers have been growing opium poppies in the country's sheltered valleys for generations. There is evidence that opium sales revenue was used by the Mujaheddin to pay for weaponry to resist the Russian army after the Soviet invasion of 1979. The same source funded warlord rule in the 1990s and Al Qaeda and Taliban activities in the late 1990s and early 2000s.[20] Production was stepped up in the dying days of the 1980s as a way of rebooting the agriculture sector after the devastation caused by the Soviet invasion of 1979 and the subsequent decade of conflict. Livestock had been killed. Irrigation systems were destroyed. Fields that once grew wheat were mined and became unusable. But opium poppies were reasonably resilient. They did not require much water, they were hardy and pest-resistant, and there was a strong and ready market for the opium resin produced by the plants, thanks to earlier bans on cultivation enforced by Iran in the 1950s and Pakistan two decades later. Afghan producers found the poppy a relatively simple plant to grow, requiring little husbandry, and the resin, collected at harvest time, was easy to store and sell. As

---

17 Farrell, *Unwinnable*, p.226.
18 Telegram, US Embassy, Kabul to State Department, 001284, subject: PRT/Lashkar Gah – UK Officials Discuss Transition with Provincial Council and Mullahs' Council, dated 24 March 2006, <https://wikileaks.jcvignoli.com/cable_06KABUL1284?hl=Gordon%20Messenger>, accessed 4 April 2023.
19 UN Office on Drugs and Crime, *Afghanistan Opium Survey 2005*, published November 2005, <https://www.unodc.org/documents/crop-monitoring/Afghanistan/afg_survey_2005.pdf>, accessed 24 March 2023.
20 Rubin R. Barnett, 'Road to Ruin: Afghanistan's Booming Opium Industry', Centre for American Progress, 7 October 2004, p.2, <https://cdn.americanprogress.org/wp-content/uploads/kf/ROADTORUIN.PDF>, accessed 6 July 2024.

a result, opium production increased steadily and by the mid-1990s Afghanistan was the main source of the world's supply of heroin, which is refined from the opium derivative, morphine.[21] The Taliban initially frowned on opium production. On coming to power in 1996, their first thought was to ban it. However, the impact on the livelihood of poor subsistence farmers who relied on the opium trade to eke out a living, was so great that they quickly reworked the policy and adopted a more laissez-faire approach. This evolved into taxing the farmers on their poppy profits, and at the same time charging the traffickers for providing them with security to move their wares to market. In 1999, Mullah Omar, attempting to gain international legitimacy for the movement, again banned cultivation. This cut poppy growing to practically zero in a single season, but once again it caused massive hardship for the farmers and labourers who depended on it for their livelihoods.[22] The Taliban dithered over imposing this second ban – precisely because they understood how unpopular it would be.[23] This reflected the traditional way in which poppy production was funded. With significant profits to be made, many farmers borrowed relatively large sums of money from the traffickers to buy land and the seed to sow on it. These loans were intended to be repaid in opium paste when the crop was harvested. In the meantime, the smugglers demanded insurance against default and it was common practice for farmers to offer up a daughter as collateral. If the crop failed, or if it was destroyed, these so-called 'loan brides' would have to be surrendered, entering into a life of slavery and sexual abuse while the farmer and his remaining family faced ruin. In these circumstances, it is not difficult to understand why, despite the Taliban's heavy-handed clampdown, reinforced with threats of beatings and imprisonment, some farmers returned to sowing poppy seed the following year. Recognising the significant political damage that was being done to their cause by continuing to enforce prohibition whilst failing to create replacement livelihoods for the farmers and their families, the Taliban again rescinded the ban in September 2001, just ahead of the US-led invasion.[24] It was not long before opium production was back to and exceeding its previous record yields.[25]

The political price of destroying the sole source of livelihood for a large segment of the population proved too great for even the Taliban to ignore.[26] Yet some parts of the British establishment sought not only to use counter-narcotics as part of the case for going to Afghanistan, but also to put pressure on the Afghan government to go where the Taliban had feared to tread. The FCO and MI6 were among the staunchest enthusiasts for bearing down on the illegal narcotics. Some officials argued, from time to time, that this was the main reason for being in Helmand. The Secret Intelligence Service played a leading part in setting up a direct-action operation known as Operation Emperor which was designed to train Afghan military teams to eradicate poppy nationwide. However, when the Prelim Ops team produced the Helmand Plan, they recognised

---

21   Graham Farrell and John Thorne, 'Where have all the flowers gone?: evaluation of the Taliban crackdown against opium poppy cultivation in Afghanistan', p.81. *International Journal of Drug Policy,* 16 (2005) pp.81–89, <https://www.researchgate.net/publication/28576871_Where_have_all_the_flowers_gone_Evaluation_of_the_Taliban_crackdown_against_poppy_cultivation_in_Afghanistan>, accessed 7 July 2023.

22   Luke Harding, 'World's opium source destroyed', *The Observer* (1 April 2001), <https://www.theguardian.com/world/2001/apr/01/internationalcrime.drugstrade>, accessed 6 July 2023.

23   Farrell, *Unwinnable,* p.131.

24   Vanda Felbab-Brown, 'Pipe Dreams: The Taliban and drugs from the 1990s into the new regime', *Small Wars Journal,* 15 September 2021. <https://smallwarsjournal.com/jrnl/art/pipe-dreams-taliban-and-drugs-1990s-its-new-regime>, accessed 06 July 2024.

25   UN Office on Drugs and Crime, *Afghanistan Opium Survey 2005,* published November 2005.

26   Vanda Felbab-Brown, 'Pipe Dreams: The Taliban and drugs from the 1990s into the new regime', *Small Wars Journal,* 15 September 2021. <https://smallwarsjournal.com/jrnl/art/pipe-dreams-taliban-and-drugs-1990s-its-new-regime>, accessed 06 July 2024.

the risk of alienating local people by being seen to push too hard on counter-narcotics. Noting that drugs permeated all aspects of life in the province and underpinned the local economy, they pointed out that any interventions to eradicate poppy should be sequenced with other counter-narcotics activities to 'avoid significant and deleterious reductions in household incomes'. There must be proper coordination of poppy-eradication operations in order to avoid 'undesirable effects' on other strands of UK activity.[27] The likelihood that counter-narcotics activity would increase the physical risk to Government of Afghanistan and international personnel was rated as 'high'.[28] For that reason, they placed considerable emphasis on efforts to develop alternative livelihoods in an attempt to wean farmers away from poppy and encourage them to grow other crops.[29] However, in reality, given the relative values of opium resin and alternative crops – poppy was worth 10 times more per acre than wheat – this was never likely to be a realistic short or medium-term proposition.

Although they had accepted the broad thrust of the Helmand Plan, including the need to provide an alternative to poppy production, deep down the FCO and the Security Service behaved as if they were oblivious to, or uncaring about, the correlation between poppy and the livelihoods of local people. In the West, if you miss a mortgage payment it affects your credit rating and eventually the bailiffs may come along and remove some of your goods or repossess your house. In Helmand, the money lenders and debt collectors carried AK-47s, and they were not shy about using them. For an Afghan, therefore, anything that got in the way of paying off debt was likely to be resisted, even to the point of taking up arms against the source of the problem. In these circumstances, it was not difficult for the Taliban to persuade many local farmers to resist the British presence. As Wakil Haji Mohammed Naim, a tribal elder in Musa Qal'eh, told The Times, after the fighting there in 2006: 'Most of the fighters weren't real Taliban… [they] were local men who were angry with the Government…'[30]

Protecting the Weak

Hamid Karzai's appointment of Engineer Mohammad Daoud to be the Governor of Helmand Province, did his friend and fellow Pashtun no favours. To use a sporting metaphor, it was a 'hospital pass'.[31] Daoud was, without doubt, a good man, free from the baggage of corruption that had dragged down his predecessor. But in the complex world of Afghan tribal politics, he was a lightweight. He had been persuaded by the President to leave the relative comfort of Kabul for his native Helmand and assume the Governorship, partly on the basis of a promise that he would be supported by thousands of British soldiers. At the time he accepted the job, in late December 2005, the force had been due to arrive the following month. He quickly realised there were two big problems with this. First, British Defence Secretary, John Reid's decision to delay the deployment to encourage the Dutch to commit, meant the troops would not arrive until April; and secondly, that although the force would consist of 3,500 personnel, only a little over 600 of them would actually be fighting troops.

---

27 Joint UK Plan for Helmand p.10.
28 Joint UK Plan for Helmand, Annex A, p.3.
29 General Gordon Messenger, interview with author.
30 Anthony Loyd and Tahir Luddin, 'After the fighting and dying, the Taliban return as British depart', *The Times* (30 October 2006), <https://www.thetimes.com/article/after-the-fighting-and-dying-the-taleban-return-as-british-depart-2r9xl877xsr>, accessed 25 March 2023.
31 In football or rugby, a hospital pass is a poorly-executed or inaccurate pass that places the receiver of the ball in danger of being heavily tackled by an opposing player.

Brigadier Ed Butler sensed Daoud's bitter disappointment when he explained to him, at one of their early meetings, that most of the 16 Air Assault Brigade soldiers arriving in the province were actually support personnel, such as engineers, signallers, logisticians and medics, who would not be getting directly involved in combat. Butler recalled:

> In the Afghan army, if a commander has a force of 3,500, that means 3,500 men lined up with rifles and bayonets ready to fight. It took a bit of explaining to get across the idea that in the British army we have the 'teeth and tail' concept, and that a very long tail is required to provide proper support for the teeth. To say he was underwhelmed would be a fairly massive understatement.[32]

The Governor's displeasure was understandable. He knew that the Taliban had been recruiting in the province since 2004, helped in their task by the heavy-handed approach of SMA and his henchmen. He also knew he was weak. He did not have SMA's militia, nor yet the loyalty of the ruthless head of intelligence, Dad Mohammad Khan of the National Security Directorate, who had been happy to use a range of nefarious methods to compel people to do Akhundzada's bidding. He did have a small number of newly-trained Afghan National Army (ANA) troops and some police, but the soldiers were fresh out of training and the police were largely unreliable. As Daoud himself said: 'Officially, we had 1,700 policemen in Helmand, but actually we had only 250. The rest answered to warlords'.[33]

About a month before the first British troops walked down the ramp of their C-130 transport aircraft at Camp Bastion, Governor Daoud ordered the Afghan Army to establish a 'fort' near the town of Sangin, about 90km north of Highway 1. This was in response to the murder of four of his provincial administrators in the area. The base was later designated as Forward Operating Base (FOB) Wolf, and then renamed FOB Robinson, in memory of US special forces soldier, Staff Sergeant Christopher Robinson (20th Special Operations Group), who had died in the district in March of that year. Sangin was the centre of the Helmand opium trade and an area where the Taliban had been working hard to build relationships with the locals. It was an obvious place for the insurgents to seek to challenge the Governor's authority and Daoud believed the creation of a fixed security outpost would send a strong message to the Taliban and the locals that he was in charge. He was wrong. Instead of providing a symbol of security for local people, it represented a threat to the poppy growers and opium traffickers, who the Taliban had promised to protect…for a price. It was not long before the insurgents – probably a mix of core Taliban and aggrieved local farmers – began to threaten the base.

Daoud was now even more worried. The loss of the 'fort' or any of the Government offices, known as District Centres, would be a serious blow to his authority and reputation, and that of the Kabul Government. No sooner had Butler arrived than he came under pressure to deploy troops to Sangin. 'Right from the start Daoud was telling me that I had to back him up'.[34] Lieutenant Colonel Stuart Tootal, at Camp Bastion, felt the same political weight begin to press down on his shoulders. Despite the fact that he only had a single Company Group in theatre at that time, 'there was increasing pressure for us to take over command of the base'.[35] Tootal's plan, agreed by Task Force Helmand headquarters and PJHQ, based on the tightly-controlled cap on troop numbers,

---

32 Brigadier Ed Butler, interview with author.
33 James Fergusson, *A Million Bullets – The Real Story of the British Army in Afghanistan* (London: Transworld Publishers, 2008), p.154.
34 Brigadier Ed Butler, interview with author.
35 Tootal, *Danger Close*, p.35.

called for him to deploy his initial resources to FOB Price, near Gereshk. From there he was to begin to establish a security effect, patrolling the road into the town. The presence of British troops was intended to deter the insurgents and, at the same time, reassure the locals. The last thing he needed at this early stage of the operation, with most of his battlegroup still in the UK, was to have to split his meagre in-theatre resources and become fixed at two locations, miles apart. Not only did he have insufficient troops for the two tasks, but he was also worried that he did not have the airframes and operating hours necessary to keep both locations properly supplied.[36] Resupply by road was not a great alternative. There were few logistics vehicles available and road convoys could be attacked, either by IEDs or ambushes or a combination of the two. This meant they would need strong escorts which would, in turn, suck away more scarce combat power. PJHQ insisted, perhaps understandably given that the mission was still in its infancy, that TFH should stick to the original plan. Daoud's request was declined. But the geopolitical situation on the ground was changing fast and crying out for a rethink. Sangin was a problem but there was not much Task Force Helmand could do about it in the short-term and this undoubtedly soured the relationship with Daoud, who was frustrated and felt let down and exposed. He was disillusioned from the start and the British were never able to gain his full confidence.[37] Eventually, a small detachment of under-trained and lightly-equipped ANA troops was sent to FOB Robinson, allowing a Canadian unit in occupation to return to Kandahar.

On 7 and 14 April, suicide bomb attacks outside the PRT base in Lashkar Gah caused injuries but no deaths. Meanwhile, Defence Secretary, Dr. John Reid, arrived in Afghanistan on 23 April to see things for himself. He met Afghan politicians in the capital and was briefed by Brigadier Butler, who brought him up-to-date with the deployment. After the standard PowerPoint presentation, Reid dismissed his aides and asked for a one-to-one discussion with Butler. 'He asked about the mission and I explained that I had, in effect, a number of potential tasks including counter-terrorism, counter-narcotics, counter-insurgency, peace support, peace-building and nation-building. These were all conflating and I didn't have sufficient resources', the Brigadier recalled. Reid was reportedly aghast and claimed he had no idea the Task Force was facing such a multitude of demands. Butler felt the Secretary of State had been protected from the reality of the deployment by senior military officers in Whitehall, who thought they should be making political judgements and giving ministers political, as opposed to purely military advice.[38]

On 29 April, five days after the Defence Secretary departed for the UK, A Company, 3 Para conducted their first patrol from FOB Price into Gereshk. This turned out to be uneventful. However, as the paratroopers, weighed down with heavy body armour, weapons, water and extra ammunition, trudged wearily back to the FOB at the end of the patrol, the town of Baghran, 80km north of Gereshk, was falling to a Taliban attack. This was quickly reversed by government-supporting militias who pushed the insurgents out of the town and back into their mountain strongholds. But it was a combat indicator that the Taliban were determined to challenge Daoud's position, not in Laskar Gah, but in the north. At the same time, despite the presence of A Company, the area around Gereshk was beginning to look more dangerous. On 30 April, a day after the Battlegroup's first patrol, an ANA convoy on Highway 1, on the outskirts of the town, struck an IED, killing four and injuring a further three soldiers. The following day, a 3 Para patrol came under fire as it left the town. Thankfully, there were no casualties.

The first few weeks of the Battlegroup's deployment passed quickly, and mostly without significant incident, although it was clear by that point that Taliban activity was on the rise. On 17 May,

---

36 Tootal, *Danger Close*, p.36.
37 Brigadier Ed Butler, *Setting Ourselves Up For A Fall in Afghanistan,* p.52.
38 Brigadier Ed Butler, interview with author.

the Joint Operations Centre (JOC) at Bastion received a message that the District Centre in Musa Qal'eh, was under attack. The beleaguered ANP garrison reported that 30 of its number had been killed and it believed the position was on the verge of being overrun. The situation was restored with the despatch of 200 ANP, backed up by 3 Para's Pathfinder Platoon. Reporting on the action, Tim Albone of the *Sunday Times*, described how the Pathfinders, about 30-strong, dashed through the mountains in their unarmoured WMIK Land Rovers to help to repel the attackers.[39] By dawn on 19 May, the paratroopers were perched on high ground above Musa Qal'eh from where they could see Afghan National Police storming out of the town in Toyota pick-up trucks in pursuit of the Taliban, who had decided to flee as the relief force arrived. The Pathfinders followed the ANP as they chased the insurgents towards the town of Baghran. The Taliban attempted to make a stand but a show of force by an American B-1 bomber appeared to shatter their morale and they broke contact and disappeared. On the way back to Musa Qal'eh the Pathfinders were ambushed as they moved through a gorge near a village called Paysang. Once again, coalition airpower in the form of French Super Etendard aircraft, flying from the aircraft carrier, Charles de Gaulle, in the Indian Ocean, and US A-10 Thunderbolt ground-attack aircraft, known as Warthogs, were sufficient to discourage the attackers. The patrol arrived at the Musa Qal'eh District Centre without loss.[40] The intention was for the small, elite unit to stay there only for as long as it took to get an Afghan force into the town. But with no indigenous troops forthcoming, the Pathfinders would be required to remain in Musa Qal'eh until they could be replaced. On 19 May, a small French special forces convoy was badly mauled in an ambush as it made its way from Kajaki Dam to FOB Robinson, leaving three dead. ANA soldiers travelling with the convoy were also engaged, leading to about 20 further fatalities.[41] It was now clear that these attacks were not a series of isolated incidents but part of a concerted effort by the Taliban, a spring offensive that appeared to be focused on undermining the authority of the Karzai administration and ejecting the foreign troops, not just in Helmand but throughout the south.[42]

The tactical situation on the ground was now much different from that on which the British deployment had been planned and resourced. The 'stable but fragile' image that had been described by MOD officials when they briefed the House of Commons Defence Committee at the beginning of the year had cracked.[43] In its place was an unstable and highly-volatile environment that seemed to be growing more dangerous and disruptive by the day. Brigadier Butler's prophesy about the Taliban's likely reaction to the arrival of the Task Force was proving to be correct. But there was no comfort to be drawn from being right.

The decision to commit the Pathfinder Platoon to help the Afghans to secure the Musa Qal'eh District Centre was a well-intentioned gesture of support. It was not intended to signal a move away from the mission to protect the Triangle. Nevertheless, it was the point at which the fingertips of the British Task Force became trapped in the mangle that was northern Helmand. Having once agreed to hold a District Centre against the Taliban, it was going to be much, much harder to refuse to provide similar assistance in the future. Daoud had achieved a breakthrough in terms

---

39 WMIK = Weapons Mount Installation Kit. These vehicles were standard, unarmoured Land Rovers equipped with .50in and 7.62 machine guns. They were relatively nimble, capable of crossing most types of desert terrain and wadis, and the Pathfinders preferred them to heavier, slower, up-armoured vehicles.
40 Tim Albone, 'British troops in 5 day chase of Taliban', *Sunday Times* (28 May 2006), <https://www.thetimes.com/article/british-troops-in-5-day-chase-of-taliban-znqhtkp2zq7>, accessed 25 March 2023.
41 Tootal, *Danger Close*, p.48.
42 Rashid, *Descent into Chaos*, pp.362–365.
43 Martin Howard, Director General Operational Policy, MOD, Evidence to HCDC, *The UK deployment to Afghanistan, Fifth Report of Session 2005-06,* 17 January 2006, EV3, Q10, <https://publications.parliament.uk/pa/cm200506/cmselect/cmdfence/558/558.pdf>, accessed 25 March 2023.

of the British reluctance to move beyond the Triangle. He would continue to turn the handle, and the Task Force would be dragged further and further into the growing struggle for supremacy in the north. On 22 May, Now Zad was reported to be about to fall to a heavy Taliban attack. Daoud once again piled on the pressure and again Butler and Knaggs agreed to help. Tootal was ordered to plan an intervention, and later that day troops from B Company were helicoptered forward to find the situation had been resolved and the DC was still in Government hands. Tootal was unhappy about the way his battlegroup was being stretched. However, he understood the bigger-picture imperative to back up the Governor. While B Company watched and waited in Now Zad, the rest of the Battlegroup 'continued to respond to the whims of Daoud'.[44] Two days later, A Company was ordered to fly to the Baghran Valley to rescue one of Daoud's supporters who was apparently surrounded by insurgents and in danger of being killed. Meanwhile, with the Governor applying more pressure, Knaggs and Butler were now also considering establishing a permanent British presence at Musa Qal'eh and Kajaki Dam, as both were perceived to be under threat.

Before that happened, however, the US commander of Combined Joint Task Force 76, Major General Ben Freakley, demanded British help to prosecute a major offensive against the Taliban in Helmand, Kandahar, Zabul and Uruzgan. Code-named Operation Mountain Thrust, Freakley's plan was to launch a large-scale sweep across the four provinces in a bid to disrupt the insurgents in the region before NATO formally assumed responsibility for the south. With the British Task Force being pulled in every direction, Butler was reluctant to get involved and this led to a difficult stand-off with Freakley. Butler said later that the American did not understand the role of the National Contingent Commander.[45] Although the ex-SAS officer was not in the operational chain of command (as explained earlier, the Task Force was under the command of Colonel Charlie Knaggs), he (Butler) was still responsible for the British Task Force to the British chain of command and he was perfectly entitled to object if he thought the 3 Para Battlegroup was being misused. The issue was eventually resolved, but it required some creative thinking. Tootal was forced to strip out men from the Gurkha Company tasked with guarding Camp Bastion, replacing the infantrymen with support personnel and members of a Danish Armoured Reconnaissance Squadron that had been attached to TFH. This provided two additional platoons, one of which went to relieve B Company at Now Zad and the other reinforced an ANA detachment and a troop of gunners from 7RHA at FOB Robinson, south of Sangin. By doing this, he was able to free up B Company to provide a second manoeuvre sub-unit and thus allow him to contribute one company to participate in Mountain Thrust while holding a second against any other requirements that might arise.[46]

Tootal and his planning team worked-up a number of possible target options before finally settling on a strike operation against a Taliban leader, assessed as a High Value Target or HVT, believed to be hiding out in a compound near Now Zad. Operation Mutay, as the mission was named, would be the Battlegroup's first major offensive action. The soldiers were keen to be proactive for a change rather than responding to Taliban activities, and everyone involved was determined to make it a success, particularly since they knew that the Americans and the local Afghans would be watching. According to intelligence reports, the target, a mid-level commander, together with a small number of insurgents, was located in a farmer's compound about 3km east of the town. The area was heavily cultivated, the fields planted with poppy and wheat. It was crisscrossed by tracks and irrigation channels as well as hedgerows, low walls and wooded areas. A wide wadi ran roughly north-west to south-east just to the east of the objective. The trees, ditches and

---

44　Tootal, *Danger Close,* p.51.
45　Brigadier Ed Butler, interview with author.
46　Tootal, *Danger Close* p.52.

hedges would help to mask the approach of troops from the town, but they would also provide the defenders with good cover and many options for engaging the force as it moved in. Tootal was confident that he had sufficient troops to tackle the mission, providing the intelligence was accurate. After careful consideration of a range of options, he decided to use the Gurkhas and ANP, already based in Now Zad, to form an outer cordon. Patrols Platoon would move into the District Centre the day before and use the mobility provided by their WMIKs to set up a blocking position to the south. Once the area had been secured, A Company would air-assault into the area to clear and secure the compound before the Royal Engineer Search Team arrived to conduct exploitation. Apache gunships would be on standby to provide close air support if required.

At 1100hrs on 4 June, the Gurkha platoon, commanded by Lieutenant Paul Hollingshead moved out from the Now Zad District Centre, followed a short time later by Patrols Platoon in their WMIKs. Both quickly found themselves in contact. Instead of facing a small group of Taliban, the Paras and Gurkhas discovered they were up against a force of about 60, armed with rifles, RPGs and a number of PKM belt-fed machine guns, who opened heavy and sustained fire, preventing both groups from reaching their assigned positions. Meanwhile, A Company, aware that the troops on the ground were in contact, but not the extent of the fighting, landed as planned about 200 metres away from the compound, also coming under fire as they deployed. Despite this, they quickly cleared the farmstead and set a defensive perimeter while the compound was searched. The HVT was not there. Tootal ordered the Patrols Platoon to pull back into more open country where they could make use of the superior ranges of their heavier weapons systems. The Gurkhas had already manoeuvred back into the District Centre. While the search team was examining the compound, the A Company perimeter came under determined attack from multiple directions. By 1500hrs, with the sun beginning to dip, Tootal became anxious to complete the task and withdraw before he lost the light. The Royal Engineers needed more time, however, and it was agreed that they could have a further 45 minutes, after which the cordon was collapsed and the searchers and their security screen of paratroopers exfiltrated over the wadi to a Landing Zone (LZ) where they would reboard the Chinooks and head home. With assistance from an American A-10, which engaged enemy positions with its 30mm rotating cannon, the force was able to break contact and extract as planned, boarding four big twin-rotor CH-47 Chinook helicopters for the flight back to Bastion.

The objective of the mission had not been achieved but the Paras had learned many lessons which would help to shape future operations. Remarkably, the only casualty sustained by Tootal's force in five hours of heavy fighting was an Afghan Army soldier who was shot in the stomach early on in the battle. As Tootal said afterwards, the professionalism, skills and drills of the platoon commanders and soldiers had carried the day. But he also highlighted the vulnerability of vehicles operating without infantry support in close country – the same lesson the Americans and British had learned in the hedgerows of Normandy's Bocage in 1944.[47] Assessing the fight as part of an analysis of Taliban tactics for the US Marine Corps in 2009, Carter Malkasian, an Afghanistan expert, who was a Special Assistant for Strategy to the Chairman of the Joint Chiefs of Staff, General Joseph Dunford, and co-writer, Jerry Meyerle, concluded that the insurgents had demonstrated 'impressive tactical sophistication' during the engagement. They had used cover and concealment well, including prepared defensive positions, and demonstrated a willingness to manoeuvre, strong resolve and some degree of command and control. The incident had also shown that the Taliban were capable of defending important bases, particularly if they contained mid or high-level commanders. Striking the British before they had reached the compound, the

---

47 Tootal, *Danger Close*, p.69.

insurgents had managed to delay the raid long enough for the HVT to make his escape.[48] Tootal would later write: 'After Mutay, everything changed…any preconceived wishful thinking about conducting a peace-support operation fell away'.[49]

The Road to Sangin

Op Mutay was the stick that poked the hornet's nest and the Helmand Task Force was about to be stung. Northern Helmand had been a Taliban stronghold for some time, but the insurgents there appeared to have grown more numerous during June. It is likely that this was, at least in part, as a result of CJTF76's Operation Mountain Thrust. As the Commanding General, Major General Freakley, explained: 'We had identified a number of Taliban commanders in Helmand Province and we attempted to kill, wound or capture them, or to encourage them to withdraw. We probably killed 8-10'. Freakley likened the insurgents to a balloon. If you squeeze it the balloon changes shape.[50] Mountain Thrust exerted pressure on the Taliban and it is likely that some fighters moved out of Kandahar, Uruzgan and southern Helmand and into the mountainous territory in the north of the province where they would have felt more secure.

At FOB Robinson, just south of Sangin, Captain Jim Phillipson (29), from St Albans, Hertfordshire, was part of an eight-man group, known as an Operational Mentoring and Liaison Team – or OMLT (pronounced omelette) – providing embedded support and guidance for the recently-arrived ANA unit that had relieved the Canadians there. Phillipson and his group of mentors were from 7RHA, which was (and is) 16 Air Assault Brigade's organic artillery support. The 'horse gunners' are all parachute-trained. They wear the maroon beret and, on their sleeves, the winged horse, Pegasus, denoting membership of the airborne forces club.[51] Their 105mm Light Guns are air-transportable by helicopter as underslung loads, and can fire out to ranges of up to about 20km, using rocket-assisted ammunition (the exact details are classified). From a number of carefully-selected bases they could bring down accurate, almost instantaneous artillery fire to protect troops in contact across the area of operations. While some personnel were involved in mentoring an Afghan *Kandak* (battalion), others stood by to respond to calls for fire from troops operating under the protective umbrella of their guns.

Also at FOB Robinson was a small detachment from 18 Battery, 32 Regiment, Royal Artillery, who provided an Intelligence, Surveillance, Target Acquisition and Reconnaissance (ISTAR) capability using their Desert Hawk drones. These small, battery-powered remotely-piloted aircraft, made by the American aircraft company, Lockheed Martin, have a wingspan of just over a metre, and carry sensors that can beam back imagery to a base station. They are hand-launched and can loiter over a target area for more than an hour, flying a pre-programmed route. They can also be operated manually using a device that looks a bit like a PlayStation controller. On the afternoon of Sunday, 11 June, the 18 Battery detachment had a problem. One of their Desert Hawk drones had gone missing in the green zone. It was believed to have crashed on the far bank of the Helmand

---

48 Carter Malkasian and Jerry Meyerle, *Ambush in Now Zad, Helmand, June 2006,* in research paper on Insurgent Tactics in Southern Afghanistan 2005-2008, sponsored by the US Marine Corps Intelligence Agency, August 2009. <https://nsarchive2.gwu.edu/NSAEBB/NSAEBB370/docs/Document%205.pdf>, accessed 6 April 2023.
49 Tootal, Danger Close, p.70.
50 Lieutenant General Ben Freakley, interview with author.
51 In 2006 they would have worn the 'Screaming Eagle' 16 Air Assault Brigade Tactical Recognition Flash, which was replaced by the Pegasus emblem in 2015.

River… and they wanted it back. A patrol was organised and set out from the FOB to recover the UAV. There were just a couple of hours of daylight left in which to complete the task. Having failed to locate the drone, and with the light fading, they were returning to base when they were ambushed, one member of the patrol being hit in the chest by AK-47 rounds. Phillipson was part of a rescue force despatched to assist the patrol. He was cut down by Taliban fire and killed instantly as he moved towards the ambush site. His body was recovered by his comrades, covered by fire from the 105mm Light Guns at the FOB. A second relief force also came under heavy fire and sustained injuries before contact was broken and the patrol and the rescuers were able to work their way back to the base. Phillipson's body and two wounded soldiers were airlifted to Bastion by helicopter.

The first fatality, and the recent up-turn in Taliban activity, provided brutal proof of what all the British troops in Helmand already knew – that they were fighting a bold, motivated and well-connected insurgency, that had achieved a considerable degree of popular support. Despite this, there were few signs yet that the penny was dropping in Whitehall. The new Defence Secretary, Des Browne, who replaced John Reid on 5 May, arrived on his first visit to Helmand on 12 June, meeting Task Force personnel at Bastion and flying forward to Lashkar Gah. Tootal explained the Battlegroup's recent activities and was surprised when the politician 'pursued an aggressive line of questioning about why we were planning to do strike ops instead of development'. Browne was also curious as to why the military rather than the development authorities were leading operations.[52] This was clear evidence that the Secretary of State had not been briefed on, did not understand, or had chosen to ignore the prevailing situation on the ground. Having just lost a valued officer to Taliban fire, Tootal's response may have lacked diplomacy but it went straight to the heart of the matter. 'Because, sir, this is Afghanistan and we are in the middle of a vicious counter-insurgency. The Taliban are trying to kill my soldiers', he retorted, with an edge to his voice that the minister could not have missed.[53] He could have added that the military were leading because the civilians were unable or unwilling to leave the relative safety of Lashkar Gah.[54] Browne left, perhaps a little wiser regarding the true situation facing the Task Force, while Tootal went back to planning to take over Musa Qal'eh and how to secure Kajaki Dam against a growing number of insurgent attacks. But before the force could take on either of these tasks, it would have to go to Sangin.

The town of Sangin was a dangerous place even without the Taliban. It was at the heart of the province's opium trade and the scene of an inter-tribal turf war that had been raging there for some time before the Task Force arrived. The Ishaqzai had been influential in Helmand under the previous Taliban rule, but they had been usurped by the Alizai, who enjoyed the support of Governor, Sher Muhammad Akhundzada. The Alizai proceeded to marginalise and 'tax' the Ishaqzai, stoking up resentment which eventually boiled over into bloody clashes. The Taliban, sensing an opportunity, exploited the conflict by offering support to the Ishaqzai. This, in turn, expanded Taliban influence in Sangin where the Ishaqzai were in the majority.[55] When Government forces began a poppy eradication programme in the district, threatening the livelihood of Ishaqzai farmers and opium traffickers, the Taliban and the Ishaqzai were quick to respond and the district spiralled into violence, focused on the Government and its supporters.

One target for this hostility was the provincial intelligence chief, Dad Mohamed Khan, a particularly unsavoury character whose heavy-handed approach had alienated many local people.

---

52   Tootal, *Danger Close*, p.79.
53   Tootal, *Danger Close*, p.79.
54   Tootal, *Danger Close*, p.79.
55   Giustozzi, *Koran, Kalashnikov and Laptop*, p.61.

To make matters worse, the district Chief of Police was believed to have abducted and raped children from the town. On 18 June, a rival warlord and leader of the Ishaqzai, no doubt hoping to take advantage of the deteriorating security situation, decided to get even. With Taliban support, he ambushed and killed about 40 of Khan's supporters. Khan's son was wounded in the attack. The survivors, including the police chief, took refuge in the District Centre. Daoud immediately called on the British to mount a rescue mission to extract them before the compound was overrun. Butler, who had by now been restored to his rightful place in direct operational command of the Task Force, was not keen to accede to Daoud's latest demand. Both he and Tootal could see the negative implications of seeming to take sides in an inter-tribal feud and, in particular, the poor optics of supporting Khan who was despised by many local people. In addition, he was concerned about putting a force into an unsecured LZ where the risk of losing a Chinook was high.[56] Tootal had worked-up a risk analysis which included a worst-case scenario of losing up to 50 soldiers if a helicopter was shot down.[57] The two men would also have been aware of the political fall-out at home of such a mass-casualty event, and how that might impact on the deployment overall. However, Daoud, perhaps sensing that he was facing firmer resistance, played the humanitarian card. He told Butler that Khan's teenage son was in imminent danger of death and needed to be evacuated to proper medical care as soon as possible. It was a hard decision and Butler agonised over it for some time, referring up to the British Ambassador in Kabul for a diplomatic view, and to PJHQ for national chain of command guidance.

With dawn fast approaching to rob them of the cover of darkness, and Daoud on the phone telling him the DC was about the be overrun, Butler had to make a choice. He chose to go. Within an hour, A Company were in the air, thundering over the desert towards the town. The Paras fully expected to be going into a 'hot' LZ, but to their relief no bullets or RPGs greeted their arrival, and the force was able to secure the District Centre unopposed. There they found Khan's group and his wounded son, aged about 15, who had been hit in the stomach by a rifle bullet, but did not seem to be about to expire. The patient, his father and a group of about 20 of his supporters were picked up by helicopter and flown to Camp Bastion. A Company were to remain at the District Centre to await a force of ANP that Daoud promised would arrive within three days to reinforce the garrison and allow the Paras to return to Bastion. The ANP never turned up. A Company found themselves stuck holding another fixed position, a new target for Taliban aggression, and the Battlegroup now had one less sub-unit available for other tasks. Butler admits he was 'duped' by the Governor over going to Sangin. As A Company discovered when they arrived, the District Centre was not about to be overrun and Khan's son was not on the verge of death.[58] It was a lesson in Afghan duplicity, and also an indication of just how desperate Daoud had become to keep what little local support he had on-side.

A few days later, on 27 June, the drug town would be the scene of another tragedy that would claim the lives of two British special forces soldiers – Captain David Patton (38), of the Special Reconnaissance Regiment (SRR), who was from Aghadowey, near Coleraine, County Londonderry, in Northern Ireland, and Sergeant Paul Bartlett (35), of the Royal Marines' Special Boat Service (SBS), from Poole in Dorset. They were members of a 16-man team from C Squadron, SBS and the SRR, taking part in Operation Ilios, which was planned to capture four Taliban leaders in compounds on the outskirts of Sangin. The patrol was ambushed by 60–70 insurgents, and called for help from the Gurkhas at FOB Robinson. The Gurkhas had responded and the team had extracted back to the FOB, but two of the special forces soldiers were reported missing. The

---

56 Butler, interview with author.
57 Tootal, *Danger Close,* p.86.
58 Brigadier Ed Butler, interview with author.

presence of the patrol was not known to Task Force Headquarters.[59] This was not unusual for special forces operations. The practice was, however, a matter of some frustration for conventional forces. It made battlespace management difficult, increasing the risk of 'blue-on-blue' and 'green-on-blue' incidents.[60] It also meant that the Task Force had no contingency plan to support the mission if it went wrong. Nevertheless, with British troops unaccounted for, Tootal launched B Company to Sangin, with orders to search for the missing soldiers. Landing a kilometre away, the Paras swept towards the ambush sight and before long one of the platoons found the men, both deceased, surrounded by many dead Taliban.[61] The incident heralded the start of a period of hard and bloody fighting at Sangin. As B Company made its way back to Bastion by Chinook, A Company's commander, Major Will Pike was told by a local elder, who turned up, unannounced, at the District Centre, that the garrison would be attacked if it remained there.

The Mirror Crack'd…

Before that happened, however, another incident, 100km to the south-east of Sangin, would bring home to Whitehall and to the British public, the true reality of the mission in Helmand and the fact that it had gone well beyond the peace-support task described by John Reid when he briefed Parliament back in January of that year. While Will Pike was receiving the elder's warning in Sangin, a patrol from C Company, under Major Paul 'Paddy' Blair, including Royal Irish Regiment soldiers of Ranger Platoon, was setting off to patrol from FOB Price to the nearby village of Zumbelay, accompanied by *Sunday Times* journalist and veteran foreign correspondent, Christina Lamb, and her photographer, Justin Sutliffe. Lamb's graphic report of the patrol's life-or-death struggle in the fields, hedgerows and irrigation ditches outside the village, made a mockery of the idea, still being peddled by the MOD and NATO, that the situation was 'stable but fragile'. The words and pictures beamed back by Lamb and Sutliffe revealed the true reality of what the Task Force was dealing with in southern Afghanistan.

Lamb had been embedded with C Company at FOB Price and jumped at the chance to join a mobile 'hearts and minds' patrol heading to Zumbelay, to the east of the base, to assess the village's development needs. A convoy of about 15 WMIKs, Snatch Land Rovers and four-wheel-drive Pinzgauer trucks, left the FOB in the early afternoon. It was a warm day with the mercury indicating an ambient temperature of about 55 degrees Celsius. The convoy had made slow, deliberate progress from the FOB, taking about 90 minutes to complete the 7–8km journey, crossing the Helmand River and following Highway 1 for a short distance before turning north towards the village. Stopping in the desert, about a mile short, the patrol dismounted. Their vehicles were parked up in a Zulu Muster and the Fire Support Group,[62] including WMIKs with heavy machine guns and a section of mortars, moved off to establish an overwatch position on, and just behind, a nearby ridgeline. The remainder, including the journalists, approached the village on foot.

Christina Lamb noted afterwards that as they neared the collection of compounds it was unusually quiet. There was no sign of the hordes of smiling children who usually mobbed visitors,

---

59 Royal Marines History website, <https://www.royalmarineshistory.com/post/operation-ilois-ambushed-by-the-taliban>, accessed 10 April 2023.
60 Blue-on-Blue = friendly fire – coalition on coalition. Green-on-blue = host nation on coalition
61 Tootal, *Danger Close*, p.94.
62 Zulu muster = a holding area for troops and/or vehicles a short distance from the immediate area of operations. Fire Support Group = a grouping of heavy weapons including .50in HMGs, GPMGs and mortars, used to provide local support for troops manoeuvring on the ground.

demanding sweets or pens or cash. There were very few villagers about, and those who were seemed unwilling to engage in conversation. Eventually halting on a raised bank at the edge of a field, under the shade of a Mulberry tree, the patrol commander chatted through an interpreter with an old man, sporting a long white beard. The man did not appear to be very keen to see them. He told them the other elders were at the mosque, praying, and that they should come back later. As they got up to leave, the man pointed in the opposite direction to the way they had come and suggested that if they followed the track, they would find a bridge. They had moved 200 metres along the path when they heard gunfire from the ridge where the FSG was deployed. As they set off again in search of the bridge there was a further burst of automatic fire, this time from much closer to them. Lamb threw herself down and struggled to put on her helmet before following the soldiers as they moved across the fields, stumbling in the furrows that had been baked concrete-hard by the sun.

The patrol had scattered as the first shots flew in their direction, taking cover where they could, including in some of the deep ditches that crossed the land. Out of sight of each other, and with their personal radios failing, they began to release canisters of red and green smoke to mark their positions, calculating that the risk of friendly fire was greater than providing target indications for the enemy. 'The 8ft deep irrigation ditches that criss-crossed the fields had turned into trenches. In and out of them we climbed, slipping and falling in the muddy water as the paras tried to regroup, yelling instructions I did not understand', wrote Lamb.

The seasoned reporter was a veteran of the earlier war between the Mujaheddin and the Soviets, when, at the age of 22 she had had a narrow escape after being trapped in a trench by Russian tanks. But this was the first time in her life that she thought she would not survive. Worse, she looked at the taught, worried faces around her and could see that the soldiers thought that too.[63] For two hours, Lamb, Sutcliffe and the patrol found themselves under relentless fire from rifles, rockets, mortars and the fabled 12.7mm DShK Russian-made heavy machine gun. With no air cover available (it was busy dealing with an incident at Sangin), it was the FSG and their own WMIK-mounted .50in Browning Heavy Machine Guns that finally turned the tide. The withering firepower of the big American-designed belt-fed weapons, little-changed from their introduction during the Second World War, supplemented by the smaller but equally-lethal 7.62mm calibre GPMGs, helped to supress the attackers, creating an opportunity for the patrol to regroup and reorganise. With daylight fading, the arrival, at 8.30pm, of a pair of Apache attack helicopters, their deadly 30mm cannon supplementing the FSG, finally allowed the patrol to break contact and move back towards their vehicles and relative safety, taking a long and circuitous return route to FOB Price. Back-briefing Tootal on the outcome, the patrol commander, Major Blair, put it succinctly: 'It was a bit cheeky, Colonel. I am amazed we didn't lose anybody'.[64]

That the patrol had survived with no casualties was a remarkable achievement, given the weight of firepower that had been directed towards the troops, and the need to look after two non-combatants. It was another tribute to the training, courage and skills of the soldiers involved – and, perhaps, the poor marksmanship of the Taliban fighters. But Lamb's vivid account of the ambush, spread across five pages of the *Sunday Times*, and illustrated with Sutcliffe's photographs, was to have weighty repercussions in London. The MOD was horrified. Mark Laity, the NATO spokesman in Kabul, felt it had been a PR disaster and told Lamb so when he met her later at ISAF headquarters.[65] It was, according to Laity, the moment when the UK's Helmand narrative fell in tatters. The suggestion that the British force was there for peacekeeping, that security in

---

63   Christina Lamb, 'Have you ever used a pistol?', *Sunday Times*, 2 July 2006, <https://www.thetimes.com/article/have-you-ever-used-a-pistol-5btnlkwfkkm>, accessed 10 April 2023.
64   Tootal, *Danger Close,* p.100.
65   Mark Laity, interview with author.

Helmand was 'stable but fragile' and that 650 fighting troops were sufficient for the task, was no longer credible.[66]

The MOD's first reaction was to 'rubbish' Lamb's story as 'an exaggeration'. But the media were well aware of the *Sunday Times* journalist's credentials and were inclined to take her word rather than that of the MOD spin doctors. No doubt under pressure from their political masters, the Defence Press Office tried to impose a media black-out on Helmand. However, they did so without taking account of the ingenuity of the British infanteer. Angry that their plight was not being reported back home, some soldiers took matters into their own hands. Deciding they could do their own reporting, they began to post video clips of their firefights on YouTube. The MOD had lost control of the Helmand narrative, thanks to the power of nascent social media, and this was to have deep-reaching implications for the future of the campaign.

In Sangin, meanwhile, the warning of a Taliban attack, passed on by a local elder, proved accurate and deadly. On 1 July, the day before Lamb's article hit the newsstands, two British soldiers and their Afghan interpreter – Corporal Peter Thorpe, Lance Corporal Jabron Hashmi, and Dawood Amiery – died when a Chinese-made 107mm rocket exploded in a small building in the District Centre compound. The three were members of a specialist Light Electronic Warfare Team (LEWT), listening in on Taliban radio traffic. Thorpe was a Royal Signals soldier and Hashmi was from the Intelligence Corps. They died from devastating injuries caused when the rocket detonated against a wall, sending red-hot shards of shrapnel in all directions. A number of other soldiers were wounded in the blast, some seriously, but with the base now under heavy small-arms and mortar fire, it was deemed too dangerous for a helicopter to get in to evacuate the dead and wounded until the following day.

Reinforcements

On 10 July 2006, at 4.28 in the afternoon, the Speaker of the House of Commons, Michael Martin, called the Defence Secretary to the Despatch Box. Des Browne had requested a slot on the Order Paper to make an Oral Statement about troop levels in Afghanistan. Coincidentally, the previous business of the House had been a Home Office statement about counter-terrorism, involving Browne's immediate predecessor, John Reid. The MOD announcement, which included 900 additional troops for Helmand, came as no surprise to MPs. Browne's junior Defence Minister, Tom Watson, had telegraphed it the previous week when he told a Defence debate that Chiefs had requested more troops and equipment and that Browne would be announcing his response as soon as possible.[67] The immediate reinforcements included a company from the Royal Regiment of Fusiliers and two additional platoons from 1st Battalion, Royal Irish Regiment. There would also be a large number of Royal Engineers, who would push ahead with development tasks; a composite company of Royal Marines from 3 Commando Brigade, to protect the engineers; various other specialist capabilities; more helicopters and an additional C-130 Hercules to help with logistics.[68] In Kabul, Lieutenant General David Richards, who was to assume responsibility for the south of

---

66   Mark Laity, interview with author.
67   Tom Watson, Parliamentary Under-Secretary of State for Defence, Defence Debate, House of Commons, 4 July 2006, *Hansard*, Col 517, <https://hansard.parliament.uk/commons/2006-07-03/debates/06070310000002/BritishForces(Afghanistan)>, accessed 10 April 2023.
68   Des Browne, Statement: Afghanistan (Troop Levels), House of Commons, 10 July 2006, *Hansard*, Col 1132-1133, <https://hansard.parliament.uk/commons/2006-07-10/debates/06071010000002/Afghanistan(TroopsLevels)>, accessed 10 April 2023.

the country at the end of the month, was jubilant. 'Perhaps Ed Butler and I are being listened to after all', he recorded in his diary.[69]

Or perhaps the Chiefs and politicians had finally been shamed into correcting their original error. No single event had sparked the decision to increase the size of the force. Not the Zumbelay ambush nor Christina Lamb's graphic report. Not the tragic deaths of Captain Phillipson, Captain Patton and Sergeant Bartlett, or of Corporal Thorpe and Lance Corporal Hashmi, or Private Damien Jackson, who fell to Taliban small-arms fire in Sangin on 5 July. Not Tootal's sharp words with Browne during his earlier visit to the province. It was the cumulative effect of all of these, and the growing political storm, stoked by an increasingly angry media, reacting to the MOD's attempts to besmirch the reputation of one of their own. With Opposition MPs calling for more troops to be deployed, and the tabloids baying for blood, ministers and senior generals were forced to admit that their gamble over numbers was now a busted flush.

Of course, that is not how Browne chose to 'spin' the situation when he addressed Parliament. Instead of coming clean, he first pointed the finger of blame at his military advisors. 'The original force package', he explained, 'was designed by the military and endorsed by the Chiefs of Staff'. He was, in effect, implying that if the judgements about force levels had been wrong at the outset, that was the fault of the military planners and advisors, not the politicians. That statement may have had some merit. If the military had pitched their advice on initial force levels based on what they thought the politicians were prepared to sanction, rather than their best judgement about what was actually required to achieve the political objectives, that represented a significant failure of the military-political constitutional relationship. Browne then went on to provide an explanation for why the force structure now needed to be adjusted and strengthened. The original intent had been to tackle the challenges incrementally, spreading security and reconstruction outwards from the so-called 'lozenge'. This was an accurate description of the plan as it was first envisaged. However, Browne then suggested that the decision to go north was the result of the commanders on the ground spotting an opportunity to 'reinforce the position of the local Governor and the Afghan army and police by… challenging the impunity of the Taliban there'. In doing so, the Task Force had been able to move more quickly towards achieving its ultimate objectives, but also found itself 'extended'.[70] This was a very nuanced explanation for what had actually happened and certainly did not reflect the reality of the situation faced by the task force commander, who had, been dragged north by a combination of the Taliban, an increasingly embattled and vulnerable Provincial Governor, and the Afghan President.

As far as the military mission was concerned, Task Force Helmand's job was 'to support the Government of Afghanistan *and* its development objectives'. That implies two main tasks: to provide military backing for the Government, including the provincial administration that was headed by the Governor; and to support the Government's development objectives. Both of these tasks were reliant on a relatively stable security environment. The original plan called for security to be achieved in the triangle of Bastion – Laskar Gah – Gereshk to enable the Government to begin its development work, assisted by the PRT. But the Taliban opted not to comply. Instead of making life difficult around the provincial capital, they chose to challenge the Government further north, first in the Sangin Valley, close to the insurgents' mountain stronghold, and where they had built up support among the locals against the 'foreign invaders', and then at Musa Qal'eh and Now Zad. The dilemma facing Butler was clear, but that did not make it any easier to resolve. Should he stick with Plan A and continue to focus on the triangle, where it was still relatively

---

69 Richards, *Taking Command*, p.230.
70 Des Browne, Statement: Afghanistan (Troop Levels), House of Commons, 10 July 2006, Hansard, Col 1132-1133.

quiet, or should he accede to the Governor's wishes and head north to deal with the growing threat while it was still above Highway 1 and well away from Lashkar Gah and Gereshk? For Butler, the way ahead represented a nigh-impossible choice. He knew he would be damned whichever way he chose to jump. Doctrinal purists, of which there were many, and not all of them tucked away in the groves of military academe, would claim he was breaking the first principal of war by failing to maintain his original aim. But few of them would be defending him for sticking to his guns when the Governor and the President were declaring mission failure and criticising the British for not living up to their promises of support. In the circumstance, the Keynesian mantra 'when the facts change, I change my mind' seemed much more apposite.

Butler's judgement about the Taliban's violent reaction to the arrival of British troops had been proved right. He now needed to make sure that his next decision was equally correct, not just in terms of the mission, but also in relation to the troops under his command. In his mind, he had always considered that the Task Force would have to go north at some point. The ink spot concept was built around the idea of slowly and gradually expanding security and stability outwards from a central point. The development effort could not become fixed on one small area, otherwise the wider province would remain a lawless, ungoverned space. However, the process of expansion was supposed to be incremental and conditions-based. In order to win hearts and minds in Sangin, Musa Qal'eh, Kajaki and Now Zad, the British and their Afghan hosts had to be able to point to success in Lashkar Gah and Gereshk.

During the early planning it had been recognised that the Sangin Valley was the source of much of the trouble in Helmand. Apart from its links to opium production and criminality, it was the path the Taliban had to take to move from their mountain hideaways to the main population centres, and it was one of the main channels along which supplies were moved from Pakistan to Helmand and beyond. The Sangin Valley represented 'vital ground' for the insurgents and, at some point, it would have to be addressed. But, in an ideal world, that would only happen when the time was right and the necessary resources were in place. It was not a task he had expected to pursue early in the deployment, before the whole of the Task Force had even arrived in-country, Butler explained:

> The intent was always to push up and target the Sangin Valley because that was where the threat was going to be coming from. But it was all about timing. We had planned to go there when we had the troop numbers to ensure success and when we had something to show the locals in terms of what could be achieved in Lashkar Gah and Goreshk.

However, the Task Force was now faced with a different scenario. 'It was becoming clear that if we stayed below Highway 1, the Taliban, in my judgement, were going to come south and we would have to fight them in Lashkar Gah and Gereshk. We had already seen car bomb attacks in the provincial capital'.[71] These were both much larger population centres were the implications of high-intensity war-fighting, such as occurred further north, would be far more damaging and dangerous for local people and businesses.

The decision to depart from the original plan was not taken lightly. It was not, as some have claimed, the result of a 'gung-ho' former special forces officer and his band of glory-seeking Paras going looking for trouble. Neither was it a simple expedient to keep Daoud and, by extension, Karzai happy, although the politicians were significant figures in the debate that would lead to the establishment of the so-called, and much-maligned, Platoon House strategy.

---

71 Brigadier Ed Butler, interview with author.

Butler's move north to establish a British presence in the District Centres at Now Zad, Sangin and Musa Qal'eh, has come in for some fairly trenchant criticism over the years since 2006. His boss at HQ ISAF, Lieutenant General David Richards, later said his subordinate had 'gone rogue'.[72] Mark Etherington, a former Para himself, who had gone over to the 'dark side' by swapping his maroon beret for a civil service job focusing on post-conflict stabilisation and development, was clear that his former regimental comrades 'wanted to go up north and mallet the Taliban'.[73] Mark Laity, former BBC Defence Correspondent and the NATO spokesman in Kabul from May until October, 2006, took the same line. 'The original plan was based on securing the provincial capital, Laskhar Gah, and ensuring freedom of manoeuvre on Highway 1. The Paras were not meant to do anything more than that. They chose to go north because they wanted a fight'.[74]

These charges are strongly refuted by Butler. Pointing to the original mission statement, he is clear that his job was to support the government in Kabul and Helmand. Although it would mean a departure from the agreed plan, there was little point in holding the force in the south when the real threat to governance was in Sangin, Now Zad and Musa Qal'eh. Karzai and Daoud were putting him under immense pressure to act and, he argues, he had little choice but to agree. Had he refused, he was in no doubt that the Taliban would have taken over the towns and the British mission would have been seen to have failed before it had really got going. In any case, he was pretty sure that Karzai would have gone over his head to Blair, or his foreign affairs advisor, and the end result would have been the same. He would have been ordered to go north. But the delay would have made the task of securing the District Centres more difficult. The Task Force would have had to fight to eject the intruders and continue to fight to keep them from returning. At the same time, the British would have lost what was left of the Afghan political leadership's confidence:

> Karzai and Daoud made it absolutely clear to me that if the black flag of Mullah Omar was allowed to fly from any of the District Centres, their personal credibility and that of the Kabul Government, would be in shreds. The symbolism of the Taliban flag fapping in the breeze over the seats of district governance would be a clear and unassailable sign that the writ of the Kabul administration did not run in Helmand, and also a massive propaganda coup for the insurgents.[75]

The Helmandis would conclude that if Karzai and Daoud could not secure their own government offices, they had little chance of being able to deliver on their promises of economic and social development. If that happened, Daoud had told Butler, he (Daoud) – and the British Task Force – might as well pack up and go home.[76]

It is clear that the soldiers of 3 Para went to Helmand hoping to see some action. In Stuart Tootal's account of the deployment he notes: 'All they wanted to do was to go on operations and be tested in combat'. The battalion had seen relatively little action since the Falklands War, 24 years earlier, and there was some concern that Afghanistan might turn out to be 'another damp squib'.[77] However, that is not the same as deliberately seeking out trouble. Although Tootal shared some of his soldiers' doubts, he told a families' briefing, before he left for Afghanistan, that they 'were not looking for trouble' but they would be more than capable of looking after

---

72   Lieutenant General David Richards, quoted in Fairweather, *The Good War*, p.200.
73   Farrell, *Unwinnable,* p.171.
74   Mark Laity, interview with author.
75   Brigadier Ed Butler, interview with author.
76   Brigadier Ed Butler, interview with author.
77   Tootal, *Danger Close,* p.20.

themselves if trouble found them.⁷⁸ Butler also rejects the characterisation of the Brigade as 'glory-hunters'. 'Stuart Tootal and I had tasted combat. We had already been blooded. I had lost people and I knew the true consequences of war. So, I was naturally more conservative than other people who had not commanded in combat and wanted to prove themselves. Stuart and I had nothing to prove'.⁷⁹

Desmond Bowen, the MOD's Policy Director, and also a former Parachute Regiment officer, observing the situation from Whitehall, saw Butler as 'the villain of the piece', but was also critical of the MOD's decision-making process. He believed Butler got 'carried away with Mission Command' and senior officers in PJHQ and in Whitehall were reluctant to overrule him.⁸⁰ Mission Command is the British Army's conceptual approach to exercising command on operations. It is based on allowing the person on the spot a considerable degree of latitude to decide how best to achieve the desired outcome. The superior headquarters sets the mission and tasks, but then allows the subordinate commander, who is closest to the situation on the ground, to work out how best to deliver the required effects. That does not mean the lower commander can do what he or she wishes. The plan must be agreed with the higher headquarters, and the senior commander can order amendments and set control measures, although these are expected to be kept to the minimum required for the successful prosecution of the mission. Chief of the General Staff during the planning for the deployment, General Sir Mike Jackson, supported Bowen's view when he told the Defence Select Committee '…you take a very deep breath before you start disagreeing with the commander on the ground'.⁸¹ For Bowen, however, the problem was not just the decision itself, but the process by which it had been reached and agreed. 'The amount of slow deliberation at the very top, over every operational decision, was negligible and was probably inadequate in this case', he noted. 'Indeed, part of the problem was flagging up the key issues for strategic decision in the welter of real-world activity'.⁸² He is clear, however, that by going along with Daoud's demands and shifting the focus of the force from the Bastion – Lashkar Gah – Gereshk triangle, Butler was actually making a strategic change to the mission, something which should have been referred to ministers for approval.⁸³

There is a difference of opinion regarding whether or not ministers were brought into the decision-making. John Reid told the House of Commons Defence Committee on 8 February 2011 that although 'it was a decision that changed the strategic nature of the mission', neither he nor his successor, Des Browne, had been consulted about the move north:

> I recall being briefed by PJHQ…that Governor Daoud needed to be discouraged from making gestures – for example, the idea of a forward operating base at Sangin – that were unsustainable. I understand from enquiries that I made…that the matter [the decision to establish Platoon Houses] was not referred to the Secretary of State for Defence who succeeded me.⁸⁴

Des Browne, giving evidence to the Defence Select Committee's enquiry into Operations in Afghanistan on 29 March 2011, confirmed that this was the case. 'A tactical decision was made… to deploy forces beyond the lozenge. It was all briefed to me retrospectively and it has subsequently

---

78 Tootal, *Danger Close*, p.31.
79 Brigadier Ed Butler, Interview with author.
80 Desmond Bowen, interview with author.
81 General Sir Mike Jackson, Evidence to HCDC, 15 March 2011, EV114, Q523, https://publications.parliament.uk/pa/cm201012/cmselect/cmdfence/554/554.pdf. Accessed 14 April 2023.
82 Desmond Bowen, interview with author.
83 Desmond Bowen, interview with author.
84 Lord Reid, Evidence to HCDC, 8 February 2011, EV91, Q415, <https://publications.parliament.uk/pa/cm201012/cmselect/cmdfence/554/554.pdf>, accessed 14 April 2023.

been described by those who were in command in military terms as an operational decision and that is how I perceived it'.[85] However, Butler told the same Committee: 'Anyone who says they were not aware, either military or political, is, I would say, incorrect'.[86] Lieutenant General Sir Rob Fry said that from his experience it was 'inconceivable' that a subject of such significance would not have been briefed to ministers.[87]

The available evidence confirms that Butler did not make the decision in a vacuum. It was the result of much deliberation and debate, during which he had consulted with all relevant Government departments and his chain of command. The issue was discussed at the Helmand Executive Group, a cross-Government meeting involving representatives from the FCO, DfID and the military, which took place at Lashkar Gah. It was considered on a weekly basis at the Kabul Steering Group, a multi-agency gathering, involving the UK ambassador, DfID and Security Service representatives, which was designed to ensure clarity of purpose across the various lines of operation (i.e. diplomatic, security, military, economic and social development). This meeting was also connected by video link to the Afghanistan Steering Group in London (when the technology allowed), ensuring that key Whitehall departments were 'in the loop'. 'We were very clear at every stage of this period, from mid to late April, when Baghran fell, that if we were going to fulfil the mission we were going to have to deploy north', explained Butler. He believed that the Task Force was facing mission failure in month two if it did not act.[88]

Ahead of the decision to occupy the District Centre in Sangin, Butler had discussed his options with Major General Peter Wall, the Deputy Commander of Joint Operations at PJHQ, who happened to be visiting the theatre at the time. Wall could see the dilemma faced by his subordinate and agreed that he had little choice but to meet Daoud's request.[89] On 24 May, two days before the first moves took place to establish the Platoon Houses, Butler returned to the UK and briefed the Chiefs of Staff on his plan. He did so at the weekly meeting known as OPCOS – Operational Chiefs of Staff. This was a highly-classified meeting which took place in a secure conference room that was regularly swept for listening devices and all attendees were relieved of their mobile telephones before entering. An off-shoot of the Chiefs of Staff Committee, OPCOS focused on current operations. It was chaired by CDS and attended by the Service Chiefs as well as the Policy Director (or a substitute, often the Director General Operational Policy) and representatives of the Intelligence Services.[90] The Chief of Joint Operations usually joined the meeting via secure video link from Northwood. These meetings were routinely followed by a discussion with ministers, known as COSMIN (Chiefs of Staff – Ministers) at which the ministerial team was briefed on the key issues emerging from OPCOS. Des Browne was present. Although not a decision brief as such, the formal adoption of the Platoon House strategy was consequent upon that meeting.[91]

---

85   Lord Browne, Evidence to HCDC, 29 March 2011, EV120, Q562, <https://publications.parliament.uk/pa/cm201012/cmselect/cmdfence/554/554.pdf>, accessed 14 April 2023.
86   Brigadier Ed Butler, Evidence to HCDC, 16 December 2014, p.19, Q41, <https://committees.parliament.uk/oralevidence/4405/pdf/>, accessed 14 April 2023.
87   Lieutenant General Sir Rob Fry, Evidence to HCDC 16 December 2014, p.26, Q58. <https://committees.parliament.uk/oralevidence/4405/pdf/>, accessed 14 April 2023. (NB: Fry had moved to a new position in Baghdad by the time the Platoon House decisions were taken, and was speaking on the basis of his experience of the senior decision-making processes in the MOD).
88   Brigadier Ed Butler, interview with author.
89   Brigadier Ed Butler, interview with author.
90   General Sir Nick Houghton, Evidence to the HCDC, 11 May 2011, EV147, Q679, <https://publications.parliament.uk/pa/cm201012/cmselect/cmdfence/554/554.pdf>, accessed 02 July 2024.
91   General Sir Nick Houghton, Evidence to the HCDC, 11 May 2011, EV147, Q679, <https://publications.parliament.uk/pa/cm201012/cmselect/cmdfence/554/554.pdf>, accessed 02 July 2024.

It is clear from this that Des Browne was briefed on the plan before it was put into operation. To be fair to him, he was relatively new to Defence and it may have seemed as if it was a tactical decision, particularly as it was presented by the tactical commander. However, there would have been other ministers and officials present, who had been in Defence much longer than Browne, who should have recognised the strategic significance of what was being proposed, and could have challenged the decision if they were uncomfortable about it. No one did. This would appear to support Desmond Bowen's criticism of the high-level decision-making in the MOD at that time.

General Richards, giving evidence to the Defence Select Committee on 11 May 2011, denied that Butler's decision to go north represented a change of mission. It was, he explained, a change of tactics. Although he did not agree with the Platoon House concept, he was 'very forgiving' of Brigadier Butler's need to respond to some very strong political pressure, largely from Governor Daoud but also from President Karzai, who felt that, at the very moment NATO was on the brink of taking over responsibility, things were beginning to slip away from him and towards a resurgent Taliban.[92] General Sir Peter Wall, Chief of the General Staff, told the Committee any suggestion that the decision had been a 'whim by Brigadier Butler on the day' was a falsehood:

> Everybody else, as far as I know, was aware [of the proposal] – they were closely involved. The military tactical risks were considered. It was accepted that this could be done at measured risk for a limited time frame, and that we would start to have real logistic stresses if it then got extended beyond a short-term period to shore up security of the district centres, essentially to keep Governor Daoud in power.[93]

Wall was clear that if they had 'stuck to Plan A' and taken no account of a changing situation – which is not normally a recognised military approach – the result would have been political failure. 'We would have had a significant credibility problem in terms of the UK initiative in the south, and in the wider integration of the two missions (ISAF and OEF)'. There would still have been 'a hell of a fight with the Taliban' but probably closer to Gereshk and Lashkar Gah in the main population centres rather than in remote northern villages.[94]

Although some were advising strongly against the decision to go north, and many have since questioned it, albeit with the benefit of hindsight, it is not clear that the move was the wrong call in the circumstances at that time. The consequences of not doing so – the fall of Governor Daoud and the very obvious failure of the UK mission – were unthinkable. If it was an error, the blame must be shared among a number of senior political, policy and military figures. But Brigadier Ed Butler is not one of them. As the tactical commander, he was simply reacting to the situation on the ground. He was entitled to adjust his tactics in the light of the local political imperatives and the actions of the enemy. It was up to his superior headquarters – in this case PJHQ – to 'rein him in' if it felt he was drifting away from the original intent or moving beyond what was considered militarily coherent, given the resources available. The fact that PJHQ in the form of Lieutenant General Nick Houghton (CJO from April 2006) and Major General Peter Wall, the Chief and Deputy Chief of Joint Operations at the time, both very experienced operators, did not do so, suggests they had been convinced it was the right move in the circumstances. Superior

---

92 General Sir David Richards, Evidence to HCDC, 11 May 2011, EV145, Q676, <https://publications.parliament.uk/pa/cm201012/cmselect/cmdfence/554/554.pdf>, accessed 3 July 2023.
93 General Sir Peter Wall, evidence to HCDC, 11 May 2011, EV145, Q676, <https://publications.parliament.uk/pa/cm201012/cmselect/cmdfence/554/554.pdf>, accessed 3 July 2023.
94 General Sir Peter Wall, evidence to HCDC, 11 May 2011, EV145, Q676, <https://publications.parliament.uk/pa/cm201012/cmselect/cmdfence/554/554.pdf>, accessed 3 July 2023.

commanders sitting in a Cold War underground bunker in Northwood, 3,000 miles from the fighting, did not have the same situational awareness, or the same weight on their shoulders, as the man on the spot. Understandably, as General Jackson pointed out, this meant they were sometimes reluctant to overrule the theatre view. But, as General Wall explained, the Task Force planners had done a detailed assessment and PJHQ was satisfied that the deployments to Sangin, Musa Qal'eh and Now Zad, could be done, at some risk, for a short, time-limited period. This was the original proposal. It became a problem, and created serious logistical and other stresses, partly because of the ferocity of the Taliban response, which went far beyond expectations, and partly because it proved impossible to relieve the British garrisons with suitably-trained ANA and ANP personnel. Daoud was unwilling to stake his future on the capabilities of his own partly-trained forces, and demanded that the British should stay put.

It seems unlikely that both the Task Force and PJHQ failed to consider, and factor into the decision, the possibility of becoming fixed in the Platoon Houses. The Army's decision-making model calls for close consideration of all the pertinent factors and it is implausible to conclude that they would have overlooked such a potential outcome. It is much more likely that the possibility had been included in the deliberations, but was outweighed by the risk of mission failure. In other words, the risk of becoming fixed in the District Centres was considered more acceptable than allowing the Taliban to hoist their black flags over them.

Part 3

8

The Taliban

In the early hours of 27 September 1996, as the Taliban marched, victorious, into Kabul to seize power, a group of fighters broke away from the main body. They made their way to the UN compound where the former General Secretary of the People's Democratic Party of Afghanistan and President towards the end of the Soviet era, Dr Mohammad Najibullah, had been sheltering since 1992. Showing no regard for international diplomatic protocols, they smashed down the gates to the compound – the civilian guards had already fled – dragged Najibullah into a pick-up truck and took him to the Presidential Palace where he was tortured, castrated and hanged by a wire noose from a traffic control stand in the street at Ariana Square.[1] Some accounts claim that his genitals were stuffed into his mouth.

As James Fergusson has noted, it was 'a terrible moment of truth for the world'.[2] Across the globe, people were stunned by the barbarism. Even some members of the Taliban leadership were taken aback by the brutality and savagery of this act of revenge. Together with other excesses, such as the alleged slaughter of Hazaras in Mazar-e-Sharif in 1998, in which, according to Human Rights Watch, scores, perhaps hundreds, of Hazara men and boys were 'summarily executed',[3] the killing of Najibullah would help to turn the movement into an international pariah, an image that would hang over it for the next two decades and beyond. These seemingly gratuitous acts of violence and cruelty, together with the much-publicised clampdown on the rights of women and girls, the prohibitions on music and kite-flying, and public hangings, floggings and stonings of alleged transgressors, were to condition much of the international community's understanding of, and response to, the movement in the years ahead. But the Taliban did not start out that way. The movement was not conceived as a platform for what many considered to be a wrong-headed, extreme interpretation of Islam that subjugated women and handed out cruel and inhuman punishments for perceived breaches of religious edicts. It was, in fact, born as a response to the warlord-ism and banditry that flourished across the country in the wake of the Soviet invasion and the subsequent civil war.

The Soviet Union had marched into the so-called Democratic Republic of Afghanistan in 1979 and installed a puppet regime, led by communist placeman, Babrak Kamal. The Afghan people did what they always do when foreigners invade: they fought back. For the next 10 years the countryside was engulfed in a bitter conflict, with groups of Mujaheddin fighters, funded and supplied by the West, taking on the might of the Russian military – rifles, RPGs and later American-made Stinger shoulder-launched anti-aircraft missiles, against tanks, fast jets and the fearsome, rocket-firing Mil Mi-24 'Hind' attack helicopters.

---

1   Fergusson, *Taliban*, p.43.
2   Fergusson, *Taliban*, p.43.
3   Human Rights Watch, November 1998, Volume 10, No. 7, <https://www.hrw.org/legacy/reports98/afghan/Afrepor0.htm>, accessed 28 March 2023.

In the face of the Mujaheddin's determined resistance, as well as international sanctions and boycotts, and with the emergence of reforming leader, Mikhail Gorbachev, the Soviet Union eventually withdrew in 1989, the last military vehicle crossing the bridge over the Oxus River (also known as the Amy Darya River) into the then Soviet Republic of Uzbekistan, on 15 February of that year. The enemy had departed, leaving a fragile regime in Kabul. Kamal's government was weak and poor. A decade of fighting had crippled Afghanistan and its economy. There was little work for the returning fighters. The new political leadership had no money and little power or influence beyond the capital. Civil War followed as powerful groups of rival warlords clashed in a fight for ascendency, and Afghanistan once more became a strife-ridden nation in which there was little regard for the normal rules of society. Nowhere was this lawlessness more pronounced than in the traditionally-conservative south.

In the countryside of Kandahar and Helmand the Mujaheddin groups, who had originally banded together in a powerful united front against a common enemy, were now turning in on themselves in a series of bloody turf-wars. Below these warlords was a layer of more junior ex-fighters. In the absence of paid employment, many of them had resorted to brigandry. They extorted 'tolls' at gun-point from the drivers of goods vehicles carrying freight to and through the country, and also from local farmers trying to convey their produce to market. Food and goods became scarce as many truckers and farmers found the tolls being exacted by these gangsters, at a series of checkpoints along Highway 1, were often more than the value of their cargoes.[4]

But not all the former Mujaheddin had evolved into outlaws. Some, like Abdul Salam Zaeef, had returned to their religious studies after fighting the Russians, and were eking out a living as best they could. By 1993, Zaeef had found a position as a mullah in a small village mosque about 30 miles west of Kandahar. Another former Mujaheddin-turned-cleric was a one-eyed man called Mohammad Omar. Accounts of Omar's early life do not always align in terms of key details. One version claims he was born in Uruzgan.[5] Another suggests his birthplace is Chah-i-Himmat in the Kharkez district of Kandahar Province.[6] However, both the CIA and Pakistani journalist and acknowledged Taliban expert, Ahmed Rashid, believe he was born in the village of Nodeh in Kandahar.[7] When the Russians left, he settled in Sangisar, putting away his rifle and opening a small madrassa, making a living by preaching and teaching the Diobandi beliefs.[8] It was these two men, together with a small group of their former Mujaheddin comrades, incensed by the lawlessness they saw going on around them, and the dreadful toll it was taking on their friends and relatives, who created the movement that would become the Taliban.

Mullah Omar had been known as a courageous fighter, but he did not stand out as a great leader or orator. He had initially questioned his friends' proposal that he should be in charge of the new movement. However, he was eventually persuaded to accept the role, telling Zaeef that 'everything that happens depends on God'.[9] Having begun as a small local collective, dedicated to

---

4   Fergusson, *Taliban*, p.10.
5   Fergusson, *Taliban*, p.15.
6   Who's Who in Afghanistan, <https://www.afghan-bios.info/index.php?option=com_afghanbios&id=1298&task=view&total=3195&start=2127&Itemid=2>, accessed 30 March 2023.
7   Rashid, *Taliban*, p.23, and CIA biography, National Security Archive, <https://nsarchive2.gwu.edu/NSAEBB/NSAEBB55/ciaomar.pdf>, accessed 1 April 2023.
8   Diobandism, is a school of Islamic thought which originates from a religious college in the town of Dioband in India's Uttar Pradesh during British rule. It is characterised by strict mental discipline, learning the Koran by rote, the belief that adherence to Sunni law – Sharia – is the path to salvation, and upholds the idea that global jihad is a sacred duty to protect Muslims across the world. <https://theconversation.com/talibans-religious-ideology-deobandi-islam-has-roots-in-colonial-india-166323>, accessed 30 March 2023.
9   Abdul Salam Zaeef, *My Life With The Taliban* (London: Hurst and Co, 2011), p.64.

standing up to the bandits in one tiny corner of Kandahar Province, this 'Mullahs' Revolt' as it is sometimes called, quickly gathered support and momentum. From its original roots in Maiwand and Panjwayi, it grew rapidly, attracting popular backing throughout the province, and, before long, from Pakistan.

Finance came largely from two sources – the local trucking mafia, who were keen to open up smuggling routes from Afghanistan to the Central Asian Republics and Iran and were happy to pay a single toll rather than be extorted every few miles; and from Pakistan's fabled intelligence arm, the ISI (Inter-Service Intelligence). Pakistan feared Indian interference in Afghanistan and felt the Pashtun-dominated Taliban would resist any attempt by New Delhi to gain undue influence there. An attack on the border town of Spin Boldak cleared out the local warlords, but also provided access to a massive arms dump where they seized vast quantities of weapons, ammunition and vehicles. As the Taliban continued their conquest, many of the local strongmen were quick to recognise the power of this popular rising and either switched their allegiances to Omar and his group or moved their 'businesses' elsewhere.

On 5 November 1994, Kandahar City fell to the new movement, now equipped with tanks, armoured personnel carriers and artillery they had captured along the way. By this point, although some Afghans were concerned about yet another armed band, many more, especially those still under the yoke of the warlords and bandits, were relieved that a force was finally taking on the outlaws and bringing security to large swathes of the country. Men and women were once more able to move about in Taliban-controlled areas without fear of rape, kidnap or murder. Just four months after Zaeef and Omar set up their first checkpoint in Kandahar, the Taliban had become a national movement. By September the following year, Kabul had fallen at the second attempt, although a loose confederation of mainly Shi'ite Tajiks, Hazaras, and Uzbeks – the Northern Alliance – led by Abdul Rashid Dostum and Ahmed Shah Massoud, continued to mount a resistance in the north from their sanctuary in the Panjshir Valley, in the foothills of the Hindu Kush; and in Herat, Nimroz and Farah, under the leadership of Ismael Khan. The Northern Alliance, also known as the United Front, was backed by Iran, Turkey, India, Russia and four of the Central Asian Republics, Uzbekistan, Kazakstan, Kyrgyzstan and Tajikistan.

Many of the first-generation Taliban fighters were orphans, having lost their parents and their homes in the fighting during and after the Soviet invasion. With few orphanages in Afghanistan or in the frontier provinces of Pakistan, where many refugees ended up, the madrassas – religious seminaries – were the only institutions prepared to take in the young boys, providing them with food, lodgings and a deeply religious education. The word 'Taliban' is the plural form of the Pashtu term, Talib or student (literally, 'knowledge-seeker'). The name also points to a key source of recruitment to the movement, and the glue that held it together – a powerful blend of religion, ethnicity and the Pashtun's historic hatred of foreigners. By the mid-90s the boys who had survived the turmoil of invasion and conflict had become fighting-age men, tough and disciplined by their years of strict adherence to the Deobandi code, and keen to uphold the extreme religious and cultural beliefs and customs that had been instilled in them in the Islamic colleges.

Mullah Omar and the other leaders were always inwardly-focused. They wanted to bring their brand of religious fundamentalism to the whole of Afghanistan, and that is where their ambition ended. Omar's Taliban had no interest in exporting terrorism abroad.[10] As he explained to journalists in 2007: 'We have set the expulsion of American troops from Afghanistan as our target'.[11]

---

10   Fergusson, *Taliban*, p.91.
11   Ishmail Khan and Carlotta Gall, 'Taliban Leader Promises More Afghan War', *The New York Times* (5 January 2007), <https://www.nytimes.com/2007/01/05/world/asia/05taliban.html?searchResultPosition=1>, accessed 30 March 2023.

The Taliban's fight with the West after 9/11 was based on a typically-Pashtun desire to expel the invading foreign forces from their country. However, they had made the mistake of offering sanctuary to another Islamic movement that was absolutely focused on waging holy war on the streets of America and those of its allies – Osama bin Laden's Islamic Salvation Foundation or Al Qaeda (The Base).

Bin Laden, the son of a wealthy Yemeni construction magnate who had been born and raised in Saudi Arabia, arrived in Afghanistan in 1982, one of thousands of Arabs who crossed the Persian Gulf to fight the *infidel* Russians. He returned home in 1990, and went back into the family business before the Iraqi invasion of Kuwait sent shock waves rippling around the Gulf and far beyond. Bin Laden tried to persuade the Saudi Royal Family to raise a force from the Arab veterans of the Afghan War to defend the nation against possible Iraqi aggression. Incensed when his suggestion was ignored in favour of inviting in the US and its allies, he launched a vitriolic campaign of criticism against the Royals and began to lobby the *ulema* (religious leaders) to issue *fatwas* (religious rulings) against non-Muslims being based in the country. The Saudis retaliated by declaring him *persona non grata* and later by revoking his citizenship. No longer welcome in his own homeland, he moved on to take part in a growing Islamic revolution in Sudan before returning to Afghanistan. In May 1996, he turned up at Jalalabad in a chartered aircraft with dozens of militants, bodyguards, three wives and 13 children.[12]

Bin Laden set about ingratiating himself with the Taliban leader, pouring millions of dollars of his own fortune into the movement's coffers. He built a house for Omar's family in Kandahar, imported a fleet of Toyota Hilux pick-up trucks from Dubai, and promised to pay for all kinds of good works, including building mosques and schools.[13] He also acted as a financial conduit, channelling money to the Taliban from wealthy donors in the Gulf States. Rashid believes the two men formed a friendship but James Fergusson contends that their relationship was more transactional, based on bin Laden's money and how that could support Omar's impoverished movement.[14] Whether it was a genuine friendship or purely the result of financial expediency, bin Laden was granted Omar's protection under the Pashtun creed of *nanawatai* (sanctuary). By August of 1996 he issued his first declaration of jihad against the Americans who, he claimed, were occupying Saudi Arabia.[15] That same year, a CIA assessment named bin Laden as 'one of the most significant financial sponsors of Islamic extremist activities in the world today'.[16] The financial support of bin Laden and other Arab benefactors meant that the Taliban's Afghanistan, was not, as many think, a state sponsor of terrorism, but actually a state sponsored by terrorism.[17]

Bin Laden was a liability for Omar and the Taliban, almost from the moment he returned to Afghanistan in 1996. He was already under CIA scrutiny after his activities in Sudan. The thousands of Arab and other foreign fighters he brought to Afghanistan for training at numerous camps he had established in the south and east of the country, created even more unwanted attention. The Arabs were not well-liked by the Afghans. They were thought to be too anxious to flaunt their wealth, and most practiced a form of Islam – Wahabism, an ultra-conservative branch of Salafism – which was viewed with some suspicion by the Afghan mullahs. Wahabis take their name from eighteenth century Arab scholar, Muhammad ibn Abd al-Wahab, who believed in the purification

---

12 Rashid, *Taliban*, p.133.
13 Fergusson, *Taliban* p.95.
14 Rashid, *Taliban*, p.133 and Fergusson, *Taliban*, p.95.
15 Rashid, *Taliban*, p.133.
16 CIA Assessment, The National Security Archive, Volume I: Terrorism and US Policy, <https://nsarchive2.gwu.edu/NSAEBB/NSAEBB55/index1.html#I>, accessed 31 March 2023.
17 Fergusson, *Taliban*, p.95.

of Islam from 'heretical innovations' through violence. The Wahabi interpretation of Sharia resembles the Hambali school, a tradition alien to the Hanafi Islam embraced by most Afghans.

Signs of a significant fracture in the Taliban-Al Qaeda relationship first began to surface in the wake of the simultaneous attacks on the US embassies in Nairobi in Kenya and Dar-es-Salam in Tanzania, on 7 August 1998. Over 200 people died and more than 5,000 were injured in the dual bombings. An FBI investigation linked some of those responsible to Al Qaeda training camps in Afghanistan.[18] The US retaliated on 14 August, launching 70 Tomahawk cruise missiles at bin Laden's camp near Khost, close to the Pakistan border, south of Kabul. This was part of what became known as Operation Infinite Reach.[19] A few months later, the US authorities offered a bounty of $5m for information leading to bin Laden's capture. They dearly wished to see him tried in an American court and they worked hard to persuade the ISI to help them to bring him into custody. The ISI politely refused.[20]

The US also put pressure on the Saudi authorities to cooperate in his capture. A member of the Royal Family, Prince Tukri, visited Kandahar for talks with Omar. These discussions ended badly for all sides. Not only did the Taliban leader refuse to hand over bin Laden, who, he said, was his guest, but he proceeded to insult the Saudi royals. This provoked the Saudis into suspending diplomatic relations with Afghanistan and putting a block on further financial backing.[21]

Until this point, the Taliban leadership had not been particularly antagonistic towards the Americans. In fact, they had been in talks with a US-backed company called Unocal about the possibility of building a pipeline through the country to transport gas from Turkmenistan to Pakistan. However, with the US's retaliatory strike at Khost perceived as an attack on their sovereign territory, the attitude towards America hardened, along with the rhetoric. They became much more critical of the US, the Saudis, the UN and other regimes, and they dug in their heels over bin Laden. He was their guest and it was against Afghan tradition to expel guests, they explained.[22]

Although they were not prepared to hand over bin Laden to the US, the Taliban did insist that he moved from Jalalabad to Kandahar, ostensibly for his own safety, but also so they could exert some control over him. In a bid to strengthen his position with Omar, bin Laden sent hundreds of his Arab fighters to help the Taliban assaults in the north in 1997 and 1998. Some of these foreigners may have been involved in the massacre of Hazaras in Mazar-e-Sherif in August 1998.[23] As the US stepped up their campaign to have bin Laden extradited, however, Omar began to see his Saudi guest less as an asset and more as a dangerous millstone that had the potential to drag the Taliban movement down. With that in mind, a communication channel was opened with the State Department in Washington, as Omar sought a way out of his dilemma without losing influence or face in the wider Islamic world.[24] Discussions were still taking place in September 2001

---

18 FBI archive, <https://archives.fbi.gov/archives/news/testimony/al-qaeda-international>, accessed 31 March 2023.
19 Major Todd R. Phinney, USAF, *Operation Infinite Reach – Airpower versus Terrorism,* Air University Press, 2007, <https://media.defense.gov/2017/Dec/27/2001861438/-1/-1/0/T_0009_PHINNEY_AIRPOWER_VERSUS_TERRORISM.PDF>, accessed 31 March 2023.
20 Rashid, *Taliban,* p.138.
21 Major Todd R. Phinney, USAF, *Operation Infinite Reach – Airpower versus Terrorism,* Air University Press, 2007, <https://media.defense.gov/2017/Dec/27/2001861438/-1/-1/0/T_0009_PHINNEY_AIRPOWER_VERSUS_TERRORISM.PDF>, accessed 31 March 2023. Rashid, *Taliban,* p.138.
22 Rashid, *Taliban,* p.149.
23 Rashid, *Taliban,* p.139.
24 Telegram, US State Department to US Embassy, Islamabad, 23 August 1998, National Security Archive, George Washington University, <https://nsarchive2.gwu.edu/NSAEBB/NSAEBB134/Doc%202.pdf>, accessed 2 April 2023.

when the Twin Towers of New York's World Trade Centre came tumbling down, paving the way for the end of Taliban rule in Afghanistan.[25]

The US had not responded militarily to Al Qaeda's bombing of the USS *Cole* in the Port of Aden, in Yemen, in October 2000, in which 17 of the ship's crew died and nearly 40 more were injured. As Secretary of State, Condoleezza Rice, told the National Commission on Terrorist Attacks Upon the United States, President Bush 'did not want to respond to Al Qaeda one attack at a time'. He was 'tired of swatting flies'.[26] Instead, America had decided to topple the Taliban using other means. A week before the hijacked planes crashed into the Twin Towers, an interagency meeting agreed to provide the CIA with $125m to arm the Northern Alliance. Before that could happen, however, the 9/11 attacks brought a response of a completely different magnitude. Within weeks Bush had unleashed a devastating aerial bombardment on Afghanistan, and sent CIA and special forces operatives into the country to support the Northern Alliance in their fight to overthrow the Taliban administration and to kill or capture bin Laden.

Although the Taliban's only attacks on America had been with words, Bush and many of his senior advisors, including Defence Secretary, Donald Rumsfeld and Vice President, Dick Cheney, saw the Taliban and Al Qaeda as two peas in the same pod. As a US diplomat told a British Foreign Office conference at Weston Park, as far as America was concerned 'the Taliban and Al Qaeda are one enterprise'.[27]

The overthrow of Mullah Omar's administration was a short, bloody and uneven fight. Even with their tanks, truck-mounted Katyusha-type multi-barrelled rocket launchers and artillery, the Taliban were no match for American technology. Working in support of Northern Alliance fighters, the US deployed precision 'smart' ordnance, cued by special forces soldiers, to hit specific buildings or even individual vehicles that had been 'illuminated' from the ground by laser target designators. The ground troops laid the laser beam, invisible to the naked eye, onto the target and the bombs locked on to the beam and followed it to their marks. They also made extensive use of 'dumb' BLU-82 'Daisycutter' 15,000lb bombs, pushed out of the back of C-130 Hercules aircraft on parachutes, and designed to explode just off the ground, causing devastation over a blast radius of 300 metres. The 'Daisycutters' with their characteristic bright detonation flash and thunderous report, audible over long distances, would have had a psychological as well as a physical effect on the Taliban combatants.

By 9 November, Kabul had been taken. A month later Omar fled from Kandahar, apparently escaping by night on a motorcycle, and bin Laden eventually made his way into exile in Pakistan. The international community used a hastily-convened summit in Bonn to install a new regime in Kabul. The urbane Pashtun, Hamid Karzai, with his almost flawless command of English, was appointed as chairman of the interim administration, pending democratic elections. Mohammed Fahim, a Tajik was to be vice-chairman and Defence Minister; Dr Abdullah Abdullah (Tajik) would take on the Foreign Affairs portfolio while Younus Qanooni (Tajik) would be the Minister of the Interior; Abdul Rahim Karimi (Uzbek) would be Justice Minister; and Sima Samar (Hazara) would hold the Women's Affairs post. The entire administration was a carefully-balanced mix of Afghan ethnicities, with Pashtuns, Tajiks, Hazaras and Uzbeks all well-represented across the ministries.

---

25   Rashid, *Taliban,* p.140.
26   Condoleezza Rice, Secretary of State, National Commission on Terrorist Attacks Upon The United States, Ninth Public Hearing, 8 April 2004, <https://www.9-11commission.gov/archive/hearing9/9-11Commission_Hearing_2004-04-08.htm>, accessed 1 April 2023.
27   Ahmad Rashid, *Descent Into Chaos* (London: Allen Lane, 2008), p.60.

The Bonn conference also created an international military force that was designed to support the administration until it was able to train up its own army and police forces. The International Security Assistance Force (ISAF), as it was tagged, was established and empowered under United Nations Security Council Resolution 1386, of 20 December 2001, for an initial period of six months. Its agreed role was to ensure that the Interim Administration and United Nations personnel could operate in a secure environment. Unfortunately, the ISAF mandate was confined to 'Kabul and its surrounding areas' and did not allow it to function outside the capital.[28] This restriction would have unfortunate consequences for security beyond Kabul, a limitation that would not be removed until 2003 when a new UN resolution expanded the ISAF writ nation-wide.

While many Afghans initially celebrated the demise of the Taliban, it was not long before some began to yearn for their return. Without the religious extremists to keep order, and with the interim authority and its international supporters focused on building new institutions in Kabul, security across the country rapidly returned to the low levels seen before Omar and his men took control. Warlords once again held sway in the cities, towns and villages, particularly in those provinces furthest away from the capital, where the writ of Government did not run. Corruption became rife among public officials, including provincial and district governors and police chiefs. Farmers once again turned to poppy production to make ends meet. The opium producers and traffickers found themselves back in business, and business was very good.

According to the UN Office on Drugs and Crime (UNODC), by 2003 Afghanistan was again producing three-quarters of the world's illicit opium, delivering an estimated $2.3bn in income for farmers and traffickers at a time when the total GDP of the country was about $4.5bn or $200.5 per capita.[29] Poppy cultivation had increased from 74,000ha in 2002 to 80,000ha 12 months later and was spreading to new areas. There had been reductions in Helmand and Kandahar, but increases in provinces such as Badhakshan. Opium production had shown a corresponding increase, rising from 3,400m tonnes in 2002 to 3,600m tonnes in 2003. There was, said UNODC's Executive Director, Antonio Maria Costa, 'a palpable risk that Afghanistan will again turn into a failed state, this time in the hands of drug cartels and narco-terrorists...'[30]

There was no seat at the Bonn conference table for Mullah Omar or any of his surviving lieutenants. They, together with thousands of their foot soldiers, had gone into hiding in the Pakistan border lands...licking their wounds and considering their future. The movement had been comprehensively battered by a potent combination of American airpower and Northern Alliance zeal, determination and a lust for revenge. But it had not been destroyed. The brain still lived, the heart still pounded, and it was not long before new blood, rich with the oxygen of religious fervour, began to course through the arteries and veins. The body, bruised and battered, began to sprout fresh arms and legs as the next generation of fighters heard the call and came forward. Like a snake, the Taliban cast off its old skin and began to emerge into the light with a fresh coat, bright eyes burning with the fire of Deobandi ideology, and a new desire to expel the invaders and return Afghanistan to their vision of what an Islamic republic should be. Once again, students from the Deobandi madrassas in Pakistan, as well as village mullahs and the people who aligned with them, flocked to the cause, willing to lay down their lives for the movement.[31]

---

28 UNSCR 1386, 20 December 2001, <https://documents-dds-ny.un.org/doc/UNDOC/GEN/N01/708/55/PDF/N0170855.pdf?OpenElement>, accessed 1 April 2023.
29 World Bank, <https://data.worldbank.org/indicator/NY.GDP.PCAP.CD?end=2021&locations=AF&start=1994>, accessed 1 April 2023.
30 UNODC, Afghanistan Opium Survey, 2003, <https://www.unodc.org/documents/crop-monitoring/Afghanistan/Afghanistan_survey_2003_full_report.pdf>, accessed 1 April 2023.
31 Giustozzi, *Koran, Kalashnikov and Laptop*, p.15

But the force that emerged from the defeat of 2002 – what Antonio Giustozzi has called the neo-Taliban – was a different organism. Although many of the original leaders remained, there were some significant disparities apparent as the organisation began to regenerate. American journalist, Gretchen Peters, describes the emerging organisation as 'fragmented and transnational'.[32] It had moved away from some of the attributes and political aspirations that had characterised its predecessors. It developed a more flexible approach to the use of imported technologies and techniques. Having previously banned television and photographic images, it began to lift the restriction and to make use of documentary videos as part of its propaganda campaign. Some insurgents now carried video cameras on operations to record their activities and incorporate the footage into future productions. It became more integrated into the international jihadist movement. Rhetoric began to feature concepts such as a 'global Christian war against Islam' and highlighted solidarity with other jihadist groups.[33]

There were signs, too, that the new fighters were willing to be more tolerant of local opinion, a nod towards the British counter-insurgency doctrine of seeking to win the 'hearts and minds' of the people. Reacting to complaints that villagers were being killed or injured – collateral damage – in their attacks on coalition forces, they began to warn locals about impending operations, even though this made the assaults less effective. The absence of people in usually-busy bazaars became a classic 'combat indicator' to Western forces that an attack was imminent.

They did not 'tax' travellers at checkpoints, immediately differentiating themselves from many local police officers, who did. They stopped looting farmers' harvests, preferring instead to benefit from the profits of narco-criminality by hitting the pockets of the opium traffickers, levying charges in return for protecting their convoys. As a result of these new behaviours, many villagers, including those in Helmand, began to see them as protectors of their livelihoods, rather than a threat to them. Significantly, with the flow of cash from Saudi benefactors beginning to reduce, the new Taliban were also more heavily reliant than their predecessors had been on opium as a source of funding.[34]

In some areas, fighters who called themselves Taliban (or who were referred to as such by locals), had few links with and little allegiance to Mullah Omar and his core group. These bands, often closely associated with corrupt local officials, were just as likely to fight with local rivals (who also called themselves Taliban) as with the forces of the legitimate government, and were involved in a broad range of criminal activities, including kidnapping and racketeering. As Colonel Gordon Messenger noted, when he arrived in Helmand in late 2005, it was important to use care when referring to the Taliban because lots of different groups were involved in fermenting violence. These included tribal leaders, who were not formally part of the insurgency; local farmers who feared poppy eradication would cut off their main source of income; and even members of the unofficial militia that had been loyal to the deposed Governor, Sher Mohammad Akundzada.[35] There was a greater reliance on a 'free market' approach to insurgency, with evidence of payments to part-time fighters – piece-workers – with agreed rates of pay for actions such as firing rockets at an enemy base or carrying out targeted assassinations.[36]

Despite the mauling they had received at the hands of American airpower, Taliban violence never really ceased. In the mountainous east and south-east of the country, hard up against the Pakistan border, attacks on Afghan Army border posts occurred during the first eight months of

---

32 Gretchen Peters, *Seeds of Terror*, p.104.
33 Giustozzi, *Koran, Kalashnikov and Laptop*, p.15.
34 Gretchen Peters, *Seeds of Terror*, p.104.
35 General Sir Gordon Messenger, interview with author.
36 Giustozzi, *Koran, Kalashnikov and Laptop*, p.14.

2002. The authorities initially put these down to the death-throws of the Taliban and Al Qaeda, carried out by small cells of fighters who were unable or unwilling to flee to Pakistan. However, a spate of attacks in Kabul in the late summer suggested that a new insurgency was under way. At this point most of the incidents appeared to be against police and militias.

American military installations were sometimes subjected to sniping and rockets, although there were a few reports of US Army patrols coming under fire. Much of the activity was limited to Kunar, Paktia, Paktika and Khost; all mountainous provinces close to the porous border with Pakistan, making it easy for the attackers to strike and then fade away to the safety of the neighbouring territory. By September, however, a recruiting drive was reported in Pakistan and Afghanistan, while propaganda pamphlets were being distributed in the villages and training bases were springing up in the lawless tribal areas of Pakistan.[37]

Taliban activity increased throughout the autumn, with improvised explosive devices being planted on some roads and rocket and mortar attacks on US bases becoming more frequent. Border posts in Kandahar and Helmand were now being hit regularly by small groups of insurgents. In January 2003, US forces clashed with an 80-strong Taliban unit near Spin Boldak.[38] The insurgents' build-up continued during the spring of 2003 when US bases began to be attacked with salvos of rockets and more sophisticated ambushes took place involving groups of up to 50 fighters. Despite this, US Defence Secretary, Donald Rumsfeld, visiting troops in Kabul on 1 May 2003, felt confident enough to say that 'major combat' was at an end. Talking to reporters during the visit he said: 'We are at a point where we have clearly moved from major combat activity to a period of stability and stabilisation and reconstruction activities'.[39] No one told the Taliban, who carried on striking at Afghan and US forces over the summer, now deploying groups of up to 150.[40] In June, an audio tape, reputed to be from Mullah Omar, announced the formation of a new 10-member leadership council 'to expedite jihad against occupation forces'.[41] This was the birth of the infamous 'Quetta Shura', the Taliban's policy-making and leadership forum.

By the end of the summer, Western diplomats were reporting that the Taliban were trying to destabilise the south of the country. The Government had failed to extend its writ in isolated parts of the southern provinces and the Taliban were attempting to fill the vacuum.[42] At the same time, the insurgents had created a new stronghold within Afghanistan at Dai Chopan in Zabul where as many as 1,000 fighters were rumoured to be based. As summer turned to autumn, the province had largely fallen under Taliban control while in Kandahar the presence of the insurgents was also growing. The following year, they established themselves in Uruzgan and Kandahar and by the spring of 2006 they had succeeded in virtually eliminating Government presence in the countryside of southern Ghazni, much of northern Paktika, some areas of Paktia and Khost and most of southern and central Helmand.[43]

---

37 Giustozzi, *Koran, Kalashnikov and Laptop*, p.2.
38 'Military Fights largest Afghanistan battle since March', *Tampa Bay Times* (29 January 2003), <https://www.tampabay.com/archive/2003/01/29/military-fights-largest-afghanistan-battle-since-march/>, accessed 1 April 2023.
39 'Rumsfeld: Major Combat Over in Afghanistan', *CNN* (1 May 2003), <https://edition.cnn.com/2003/WORLD/asiapcf/central/05/ 01/afghan.combat/>, accessed 1 April 2023.
40 Giustozzi, *Koran, Kalashnikov and Laptop*, p.3.
41 'Taliban Raids Widen in Parts of Afghanistan', *The New York Times* (1 September 2003), <https://www.nytimes.com/2003/09/01/world/taliban-raids-widen-in-parts-of-afghanistan.html>, accessed 1 April 2023.
42 'Taliban Raids Widen in Parts of Afghanistan', *The New York Times* (1 September 2003), <https://www.nytimes.com/2003/09/01/world/taliban-raids-widen-in-parts-of-afghanistan.html>, accessed 1 April 2023.
43 Giustozzi, *Koran, Kalashnikov and Laptop*, p.3.

By now it was clear to most neutral observers that the Taliban were back in strength, and that a new, powerful insurgency was under way, particularly in parts of central, southern and eastern Afghanistan. However, American military officers in Kabul sought to play down the threat, perhaps lulled into a false sense of security by the fact that the 2004 and 2005 presidential and parliamentary elections had passed without significant insurgency interventions. This was a mistake. As Giustozzi argues, the Taliban's decision not to disrupt the elections was a manifestation not of their military weakness but of their new-found wish to listen to the people. The insurgency implemented what amounted to a form of self-imposed truce during both elections. They continued to threaten to kill candidates who were opposed to them, but they did not attempt to attack polling stations during the voting periods, recognising the strong desire of Afghan people to elect a president and a government.[44]

There was also evidence that the insurgents were becoming more tactically aware, suggesting, perhaps, that they were importing skilled fighters and trainers from elsewhere, including the Middle East and Chechnya. Some basic skills such as marksmanship did not improve much among the rank and file, but they did appear to get better at launching ambushes and introducing specially-trained snipers and mortar teams. By the spring of 2006, they were demonstrating considerable advances in this form of attack. This was brought home on 19 May 2006 when a patrol of 3rd Battalion, 7th Special Forces Group, from Fort Bragg, North Carolina, accompanied by some Afghan National Army soldiers, was moving through a mountainous area of Uruzgan province. As they transited along one of the many valleys in the area, they came under heavy fire from up to 200 Taliban fighters from positions on the hillside overlooking the road. The ambushers had established themselves in an L shape with a blocking group in place. This was to prevent the patrol from making its escape by simply driving through the ambush while the main body hit the convoy from the flank.

Once halted, the attackers used 12.7mm Russian DShK heavy machine guns to rake the vehicles and suppress defensive fire. The enemy then moved to surround the trucks and the special forces soldiers found themselves under heavy and accurate fire from all sides. Into the chaos the Taliban introduced mortars, fired from the reverse slope of a hill and thus invisible to the Americans. As the light faded, the US soldiers could see commanders with binoculars directing the Taliban fire from a series of stone-built sangars, high up on the hillside. The attackers eventually withdrew, leaving one US serviceman dead and a number wounded. Troops clearing the attack site later found prepared positions, specialised sniper rifles, fitted with 10x optical sights, and camouflaged 'ghillie suits'. Another telling aspect of this attack was the reaction of local farmers. A group of men who had been working in nearby fields on the valley floor, seeing the ambush being sprung, and acting spontaneously, without any prior arrangement with the Taliban, went home, collected their rifles and returned to join in the fight. They formed a second stop group which prevented the patrol from retreating back the way they had come. When questioned afterwards, the villagers denied they had acted in concert with the Taliban. They were not particularly supportive of the insurgents but they had seen a fight and they wanted to get involved.[45] If accurate, this is a good indication of the Pashtun's warrior spirit and will to fight.

It is clear that the Taliban was a resurgent force and growing stronger between 2003 and 2006. There had been opportunities for the Kabul administration, with the support of their foreign allies, to snuff out the rebirth before it took a firm hold. If Karzai had acted in 2003 and 2004 there was a chance that he could have rescued the situation, turned the people away from the fundamentalists

---

44 Giustozzi, *Koran, Kalashnikov and Laptop,* p.114.
45 David Kilcullen, *The Accidental Guerilla – Fighting Small Wars in the Midst of a Big One* (London: C Hurst and Co, 2009), pp.39–40.

and established the firm but fair hand of legitimate, democratically-elected government in the southern and eastern provinces, where Mullah Omar's movement had traditionally drawn much of its strength. But with his US allies now firmly focused on Iraq; with some of the key warlords gaining legitimacy by being brought into government; with corruption growing by the day; with NATO focused first on the north and west; and with the opium-economy once more flourishing, these opportunities were not taken. The Taliban were allowed to grow and spread, and the south was about to explode in bloody battle.

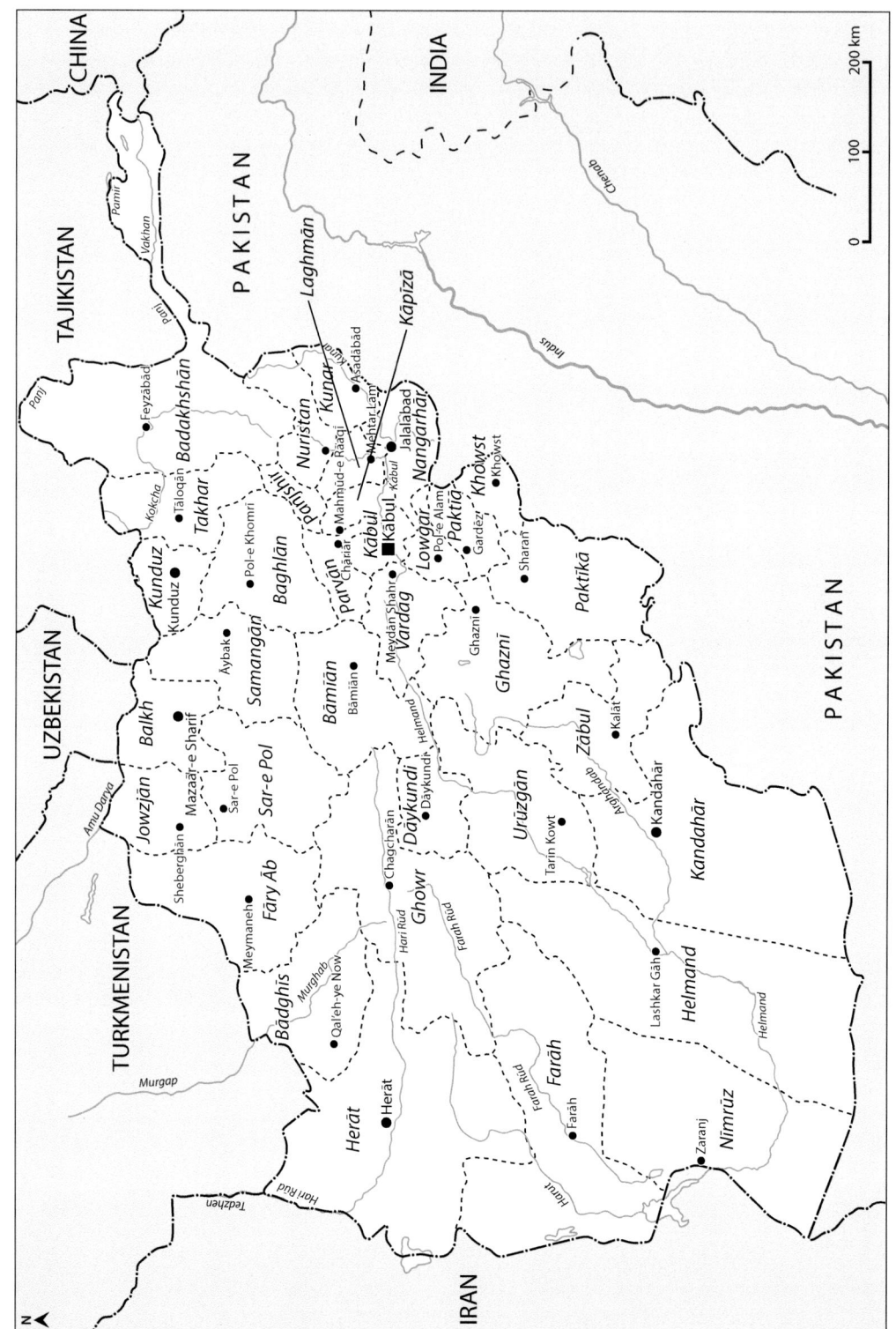

Afghanistan. (Map by George Anderson)

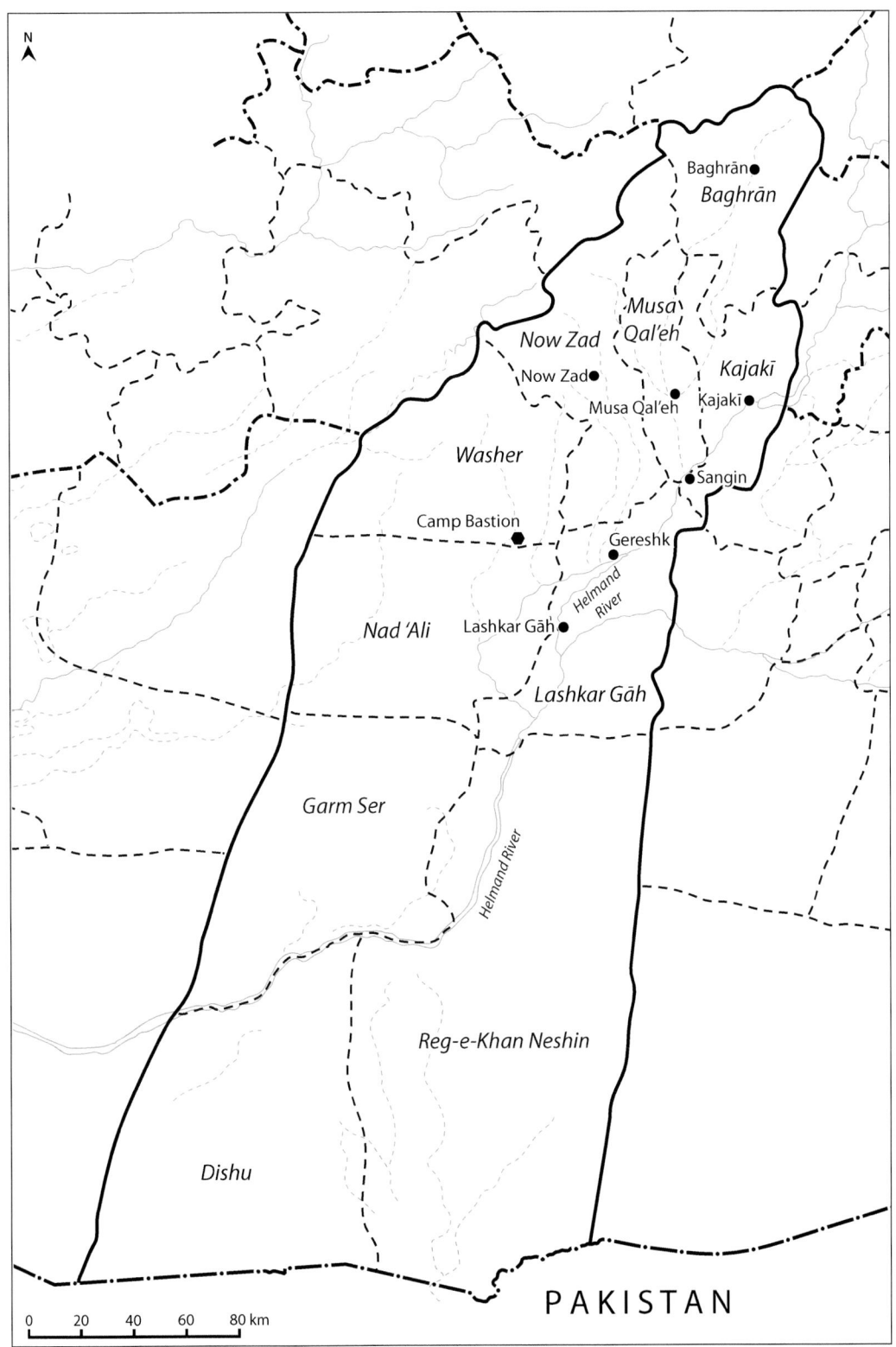

Helmand Province. (Map by George Anderson)

Musa Qal'eh and the District Centre. (Map by George Anderson)

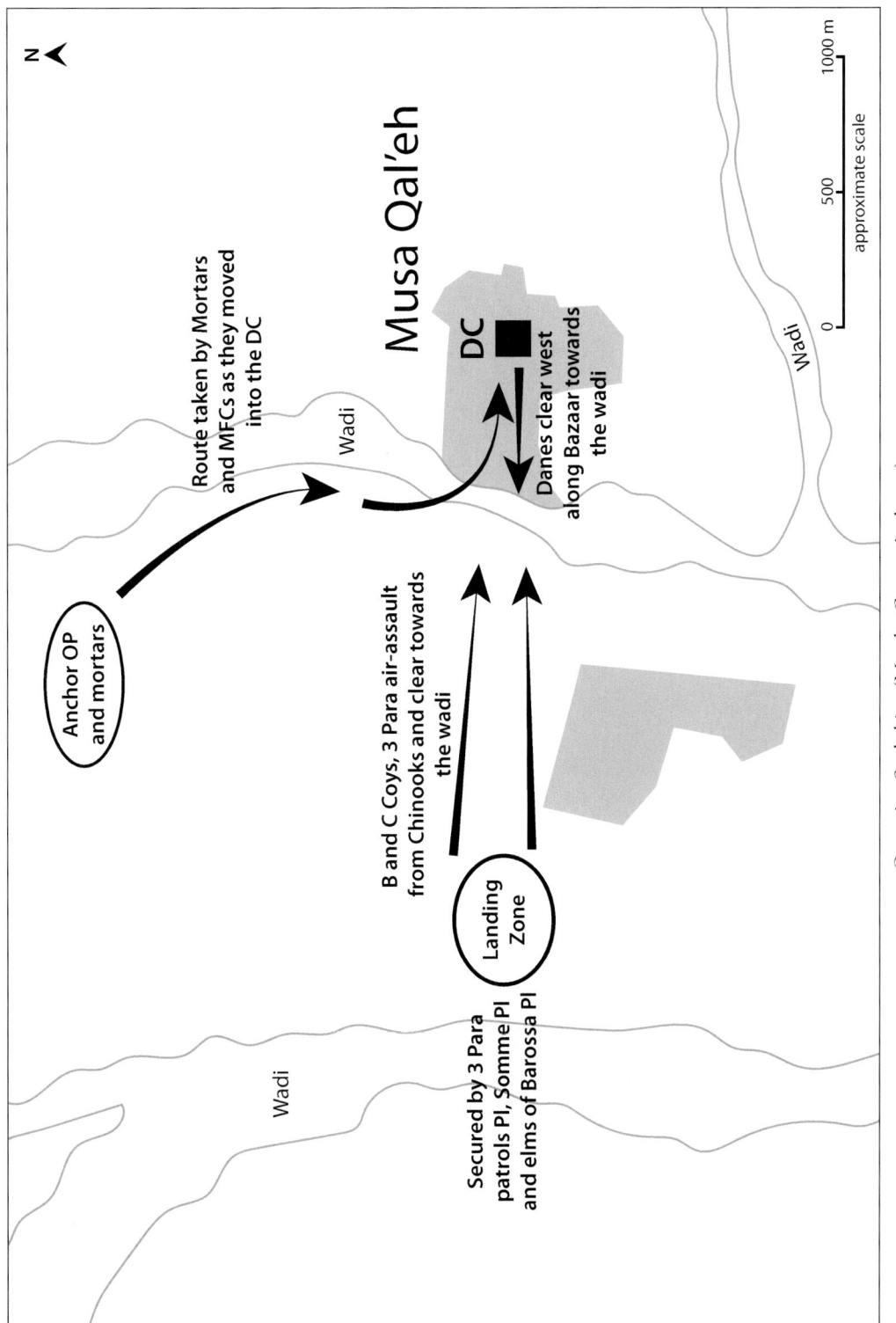

Operation Snakebite. (Map by George Anderson)

An 81mm mortar firing at night at Musa Qal'eh. (Photo: Danny Groves)

The Alamo. Danish Eagle armoured vehicles parked up alongside. (Photo: Danny Groves)

A CH-47 Chinook helicopter lands in the Helmand desert to drop off a replacement Pinzgauer vehicle during the insertion phase of Operation Snakebite. (Photo: Danny Groves)

Mortar Fire Controllers, Corporal John Harding (left) and Lance Corporal Rab McClurg, Musa Qal'eh, 2006. (Photo: Danny Groves)

Royal Irish Regiment mortar detachments at Musa Qal'eh. From left to right: Corporal John Harding, Ranger Ricky Armstrong, Ranger Adam Dunlop, Ranger Jason Mooney, Corporal Danny Groves, Lance Corporal Rab McClurg, Ranger David McFarland, Ranger Smith. Seated: Ranger Dougie McLaughlin and Ranger Crockard. (Photo: Danny Groves)

Bedding-in the mortar base-plate during the insertion phase of Operation Snakebite. (Photo: Danny Groves)

Easy Company, 3 Para Battlegroup, Musa Qal'eh, 2005. This photograph was taken after the ceasefire. (Photo: Stephen Gilchrist)

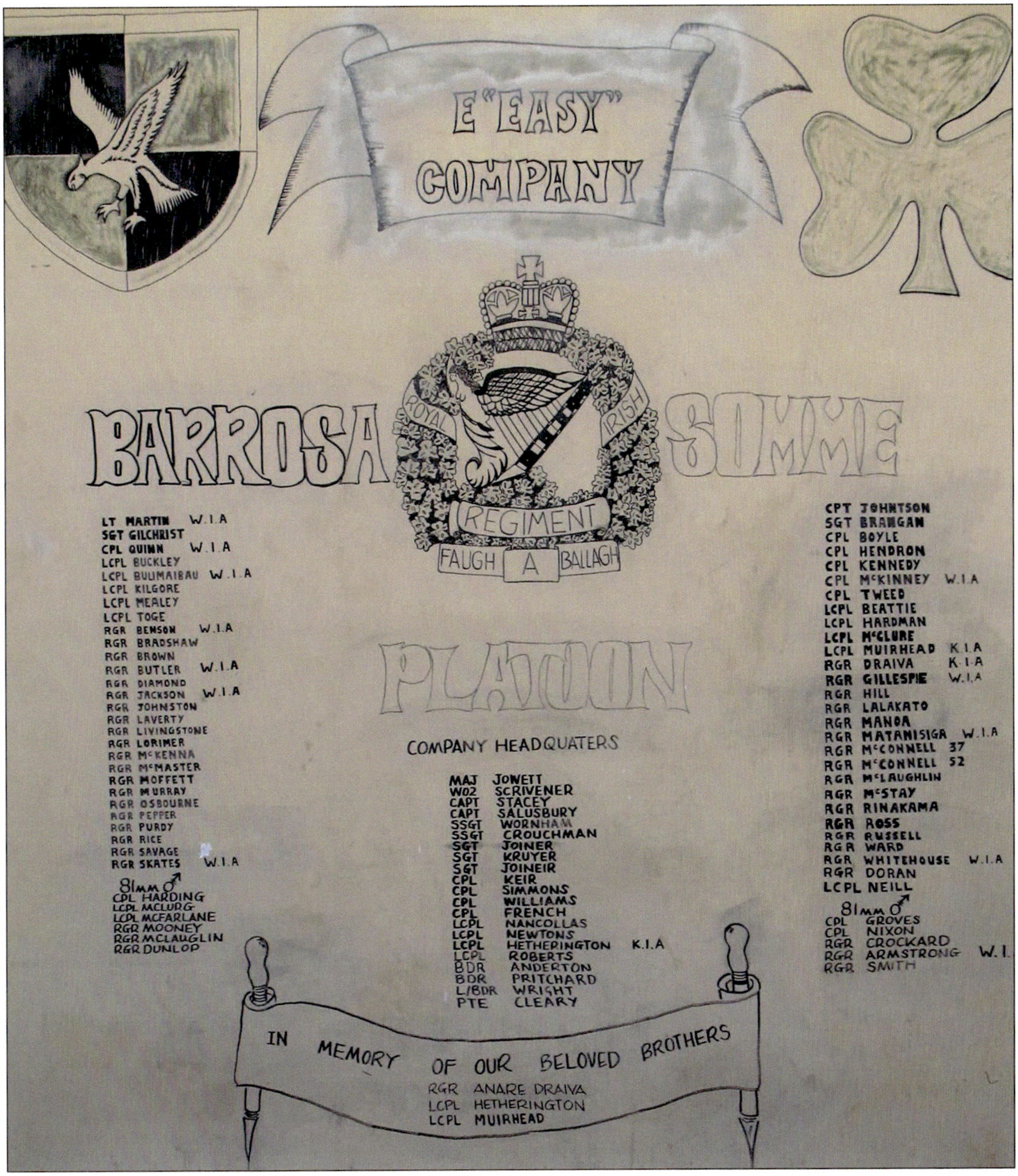

The Easy Company mural, painted on the wall of a building in the District Compound at Musa Qala. (Photo: Danny Groves)

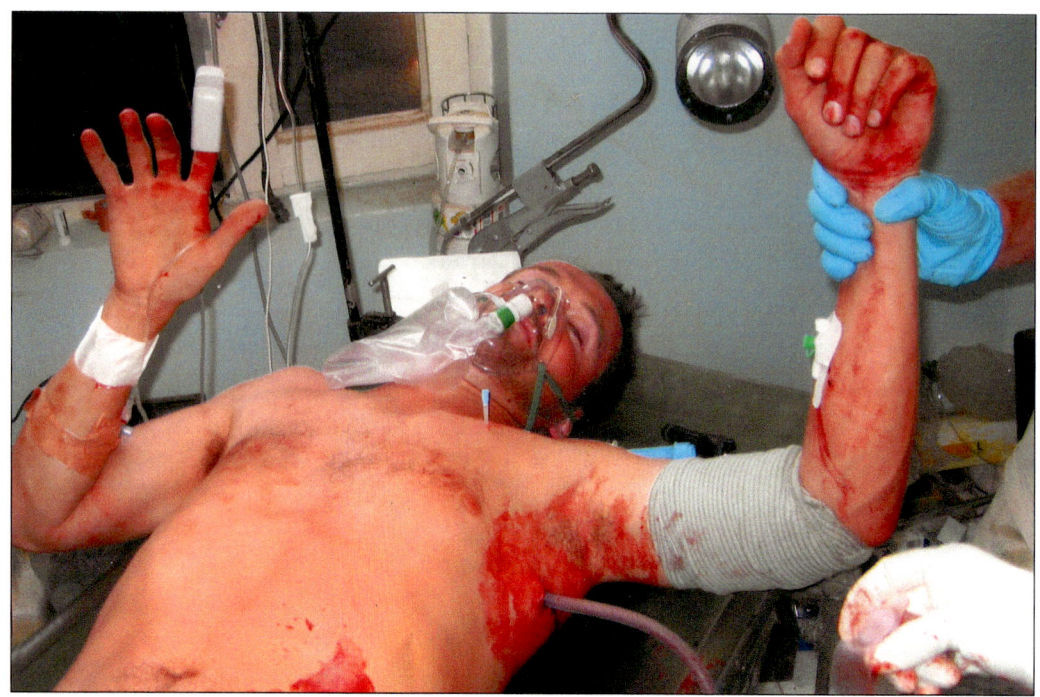

Lieutenant Paul Martin receiving emergency treatment at the medical centre, Musa Qal'eh, after being injured by shrapnel on the roof of The Alamo. (Photo: Danny Groves)

"Moonbeam". Lance Corporal Paul Muirhead, who died of wounds after being injured in a mortar attack at Musa Qal'eh. (Photo: Danny Groves)

Ranger Ricky Armstrong. (Photo: Ricky Armstrong & Danny Groves)

The remains of the sangar in which Ranger Anare Draiva died and Lance Corporal Paul Muirhead was fatally wounded in a rocket attack. (Photo: Danny Groves)

Ranger Jason Mooney. (Photo: Danny Groves)

An Afghan "jingly truck" with Easy Company soldiers on board, followed by a Pinzgauer, carrying members of the Mortar Detachments, drives through the Helmand desert on the way back to Camp Bastion at the end of the siege. (Photo: Stephen Gilchrist)

Sergeant Stephen Gilchrist, Ranger Paul Johnston and Ranger William McMaster help to paint out the Easy Company mural just before leaving the compound at the end of the siege. (Photo: Stephen Gilchrist)

Ranger Anare Draiva, who died in a rocket attack at the District Centre, Musa Qal'eh. (Photo: Danny Groves)

Platoon Sergeants Stephen Gilchrist (left) and PJ Brangan, stand by the Easy Company mural.
(Photo: Stephen Gilchrist)

The Bastion Memorial at the National Arboretum, Alrewas, Staffordshire, bearing the names of members of the UK armed forces who made the supreme sacrifice during the campaign in Afghanistan.
(Photo: author's collection)

Outdoors sleeping accommodation, next to the former medical clinic at the south of the compound.
(Photo: Davy Pepper)

Part of the Bastion Memorial bearing the names of members of the UK armed forces who died in Afghanistan during Operation Herrick IV in 2006. Included are four of the fatalities from the fighting at Musa Qal'eh: Private Barrie Cutts, Royal Logistics Corps; Lance Corporal Jon Hetherington, Royal Corps of Signals; Lance Corporal Paul Muirhead and Ranger Anare Draiva, Royal Irish Regiment. Also on the plaque are the names of Lance Corporal Luke McCullagh, Royal Irish Regiment, who died of injuries received at Sangin, and Captain David Patton, formerly of the Royal Irish Regiment but serving with the Special Reconnaissance Regiment, who also died at Sangin. (Photo: author's collection)

Part 4

When you're wounded and left on Afghanistan's plains,
And the women come out to cut up what remains,
Jest roll to your rifle and blow out your brains
An' go to your Gawd like a soldier.
                                        Rudyard Kipling[1]

---

1   Rudyard Kipling, *The Young British Soldier,* Kipling Society, <https://www.kiplingsociety.co.uk/poem/poems_youngbrit.htm>, accessed 4 July 2024.

9

Musa Qal'eh – a Modern Rorke's Drift?

The Siege of Musa Qal'eh took place in Helmand Province in southern Afghanistan, in 2006. For more than five weeks in high summer, when daytime temperatures could push the mercury up to 50 degrees Celsius and beyond, soldiers of The Royal Irish Regiment, together with members of the Afghan Police and a small contingent of paratroopers, signallers, gunners, and medics, cut off and isolated in a mud-brick compound, held their ground. They did this in the face of repeated and heavy assaults by well-armed, tenacious and highly-motivated Taliban insurgents, intent on killing them or driving them out. The fighting was brutal, with no quarter given by either side. The Taliban were determined to fly their flag over the compound. By doing so, they hoped to undermine the standing of the Provincial Governor, and the fledgling government in Kabul, in the eyes of the local population. At the same time, by inflicting heavy losses on the garrison, and other British troops deployed in the north, in Now Zad, Sangin, and Kajaki, they sought to persuade the force to pull back to the relative safety of Lashkar Gah and Goreshk. With Britain still heavily engaged in an increasingly unpopular and politically-damaging war in Iraq, they calculated that Prime Minister, Tony Blair, and his Cabinet, would have no stomach for high casualty numbers, and might even be persuaded to leave Afghanistan. With that in mind, they threw everything they had at the position, making its conquest their 'main effort' in the north of the province.

Maintaining a high tempo of attacks, they would launch nine or 10 serious firefights each day, using a formidable assortment of weapons. There were times, and not a few, when only the massive firepower of coalition fast jets, with their 1,000lb bombs and depleted uranium-tipped cannon shells, supplemented by British artillery, based out in the desert, and the garrison's own 81mm mortars, kept the insurgents from breaching the defences and massacring the occupants. If that had happened, it is not fanciful to suggest that the Taliban could have achieved their strategic aim. With multiple bodies of British soldiers displayed across the world's media, it is entirely conceivable that Prime Minister, Tony Blair, would have been forced, by popular opinion, to end his Afghanistan odyssey. If the UK had pulled out, NATO would have been left in disarray. The Karzai administration would have been made to look weak and unable to govern. The Taliban might even have been gifted sufficient momentum to push on and retake control of the whole country, as they would do in 2021. The human cost of holding the position was significant for both sides. The number of Taliban dead and wounded may never be known for certain, but it was believed, at the time, that their casualties ran into several hundreds. The British losses totalled 14 of whom three were fatalities – Lance Corporal Jon Hetherington, Royal Signals, Lance Corporal Paul Muirhead and Ranger Anare Draiva, both Royal Irish Regiment.

Some commentators have described the events at Musa Qal'eh as the modern-day equivalent of Rorke's Drift, in January 1879, when 139 soldiers, mainly from the 24th Regiment of Foot, held off determined attacks by the Zulu warriors of the uNdi Corps under Prince Dabulamanzi kaMpande, a half-brother of Cetshwayo kaMpande, the Zulu king. Celebrated BBC War Correspondent, Martin Bell, called it 'The Rorke's Drift of our times'.[1] Ten years after the fighting, in August 2016, the Daily Mail was still using the imagery of the blockbuster film, Zulu, starring Michael Caine, to describe the ordeal of the soldiers who were there.[2] There are certainly some similarities. But overall, the comparison is not valid. In both cases, a small, lightly-armed British force was defending a compound. They were cut off from supplies and reinforcements by the enemy, who had surrounded them. The British were heavily outnumbered. They sustained fatal casualties but inflicted far greater damage on the enemy. They ran low on food, water and ammunition before their bravery, endurance and determination finally convinced the attackers that the cost of taking the positions was too great. But there are also many dissimilarities. The Zulus were mostly armed with short spears, known as assegais, and defended themselves with cow-hide shields that provided no protection at all against the British .577in bullet, propelled by 85 grains of black powder, that developed a muzzle velocity of 1,300ft/s. The British carried single-shot Martini-Henry falling-block, breach-loading rifles, and were trained to shoot straight, and also to use the bayonet and the heavy rifle-butt in close quarters fighting. They could fire at a rate of up to 12 rounds a minute, and when grouped in ranks, the effect of their volley fire was devastating against tightly-packed waves of native fighters – similar to that of a machine gun.

At Rorke's Drift, the defenders had clear, wide fields of fire in most directions which meant they could individually engage the enemy at the full effective range of their rifles – 400 yards. At Musa Qal'eh, the British position was in the middle of a town, surrounded and overlooked by numerous buildings, alleyways and rat-runs, which provided the attackers with good cover, in many places almost to the compound wall. Many of the exchanges took place at ranges measured in feet.

The Zulus did not like to use firearms. They believed they were cowardly weapons and that warriors should fight face-to-face and hand-to-hand. In Afghanistan, the enemy, like the Zulus, were wily and courageous fighters, but they had no such hang-ups about using modern weaponry. They were armed with up-to-date and reasonably reliable automatic assault rifles, heavy and light machine guns, rockets, rocket-propelled grenades (RPGs), recoilless rifles, mortars and hand-grenades, and they knew how to use them. Although in the early days they made little use of modern tactics, later on they showed that they understood how to employ fire-and-manoeuvre, together with cover and concealment, to minimise the effects of defensive fires, although they did not always practice what they had learned. The defenders were similarly armed, but in addition to their own organic firepower, they could call on air and artillery support. It was possible, at some risk, to resupply the garrison, and for casualties to be evacuated by helicopter. However, there were times when the risk of losing an airframe was deemed to be too great and casualties had to wait, sometimes for many hours, before they could be airlifted to hospital.

But there are two other ways in which the events were significantly different. The defence of Rorke's Drift lasted for about 12 hours. The Royal Irish Regiment's part in the Siege of Musa Qal'eh went on for 37 bloody days. The defenders of Rorke's Drift were awarded 11 Victoria Crosses and five Distinguished Conduct Medals. Despite the viciousness of the fighting, the fortitude of the garrison, and many individual and collective acts of bravery, no Royal Irish Regiment soldier who fought at Musa Qal'eh – indeed no member of the garrison, irrespective of cap badge – received an honour or award, save for the Operational Service Medal with Afghanistan clasp.

---

1   Martin Bell, in Adam Jowett, *No Way Out* (London: Pan Books, 2019), cover.
2   'Miracle Escape of the new Rorke's Drift Paras', *Daily Mail* (6 August 2016), <https://www.dailymail.co.uk/news/article-3727024/Cut-Surrounded-Outnumbered-Just-88-British-soldiers-resigned-defeat-fighting-500-Taliban-54-days-against-odds-Miracle-escape-Rorke-s-Drift-Paras.html<, accessed 7 February 2024.

This was the same campaign medal that was issued to every service person and civil servant who completed a minimum of 28 days in that theatre, regardless of whether or not they had been involved in combat operations.[3]

The Operational Honours List for Operation Herrick IV, published in the London Gazette on 15 December 2006, contains the names of 77 recipients of gallantry and other awards. The Brigade Commander, Brigadier Ed Butler was made a Commander of the Order of the British Empire (CBE). The 3 Para Battlegroup Commander, Lieutenant Colonel Stuart Tootal and the Officer Commanding C Company, Major Paddy Blair, The Parachute Regiment, both received Distinguished Service Orders (DSO). Royal Irish Regiment Captain Doug Beattie was awarded a Military Cross (MC) for his work mentoring members of the Afghan Army. Lance Corporal Luke McCulloch of Ranger Platoon, killed whilst serving with C Company at Sangin, received a posthumous Mention in Despatches (MID). Another Royal Irish Regiment officer, Major Sean Burke, was made a Member of the British Empire (MBE) for his work within the headquarters of the International Security Assistance Force in Kabul.[4] But the gallantry of the soldiers who fought at Musa Qal'eh went entirely unrecognised by the Army, the MOD and the country.

This apparent failure of the Operational Honours system was, and remains, a subject that invokes considerable ire among many of the veterans of Somme and Barossa Platoons and the mortar detachment as well as the man who commanded their parent unit, Lieutenant Colonel (later Brigadier) Michael McGovern. For him, it remains a matter of 'profound disappointment' that none of his Royal Irish Regiment soldiers who fought at Musa Qal'eh was recognised in the roll of honours that followed the deployment:

> Many people believed the Royal Irish elements at Musa Qal'eh deserved some sort of recognition, and there was palpable shock when that did not happen. It became a massive issue, so much so that the 16 Air Assault Brigade Commander for Herrick VIII (the next Afghanistan deployment on which Royal Irish Regiment soldiers served), told me that the unit would not be forgotten again.
>
> People should be in no doubt about the bravery and courage displayed by some very young men in very arduous circumstances. They did not have the experience of 10 previous Afghanistan deployments to draw on. They were the new kids on the block and few who were not there can know how hard it was for them, day after day.[5]

The MOD has refused to discuss this issue, citing an exemption under the Freedom of Information Act relating to the Honours and Awards system. Responding to a request from the author, seeking information about the number of citations written in respect of Musa Qal'eh, the Defence People Secretariat (the part of the MOD responsible for civilian and military personnel policy) would only say that the Operational Honours list for Herrick IV was published in December 2006 and that none of the unsuccessful recommendations for honours was retained on the file.[6]

However, commenting on the issue in a podcast, hosted by former Parachute Regiment sniper, Hugh Keir, the Easy Company CSM, WO2 (now Major) Jo Scrivener, revealed that citations had

---

3 British troops under NATO command were also awarded, but are not allowed to wear, the NATO non-Article 5 medal with ISAF clasp.
4 The London Gazette, Supplement 58183, Page 17355, dated 15 December 2006, <https://www.thegazette.co.uk/London/issue/58183/supplement/17355>, accessed 13 April 2025.
5 Brigadier (Retd) Michael McGovern, former Commanding Officer, 1st Battalion, The Royal Irish Regiment, interview with author.
6 Letter from Defence People Secretariat, responding to author's FOI Request, dated 31 March 2025.

been written to recognise a number of members of the garrison. According to this well-placed and well-regarded source, who claims he saw the citations, many of the soldiers of Somme and Barrosa platoons who fought through the siege deserved to be recognised:

> There were some acts of bravery [at Musa Qal'eh] that were unparalleled on that tour. There were some brave people who did extraordinary things and who should have been awarded decent medals and they weren't. Unfortunately, 16 Air Assault Brigade went home [by the time Easy Company extracted from the District Centre] and the citations were given to the next unit [3 Commando Brigade] to process.

Because of this, Scrivener has suggested, any awards for the Musa Qal'eh men would have had to come out of the following Brigade's (3 Commando Brigade) allocation.[7] Unsurprisingly, that did not happen. Formally, there were no 'allocations' for Operational Honours and awards, but there were certainly no incentives for any brigade to recognise the acts of its predecessor.

The former Royal Irish CO finds Scrivener's explanation to be unconvincing:

> Honours and Awards are not a responsibility that a commanding officer leaves to the next unit. Part of the process, when you return from operations, is to write up those who are deserving of recognition. You have a moral responsibility towards those who fought for you to see their efforts are properly rewarded. 3 Para had a responsibility towards the young men who had fought for them at Musa Qal'eh and elsewhere and they did not discharge it. To me, that is a matter of profound disappointment and injustice. It was not well done. It was a matter of embarrassment to the country and the army. It was simply wrong.[8]

The truth is that despite the daily heroics of the young Royal Irish soldiers, and their compatriots from the Parachute Regiment and other cap badges, the Siege of Musa Qal'eh was an embarrassment for the Blair administration. They had told the British public the troops were being deployed on a peace-support mission. The reality was that the small force became entangled in some of the toughest and most brutal fighting experienced by the British Army since the Korean War – the sort of intense, bloody, no-quarter-given combat the men of one of The Royal Irish Regiment's antecedents, the Royal Ulster Rifles, who fought against human waves of Chinese and North Koreans at the Imjin River, in 1951, would have recognised. As Michael McGovern put it: 'I think, at that time and since, there were people who were more than happy to move on from Musa Qal'eh'.[9]

A Rickety Afghan Town

Even before war came to Musa Qal'eh, the town had little to recommend it to Western eyes. A small, unassuming settlement, dependent on agriculture and opium for its existence, it was located on a slightly elevated site, a short distance due east of the Musa Qal'eh River. The river, a main tributary of the Helmand Rud, was a significant water course in its own right. Flowing south from its source in the foothills of the Hindu Kush mountain range, it provided vital irrigation for the

---

7   WO2 (now Major) Jo Scrivener, CSM, Easy Company, An Untold, Unbelievable Military Story, H Hour Podcast, Hugh Keir, 5 February 2025, <https://substack.com/@hughkeir/note/p-157271203?utm_source=notes-share-action>, accessed 20 February 2025.
8   Brigadier (Retd) Michael McGovern, interview with author.
9   Brigadier (Retd) Michael McGovern, interview with author.

crops – mostly maize, wheat…and poppy – that grew vigorously in the nearby fields, creating a verdant, productive strip that seemed quite incongruous alongside the arid desert plains from which it was approached. Sangin, the opium capital of Helmand, lay 20 miles further south, while the Kajaki Reservoir and its important hydro-electric plant was 15 miles east. Now Zad was about the same distance to the north-west.

Sitting at the confluence of two riverbeds or wadis, Musa Qal'eh appeared to be just another rickety Afghan town of residential compounds and poorly-maintained low-rise commercial units. By the late summer of 2006, however, a visitor there would have noticed that the buildings closest to the centre were in a bad shape, even by local standards. Many of them were in a state of collapse, and of those that still stood, most were damaged to some degree, often pock-marked and shrapnel-scarred as if some giant hand had hurled rocks at them in a fit of temper. A closer look would have revealed that there were few signs of 'normal, daily life', whatever that was supposed to be. No cars drove along the narrow, dusty streets. No children played by the roadway. No artisans laboured in the numerous small workshops. No farmers tended the fields. The bazaar, usually the centre of activity in Afghan towns, was deserted. The silence was punctuated only by the breeze, rustling the leaves of the trees, the bushes and the crops growing in the green zone to the east of the river, and the occasional dog, barking in the distance. And it was hot…really hot. The kind of searing heat that causes perspiration to seep from every pore, soaking clothes, tracing rivulets down dust-covered skin, and leaving un-acclimatised humans exhausted by even the slightest exertion.

But first impressions can be deceiving. The peace and quiet described above were fleeting. For Musa Qal'eh, in that long, hot summer, was a war zone – a place of death and destruction. Its streets had become a battlefield over which two opposing forces and two competing ideologies fought daily battles to the death in a no-holds-barred struggle for control of a small, seemingly insignificant, piece of Afghan dirt. Before the fighting began, the sprawling town of one and two-story, flat-roofed buildings, had a population of 15,000–20,000 people. It also had thriving bazaars, and two mosques, all built from the same brown, sand-coloured bricks-under-mud rendering that is typical of construction throughout the province. Pounded daily by mortars and artillery, as well as countless bombs and depleted-uranium-tipped cannon shells, fired from coalition aircraft, many of the town centre buildings had been turned to dust, and the local people had long gone. Now, the damaged buildings, narrow streets and alleyways provided shelter for new residents – Taliban insurgents, intent on dealing death to the foreign infidels based there.

The main focus for the violence was the town's District Centre, or DC – the seat of governance and a symbol of the tenuous political power that flowed from Kabul, through Lashkar Gah and out across Helmand. It was from here that the police, the judges, the doctors, the civil servants and the elected representatives of the area were supposed to provide public services such as health, education, justice and economic development. But all these things had shuddered to a halt in June when the Taliban had arrived and threatened to take over the complex. The judge, the doctors and the nurses had fled. Only the police chief, and a handful of unreliable and ill-equipped Afghan National Police remained. Some of these, without uniform and thus wearing civilian garb, were difficult to tell apart from the enemy.

The DC was a small compound, measuring no more than 200m from north to south and about 150m from east to west. It was located prominently, as befitted its status, at the eastern end of the main bazaar, a half-completed minaret in the centre of a small roundabout guarding the way to its front gate. Surrounded by a mud-and-brick wall which was mostly about 10ft (3m) in height, but in some parts quite a lot lower, topped with razor wire here and there, it was overlooked on three sides by buildings, some of them coming to within a few feet of the boundary. These provided covered approach routes that would allow insurgents to creep, often unseen, to within grenade-throwing range of the beleaguered garrison. The location may have been a good place to site a District Centre but it was an exceptionally poor choice as a defensive position. Certainly, no one with a military brain would have selected it for that purpose. As Parachute Regiment Major Adam Jowett, considered his predicament, shortly after arriving there that August, he was certain that if he had chosen it as a base in a Staff College exercise his instructors would rightly have torn him to shreds.[10] As the days went by, Jowett, not yet fully understanding the political realities of his situation, asked for permission to move to a more defendable location. The request was refused.[11] The DC was too important as a symbol of Afghan governance. Neither the Provincial Governor, nor the President would countenance such a move. It had to be held at all costs. The defenders would have to make the best of a bad situation.

The complex had been built with American aid money, and included a police station, a medical facility and a small jail. When British troops first occupied the DC, there were prisoners still locked up in the cells there, guarded by a small team of Afghan warders. The inmates would have a long wait for justice. The local judge had left, at the first sign of trouble, for the relative safety of Lashkar Gah. Five guard positions – sangars – provided overwatch. Sangar 1 was above the main gate, which looked west, along the bazaar towards the wadi and the green zone. Sangar 2 was in the north-west corner, near a position known as The Outpost. Sangar 3 was opposite Sanger 1 on the north-east corner. A fourth was on the south-east boundary and a fifth to the south-west, overlooking the remains of what had been a mosque until it had come off second best in a tussle with a coalition bomb. In addition, there were a number of stand-to fighting positions along the walls. The construction of the fighting positions was rudimentary at best, owing little to the contents of the Army's field fortifications manual. Although some of the sangars had been built of concrete breeze blocks, bonded with cement, most were just chest or shoulder-high sandbag walls with, in some cases, corrugated iron – or 'wriggly tin' – and camouflage nets overhead to provide some shade from the baking Afghan sun. Hessian sheets had been strung between posts here and there to provide anti-sniper screens. The sandbags and breeze blocks might have stopped rifle bullets, but there was little in the way of hard overhead protection against shrapnel from airburst RPG rounds or near or direct hits from mortars, recoilless rifles or missiles. At one place an old sofa had been stuffed into a hole left by a Chinese rocket. Although not bullet-proof, the improvised plug did help to ensure that Taliban snipers could not use the breach to spot movement and possible targets.

The garrison had been forced to do the best they could with the materials they had to hand. There was no prospect of risking a helicopter just to bring in defence stores, and earlier resupply by road had tended to prioritise food and ammunition.[12] Vulnerable points outside the walls were protected by carefully-positioned Claymore anti-personnel mines, which were rigged, as the law required, to be command-detonated. This meant that instead of being fired by a trip-wire they were attached to a manual firing device, known as a 'clacker' and could be exploded, when required, from a safe distance. The Outpost, so-called because it was on the outside of the northern wall, with an alley running between it and the compound, was a three-story building with two firing positions on the roof, affording views over the main Helicopter Landing Site (HLS). Usually held in section-plus strength, about 10 men, augmented by some ANP, access was gained by clambering over an improvised ladder, laid horizontally to bridge the gap between the compound wall and the building. Once inside, the section had to climb up two further ladders to reach the roof, where two sandbagged sangars had been built. One of the garrison's two .50in heavy machine guns was mounted there. It was just about tolerable to be there during the day. However, some soldiers were less enthusiastic about occupying the Outpost during the hours of darkness when they felt much more vulnerable to Taliban attack. Ranger Davy Pepper described it thus:

---

10   Jowett, *No Way Out,* p.57.
11   Jowett, *No Way Out,* p.188.
12   Jowett, *No Way Out,* p.58.

We were outside the main compound. I could see into the buildings opposite…and anyone there could see me. The outpost was one of the first positions to come under fire in any attack. When you were on guard, you were in the sangar on your own, although there were other people nearby and you had night-vision – a CWS (Common Weapon Sight). I won't lie, as a 20-year-old kid, I found the nights a bit scary. But with contacts coming so frequently, sometimes you didn't have much time to think about being scared.[13]

Another key position, roughly at the centre of the compound, was known as the Alamo. This gave good all-round visibility and was an obvious place from which to command the DC during attacks. Its roof provided an elevated platform from where the Joint Tactical Attack Controllers (JTAC) could observe and direct fire from supporting artillery and aircraft. However, being close to the centre of the complex, it was also a bullet magnet and life there could become very uncomfortable very quickly during a firefight. The second .50in heavy machine gun was located here, although it was later damaged and became unserviceable. Taking its name from the mission compound near San Antonio where Davy Crockett, Jim Bowie, Lieutenant Colonel William Travis and a small force of Texans held off the Mexican forces of Santa Anna in a 13-day siege, in 1836, the Musa Qal'eh Alamo had once housed the town's jail. However, it was now the final fallback position in the event that the walls were breached and the compound overrun. This was to be the rally-point where the defenders, like the Texans, would make their last stand, until they had been relieved by a rescue force…or killed. No one talked about surrendering.

The Joint Operations Centre or JOC was in a separate building, north of the Alamo, housing radios, signallers and small intelligence and electronic warfare teams. With a fighting position on the roof, this building was also where the men on Quick Reaction Force (QRF) duty stood by, under cover, to reinforce the fighting positions, carry ammunition or assist with recovering the wounded. At the southern end of the compound, hard up against the boundary wall, was the old health clinic, which had been turned into sleeping accommodation, mostly used by the men of Barrosa Platoon. This was also where the Regimental Aid Post (RAP) – a small room with a single, makeshift operating table – was located.

Two cramped helicopter landing sites (HLS) had been identified within the walls. While these were suitable for small aircraft such as the British Lynx, neither had sufficient clearance to accommodate the large, twin-rotor Chinooks that were to evacuate casualties and provide resupply of food and ammunition. As a result, the main HLS had to be located outside the northern wall – again overlooked and very difficult to secure within the rules of engagement that were in effect at the time.[14] Each time an aircraft was scheduled to land a rifle platoon had to push out beyond the compound to provide a security cordon. The helicopter pilots hated and feared it in equal measure. One of them, Royal Marine Major, Mark Hammond, described it as 'the worst HLS in Helmand'. Surrounded by high ground, with a very tight and dusty touch-down spot, it was, in his word, 'hideous'.[15]

---

13   Ranger Davy Pepper, interview with author.
14   During the early occupation of the DC, the garrison could only fire on, or call in air or artillery support against, targets that were posing an active threat. This meant they had to actually be in contact or identify a probable threat (i.e. sight armed insurgents in a threat posture), before authorising the release of ordnance by aircraft, or from the guns of 7RHA. It would have been possible to secure the HLS by the use of what was known as 'preliminary fires'. This meant calling down fire on suspected enemy positions and forming-up points before they had engaged, but legal authority for this had to be sought in advance and was not always forthcoming.
15   Hammond, Mark, *Immediate Response* (London: Penguin Books, 2018), pp.71–72.

10

Basra, Baghdad, Bastion…

The years leading up to the Afghanistan deployment in 2006 had been a busy period for the British Army. The 1st Battalion, The Royal Irish Regiment, was no exception. The unit had been part of 16 Air Assault Brigade since the formation's birth in 1999, one of the key structural changes to the army that flowed from the Blair government's Strategic Defence Review the previous year. The Brigade had been created from the amalgamation of elements of the old 5 Airborne and 24 Airmobile Brigades. Like its predecessors, it was intended to be a rapidly-deployable force, able to operate across the entire spectrum of modern conflict, from counter-insurgency to high-intensity combat and everything in between. Under this concept, the Brigade's two Parachute Regiment battalions would provide an airborne element while the Royal Irish would deliver an air-assault capability, deploying down the rear ramps of Hercules transport aircraft or from Chinook helicopters.

It was in this role that the battalion had taken part in all of Blair's wars, including Operation Agricola (KFOR, Kosovo), in 1999; Op Palliser (Sierra Leone), in 2000; and Op Telic (the invasion of Iraq) in 2003. By the summer of 2005 they were back in Iraq, this time as the Rear Operations Battlegroup, charged with guarding the British logistics base and the Multi-National Division (South-East) (MND(SE)) Divisional Detention Facility at Shaibah, a former RAF station, south-west of Basra and just north of the town of Az Zubayr. They were also responsible for providing security for the Senior British Military Representative and his staff at Maude House and other operations in Baghdad's Green Zone.[1]

The high tempo of operations had been wearing for the soldiers, but it had also brought important benefits. As 2005 rolled into 2006, the battalion was at the top of its game, well-trained, fully-recruited and with a high proportion of soldiers who had recent operational experience. As the unit resubordinated to 16 Air Assault Brigade, the then-Commanding Officer, Lieutenant Colonel (later Brigadier Retd.) Michael McGovern, felt his men were looking forward to the challenge of their return to operating in that role:

> The boys were understandably tired when they came back from Iraq but after a period of leave and rest, they quickly gained a new lease of life. The move back into the 16 Air Assault Brigade ORBAT was viewed as a positive thing by everyone with any relationship to the regiment. We knew the nature of the beast; we knew the requirements of the role; and we absolutely felt that was our rightful place because of the nature of the battalion and the strengths of the young men and women who were part of it. Without wishing to sound arrogant, we

---

1 Maude House was named after General Sir Stanley Maude, who led the joint British and Indian force that captured Baghdad from the Ottomans in 1917.

really felt we were the match of other units in the brigade and that being part of it was a good use of an Irish infantry battalion.²

The Brigade appears to have held a similar opinion. When 3 Para was selected to form the infantry core of the Battlegroup to go to Afghanistan in the spring of that year, it was no surprise that Brigadier Ed Butler turned to the Royal Irish to make up manning shortfalls. A composite platoon – Ranger Platoon – was duly attached to 3 Para. As his battalion was beginning to reestablish its position within the Brigade, it was important to the Commanding Officer, that his unit was involved in the Afghanistan deployment in some way. 'I wanted the Royal Irish to be part of it and a platoon seemed like a good way to achieve that objective', he explained. With a reputation to uphold, it was also critical to ensure that troops of the right calibre were selected for the task. Ranger Platoon was deliberately established as 'an all-volunteer platoon of super, high-powered, highly-competent soldiers',³ who were pleased to find themselves serving under fellow Ulsterman, 3 Para's Major Paddy Blair. Having been attached to the Battlegroup from early in the pre-deployment phase, the Ranger Platoon soldiers benefitted from being able to complete their work-up training with C Company, and by the time they arrived in Helmand, they were thoroughly and deeply integrated with their Parachute Regiment comrades. These Royal Irish Regiment soldiers would find themselves heavily engaged in the fighting around Sangin and Garmsir.

When additional support was called for, ahead of Defence Secretary, Des Browne's announcement of reinforcements, in July, it was to the Royal Irish that the Brigade looked once more for support. A further two platoons and a mortar section were despatched to Helmand at short notice. Again, Lieutenant Colonel McGovern sought to ensure that the cream of his battalion was selected. 'I was in no doubt that we would not be sending people over whom there was any kind of a question mark. On an individual basis, the soldiers that went were extremely able and highly-regarded'.⁴

Corporal Danny Groves (26), commanding the mortar section, had just returned from Iraq and was enjoying some long-awaited post-operational tour leave with his girlfriend when his phone rang. It was the Mortar Platoon's second-in-command and he was seeking volunteers. Groves was by now an experienced soldier, having just completed two tours in Iraq as well as two deployments to Northern Ireland. The most recent of these had been as a member of the Close Observation Platoon, crawling around in the South Armagh hedgerows, keeping an eye on suspected terrorists. He was aware of the soldier's rule about never volunteering for anything, but the opportunity to go to Afghanistan was not to be missed. 'I thought at the time, if it's not me, it'll be someone else. I was single and young and I wanted to go. I said "yes".' The decision pleased his superiors but it did not go down well with his girlfriend. 'She thought I had five weeks' leave. Now, two weeks into it, I had to tell her I was off again – and to Afghanistan of all places'.⁵

One of the most experienced soldiers in Musa Qal'eh that summer was Corporal John Harding. A senior corporal, on the cusp of promotion to sergeant, he was at the pinnacle of his craft – a Mortar Fire Controller *par excellence*. Harding was 29 years old when he went to Musa Qal'eh, and he had seen some hard soldiering since joining the Army 10 years before. He had crossed the Iraqi border with the battalion in 2003, and had been in Kosovo in 1999 and Sierra Leone in 2000. A man bred for action and adventure, he had found the low-key 2005 deployment to Iraq to be 'just

---

2   Lieutenant Colonel (now Brigadier Retd) Michael McGovern, Commanding Officer, 1st Battalion, The Royal Irish Regiment, interview with author.
3   Lieutenant Colonel Michael McGovern, interview with author.
4   Lieutenant Colonel Michael McGovern, interview with author.
5   Corporal Danny Groves, interview with author.

awful'.[6] When the opportunity came to volunteer for Afghanistan, he was right at the front of the queue. Having put his name down for possible deployment while still in Iraq, he was back in the UK when he learned he would be part of the reinforcements heading for Helmand that summer:

> I was sitting in the Mortar Platoon office at Fort George on a Friday afternoon when I got a call from the Ops Officer telling me that I needed to put together a mortar team to deploy on Sunday. That was the air assault way. We didn't go on the Sunday. Instead, we headed for Germany where we completed a fairly generic pre-deployment training package.[7]

Harding was relaxed about the lack of theatre-specific preparation. 'The thing that stood us in good stead was our baseline training. I felt ever so comfortable with my basic skills and drills'.[8]

Lance Corporal Rab McClurg (21), had joined the Army as a boy soldier at 16. He had just missed the invasion of Iraq in 2003, but had gone there in 2005, and found it 'all a bit benign and boring'. As that tour was coming to an end, he began to hear rumours about a possible deployment to Afghanistan. Another mortarman by trade, when he returned to the UK in early 2006, he had gone immediately on a Mortar Fire Controller course and by the time he returned to the battalion, he was craving an opportunity to gain some further operational experience. 'Iraq had been tedious but Afghanistan sounded exciting', he recalled. He put his name down to be a section 2ic (second-in-command). He was not the only one:

> The response to the call for volunteers had been so great the battalion had to run a selection course to decide who to take. About half-way through the course, they concluded that they also needed a mortar team, and since I was already a volunteer and a newly-qualified MFC, I was switched across and teamed up with Corporal John Harding as his bravo.[9]

Paul Martin was a 26-year-old Lieutenant, enjoying a six-week exercise in Jamaica, with B Company, when the call came. A farmer's son from Lisburn, he had chosen soldiering over running the family farm. After studying finance at Dundee University, on the east coast of Scotland, he headed for Sandhurst, commissioning into The Royal Irish Regiment in August 2004. Disappointed to miss out on an Op Banner tour in his native Northern Ireland that year, he had deployed to Iraq in 2005 and had relished the opportunity to command his Rangers in an operational, albeit relatively peaceful, environment, where they had experienced 'a few 'scrapes but no casualties'. Exercise Red Stripe, on the Caribbean island of Jamaica, seemed like the perfect reward after six months of escorting convoys between Basra and Al Amarah, guarding the Detention Centre at Shaibah Logistics Base, and providing security at Maude House in Baghdad:

> We were in barracks at Port Antonio when the CO, Lieutenant Colonel Michael McGovern, arrived, bringing exciting news. Things were not going well in Afghanistan. The 3 Para Battlegroup was in desperate need of reinforcement and casualty replacements, and the Royal Irish had been asked to provide the manpower and deploy as quickly as possible.[10]

---

6   Corporal John Harding, interview with author.
7   Corporal John Harding, interview with author.
8   Corporal John Harding, interview with author.
9   Lance Corporal Rab McClurg, interview with author. (MFCs operate as a two-man team, Alpha and Bravo. Alpha is senior and in a command role. The Bravo provides support and can take responsibility for calling down fire missions on his own targets during busy periods).
10 Lieutenant Paul Martin, interview with author.

McGovern asked the young officer to command a platoon, but he was clear that he was not ordering him to do so. It had to be voluntary. 'I jumped at the opportunity. There were lots of Lieutenants he could have chosen and I was incredibly humbled that he had asked me'.[11]

At 21 years old, Ranger Paul 'Jonty' Johnston had been in the Army for four years and, like Paul Martin, Danny Groves, and Rab McClurg, he had seen action in Iraq in 2005, coming under fire while driving along the notorious Route Irish between Camp Victory at Baghdad Airport and the so-called Green Zone in the centre of the city, where the main coalition headquarters was located. Despite this, his time in Iraq had not been particularly exciting. 'I found it a little surreal to sit by the swimming pool at the back of Saddam Hussein's Republican Palace as American servicewomen walked about in bikinis with M16 rifles slung over their shoulders'. It was not what he had expected from an operational deployment. The trip to Jamaica had provided some compensations, but he knew that the real action was going on in Helmand:

> This was before we had smart phones so the only sources of information were television, radio and the newspapers. I had been glued to the TV at every opportunity and I could see that Afghanistan was high on the news agenda.
>
> The CO called us all together in the cookhouse and gave us an outline of what was going on in Helmand. At the end of the talk, he explained that the battalion had been asked to form two additional platoons to support 3 Para, and he called for volunteers.
>
> I was the first one. I practically ran to the Company Commander, Major Weir,[12] to tell him to put my name down. He wasn't surprised that I wanted to go.[13]

Ranger Davy Pepper (20) had been too young to deploy on Operation Telic 1 (the invasion of Iraq). He joined the Army in September, 2002, arriving at the battalion in March the following year, and spent some time in Cyprus while the others were in Iraq. He took part in Op Telic VI in 2005, finding his time there 'very routine'. 'Down in Basra it felt like a Northern Ireland tour – except we were in the desert. We were doing lots of vehicle patrols, providing escorts for road moves, and guarding the camp at Shaibah'.[14] But a four-week rotation to Baghdad, was more interesting. 'There was a lot more going on there at the time. There were explosions and small-arms fire and the Americans seemed to be losing a lot of troops. We received intelligence reports every day that mentioned US losses, but we didn't see any action'.[15]

A yearning for adventure and an opportunity to escape from barrack life in the UK persuaded Sergeant PJ Brangan (31) to put his name down for the Afghanistan tour. By 2006 he had been in the Army for 11 years. Like many Royal Irish soldiers, he hailed from the Irish Republic, deciding on a military career after moving to Maidstone in Kent to train to be a mental health nurse. He had joined his local Territorial Army (now Army Reserve) unit for something to do in his spare time but found that he was spending more time as a soldier than he was as a nurse. He decided to switch direction and joined the Regular Army in February 1995. By 2006, he was a seasoned veteran with tours of duty in Northern Ireland, Macedonia and Iraq under his belt. 'I was in Iraq, towards the end of the 2005–6 deployment when a call came for volunteers and I put my name in the hat. I just wanted to get away as much as I could'.[16] Brangan returned to the UK and began his

---

11 Lieutenant Paul Martin, interview with author.
12 At the time of writing Maj General (Retd) Colin Weir.
13 Ranger Paul Johnston, interview with author.
14 Ranger Davy Pepper, interview with author.
15 Ranger Davy Pepper, interview with author.
16 Sergeant PJ Brangan, interview with author.

post-operational tour leave when a summons to the battalion's Regimental Sergeant Major's office confirmed that he would be going to Afghanistan.

Sergeant Stephen Gilchrist volunteered because he had not managed to complete the Iraq tour. He had been injured and had returned to the UK for rehabilitation. 'I felt I needed to get another full deployment under my belt so I put my name down for Afghanistan, not realising the full story behind it'. Gilchrist, or Gilly, as he was known to everyone in the battalion, was attached to A Company. While B Company had gone off to Jamaica, he and the rest of A Company had been hosting members of the Jamaican Defence Force on an exchange visit, which had included conducting internal security training at the Urban Warfare Facility at Lydd. The training package completed, he went off on summer leave, putting all thoughts of Afghanistan out of his head as he travelled to New Zealand to visit his sister. 'I'd only been there a short time when I got a call from PJ Brangan telling me I had been selected to deploy on Op Herrick and I needed to get myself back ASAP because we would be leaving for Afghanistan very soon'.[17]

On returning to the UK, Lieutenant Martin, Sergeant Gilchrist, and the B Company contingent (those who would form Barrosa Platoon) completed a short pre-deployment training package at Lydd Camp in Kent (known as OPTAG – Operational Training and Advisory Group), while the soldiers destined for Somme Platoon did the same in Germany. The training was cursory and, not particularly mission-specific, probably reflecting the expected nature of the role in Helmand. 'We had lots of lectures and we covered things like urban patrolling, vehicle checkpoints and public order training – all the sorts of stuff you'd expect to do for a tour of Northern Ireland', recalled Ranger Pepper.[18] From there they eventually made their way to RAF Brize Norton, in Oxfordshire, where they boarded an elderly Tristar aircraft bound for Kabul. After a few hours at Kabul International Airport – KIA to the soldiers – just enough time for the troops to find their way to the cookhouse, get a meal, find a toilet, and get back to the flight line – the new arrivals were back in the cavernous hold of a RAF Hercules and on their way to Camp Bastion.

Corporal John Harding probably spoke for many when he expressed surprise at the sight that greeted him as he walked down the cargo ramp at their destination after 40 minutes in the air:

> We seemed to be in an empty bit of desert. There was no runway – we had landed on a temporary gravel airstrip. There were no buildings – just a few tents and ISO containers, and the beginnings of some Hesco shelters. There was no reception party – not even the usual RAF or RLC movements staff.[19]

The men unloaded their kit by the side of the landing strip and, as the light was fading, Harding decided to try to find someone who could point him in the direction of the accommodation. A nearby tent, adorned with antennae seemed the logical place to start. Going inside, Harding found himself in the Battlegroup operations room. But it was not like any ops room he had ever seen before. There was hardly anyone there. '3 Para had become so stretched they had been forced to send anyone with a pulse out onto the ground'. Harding could see desperation in the Paras' faces. 'The unit's QM seemed to be in charge, which was definitely not part of his normal job description'.[20]

Initially, it had been thought that while the mortar section and the Mortar Fire Controllers would probably be deployed to one of the District Centres to provide organic indirect fire support,

---

17 Sergeant Stephen Gilchrist, interview with author.
18 Ranger Davy Pepper, interview with author.
19 Corporal John Harding, interview with author.
20 Corporal John Harding, interview with author.

the two platoons – now named Somme and Barrosa in honour of two of the regiment's greatest battle honours – would be broken up and used to provide individual battle casualty replacements (BCRs) to fill gaps in the Parachute Regiment companies caused by injuries or deaths. There had already been a few casualties and more were expected. However, that plan seemed to have been overtaken by events. 'The QM turned around and asked if the mortar section had arrived. When I told him they had he said 'Thank God you're here. You're going to Musa Qal'eh…and you're going tonight. We're in real trouble up there".[21] The mortars did not go to Musa Qal'eh that evening. But they were badly needed there.

Band of Musa Muckers[22]

16 Air Assault Brigade's Pathfinder Platoon was regarded as an elite team of specialists. Lightly-armed, their primary role was to act as the Brigade's eyes and ears, dropping ahead of the main body, using advanced HALO (High Altitude, Low Opening) or HAHO (High Altitude High Opening) techniques, to mark drop zones and helicopter landing sites for airborne operations. In Afghanistan, the platoon would not be going to war by parachute. Instead, it was intended that they would provide a mobile force, using the excellent cross-country characteristics of their unarmoured WMIK Land Rovers, to rove over the area of operations, providing a reconnaissance and intelligence-gathering capability. They could also act as quick-reaction troubleshooters if required. It was in this latter role that the small band of highly-motivated and well-trained paratroopers had been despatched to Musa Qal'eh on 17 May to support pro-Government militia fighters and a detachment of Afghan National Police in the District Centre who had been attacked by the Taliban. After the intruders had been driven off, a US infantry company took over the position temporarily before the Pathfinders returned to the town on 14 June to allow the Americans to depart. The plan was to hold the compound for a few days before handing over to A Company, 3 Para, then in Sangin. However, as the situation in Sangin deteriorated, A Company could not leave so the Pathfinders had to 'stag-on',[23] initially reinforced by 6 Platoon, B Company, and later by a troop of gunners from I Battery (Bull's Troop), 7RHA.[24]

In the coming weeks, the Pathfinders and gunners witnessed a growing insurgency as attacks on them increased in frequency and ferocity. Involved in daily battles, the small band of defenders, supported by coalition air power and artillery, returned Taliban fire with interest, but they were lightly-armed and not ideally suited to garrisoning the position in the long term. After four weeks, food and ammunition were running low. The men, and their equipment, were feeling the strain.

Battlegroup commander, Lieutenant Colonel Stuart Tootal, wanted them out so they could get back to providing his eyes and ears throughout the AOR. He was also aware that the troop of gunners there – G Troop, under Lieutenant Pete Airey – would be more profitably employed in their primary role, providing artillery support across the force. Operating in the infantry role, they had left their 105mm Light Guns in the desert. During their time in the DC Lieutenant Airey and his men had been conducting foot patrols in the town, and had come under some fairly intense Taliban fire. They expended more than 10,000 rounds of small-arms ammunition and 76 40mm grenades from underslung launchers fitted to their SA80 rifles. They also had the unique

---

21   Corporal John Harding, interview with author.
22   The title of Corporal Danny Groves' daily journal of his time at Musa Qal'eh.
23   To be 'on stag' is Army jargon for being on guard. To 'stag-on' means to continue with a task with no end in sight.
24   Patrick Bishop, *3 Para* (London: Harper Perennial, 2008), p.159.

experience, certainly in terms of the Afghanistan campaign, of being at both ends of a 105mm gun barrel, having been supported, during some of their contacts, by a US artillery battery, firing similar weapons.[25]

With growing calls on his resources, resulting in the Battlegroup becoming dangerously overstretched, Tootal would have preferred to pull all UK troops out of the DC and leave it under the control of Afghan forces. But, with political pressure mounting to ensure the Taliban did not occupy the location, it became clear that the Pathfinders could only be withdrawn if they could be replaced with troops who could be relied upon to hold the ground. With his scarce resources now spread thinly across the north of the Province, in Sangin, Now Zad and Kajaki, Tootal turned to a Danish armoured reconnaissance squadron that had been attached to the Battlegroup as part of Denmark's contribution to the NATO mission.[26]

The 140-man 1st Light Reconnaissance Squadron, known as The Griffins, a sub-unit of the Danish Guards Hussars cavalry regiment, had been conducting training in the desert, around Bastion, prior to being given its first mission. Before arriving in Afghanistan, its commander, acting Major Lars Ulslev Johannesen, had expected that this was going to involve supporting the security line of operations. That meant patrolling across the AOO, establishing observation posts and checkpoints, in the hope of deterring or interdicting Taliban fighters.[27] The Griffins were a well-equipped and highly-trained force, with excellent protected mobility, provided by their vehicles, including the Eagle (an up-armoured version of the ubiquitous US Hummer) and the Piranha, an eight-wheeled, armoured ambulance. They also wielded significant organic firepower, from numerous .50in heavy and 7.62mm M/62 light machine guns, which had been issued to the Danes at a scale the British could only dream of. The latter was an updated version of the fearsome German MG42 of Second World War vintage – old, but with a high cyclic rate of fire (1,200 rounds per minute) that sounded like ripping cotton. They had been deployed practically free of national caveats that might have limited their utility. The only stipulation by the Danish Government was that the troops could not operate directly with indigenous forces.[28]

Once they had arrived in Helmand their expected mission changed. Instead of focusing on the Bastion – Lashkar Gah – Gereshk triangle they were given three new potential tasks. The first two – conducting counter-smuggling patrols on the border with Nimruz Province or disrupting Taliban resupply activities on Highway 1 – would have suited them very well. However, the third – garrisoning the District Centre at Musa Qal'eh – was much less appealing. But this was the task most favoured by the Battlegroup. The Danes were not impressed. Like the Pathfinders, the Griffins were intended to be agile, relying for protection on their speed and manoeuvrability as much as their armour. They were good soldiers and doughty fighters, but, in common with the Pathfinders, they were not at their best in a static role, preferring to be on the move, out in the open desert, where they could see the enemy coming, and choose if, when and where to engage. The Musa Qal'eh option did not play to their strengths. They were all about mobility and they felt they would be misemployed in a fixed, ground-holding role. Their armoured vehicles would be almost useless in the restricted urban environment of the town, they argued. They could do it, but it would not be the optimum use of their capabilities.[29] This view had been passed up their national chain of command, to the Danish Contingent Commander in Kabul, and to Brigadier Ed Butler.

---

25 Major Gary Wilkinson, Battery Commander, I Battery, 7RHA, Op Herrick IV, interview with author.
26 Major Lars Ulslev Johannesen, *The Tigers and the Taliban* (Copenhagen: Story House and ISIS Audio LLC A/S, 2013), p.71.
27 Major Lars Ulslev Johannesen, interview with author.
28 Major Lars Ulslev Johannesen, interview with author.
29 Major Lars Ulslev Johannesen, interview with author.

He (Butler) understood the concerns, but pointed out that there were other, broader considerations to be taken into account.[30] Johannesen, recalled: 'I tried to reshape the mission to better suit our capabilities but, in the end, I was ordered to occupy the District Centre and that is what I did'.[31] Stuart Tootal felt the Danes took some persuading before eventually accepting the task.[32]

The operation to insert the Griffins was named Op Barabar (Pashto for even or equal). The plan was for the Danes to move from Bastion, across the desert, to Musa Qal'eh, keeping away from roads where the threat from IEDs was at its greatest. 'We knew there had been ambushes on the road, and that the off-road routes could be mined. I balanced the risks and decided on the desert option', explained Johannesen. He had mine maps that had been prepared by the UN but these were not up-to-date.[33] It had been agreed that once they had arrived on the outskirts of the town, the Pathfinders and ANP would secure the road from the DC, through the Bazaar, to the beginning of the green zone. The Griffins would then move east across the western wadi, and along the secured route into the compound.

Although the route through the desert reduced the risk of ambush or striking a Taliban roadside bomb, there were still dangers lurking below the rough, rock-strewn, dusty surface of the *Dasht-e-Margo*. On 22 July, as the Danish column, consisting of the squadron's vehicles and some additional logistics trucks, was approaching the town, one of the Eagles struck a mine. The device was not a Taliban IED but part of an old legacy minefield that had been laid by the Soviet army during their invasion in the 1980s. It was not marked on coalition maps, but locals had indicated it in their own way, by building a line of mounds, each topped with a white-painted stone. These could be seen clearly from the road, but, unfortunately for the Danes, they were almost invisible as they approached from the desert. Several other vehicles had driven over the same ground just before the strike occurred.

The Eagle was badly damaged and all three occupants were injured, although none of them seriously. They were airlifted back to Bastion. With no prospect of being able to recover the vehicle, Johannesen ordered a patrol forward to remove the sensitive encryption keys from the radios. The stricken vehicle, with its radios and Electronic Counter Measures (ECM) equipment still in place, was then 'denied' – destroyed so that it could be of no use to the enemy.[34] This was achieved courtesy of a Hellfire missile, followed by a burst of 30mm cannon shells, fired from a British Apache helicopter. The convoy moved off again towards its objective.[35]

As the Griffins approached the western wadi, the Pathfinders could see the Taliban rushing to prepare an ambush. Alerting the Danes, the Paras called in an airstrike and a Harrier jet dropped a 500lb bomb which seemed to deter the attackers for a time. The relief convoy continued slowly towards the green zone. From there, the road would take them to the western end of the bazaar. At that point, they would be about 1km from the DC. A hundred metres from the green zone, an insurgent, disguised under a blue burqa, launched an RPG at the vehicles. It missed, but was quickly followed by heavy small-arms fire from nearby buildings. The soldiers suppressed this in a few moments, but the road ahead grew narrower as it passed between low walls and ditches, reducing the Danes' ability to manoeuvre.

The advanced element reported that there were hard left and right turns ahead as the route began to enter the western end of the bazaar, meaning the convoy would have to reduce speed,

---

30 Johannesen, *The Tigers and the Taliban*, p.73.
31 Major Lars Ulslev Johannesen, interview with author.
32 Tootal, *Danger Close*, p.124.
33 Major Llars Ulslev Johannesen, Interview with author.
34 Major Lars Ulslev Johannesen, Interview with author.
35 Johannesen, *The Tigers and the Taliban*, p.89.

becoming even more vulnerable. Two oil drums spotted in the middle of the road, potential IEDs, seemed to indicate that the route was no longer viable. Johannesen had a big decision to make:

> I had the Pathfinders in the DC telling me they could see a number of Taliban, dug-in, waiting for the convoy, and the possibility of IEDs in the road. They were saying abort. I had the reconnaissance troop commander out in front, telling me we should not continue. I had another troop commander at the back urging me forward. Headquarters was pushing me to carry on.[36]

The officer needed to take a few minutes to get his thoughts together. He went back to his vehicle and conducted a mini-estimate in his head, going through all the factors, just as he had been trained to do. When that was done, the way ahead was clear. They would need to withdraw. But his new-found clarity did not make the decision any easier. 'I knew we needed to reach the DC. The Pathfinders were running low on food, water and ammunition, which was contained in the supply trucks that were part of the convoy'.[37] In the end, the deciding factor was the unacceptable risk to life and limb:

> It was obvious that if we went ahead, we were going to take casualties. Of course, these go with the job. But it seemed to me that we were likely to sustain losses that could not be justified in the circumstances. We would be of little use in Musa Qal'eh if we had lost a lot of men and vehicles on the way in.[38]

With a heavy heart, Johannesen pressed the transmit button on his radio and ordered the convoy to withdraw back out into the open desert. 'It was the hardest decision I have ever made'.[39]

Pathfinders Sergeant Major, Andy Newell, accompanying the Danes, was deeply frustrated. He wanted to walk in on his own, whatever danger lurked along the way, until good sense prevailed and he climbed back into a vehicle, still grumbling about needing to be with his men.[40] Out in the desert, in a hastily-organised overnight harbour area, with time to ponder on the events of the day, Johannesen felt he had let down the Paras and that the Danes had lost face.[41] They would have to go back. But that would require a new route and a different approach.

For their second attempt, the Griffins plotted a long and circuitous course that took them through steep, narrow mountainous passes, where they lost a supply truck, before bringing them back down towards the town from the north. Johannesen had asked for, and been given, permission to use preliminary fires. This meant he could use aircraft, artillery and attack helicopters to strike suspected enemy positions before they opened fire. An Apache gunship, using its sensors, swept the route ahead to identify potential threats. After the artillery and air strikes, the road in seemed quiet. As the convoy slowly made its way over the wadi and into the bazaar area there were no signs of enemy activity. The vehicles moved quietly, their crews using night vision equipment to pick their way along the road. One crewman from each vehicle had dismounted, moving on foot, ready to give covering fire if required. The lead Eagle was less than 100m away from the District Centre when a single shot rang out into the darkness. The men tensed, expecting this to herald

---

36 Major Lars Ulslev Johannesen, interview with author.
37 Major Lars Ulslev Johannesen, interview with author.
38 Major Lars Ulslev Johannesen, interview with author.
39 Major Lars Ulslev Johannesen, interview with author.
40 Johannesen, *Tigers and Taliban*, p.97.
41 Johannesen, *Tigers and Taliban*, p.97.

a Taliban onslaught. But no further fire followed. The shot had been discharged by a nervous Afghan police officer guarding the main gate, striking Andy Newell, on the arm. A Danish soldier sustained a damaged leg after being struck by his own vehicle in the following confusion. Both were evacuated back to Bastion by Lynx helicopter.[42] A quick assessment of the situation in the DC, the following morning, convinced Johannesen that when the Pathfinders pulled out, he and his cavalry soldiers were going to need infantry support and an indirect fire capability to try to keep the insurgents at arm's length.

The Pathfinders had been coming under increasing pressure from the Taliban, and without their own indirect fire assets, they were heavily dependent on fast air to keep them out of trouble. The Danes were better-equipped than the Paras they were replacing, particularly in relation to the firepower they could deliver through the potent combination of their heavy and light machine guns. However, the available direct-fire weapons – rifles, machine guns, anti-tank missiles – could only engage targets they could see and which were within the effective range of the individual weapon systems. There were signs that the insurgents were making more use of stand-off weapons such as mortars and 107mm rockets that could fire from longer ranges, often out of direct line-of-sight from the compound. Coalition air power was feared by the Taliban, but it could not be turned on and off like a lightbulb. Sometimes there was a delay in getting fast jets to support the Musa Qal'eh garrison and it was this gap that the mortars could help to fill. Having the ability to target enemy firing points with precision, beyond direct-fire range, would make a significant difference to the defenders' ability to keep the Taliban at bay, the OC believed.[43] When Johannesen presented his shopping list to battlegroup HQ, Tootal felt it represented not so much a request as a demand – the Danes' 'preconditions for staying'.[44] But he needed the Griffins to remain and if that meant giving them more troops, his only realistic option was to comply. This was one of the tensions involved in coalition warfare. He agreed to provide a rifle platoon and a mortar section from The Royal Irish Regiment.

Having just witnessed how difficult it had been to get the relief force into Musa Qal'eh, the garrison recognised the scale of the challenge of extracting the Pathfinders and inserting reinforcements and vital supplies. They recommended a battlegroup-level operation.[45] However, back at Bastion, staff officers at Battlegroup Headquarters disagreed. They felt the men in the DC were over-estimating the strength of the insurgents and that the Relief-in-Place (RIP) could be completed using the garrison's own resources, supported by air and artillery, with Scimitar and Spartan tracked reconnaissance vehicles of the Household Cavalry Regiment providing distraction to the west.[46] Events would demonstrate that, as usual, the men on the spot had a much better appreciation of the situation than their headquarters colleagues.

Operation Nakhod, as the extraction was named, took place, in daylight, on 1 August 2006 and was an unmitigated disaster. The plan was for three troops of D Squadron, Household Cavalry Regiment, to distract the Taliban by approaching from the west. This would, it was hoped, draw away some of the insurgents from the centre of town and make it easier for the Pathfinders to pull out. Meanwhile, the Danes and Paras would move out from the compound, cross the western wadi and clear and secure the route to and from a helicopter landing zone, 5km from the DC, into which supplies would be dropped by Chinook. The Danes would collect the stores and move them back to the DC (requiring a number of return trips to lift several tons of food and ammunition)

---

42 Johannesen, *Tigers and Taliban*, p.120.
43 Major Lars Ulslev Johannesen, interview with author.
44 Tootal, *Danger Close*, p.154.
45 Major Lars Ulslev Johannesen, interview with author.
46 Major Lars Ulslev Johannesen, interview with author.

while the Paras held the LZ. Once that was complete, the Danes would collapse back into the compound while the Pathfinders would make their way across the desert to Bastion.

The operation went bad almost from the beginning. As the garrison prepared to move out of the compound, they could hear the sound of gunfire and explosions coming from the west.[47]

The Household Cavalry Regiment's lightly-armoured vehicles had been making their way from Now Zad towards Musa Qal'eh when they ran into an ambush. RPG and small-arms fire raked the vehicles before a massive roadside bomb destroyed a Spartan. A Scimitar was also badly damaged and abandoned at the ambush site.[48] Two crewmen and an artillery Forward Observation Officer (FOO), travelling with them, had died and a fourth soldier was severely injured.[49]

Back at the compound, the Danes and the Pathfinders, aware of the fighting, but not yet the full impact, mounted their vehicles and drove out of the main gate, through the bazaar towards the wadi and the green zone. The Griffins, in the lead, had covered about 2km when they came under fire from RPGs, rifles and machine guns. At the same time, the DC, now being held by a single troop, reported that it was under attack. The Pathfinders, who had been following the Danes towards the wadi, also came under fire. With the DC at risk of being overrun, Johannesen, and the Pathfinders' boss, Major Nick Wight-Boycott, decided there was no option but to pull back to the compound. Discussing the events later, the two men agreed that there appeared to be more than 200 Taliban fighters in the town, who had been capable of launching four separate, but obviously coordinated, and almost-simultaneous attacks.[50]

Operation Snakebite

With the Taliban clearly present in significant numbers, and obviously on the alert, Tootal finally concluded that the only feasible way to extract his Pathfinders and resupply the Danes, was to mount a battlegroup-scale operation, supported by attack helicopters, fast air and the guns of 7RHA – exactly what Wight-Boycott and Johannesen had recommended earlier. Even then, and despite such an impressive array of combat power, he could not be wholly certain that everything would go his way. After some deliberation, Operation Mar Chichel – Pashto for Snakebite – was born.

The plan for Snakebite was complex and would require careful coordination to ensure that the various moving parts came together at the right place and time to deliver the desired result. The scheme of manoeuvre described a four-phase operation. 3 Para's Patrols Platoon together with Somme Platoon and part of Barrosa Platoon, would accompany a logistics column as it drove across the desert, and then secure a helicopter LZ into which B and C Companies would air-assault. Supported by Canadian infantry in their LAVs, the rifle companies would clear two small villages and the neighbouring green zone on the western bank of the wadi. The Paras' mortar section and a second team from the Royal Irish, would provide local overwatch from high ground to the north-west of the DC, close to the Roshan mobile telephone mast that was to become well-known in future iterations of Operation Herrick. Fast jets, helicopter gunships and the guns of 7RHA would be on-call to provide support as the Household Cavalry Regiment (HCR), in their tracked Scimitar and Sultan reconnaissance vehicles, protected the path across the wadi. While

---

47 Major Lars Uslev Johannesen, interview with author.
48 Tootal, *Danger Close,* p.149.
49 MOD website, <https://www.gov.uk/government/fatalities/captain-alex-eida-2nd-lieutenant-ralph-johnson-and-lance-corporal-ross-nicholls-killed-in-afghanistan#:~:text=The%20soldiers%20were%20killed%20following,grenades%20and%20heavy%20machine%20guns>, accessed 25 January 2024.
50 Major Lars Uslev Johannesen, interview with author.

that was happening, the Danes would move out from the DC and clear a route through the bazaar down to the eastern bank of the dry watercourse. Once the secure corridor had been established, the reinforcements – Somme Platoon and the Royal Irish mortars – would move in and the Pathfinders would mount up in their WMIKs and drive out with the logistics vehicles. When they were safely through the green zone and out into the desert, the corridor would collapse, the Danes pulling back into the compound while the Paras, the HCR, the Canadians, Lieutenant Martin's Barrosa Platoon, and the logistics vehicles, would recover back to Bastion by road. The two 3 Para rifle companies would fly back by Chinook.

After acclimatisation and guard duties at Camp Bastion, Barrosa Platoon had said their farewells to their Somme Platoon colleagues and helicoptered east to Gereshk to support B Company, 3 Para. Lieutenant Martin and his men were not displeased to leave the dirty, dusty Bastion behind for the opportunity to get on with some 'proper soldiering'. 'Our deployment to Goreshk was really useful in terms of allowing us to shake out and gain experience of working together', the Platoon Commander explained. About two-thirds of the platoon had come from B Company and knew each other well, but the remainder were from other parts of the battalion and although they were all well-trained, there had been no opportunity to work as a single team prior to departure. They needed to get better acquainted and to build that mutual understanding and trust that is so vital to small-unit cohesion:

> Gereshk was quite different from being in Bastion. We were able to patrol into the local area, and begin to interact with the villagers, as well as taking on some of the more mundane tasks of QRF and guarding the base. We also conducted Vehicle Check Points, helped to recover downed UAVs and took part in a few air-mobile operations.[51]

But just as they were getting into the 'groove', they received a warning order telling them to return to Bastion and prepare to support the extraction of the Pathfinder Platoon. Platoon Sergeant, Stephen 'Gilly' Gilchrist, was not sorry to see the back of Gereshk. 'I don't think they [3 Para] really wanted us there', Sergeant Gilchrist reflected. 'Obviously, we weren't Para Regiment, and despite the fact that we had been working beside them in the same brigade for years, they looked down on us, and that was hard to take'.[52] Ranger Davy Pepper experienced some of the same attitude. As the platoon radio operator, he needed to get radios and ECM from the Paras so the Barrosa men could go on patrol. This proved to be easier said than done. 'They were pretty unwelcoming to say the least', he remembered.[53]

The platoon was helicoptered back to Bastion, landing into the hustle and bustle of a battle-group headquarters preparing to deliver mission orders. There was excitement, laced with some apprehension. Martin was dismayed to discover that his platoon was to be split, some supporting the insertion whilst the remainder would provide the infantry element for the Medical Emergency Response Team (MERT), on standby at Bastion:

> I was delighted with the mission, but disappointed that the platoon was to be broken up. I fought hard to get the whole platoon on the task, but the CO was adamant. We needed to provide support for the MERT so two thirds would go with me to Musa Qal'eh and the others would be on stand-by for MERT tasks, commanded by Sergeant Gilchrist.[54]

---

51 Lieutenant Paul Martin, interview with author.
52 Sergeant Stephen Gilchrist, interview with author.
53 Ranger Davy Pepper, interview with author.
54 Lieutenant Paul Martin, interview with author.

Lieutenant Martin prepared and delivered platoon orders and he and his men made the necessary preparations for the 70km road move north. 'It was really expeditionary. Our communications were just about working. We had no night vision capability and the mapping was pretty basic. We were told we didn't need to carry Electronic Counter Measures (ECM) because the IED threat was low, but we took man-packed equipment, just in case. And off we went'.[55]

The route took them through several small settlements and gave the Barrosa Platoon soldiers their first real opportunity to see Afghan farmers at close range. 'We had seen and interacted with the townsfolk at Gereshk, but this was really different', recalled Lieutenant Martin. 'We would drive through these eerie villages and there was a difference in the way the people looked at us. I could sense the hatred'.[56] The experience was unsettling and ensured that the guards remained on high alert when the column leaguered-up for the night under the stars. The journey took the best part of two days in vehicles that had been built for utility rather than comfort or speed. Lance Corporal McClurg, in a battered Pinzgauer truck, was concerned about the lack of protection provided by the vehicles. 'We shored them up by adding some sandbags and anything else we could find, but they were in a pretty bad state and keeping them going was a mission in itself', he recalled.[57]

Corporal Danny Groves noted in his diary:

> The journey to the lie-up position was pretty uneventful by Helmand standards. The only noteworthy event was when [Corporal] John Nixon broke one of the Pinzgauers. The patrol commander was about to destroy the vehicle but at the last minute it was decided that it could be 'CASEVAC'd' back to Bastion by Chinook and a replacement delivered the same way. We eventually reached the lie-up position [on the western outskirts of Musa Qal'eh] at about 1900, just as it was getting dark. After liaising with the artillery Forward Observation Officer (FOO) and inputting possible targets into the FCA (hand-held fire control computer), we all got our heads down.[58]

The HCR's Scimitars and Spartans, which were supposed to clear and secure the wadi, had not arrived. Most had broken down on the journey and had to be towed back to Bastion.

At 0500 the next morning, 3 Para Patrols Platoon, supported by Somme and Barrosa platoons, left to clear the wadi and the Landing Zone to the west of the town. During the planning it had been discovered that the spot chosen for the helicopter LZ might have been part of an old Soviet minefield. The Patrols Platoon Commander (Captain Tom Fehley) knew he did not have sufficient time to do a proper mine-clearance. The troops arriving in the Chinooks would have to accept some extra risk.[59] Meanwhile, the MFCs and the mortar sections moved to high ground near the Roshan Tower mobile telephone mast, which was on a promontory to the north-west of the DC. The mortar teams set up their base-plates and barrels while Harding and McClurg established the Battlegroup Anchor OP location, from where they could get eyes on the town, spread out below. From their lofty perch, the MFCs began to adjust the mortars onto various targets in and around the green zone. It was possible to land a mortar round in the general vicinity of a target by firing 'off the map', using a hand-held computer to calculate charge, range, direction and elevation. But to ensure the required accuracy, and take account of wind direction, air pressure and other factors,

---

55 Lieutenant Paul Martin, interview with author.
56 Lieutenant Paul Martin, interview with author.
57 Lance Corporal Rab McClurg, interview with author.
58 Corporal Danny Groves, personal diary entry, 6 August 2006.
59 Tootal, *Danger Close,* p.155.

the fire had to be corrected, so that the mortar bombs fell exactly where they were required. This involved firing a projectile at an intended target, spotting the 'fall of shot' (where the round had landed) and then adjusting the bearing and elevation until the rounds were striking the desired impact point.

In this case, the targets being adjusted were the objectives to be assaulted by B and C Companies as they moved to secure the western end of the route into the DC. Once the MFCs were happy that the mortars were on-target, the details were recorded so fire could be brought down quickly when required. The fact that the Paras had entrusted Harding and McClurg with this important job was testimony to the men's skills, abilities and reputations. 'We were able to adjust all targets comfortably within an hour and that was a really good standard', Harding explained. 'If they didn't know what a high-quality team they had supporting them before that, they certainly knew when we had finished'.[60]

With mortar targeting completed, the Chinooks began to arrive out to the west, and the assaulting companies dismounted, thankful to discover that there were no Russian mines present after all. The MFCs could see them form up on their line of departure, orientate themselves onto their attack bearings and commence their advance. This was the signal to begin to call down fire to suppress the enemy as the Paras moved towards their objectives. The impacts of the mortars striking the targets also helped to orientate the attacking troops by indicating the positions to be assaulted.[61] In his diary, Corporal Groves recorded that these were the first HE rounds fired in anger by Royal Irish mortarmen since the Korean War.[62]

As soon as the assault was in progress, Harding and McClurg handed over to the MFCs who were accompanying the advancing companies. Corporal Groves' section supported B Company while the 3 Para team provided cover for C Company. In addition to the mortars, fire support during the course of the assault included bombing runs by A-10 ground-attack aircraft and rocket-firing Apache attack helicopters as well as artillery fire from the guns of 7RHA.

The operation to clear the green zone took about five and a half hard, painstaking, energy-sapping hours to complete, mainly because once the rifle companies had secured a section of the route, the engineers had to check it for boobytraps and IEDs, a long, slow, but vitally important part of the plan.[63] When Tootal was content that the area was safe, the Canadians in their LAVs moved forward to occupy the open ground between the eastern edge of the green zone and the western side of the town. At this point, Groves and his team stopped firing, broke down the mortars and moved, with the MFCs, to the wadi to rendezvous with Somme Platoon in anticipation of the move into the DC. With fighting still going on seemingly all around them, the mortar team were told that they, and Somme Platoon, were to be crammed into the Pinzgauers for the journey up through the bazaar to the compound. This part of the route had been secured by the Danes. Tootal has claimed it took 45 minutes longer than expected to complete the task.[64] The Danes' OC is adamant, however, that the job was accomplished in 30 minutes, well within the original hour that had been allocated. There had been a delay, but that was down to Tootal's failure to order the Danes forward. According to the plan, they were not to commence the clearance until directed to do so by Battlegroup TAC. This was to ensure that they would not move out of the DC and thus into potential enemy fire, until the wadi and green zone had been secured.[65]

---

60 Corporal John Harding, Interview with author.
61 Corporal John Harding, interview with author.
62 Corporal Danny Groves, personal diary entry, 7 August 2006.
63 Bishop, *3 Para,* p.168.
64 Tootal, *Danger Close,* p.157
65 Major Lars Ulslev Johannesen, interview with author.

The reinforcements had been warned that they were likely to come under fire as they emerged from the wadi… and they did. The original plan called for the route to be screened by smoke to conceal the move. But the delay in clearing the bazaar had meant the smoke screen had dissipated by the time they came to make their move. Having collapsed the mortars in anticipation of the insertion, it was not possible to thicken it up again. Corporal Harding remembered:

> As soon as we broke cover from the wadi the vehicles were absolutely pummelled with heavy PKM fire. How any of us got from one side to the other unscathed, I do not know. The Pinz was a brilliant little vehicle, but it offered scant protection against machine gun fire. It had more holes in it than a golf course. The radiator was shot out, there was steam everywhere.[66]

Lance Corporal McClurg, who was driving, recalled being told to take it slow and easy, but as soon as the rounds started to slam into the vehicle 'I put my foot to the floor and hammered as hard as I could, straight up through the bazaar and into the main gate of the compound. The Pathfinders were pleased to see us'.[67]

For Sergeant Brangan, the abiding memory of the insertion was seeing the Pathfinders as they were making their way out. 'They were laughing. They were clearly happy to be leaving and that made me wonder exactly what we were getting ourselves into?'[68] It was now 1330 hours.

The way out was just as hazardous as the insertion. As the Pathfinders and the departing supply vehicles approached the wadi, they came under the same high volume of fire that had greeted the reinforcements. Unfortunately, on this occasion, the troops were not to be so fortunate. A WMIK, being crewed by soldiers of the Royal Logistics Corps (RLC), part of the resupply column, took a number of rounds, two of which hit Private Andrew Barrie Cutts (19), of 13 Air Assault Support Regiment, RLC. Lieutenant Martin was two vehicles behind, moving along a wadi when disaster struck.

> We had taken a few rounds into the side of the vehicle and returned fire. Then Private Cutts was hit in the eye and in his leg and the situation quickly became very intense.
>
> We needed to find cover so we could administer first aid so we pushed through the wadi and round behind a nearby settlement where my driver and I did the best we could to treat the wounds.[69]

But all the work was in vain. Private Cutts could not be saved and his body was transported back to Bastion with Tootal and his TAC headquarters team, as they extracted by helicopter.

After the relief of reaching the compound without casualties, the death of Cutts weighed heavily on the Royal Irish soldiers as the adrenalin-induced euphoria of the morning's events evaporated and the harsh realities of their situation began to hit home. Lieutenant Martin and his men accompanied the Pathfinders out into the desert, and after a short stop and a quick 'bonnet-brief' they agreed to push on for as long as the light held. Nick Wight-Boycott was keen to get back to Bastion as quickly as possible as some of his soldiers were due to catch a flight out for R&R.[70] After travelling about 40kms, the convoy stopped again as dusk approached. Wight-Boycott decided that he was going to carry on after dark, using night vision goggles, but that was not an option for the

---

66 Corporal John Harding, interview with author
67 Lance Corporal Rab McClurg, interview with author
68 Sergeant PJ Brangan, interview with author.
69 Lieutenant Paul Martin, interview with author.
70 Lieutenant Paul Martin, interview with author.

Barrosa men. They had not been issued with NVGs before they left Bastion and without them there was no way they could continue driving in the dark. 'When I told Nick we had no NVGs he just looked at me in disbelief. I was disappointed and embarrassed, but there was nothing I could do so we parted company. The Pathfinders carried on towards Bastion while we leaguered-up for the night'.[71] Paul Martin recalled the beauty of the Afghan sky with its blanket of bright stars, and the sadness as he and his soldiers thought about the loss of Private Cutts. 'That was the thing about Afghanistan. Every single day was colossally bad, horrific, tragic, filled with so many emotions and adrenalin…and then at night, beautiful, so picturesque'.[72]

Back at the compound, there had been little time for backslapping and glad-handing. The MFCs and Groves needed to find a suitable position in which to establish the mortar line and get the base-plates bedded in so they could support the Pathfinders on their way out… and time was slipping away from them. Together with the Danish Commander, the mortarmen walked the interior perimeter of the compound – now known as Combat Outpost (COP) Griffin – to orientate themselves and to decide where the two mortar barrels should be located. There was not much real estate to play with. According to the manual, they needed a minimum of 40 metres between barrels, but that was impossible to achieve within the cramped confines of the compound. They could only manage about 20 metres of separation. In the end they settled for a spot, to the south of the Alamo, where they had the protection of a low building, providing some cover for the mortar detachments. 'There were still going to be rounds coming in, but we had selected the position that gave us as much protection as possible, whilst allowing the mortars to engage in a 360-degree arc', recalled Harding.[73] Groves agreed it was not ideal, but it was workable, offering a modicum of protection and communications with the Ops Room and the fighting positions.[74]

Their first concern was how they were supposed to hold the DC against Taliban attack, given its location and the nearness of the adjoining buildings. As Company Sergeant Major Jo Scrivener said later, the enemy would often appear no more than eight feet away and the fighting was 'up close and hideously violent'.[75] Corporal John Harding remembered:

> It was just the worst possible place to defend. There were buildings all around that overlooked the compound. Some of them were higher than the fighting positions. We really should have found somewhere else that was more suitable. If the problem was not giving up the seat of governance, why didn't we just move the seat of governance?[76]

Apart from the obvious issues with the location, Lance Corporal McClurg's first impression of the DC was a bit more positive than that of his colleagues:

> I thought the space inside the wall was OK. I hadn't had time to consider the negatives. I was a 21 years-old lad. This was all new and exciting, and I was in the middle of it with all my best mates. I was still on a high after the drive up through the bazaar, which, at the time, I thought had been pretty awesome.[77]

---

71 Lieutenant Paul Martin, interview with author.
72 Lieutenant Paul Martin, interview with author.
73 Corporal John Harding, interview with author
74 Corporal Danny Groves, personal diary entry for 7 August 2006.
75 Warrant Officer Class II Jo Scrivener, 'An Unbelievable Military Story', H-Hour Podcast, Hugh Keir (5 February 2025), <https://open.substack.com/pub/hughkeir/p/livestream-recording-254-full-interview?r=2h98zl&utm_medium=ios>, accessed 22 February 2025.
76 Corporal John Harding, interview with author.
77 Lance Corporal Rab McClurg, interview with author.

Whatever their views about the compound, there was little time for pointless introspection. The situation was what it was. PJ Brangan was talking to his Danish opposite number at around 1545 when the Dane looked at his watch and indicated that an attack was due. Fifteen minutes later, as predicted, the Taliban launched a probing assault from the north, and the Danes reacted quickly, hammering the attackers with their .50in heavy machine guns.[78] The mortars took the opportunity to register a number of targets and, in doing so, to send a clear warning to the enemy: 'the 81s are in town'.[79] The Taliban got the message and withdrew, but returned again shortly before 1900hrs, this time firing from the east. The MFCs quickly identified the target and called in a fire mission. Watching from the sangars, the Danish soldiers reported that the position had been flattened and at least one enemy combatant had been killed. The Danes were delighted with their new firepower. However, the dense urban environment was posing problems for the defenders. It was hard to spot the fall of the HE rounds among the buildings. To compensate, the MFCs switched to firing smoke to adjust and once they were on-target, they used HE to neutralise the position. By the end of their first day in action, including supporting the Paras during their assault, Groves and his team had expended 36 rounds of HE and 24 of White Phosphorous (smoke).[80]

The following day (8 August) provided an opportunity for the newcomers to become properly acquainted with their surroundings and it was clear from early on that shade was going to be in short supply during the hot daylight hours. The mortarmen and the rifle platoon used the time to create sun-breaks and generally improve their fighting positions. The Taliban kept a low profile until early afternoon, when they launched a new attack, heralded by the whoosh-bang of a recoilless rifle round striking its target somewhere in the compound. The men in the sangars opened fire at once, followed quickly by a call for fire from the MFCs, who had spotted a firing point to the south. The incoming rocket had impacted near the Observation Post, on the roof of the Alamo, where Harding and McClurg had been positioned. They had been shaken but unhurt, and were soon back in the fight. The remainder of the day was quiet.

First Blood

The Danes had warned the reinforcements that Taliban snipers were active, and movement within the compound, especially during daylight hours, was inclined to draw their fire. Marksmanship was generally not one of the Taliban's strengths, but there was always a danger that one of them would get lucky. That fact was driven home with horrific consequences on 9 August when the Royal Irish contingent suffered their first casualties. It had been agreed with the Danish OC that, having had time to acclimatise to their new surroundings, the riflemen of Somme Platoon would take over some of the fighting positions, beginning that morning. Discussing the move the night before with his officer, Captain Mark Johnson, Platoon Sergeant, PJ Brangan, had recommended that the first position to be held by the Royal Irish would be the Outpost, and that Corporal Ally McKinney's section would be given the task. McKinney was one of the battalion's characters, but he was also very experienced and highly regarded by all. There was no doubt he was the right man for the job. 'We got Ally in and briefed him. He couldn't wait to get stuck in', the Platoon Sergeant noted.[81]

---

78   Sergeant PJ Brangan, interview with author.
79   Corporal Danny Groves, diary entry, 7 August 2006.
80   Corporal Danny Groves, diary entry, 7 August 2006.
81   Sergeant PJ Brangan, interview with author.

The next morning, Brangan, McKinney and one of the Danes were having a chat and a brew and the Corporal had quipped: 'I bet as soon as my fat arse hits the sandbags up there them Taliban bastards will engage us'.[82] It was meant as a joke, but it turned out to be prophetic. At 0830hrs, Corporal McKinney and his section walked to the northern wall of the compound, clambered across the rickety ladder and entered the Outpost, making their way up to the fighting position on the roof. At 0915hrs, Corporal John Harding, scanning his arcs through binoculars from the roof of the Alamo, watched in horror as a round struck McKinney in the head.

> He was up on the roof of the outpost, 100m from me. I was looking past the Outpost, at a potential target, when the bullet struck. I saw the round connecting with his head and him going down. I didn't know it was Ally at the time. When I saw the impact, I thought "there's no way he's alive". But he was.[83]

Sergeant Brangan heard the crack of the high-velocity rounds and seconds later, the radio message that there was a man down on the Outpost. Grabbing his body armour and rifle he sprinted to the position. After the initial shock, McKinney's section was back up from cover and returning fire, the Danes had opened up with their heavy machine guns and the noise was deafening. As he climbed up onto the roof, Brangan could see that the position was taking heavy fire:

> When I got onto the roof a lad called Armstrong had blood coming from his ear. A medic had a look, decided it was only a scratch, and put a field dressing on it. To the left I could see a body on the floor with the Danish medics working at him. I crawled over and the medic asked me if I knew the casualty. I said it was Ally and he told me to talk to him. I grabbed his hand and called his name. He squeezed my hand and I told him "you're not going to die on this roof".

Brangan held a dressing in place on his head while the medic applied a second. 'Once they had him stabilised, we moved him down into the compound and from there to the RAP, and into the capable hands of the Danish Medical Officer'.[84] Meanwhile, the JOC had sent the nine-liner MEDEVAC request to Battlegroup Headquarters, classifying McKinney as T1 (critical) and Armstrong as T3 (walking wounded). Ranger Ricky Armstrong had lost a piece of his earlobe. He was badly shaken but otherwise physically in good shape.

Rab McClurg, in one of the southern sangars, was trying to direct the mortars onto another group of attackers who were firing from dense scrub, when he heard the 'man down' message coming over the radio, followed by a call for medics:

> For many of us, and certainly for me, it was the first time we had heard that message for real. A lot of things went through my mind. Do I go and try to help? Do I stay where I am? In the end, though, I knew I had to stay focused on what I was doing at my end of the compound. We were fighting our own battle and we needed to deal with the problem in front of us. I was sure the medics would be handling events at the other end.[85]

---

82 Sergeant PJ Brangan, interview with author.
83 Corporal John Harding, interview with author.
84 Sergeant P J Brangan, interview with author.
85 Lance Corporal Rab McClurg, interview with author.

Meanwhile, the Medical Emergency Response Team (MERT) was being scrambled to airlift the casualties to the hospital at Bastion. With the firefight continuing, the LZ, to the north of the compound, was clearly going to be a dangerous place for the big evacuation helicopter to put down. It was essential to silence the attackers' fire before the aircraft could land. This was only achieved when American A-10s and British Apache helicopters, raked the firing position while the Danes' Forward Air Controller (FAC or JTAC) called in a Joint Direct Attack Munition (JDAM) strike.

The four-hour delay in getting McKinney and Armstrong airlifted out was the cause of considerable ire among the garrison. Corporal Cliff Tweed was particularly angry. McKinney was his closest and oldest friend in the platoon, and the cold, logical balancing of risk that had to be part of the process leading to the decision to send the MERT was not how he was thinking at the time. 'The delay didn't sit well with anyone, but now, having matured, I understand the concerns about the possibility of losing a Chinook and a MERT team and why it took so long to get Ally and Ricky airlifted out'.[86] The Electronic Warfare Team, listening in on Taliban radio transmissions from the JOC, reported later that one of the attackers had been killed. This was welcome news, recorded by Danny Groves in his diary.[87] He would not have been alone in hoping that the dead Taliban was the man who had shot McKinney.

Remarkably, Ally McKinney survived the head-shot. After life-saving surgery in Bastion, he received further treatment in Pakistan before being flown back to the UK, where he spent months recovering at the Queen Elizabeth Medical Centre in Birmingham. He was then admitted to the Defence Medical Rehabilitation Centre at Hedley Court, near Epsom in Surrey, where he had to relearn to walk. His eyesight was also affected. The high-velocity bullet had passed through his Kevlar helmet, entering his head above his left eye. It went through his brain before exiting from his scull above his right ear, causing significant damage on the way. In an interview for a Belfast newspaper, two years after the event, understandably, he could not recall much about the incident. 'The only thing I can remember is that I was talking to another soldier at the time'. He was told later that he was a miracle case. The injuries he had sustained would have proved fatal 99 times out of 100. If he had not turned to the right the bullet would have gone through his eye and killed him instantly.[88]

The Royal Irish soldiers were not the only newcomers to Musa Qal'eh that August. Intelligence reports suggested that the Taliban were reinforcing their presence in the town. A new commander had arrived and with him had come a significant number of much more capable foot soldiers, seemingly better trained than those encountered thus far. The Danish OC, Major Johannesen, had also noticed signs that the enemy had begun to adopt different tactics. There was a definite improvement in the enemy's fire discipline. Up until now, the insurgents had seemed to fire indiscriminately in long bursts. Their shots were mostly unaimed, and, notwithstanding the damage done to Corporal McKinney, had been largely ineffective. They had shown little understanding of fieldcraft or the use of fire and movement. Recently, however, the firing had been in short bursts and accuracy had definitely improved. It was also noticeable that their use of mortars had become more effective. At the start, they might fire five or six rounds without ever getting close to the compound. Now they seemed to be hitting the DC with at least half of the shots fired. The intelligence assessment was that taken together, these developments indicated the enemy's

---

86 Corporal Cliff Tweed, interview with author.
87 Corporal Danny Groves, diary entry, 9 August 2006.
88 'Taliban Sniper Shot Me in the Head', *Sunday Life* (27 July 2008), https://www.belfasttelegraph.co.uk/sunday-life/news/taliban-sniper-shot-me-in-the-head-but-i-wouldnt-miss-my-brothers-wedding/28443596.html, accessed 2 April 2024.

determination to capture the compound.[89] Musa Qal'eh had become the Taliban's centre of gravity in the province.

The wounding of Ally McKinney and Ricky Armstrong was proof, if any was needed, that the sniper threat was real and increasing. Danish Jaeger Corps special forces marksmen had been scanning the town through their powerful optical sights to try to identify potential firing points. They had noted a number of positions that were likely to be problematic, some less than 200m from the walls of the compound. Foot patrols sent out to check these locations reported that the Taliban had indeed been building sniper hides and it was concluded that action needed to be taken quickly to discourage the enemy from repeating their earlier success. Ominously, the patrols also reported that the insurgents who had been firing from these positions had 'policed their brass' – that is removed all their spent cases in an attempt to conceal their presence. This suggested they were dealing with shooters who had some expertise… or at least some training. As Corporal Danny Groves noted in his diary, the fact that one of the firing positions had been found less than 150 metres from the Outpost indicated that the man they were dealing with was 'no mug'.[90]

On the night of 10 August, a fighting patrol consisting of soldiers from Somme Platoon, accompanied by Danish explosive demolition experts, slipped out of the compound and placed mousehole charges on a number of buildings. These were used to blow out the rear walls so that anyone trying to use them for cover during the day would be silhouetted and thus become a target themselves. At 1730hrs the following evening, Sangar 4, in the south-east corner, spotted movement. Instead of firing right away, which was the standard operating procedure at the time, the occupants kept their safety catches on and alerted the mortar team. The MFCs – Harding and McClurg – moved to a position from where they could observe the location. It was assessed that the enemy were heading towards a target which had been recorded as Xray-64, a known Taliban firing point, about 300m due east of the Alamo. Down on the mortar line, the two 81mm barrels were laid on to the target while the MFCs kept the location under observation. They wanted to ensure that as many insurgents as possible were within the killing zone before opening fire. Captain Johnson and Sergeant Brangan arrived and manned the smaller 51mm mortars, which had been jury-rigged to fire in the indirect role.[91]

At 1735hrs radios hissed as the MFC whispered 'Fire! Cancel at my command' and the men unleashed a vicious volley – 16 rounds of 81mm and at least as many 51mm bombs – at the target. The occupants of Sangar 3 reported enemy arms and legs flying through the air as the rounds impacted. One of the Danes later described the scene as 'the most awesome display of accurate mortar fire I have ever seen'.[92] Soldiers observing from the sangars afterwards could see packs of dogs fighting over the limbs of the dead Taliban. 'The lads were whooping and cheering at the sight', recalled Rab McClurg.[93] In the safety of an armchair, in the comfort of one's own home, that reaction might seem 'unwholesome'. But in the killing fields of northern Helmand, where these soldiers were involved in a daily life-or-death struggle with a determined and seemingly heartless enemy, seeing their friends being maimed or killed, it was just another way of dealing with their fear and anxieties. There would be a time for paying due respect to a determined foe. But this was not it.

---

89 Johannesen, *Tigers and the Taliban*, p.205.
90 Corporal Danny Groves, personal diary entry, 11 August 2006.
91 The 51mm mortar was supposed to be used in the direct-fire role – i.e. line-of-sight. However, Corporal Harding had rigged up a way of using the weapons for indirect fire, utilising ranges and bearings provided by the hand-held fire control computer used for the 81mms.
92 Corporal Danny Groves, diary entry, 11 August 2006.
93 Lance Corporal Rab McClurg, interview with author.

Taliban Rocket Man

The accuracy, reach and potency of the mortars was fast becoming a major problem for the insurgents. It was denying them freedom of manoeuvre, particularly to the north, south and east, and they decided to do something about it. They had identified the position of the mortars and it received incoming fire the following day, the explosions sending showers of dirt and rubble over Corporal Groves and his team. The mortarmen took cover in a nearby ISO container as the MFCs, the snipers and the JTAC tried, without success, to identify the firing point. While they waited for a fire mission, one of the young soldiers scrawled on the walls of the ISO: 'This is where 1 Royal Irish Mortar Platoon took cover. We hid like cowardly dogs'. Squaddie humour at its best, even under fire. The soldiers giggled when they saw it. But they had little to laugh about later that evening, when it was confirmed by intelligence, via ICOM chatter, that the Taliban were so concerned about the mortar threat that they had drafted in their own indirect fire expert – from Pakistan – together with a multi-barrelled rocket launcher, to try to even the score.[94] The incoming mortar and rocket fire suddenly became much more accurate and dangerous.

Corporal John Harding had been on the receiving end of Chinese-made 107mm rockets before, in Iraq. In that conflict, the weapons had been fired without any real targeting. 'The Iraqi insurgents would lay them on a berm (a low bank of soil or sand), point them in the general direction of where they thought we were, and set them off using an electrical charge. They could go anywhere and you would have had to be really unlucky to be on the receiving end'.[95] But in Musa Qal'eh the enemy's newly-acquired multi-barrelled launcher meant the missiles could be fired, with greater precision, from up to 8km away, and, as they were mobile, the operators could 'shoot-and-scoot' – moving to a new location after every salvo. Corporal Harding:

> You have to give the Taliban credit. They had done a good estimate. They set up the rocket-launcher just out of range of our mortars and they would fire at us at one-minute intervals until all the missiles had been expended. At the same time, up to six separate mortar crews would engage. Every round that came in was super-accurate and we were massively out-gunned. They had us for a week or so. People were looking at me to solve the problem and it was so difficult.[96]

Locating the enemy can be one of the toughest battle drills, whatever weapon system the opposition is employing. Finding the Taliban rocket launcher and mortar crews was no exception, particularly in the difficult urban terrain of Musa Qal'eh. Artillery locating radar, such as MAMBA, might have made the task easier, but this equipment was not available in Afghanistan at that time. No one had thought it would be necessary for a peacekeeping operation. With no technical aids to rely on, MFCs, Harding and McClurg, reverted to an old but effective method known as crater analysis. 'We could target the rocket launcher by observing the smoke trail, which obviously led back to the point of origin. They were usually out of range of our own mortars, but I could sometimes engage using the 105mm Light Guns of 7RHA out in the desert', explained Harding.[97] But this always depended on the time it took the observers get their heads up and spot the smoke. If they were too slow, the smoke would have gone and the rocket launcher would have moved. Unless

---

94 Corporal John Harding, interview with author.
95 Corporal John Harding, interview with author.
96 Corporal John Harding, interview with author.
97 Corporal John Harding, interview with author.

fast air was overhead when the rockets were fired, there was no point calling in an airstrike because the target would have gone by the time the aircraft had arrived on task.

The rocket launcher was a problem, but the rockets were large, heavy, and difficult to move covertly along the insurgents' supply chain. The garrison calculated – correctly – that the stock of ammunition would eventually dry up. The mortar bombs, being smaller and much easier to transport, were likely to be more enduring. The Taliban mortar teams usually fired from cover, making them hard to spot. However, Harding had learned a method that could provide a good indication of bearing – the direction from which the bomb had been fired. This involved finding the crater left by the bomb's impact, analysing the shape of the hole, the splatter marks, and the indentation left by the fuse, which together gave an indication of the direction from which it had come, and then using a prismatic compass to take a back-bearing. Finding the range was more difficult, but Harding had worked out that most of the attacks were being launched from relatively close-in. It appeared that the ammunition being used was in poor condition, and the boosting cartridges (also known as augmenting cartridges), that increased the range, could not be used. Instead of firing from up to 5,000 metres away, they were having to launch from much closer to their target – around 600m. Once they had analysed three or more craters, they could triangulate the bearings and that would give them a relatively accurate location. When an incoming attack was launched, the garrison would take cover while Harding went out, found the craters, conducted his analysis, calculated range and bearing, plotted it on the map and from that produced a fire mission. Often, he could have counter-battery fire in the air within a few minutes. It was dangerous work, but it was the only way they could tackle the threat – and it was successful. The LEWT, listening in to the Taliban's radio traffic, was able to confirm many kills. As Harding said later, 'It was all about getting into my opposite number's head – trying to think like him, and beat him at his own game'.[98] They were killing the mortar crews, but the 81mm mortars were not heavy enough to put the enemy barrels out of commission. That required ordnance with more destructive power. 'When we were sure we had located a firing point, we called in fast air to drop a 500lb bomb, to destroy the barrels and base-plates', explained Lance Corporal McClurg.[99] The Royal Irish were having success with their old-fashioned methods. But, as later events would prove, although they could reduce the impact, the threat from the Taliban's indirect fire could not be eliminated entirely.

Throughout their time in COP Griffin, the Danes were never completely at ease with their mission. The OC, Johannesen, continued to believe they would be better employed out in the desert where they could make a more valuable contribution to the Battlegroup's endeavours.

He had made several requests to be relieved so the Griffins could get back to their mobile reconnaissance role. He was growing increasingly worried about the indirect fire threat posed by the Taliban rockets and mortars. 'We either have to find it [the rocket launcher] and neutralise it or we have to leave…in a hurry', he wrote.[100]

At the same time, although the Danish media appeared to be much more fixated on events in Kosovo and Iraq, word was trickling back to Copenhagen that the mission in Helmand was not quite the peacekeeping task that had been expected.[101] On 12 August, with the 3 Para Battlegroup under the growing pressure of constantly trying to do too much with too few resources, the COP Griffin garrison received word from headquarters that they were to be withdrawn. Major Johannesen was delighted with the news. Finally, he thought, he and his reconnaissance squadron could get back to doing what they did best – operating in the open terrain of the desert 'where

---

98 Corporal John Harding, interview with author.
99 Lance Corporal Rab McClurg, interview with author.
100 Johannesen, *Tigers and Taliban,* p.221.
101 Major Lars Ulslev Johannesen, interview with author.

we can determine time and place of combat'.[102] Like the Danes, the Royal Irish soldiers were not displeased to receive the news that they were to leave. For some, however, the experience of driving through a hail of Taliban bullets as they raced through the bazaar during the insertion, was not something they were desperate to repeat unless absolutely necessary. It was not lost on them that the enemy had been reinforced since their arrival and that meant the journey out was likely to be even more challenging. They looked at the Danes' armoured vehicles which would provide their occupants with good protection against small arms. The Griffins would be alright as they drove out into the desert. Then they looked at their own vehicles, which were falling apart after the insertion, offered no ballistic protection and might not even run after the punishment they had taken on the way in. Some wondered if the better option might be stay where they were.

They did not have to decide. The extraction, planned for 14 August, was cancelled at the last minute. Once again, the Provincial Governor had demanded that the District Centre had to be defended. The political reality was that there could be no question of allowing the garrison to leave if that resulted in Taliban occupation. The decision to stay put hit the Danes particularly hard. They had really believed they would be able to leave and the news that they must remain caused a serious drop in morale. As Johannesen wrote later: 'The men are tired of being here. Tired of being on the defensive. Tired of being crammed into such limited space… The District Centre begins to feel like the very prison that it is'.[103]

On 14 August, the day that had originally been fixed for the cancelled extraction, Johannesen announced that their withdrawal was to go ahead after all, and that Battlegroup HQ was planning Operation Snakebite II, later renamed Operation Atomi. Johannesen has since insisted that the decision to pull out the Danish squadron was made at Task Force Headquarters in Kandahar.[104] However, the 3 Para Battlegroup CO had a different view. As he returned from leave in the UK on 22 August, he was told that the Danes had taken a unilateral decision to pull out, driven by concerns about their ability to evacuate their wounded. He wrote: 'The difficulties associated with…helicopter evacuation had a profound effect… As the risks they faced became more apparent, they had increasingly begun to feel that their position had become untenable. The decision was backed up by their government in Copenhagen and was presented to the Task Force as a fait accompli'.[105]

There is little doubt that the Danish Government was concerned about the changing nature of the mission, which had become much more kinetic than they had expected. However, according to Major Johannesen, the Danes were ordered to leave Musa Qal'eh by Task Force Headquarters in Kandahar because their mobility and reconnaissance capabilities were required elsewhere in the province. He agreed that CASEVAC had been a growing concern. It had taken most of the day to get a seriously wounded man flown back to Bastion and this was only achieved when a US special forces Combat Search and Rescue team arrived. 'They must have been listening in on our radio traffic and heard the growing desperation in our voices', the Dane explained. 'A doctor turned up out of the blue at the main gate and said "I believe you have a patient for me?" We hadn't even had time to secure the LZ'. Johannesen was not sorry to receive the instruction to leave, but he is clear that their departure was not as a result of any decision he had made.[106]

---

102 Johannesen, *Tigers and Taliban*, p.217.
103 Johannesen, *Tigers and the Taliban*, p.225.
104 Johannesen, *Tigers and the Taliban*, p.227.
105 Tootal, *Danger Close,* p.188.
106 Major Lars Ulslev Johannesen, interview with author.

11

The Birth of Easy Company

Whatever the genesis of the Griffins' withdrawal, what is not in dispute is that the hard-pressed 3 Para Battlegroup was given only a couple of days to find replacements. With the manpower pool all but dry, the solution was always going to be sub-optimal in terms of numbers and combat power. Somme Platoon and the Royal Irish mortar detachment would be staying put, to be joined by Barrosa Platoon and a small company headquarters element. One hundred and forty Danish warriors, along with their armoured vehicles and withering firepower, were to be replaced by a force of fewer than 50. A rifle company usually consisted of three platoons, totalling 84 fighting troops plus the command group. The company that was being created would have only two platoons, or 56 bayonets. It did not take a mathematician to work out that the new garrison was going to be a lot thinner on the ground, just as it seemed the enemy was growing in strength and determination.

As 3 Para's fifth sub-unit, it was obvious to Battlegroup Headquarters that the new organisation should be christened E Company, 3 Para – or Echo Company in the NATO phonetic alphabet. However, the *Band of Brothers* television series, about the US Army 506th Parachute Infantry Regiment's Easy Company, was popular in the UK at that time and it was decided to adopt that nomenclature instead. Easy Company, 3 Para was born. The Royal Irish soldiers thought little about the title at the time. As the days went by, however, some of them felt that since they formed by far the largest element of the sub-unit, they should have been allowed to fight under their own regimental title. The Gurkhas had fought as Gurkhas. The Royal Fusiliers had fought as Fusiliers. Why couldn't the Royal Irish have been afforded the same curtesy, they wondered? But that was a debate for another time. The more immediate conundrum was how to get the Danes out and the replacements in without repeating Op Snakebite. Although that plan had proved reasonably effective, the obvious danger with doing the same thing again was that the Taliban would be wise to it. Unfortunately, there were few more attractive alternatives. After much deliberation, it was decided that they would reprise Snakebite… but with a subtle twist. Instead of having to run the gauntlet of driving through the bazaar in soft-skinned vehicles, the incoming force would be helicopttered right into the centre of town, landing on the HLS just outside the northern wall. With only a single platoon and a headquarters element being inserted, this could be accomplished in a single lift, using two Chinooks. The aircraft would need to be on the ground for only seconds. Once the incoming troops had been delivered, the Danes would drive out, protected by their armoured vehicles.

In the DC, the details of the extraction were being kept on a 'need-to-know' basis because there had been some recent leaks to media outlets, particularly in Denmark. Writing in his diary, Corporal Danny Groves noted: 'All we knew for sure was that at some stage the Danes would drive out, taking all their manpower and equipment with them, and a platoon of R Irish, along with some ANP would replace them, possibly flying in by helo. And we knew it would be happening soon'.[1] The police who had been in the compound when the Danes and Somme Platoon arrived

---

1   Corporal Danny Groves, personal diary entry, 23 August 2006.

were all local men, whose extended families lived in the province, and there was growing concern about their loyalties. The incoming police had been recruited from other parts of Afghanistan and would, it was hoped, be less susceptible to Taliban manipulation.

Major Adam Jowett had arrived in Helmand as Officer Commanding Support Company, 3 Para. But with his specialist machine-gunners and mortarmen spread out across the Task Force, he had no company to command. Instead, he had been given the post of Operations Officer, running the Joint Operations Centre (JOC) at Battlegroup Headquarters in Camp Bastion. In that role, he had not expected to be deployed into the field. The same was true for newly-promoted Warrant Officer Class 2, Jo Scrivener, known to all as Scrivs. His appointment was Operations Warrant Officer (OPSWO), Jowett's non-commissioned wing-man and fixer in the headquarters. However, Easy Company required an OC and a Company Sergeant Major (CSM) and neither man was disappointed when the CO told them to pack their kit and head for Musa Qal'eh to take up those roles. No suitable officer could be found to be the company second-in-command, so that post would be gapped. However, Jowett was adamant that if he was going to lead a small force in an isolated compound, with no guarantee of timely evacuation of his wounded, he was going to need a good medical team. This wish was granted in the form of Captain Mike Stacey, and two Royal Army Medical Corps medics, Corporal French and Lance Corporal Roberts, from the hospital at Bastion. Jowett was also allocated a Light Electronic Warfare Team (LEWT), which consisted of soldiers from the Royal Signals, the Intelligence Corps, and two Afghan civilian interpreters. Their job was to listen in on Taliban radio frequencies and provide information about what the enemy was doing. Easy Company's local radio net and the link with Bastion and Kandahar would be run by a number of signallers under Staff Sergeant Ian Wornham. An intelligence SNCO, Sergeant Freddie Kruyer, two Parachute Regiment snipers, Corporal Hugh Keir and Private Jared Cleary, and a Fire Support Team (or JTAC) made up the remainder of Company Headquarters. In total, Easy Company would number 85 soldiers consisting of the two rifle platoons (55 infantry soldiers – Corporal McKinney had not been replaced), a company headquarters element of 19, and the mortar section of two detachments, amounting to 11. That total would be augmented by the arrival of 40 Afghan police officers of as yet unknown quality, who would travel to the DC by road.

'Quite exciting' is Lieutenant Paul Martin's understated description of the insertion. 'We had little time to prepare, no rehearsals. We would be air-assaulting as close as possible to the compound, and we were warned that the LZ could be 'hot".[2] As he looked around at the young Rangers in his aircraft, Martin could see the fear in some of their faces. Ranger Jonty Johnston's lasting memory of the insertion is the amount of equipment and ammunition that each man had to carry. 'I was a GPMG gunner, so as well as the gun, I had 1,000 rounds of link in my day sack, which was crammed into the top of my bergan'.[3] When the men arrived at the flight line, they were given more ammunition. Johnston was handed another 800 rounds and most of the others were loaded down with the 'greenie' containers that held the 81mm mortar rounds. 'Our bergans were now so heavy that it was impossible to pick them up to put them on. We had to place them on the ground, with the straps facing up, then lie down on them, back first, slip your arms into the straps, and then get someone to pull you up'. When Johnston's chalk was given the order to board the aircraft, he led the way up the ramp, and kept going until he reached the bulkhead that separated the cargo hold from the cockpit. The Chinooks had been stripped of everything except their side-door and ramp machine guns, to maximise the space for the men and their equipment:

---

2 Lieutenant Paul Martin, interview with author.
3 Ranger Paul Johnston, interview with author.

> We were told to sit down with our legs open. The next guy would sit in between your legs and this was carried on the whole way down the aircraft. There were two or three rows next to me. I remember the familiar smell of burning aviation fuel and the heat of the engines as we climbed aboard.[4]

Once the troops and equipment had been loaded the big helicopters taxied out and pulled up into the night sky, the noise of the throbbing engines and the thrashing of the twin rotors making conversation almost impossible. In any case, many of the men were lost in their own thoughts – the sights and sounds they might face when the Chinooks touched down outside the Musa Qal'eh DC. The flying time from Bastion to Musa Qal'eh was about 30 minutes, but the time seemed to gallop by. Suddenly a red light came on in the cabin, giving the troops a five-minute warning. This was the signal to stand up and prepare to dismount. Then a green light. Two minutes to go. The passengers could feel the big helicopters heave and yaw as they began their final approach.

The aircraft carrying the Barrosa Platoon commander and half of his force was almost at the LZ when it was waved off due to Taliban fire, a few rounds puncturing the thin metal skin of the Chinook:

> We flew around and approached from a different direction. By now, many of us were feeling quite ill and fearful about what was to come. But the 'Ugly' callsigns were suppressing the Taliban firing points and this time we were able to land and disembark out of contact. There was plenty of firing going on, but not directly at us.[5]

Ranger Johnston heard the note of the engines change and felt the nose of the aircraft come up as the pilot killed forward motion and banged the airframe down into the Helmand sand. He was desperate to get out of the helicopter as quickly as possible:

> Having been warned we could be getting off into a fire fight, I was keen to make sure I was up and ready to exit the aircraft as soon as the rear wheels touched down. Obviously, that was the most dangerous time for the helicopter and the quicker it could get back into the air the better. We had been told that if we didn't get off in quick time, we would be taken back to Bastion. No-one wanted that.

They had been drilled that when the five-minute warning light came on, the man at the very front would be helped up by the loadmaster, and he would turn around and help the man behind him to his feet. This would be carried on all the way to the man right at the back. For some reason, however, the soldier in front of Johnston had not turned around and he was struggling to get up, under the weight of his Bergan:

> I was screaming for help but no-one could hear above the sound of the engines. Then the men in front started to get off and I was still stuck on the floor. I was beginning to panic. Thankfully someone finally saw my predicament and helped me to my feet. I ran along the cabin, down the ramp and onto the sand, just as the helicopter lifted off.[6]

---

4 Ranger Paul Johnston, interview with author.
5 Lieutenant Paul Martin, interview with author. 'Ugly' was the callsign given to the AH-64 Apache attack helicopters – eg Ugly 14.
6 Ranger Paul Johnston, interview with author.

The aircraft had been on the ground for less than a minute.

After the warnings of a 'hot' LZ, the men of Barrosa Platoon were relieved to find that the night was relatively calm and peaceful once the beat of the Chinook rotors died away. There was no crash of RPGs or the rattle of machine gun fire. No green streaks of tracer criss-crossing the darkened sky above their heads. Just the crack of small arms and, in the distance, an Apache seeking out a solidary target. With a shrug of relief, they stood up and headed for the entrance to the compound, hailed as they went by acquaintances from Somme Platoon, who were providing cover from the sangars.

It was just beginning to get light and Ranger Johnston was surprised that the first person he saw up close was an Afghan in civilian clothes, carrying an AK-47 rifle. 'In the darkness, I felt a bit confused. I didn't know whether to shoot him or not. I'm glad I didn't because it turned out that he was one of the Afghan police officers'. Apart from that, Johnston's impression was that his arrival had been 'a bit of an anti-climax'.[7]

The following morning, Sergeant Gilchrist took stock of his new surroundings. And just like Somme Platoon, before him, he was not impressed by what he saw:

> I remember thinking "this is nuts". I looked out through the main gate and I could see a tall tower that seemed to stand out above all the other buildings. If the Taliban were smart, they would use that as an aiming marker for their mortars and rockets. And it turned out that's just what they did.[8]

Lieutenant Martin was surprised to see so many vehicles, people and equipment crammed into such a small space.[9] Ranger Davy Pepper was unimpressed by the state of the compound:

> It was a shithole. Our accommodation was in a fairly large building close to the southern wall (formerly the town's medical clinic). In some places the wall was only just above head height. There were several wrecked cars and some old Soviet-era anti-tank weapons laying around. Opposite the main gate there was a large three or four storey building, looking down into the DC. A lot of fire came from that in the days and weeks ahead.[10]

Corporal Danny Groves was pleased to see his old friend, Gilly Gilchrist, that morning. But although his welcome was warm and heart-felt, he was more interested to know if the newcomer had brought any 81mm ammunition. The high tempo of Taliban attacks, and the growing dependency on the mortars to suppress the enemy, was taking a heavy toll on ammunition supplies. There had not been sufficient stocks of mortar rounds in theatre to bring the team up to full war-fighting holdings before they had left Bastion. They had received only small replenishments since their arrival. As early as 15 August, Corporal Groves had reported that stocks were beginning to run low. The situation was not yet critical but it was becoming a matter of concern, and they had been warned by the 3 Para Mortar Platoon headquarters, in Bastion, to be careful, as there was very little 81mm ammunition left in the country.[11] The good news was that many of the incoming Barrosa Platoon had brought a 'greenie' of HE rounds. The bad news was that this only amounted to 50 bombs, taking stocks up to 150 rounds of HE, 70 White Phosphorus and 50 Illumination.

---

7   Ranger Paul Johnston, interview with author.
8   Sergeant Stephen Gilchrist, interview with author.
9   Lieutenant Paul Martin, interview with author.
10 Ranger Davy Pepper, interview with author.
11 Corporal Danny Groves, diary entry, 15 August 2006.

That sounded like a lot, but at the rate the mortars had been firing, it amounted to less than 10 days' supply. They would be able to support the extraction of the Danes, but after that they were going to need a big replenishment or they would be forced to ration their fire.[12]

The Griffins Depart

Meanwhile, the Danes were preparing to leave, packing their kit, and starting to move their vehicles down from the mounds they had built to allow their mounted weapons to fire over the wall of the compound. The newly-arrived Barrosa Platoon did not yet recognise the significance of this, but Somme Platoon had seen the devastating effect of the vehicle-mounted heavy machine guns on the enemy…and they were worried. The Griffins and the Royal Irish soldiers of Somme Platoon had forged strong friendships during their three weeks together. They had shared the same privations, and the same dangers. They respected each other for their fighting abilities and spirit. The Danes knew they were leaving their friends with significantly fewer numbers, and, with the departure of their heavy machine guns, much reduced firepower.[13] Although Barrosa had brought in a couple of .50s, the garrison would now be much more dependent on the lighter 7.62mm GPMGs – capable weapons, but with less reach and punch than the big American-designed guns. Sergeant Gilchrist recalled: 'At the time, I didn't fully appreciate the impact of losing the .50s, but looking back on it, I can remember, in the days following the Danes' departure, that the Somme lads continued to be concerned that our defensive firepower had been massively diminished'.[14] Ranger Johnston shared the worries about the reduction in firepower. But he was even more concerned about the loss of the Danes' water tanker. 'They had their own water tank and you could just go up to it with your water bottle, turn a tap, and get ice-cold, clean water. I was really sorry to see that go'.[15]

The new arrivals had just half a day to acclimatise and adjust to their surroundings before the Danes pulled out. The Battlegroup operation took place, just as it had on 6 August, and by lunchtime the corridor through the green zone and the wadi had been secured. It was now time for the Griffins to leave. But first, Jowett needed to lock down the route from the DC and through the bazaar. As Somme Platoon had been there the longest, and knew all the Taliban's favoured firing positions, they would man the sangars to provide cover while Barrosa Platoon would push out along the bazaar. Once Lieutenant Martin had reported that his troops were in position, the Danes fired up their vehicles and drove out. A little later the Afghan National Police contingent arrived in their soft-skinned pick-up trucks.

The day of the Danes' extraction (23 August) was relatively quiet for the DC garrison, with only a couple of hit-and-run RPG attacks. However, during the course of the morning, the LEWT, monitoring the Taliban radio traffic, picked up a conversation between two enemy commanders, who had decided that with the Danes gone, and the DC now, apparently, being held only by Afghan forces, they would attack in the morning and would be drinking tea in the Governor's office by the evening.[16] Before that, however, later in the afternoon, the men on sentry duty at Sangar 1, heard voices and shouting coming from the bazaar in front of them. A few minutes later, four Afghan males, all carrying weapons, appeared at the western end of the market and began to walk up the middle of the road towards the compound. Ranger Johnston could not believe what

---

12   Corporal Danny Groves, interview with author.
13   Major Lars Ulslev Johannesen, interview with author.
14   Sergeant Stephen Gilchrist, interview with author.
15   Ranger Paul Johnston, interview with author.
16   Jowett, *No Way Out*, p.70.

he was seeing. 'I let them come a bit closer and then opened fire'. It was the first time he had shot at anything other than a range target:

> My heart was pounding, I was excited, and I definitely wasn't applying the principles of marksmanship. I don't think I even looked through the optical sight properly. I just wanted to get the rounds off as quickly as possible. As I pulled the trigger, I saw a man in the middle of the group go down and I shifted fire onto the others. I could see the rounds hitting the ground in front of them and the men sort of dancing as they tried to dodge the bullets, before running into cover.

That night, when the adrenalin had worn off, and as he tried to sleep, he kept thinking over and over again that he should have done better:

> It is still one of the biggest regrets of my life that I didn't get all four. They were right there, in the middle of the road, not suspecting that we were still in the compound. If I had steadied myself, held fire for even 10 more seconds, and let them come a little closer, there would have been four less Taliban for us to worry about the next morning instead of just one.

Johnston completed two further Afghanistan tours but he was never again presented with a similar opportunity.[17]

Ranger Pepper described the daily routine:

> Basically, there were two tasks. You were either on guard or on QRF. If you were on guard – there was a section allocated to each sangar – you worked one hour on and six hours off…in theory. In reality, it never worked out like that because as soon as we were contacted, everyone went to their stand-to positions and returned fire. We were being attacked on multiple occasions during the day so there wasn't much down time. On QRF the job was to be prepared to support the firing positions on the wall if required; ammunition re-supply; or to help with casevac-ing casualties from the fighting positions to the RAP.[18]

Welcome to Musa Qal'eh

As night began to give way to dawn the next morning, the newly-arrived soldiers of Barrosa Platoon were about to become acquainted with the full fury of a Taliban assault. Having been alerted to the attack via ICOM, thanks to the Taliban's poor COMSEC (communications security) practices, the men of both platoons had manned their fighting positions before the first glimmer of light appeared in the eastern sky, some making use of night vision devices to find their way to their stand-to locations. Junior commanders spoke in whispers as they ensured their men were making the best use of the available protection.

Suddenly, the stillness was rocked by a series of deafening explosions as five RPG projectiles struck various points around the compound. These were followed almost immediately by a hail of rifle and machine gun bullets as the insurgents attempted to drive the defenders down behind cover. Glimpsing over the sandbag walls of the sangars, the Royal Irish soldiers could see the muzzle flashes and streaks of green tracer as dozens of Taliban weapons delivered a high volume

---

17 Ranger Paul Johnston, interview with author.
18 Ranger Davy Pepper, interview with author.

of fire from every side. The defenders returned the favour with interest, and in just a few seconds there were shouts of 'magazine' as soldiers dropped down into cover to reload. Observing from the roof of the Alamo, Major Jowett was impressed by the way the soldiers braved the hail of incoming lead to get their heads up, identify targets and squeeze off their rounds, remembering to change firing positions to avoid providing the enemy with easy targets as they popped back up. He was also pleased to see that the Afghan police seemed to be up for the fight.[19] It was important, in this opening exchange, for the garrison to achieve fire superiority, to win the firefight, which would force the attackers to stop manoeuvring and seek cover or risk death or injury. If that could not be achieved, the insurgents would be able to close on the compound and possibly breach the defences. The garrison had developed 'breach drills' to deal with such an eventuality, but no one wanted to find out if they were effective. The integrity of the compound had to be maintained at all costs.

Meanwhile, the MFCs and the JTAC were scanning the ground, trying to establish the main axis of the enemy's advance and their key firing positions. Having been warned that the attack was imminent, coalition aircraft were already on station – A-10s from the Texas Air National Guard – waiting for targets. Jowett held back from calling them in, waiting to see if the compound's own firepower would be sufficient to force the attackers to break contact. When that no longer seemed likely, the JTAC targeted the Taliban's centre of gravity to the west and a pair of A-10s made repeated gun-runs, just beyond the boundary wall, until the enemy fire had been reduced to almost nothing.[20] By 0800 the insurgents had ended their assault and crawled back to their hiding places to lick their wounds. Despite the intensity of the firefight, the Royal Irish platoons had sustained no casualties. Everyone knew, however, that such good fortune was unlikely to last. The Taliban made five further attempts to seize the DC during the course of the day, the final attack being timed to coincide with twilight when the human eye tends to be at its least effective. The enemy's approach had varied little throughout, each fight being initiated by the whoosh and bang of RPGs, followed by small-arms fire. This would become the standard approach over the coming days.

As this stage, the initiative appeared to have swung back in the Taliban's favour. The Royal Irish soldiers and their commanders felt they were being forced to react to the enemy's moves. They dearly wanted to turn the tables and get the enemy to respond to them for a change. An opportunity to take the fight to the insurgents arose on 25 August when the LEWT picked up transmissions indicating that a group of men and vehicles were congregating in the wadi to the south of the DC. Having developed a good appreciation of the enemy's command structure, the signallers and interpreters were beginning to identify individual commanders by their voices and callsigns and they believed some of these were among the people rendezvousing in the wadi. The MFCs (Corporal Harding and Lance Corporal McClurg), and the JTAC (Bombardier Ray Anderton (7RHA) and RAF Regiment Corporal, Ade Williams), began to hatch a plan to target them with a pre-emptive strike. They could not engage unless they could positively identify the people as hostile combatants so they tasked a Harrier to get eyes on the group from high altitude, where it was invisible from the ground. The Harrier pilot, using his plane's sophisticated optical sensors, reported that the men appeared to be armed and that they were deployed in a defensive posture. This was considered sufficient evidence that the group was Taliban. After checking that there were no Afghan army or police operating in the area, the MFCs called in a fire mission. The guns of I Battery, 7RHA and the compound's own mortars hammered the target for a time before being check-fired so that the JTAC could summon fast air. A JDAM guided bomb landed amidst

---

19 Jowett, *No Way Out*, pp.84–85.
20 Jowett, *No Way Out*, p.83.

the gathering, causing carnage. The LEWT could hear the panicked radio messages as the Taliban screamed for help to recover their wounded and dead.[21]

The garrison expected a strong response. But the next day began unremarkably. The first attack commenced at 0450hrs with the usual RPGs and small-arms fire, and was swatted away. Several more firefights of a similar nature occurred in the morning and into the afternoon. During one of these, soldiers on the western wall spotted a red Toyota Hilux pick-up truck making its way, at speed, through the bazaar towards the compound. A soldier fired a warning shot but this was ignored and the vehicle continued to approach. The compound's most vulnerable spot was the main gate. A VBIED, detonated there, could have left the defences wide open. No doubt with that threat in mind, a machine-gunner engaged the vehicle, firing burst after burst until it came to a halt, smashing into a nearby building. When the contact was eventually broken, the Afghan police went out to examine the car and then moved it inside the compound, where it was discovered that the occupants were a family of Afghans. They had been stopped on the road to Gereshk by Taliban fighters and ordered to drive to the DC. Three of the occupants had been killed in the incident. There were two survivors. The men of Somme and Barrosa platoons were horrified, not just that they had been responsible for the deaths of innocent civilians, but that the Taliban had deliberately forced them to drive towards the compound, knowing that they would be fired upon. 'We had been warned, earlier, that a Taliban suicide bomber might be operating in the area', explained Ranger Pepper. When the truck failed to stop, everyone feared it was a vehicle-borne IED (VBIED), and reacted as they had been trained. 'We all felt really bad about the incident. The machine-gunner who had engaged it, never really got over the experience'.[22] 'It was not a proud day for us', admitted Lieutenant Martin, 'but I was very clear that we had opened fire in self-defence. An RPG had been fired from the vehicle, or from just behind it, as it approached the front of the DC. I stand by what we did'.[23] The garrison medics did what they could for the wounded, and the patched-up vehicle left the next day, carrying the survivors and the dead.

Meanwhile, the fighting continued. At 1900hrs the enemy returned to the fray, this time with what seemed like a much heavier onslaught. On this occasion, the insurgents seemed to be focusing much of their violence on the Outpost and the north-west corner of the compound. Company Commander, Adam Jowett, thought this was 'the heaviest weight of fire yet', as the Taliban let loose from several PKM machine guns in long, terrifying bursts.[24] It took courage for the defenders to raise themselves above the sandbag parapets and fire back as tracer carved green and red paths back and forth across the darkening sky. A gun-run by an American A-10 seemed to silence much of the fire coming from the northern end of the compound, but it soon became clear that the insurgents had managed to penetrate into the ruins of the Mosque, which was right next to the southern wall. The aircraft could not engage without undue risk to the defenders. Corporal Groves and his mortarmen were unable to help. The mosque was too close for their barrels, even when they were angled almost vertically. The solution owed more to 1916 than to 2006. Sergeant Major Scrivener and the reserve section drove the insurgents out in an old-fashioned hand-grenade duel, exchanging bombs back and forth over the wall until the enemy had been compelled to withdraw. It had been a close-run thing. At some points during the exchange the Taliban had been so near, the men in Sanger 5 could hear their shouts of *Allah Akbhar,* responding with a flood of well-chosen Anglo-Saxon oaths and a shower of bullets. Scrivener's grenade-slinging antics earned him a new nickname from the Irishmen. They christened him Michael Stone, after a loyalist terrorist

---

21   Corporal Danny Groves, diary entry, 25 August 2006.
22   Ranger Davy Pepper, interview with author.
23   Lieutenant Paul Martin, interview with author.
24   Jowett, *No Way Out*, p.121.

who had attempted to storm the funeral service for three Provisional IRA members, in Belfast's Milltown Cemetery, armed with grenades and pistols.[25]

Death Comes Calling

For most of The Royal Irish Regiment soldiers interviewed for this account, nearly two decades after the events of August 2006, their experiences had blurred into a single episode. They found it difficult to recall individual incidents, or what had happened on particular dates. However, a few events had clearly been so significant that they had seared themselves into their memories, even after the best part of 20 years. One of these occurred on Sunday, 27 August.

On the previous evening, the LEWT had picked up radio messages from the Taliban, suggesting that they were planning another heavy assault the following day. Sergeant Gilchrist was determined that the men of Barrosa Platoon were going to be ready for the battle. 'I remember telling my boys that I wanted all the GPMGs and personal weapons cleaned and oiled. No one gets their head down until the weapons are properly prepared for whatever the morning brings'.[26] Once again, the garrison stood-to before dawn and the enemy attacked, as expected, as the sun was beginning to rise. Up on the roof of the JOC, Royal Corps of Signals soldier, Lance Corporal Jon Hetherington (22), from South Wales, had joined his infantry colleagues, waiting for the fighting to start. As an electronic warfare specialist, he was not from one of the 'teeth arms' (infantry, artillery, armour), and his usual role involved listening in to the insurgents' radio transmissions to gather clues about their locations, strength, losses and future intentions. He would not normally have expected to find himself in an infantry role. But there was nothing normal about the situation in Musa Qal'eh DC at that time. The garrison was short of fighting troops, and he was a soldier before anything else. Since he was not currently needed in the Ops Room, he was helping out as best he could, adding his rifle to the garrison's firepower. In Company Headquarters, Sergeant Gilchrist and the reserve section, on standby to distribute ammunition or rush to plug a gap in the defences, heard the attack begin:

> It was horrendous. The amount of firepower going down was unreal. It was crazy, and that was my impression from inside a building. God knows what it was like for the guys outside. There was more fire than I had ever experienced before. I had never seen anything like this in Kosovo, Northern Ireland, Sierra Leone or Iraq. It was an absolutely new experience for me and I was one of the most seasoned soldiers there at that time.[27]

A few minutes into the attack, the chilling call of 'Medic, Medic' crackled through the earpieces of the soldiers' Personal Role Radios. On the roof of the JOC, Major Jowett saw a figure lying prone on the floor, a dark pool of liquid spreading out beneath him. His heart stopped for a second. This was the moment he had been hoping would never happen, although, deep down, he knew that it probably would.

Lance Corporal Hetherington was the man down. He was unresponsive and Jowett's search for a pulse was in vain. A medic was on the scene within seconds, and the casualty was man-handled down from the roof and moved to the RAP.[28] But there was no helping him. The Taliban bullet

---

25 Corporal Danny Groves, diary entry, 26 August 2006.
26 Sergeant Stephen Gilchrist, interview with author.
27 Sergeant Stephen Gilchrist, interview with author.
28 Jowett, *No Way Out,* p.131.

had entered through one armpit, ripped its way through his chest and exited by the other one. He had been wearing his ECBA – Enhanced Combat Body Armour – but it was only designed to protect the major organs from frontal or rear impacts. The upgraded Osprey body armour, which had larger plates to the front and rear and also offered better side protection, had not been issued to all of the troops at that time. As Corporal Danny Groves pointed out, however, it was unlikely that any of the body armour in British service during the campaign could have made a difference in this instance. 'He was just unlucky'.[29] Death had been practically instantaneous.

With a murderous firefight to win, no one had time to dwell on the loss. The Taliban had used their sheer weight of fire to move in close. The south-eastern sangar was being hammered from short-range, and the reserve section rushed to provide support. Once again, the insurgents were driven off by a volley of hand-grenades. But it would take withering cannon fire and rockets from coalition aircraft, coupled with the devastating impact of a single 1,000lb bomb, to convince the attackers to call off their assault. There would be five further contacts during the course of that day – all as frantic as the first – before the garrison had time to think about the death of Jon Hetherington.

Although he did not wear the Harp and Crown cap badge, the black and green DZ flash or the distinctive green caubeen-and-hackle headdress of the Royal Irish, Hetherington had been a popular comrade and his loss was a heavy blow to all – a reminder that none of them was bullet-proof. There was sadness and sorrow. But also, a renewed determination. If the Taliban had thought the garrison would be deflated by fatalities, they had badly misjudged the fighting spirit of the young men within the walls of the DC. If anything, Hetherington's death had been catalytic, creating an even stronger resolve to stand firm, fight hard, make the enemy pay… and ensure that he had not died in vain.

According to Danny Groves' diary, the next few days were relatively quiet as the insurgents seemed to switch from infantry assaults to stand-off attacks, using recoilless rifles, mortars and rockets. By now, the men had grown accustomed to the incoming missiles, and dashed for cover when they heard the report of a round being fired. The enemy's indirect fire barrage was causing damage to the buildings within the compound but so far, the troops themselves had been largely unscathed by it, although Ranger Gillespie had been nicked by shrapnel, and on 28 August Ranger Paul Johnston had been blown out of his sangar by two RPG rounds striking simultaneously. The gate sangar had been built to increase security at the main entrance. It was a sandbagged emplacement with a firing slit for a GPMG to the front, looking out towards the minaret and the bazaar. A second low line of sandbags provided a seat from which the sentries could observe their arcs without exposing their heads. The OC and the Sergeant Major, doing their rounds of the firing positions, had stopped to speak to Johnston and the Afghan policeman who was also on duty there. Sergeant Major Scrivener told Johnston to sit on the sandbags, relax, but keep a good look-out. About 15 minutes after his visitors had left, the young Ranger saw two flashes and heard a loud explosion:

> The force of the blast knocked me back over the sandbags in a cloud of dust. I got up, grabbed the GPMG and started firing towards the yellow railings in front of me. I had dust in my eyes, my ears were ringing. I turned around to shout for the Afghan to get me more link and he'd gone. I was in the middle of a non-stop, massive fire-fight and it seemed as if every Taliban weapon out there was shooting at my sangar. I just kept firing.[30]

---

29   Corporal Danny Groves, interview with author.
30   Ranger Paul Johnston, interview with author.

Miraculously, Johnston emerged from the incident unharmed. He seemed to be leading a charmed life. He had also been on the receiving end of an RPG during a tour of duty in Sangar 5, which overlooked the mosque, on the south-west corner of the compound. This position had been built into the wall, with an embrasure knocked out to provide a firing slit:

> We were in a massive contact and I was hammering away with the GPMG. There was a huge explosion as a rocket hit the wall behind me. I was knocked semi-conscious and I remember someone pulling at my legs to get me out. I was trying to tell the rescuers that I was ok but I don't think any sound was coming out. The medic came and they threw me onto the quad-bike that was used to get casualties back to the RAP. I gulped in a massive breath of air, sat up, jumped off the bike and went back to my firing point.[31]

Two days after Johnston's miracle escape at the gate sangar, the Taliban's luck changed. At about 1600hrs, a mortar round landed directly on the roof of the Alamo. 'It had been a fairly normal day', recounted Sergeant Brangan. 'The enemy mortars had been creeping closer but we couldn't identify the firing point or where they were observing us from. There was a call of 'incoming' and the Alamo took a direct hit'.[32] The position was occupied by Ranger Anare Draiva and Lance Corporal Paul Muirhead, both of Somme Platoon. The loud, booming explosion sent a huge cloud of dust and debris into the air. Before it had settled, and the all-clear had been given, the soldiers of Somme Platoon, who had QRF duty that day, were racing towards the scene, knowing that it was their friends who were in the rubble.

Up on the roof of the Alamo, the picture was not good. 'By the time I got there, they were pulling Moonbeam [Muirhead] down from the roof', remembered PJ Brangan.[33] Draiva was clearly T4.[34] His injuries were so extensive that death would have been quick. Muirhead, with an horrendous head injury, was still breathing but clearly in bad shape. With bullets continuing to whip just inches over the heads of the rescue team, both casualties were moved with as much speed as it was possible to muster, down from the roof and into the RAP. The Medical Officer, Captain Mike Stacey set to work on the living, while Draiva's body was respectfully moved to one side and covered with a sheet. Stacey classified Muirhead as T1 – critical – and a nine-liner CASEVAC request was radioed through to Bastion, seeking an immediate airlift.

The doctor had managed to stabilise the casualty, but it was clear that if he was to stand any chance of surviving, Muirhead was going to need urgent hospital treatment.[35] With the contact still raging, however, the decision to send an evacuation helicopter was not an easy one to make. Battlegroup Commander, Lieutenant Colonel Stuart Tootal, and the man in charge of the Joint Helicopter Force, Lieutenant Colonel Richard Felton, were understandably nervous about authorising the rescue flight.[36] The enemy, able to look down into the compound from surrounding buildings, were likely to be aware that they had caused casualties, and that these would need to be evacuated by air sometime soon. It would be bad enough to lose two soldiers. The loss of a Chinook, its crew, and the Medical Emergency Rescue Team (MERT) that flew with it, would be a disaster of far greater proportions.

---

31 Ranger Paul Johnston, interview with author.
32 Sergeant PJ Brangan, interview with author.
33 Sergeant PJ Brangan, interview with author.
34 T4 was an unofficial but often-used triage classification signifying that the casualty was dead.
35 Sergeant PJ Brangan, interview with author.
36 Tootal, *Danger Close,* p.197.

The senior medical officer at Bastion, Lieutenant Colonel Peter Davis, who would be the MERT doctor, was in discussion with Stacey by TACSAT and was providing medical advice to Tootal. The two clinicians agreed that Muirhead could probably survive a few more hours, which meant the airlift would at least have the protection of darkness. Jowett, meanwhile, well aware of how difficult the decision was, asked for preliminary fires to be authorised to suppress enemy fire ahead of the aircraft's arrival. He was disgusted to learn that the lawyers at Task Force Headquarters, in Kandahar, would not agree. They were unwilling to risk collateral damage unless the compound or the aircraft were actually under attack.[37] Eventually, with Jowett piling on moral pressure, the senior officers decided that the flight could go.[38] Relieved, the men of Easy Company began to prepare for the helicopter's arrival. They knew the process of getting the casualties on to the aircraft had to be slick. Any hold-up would increase the risk exponentially. The one positive to be taken from the delay in authorising the flight was that it allowed time to ensure the fire plan for the extraction was as effective as it was possible to make it. Without preliminary fires, they would have to wait until the enemy engaged before they could reply. As the Chinook neared the HLS there could be no thought of using ground-attack aircraft or artillery and even their own mortars would have to check-fire due to the risk of bringing it down by accident. At that point they would have to rely on their rifles and machine guns to suppress the Taliban onslaught.

As per their usual drills, one platoon took up cover positions in the sangars while the other organised riflemen to secure the HLS and to act as stretcher bearers to carry the living and the dead to the aircraft. The JTAC and the MFCs plotted all the likely enemy firing points and had fire missions and bombing runs ready to call in when appropriate. Watching from the wall, Sergeant Brangan saw Corporal Hendron's section push out towards a small bund-line – a fold in the ground – from where they could engage likely Taliban firing points. The makeshift body-bag containing the corpse of Ranger Draiva, and a stretcher, holding Lance Corporal Muirhead, were brought out from the RAP and placed on the ground by the northern wall. And then they waited.

The JTAC, in communication with the Chinook, gave the garrison a two-minute warning of its arrival just as the feint but unmistakable sound of the twin rotors became apparent through the still night air, growing louder with every passing second. The Taliban could hear it too and the darkness exploded into light as they opened fire. The men in the sangars, and those providing security outside the wall, did not hold back. They replied with every rifle and machine gun they could bring to bear. The mortar teams, unable to use their barrels, grabbed their rifles and added their fire to the cacophony. With 30 seconds to run, the men on the wall sangars could see the big helicopter as it made its final approach.

With such a heavy volume of fire being aimed at them, it would have been understandable if the aircraft crew had decided to abort the landing. To the eternal credit of the pilots, looking into the jaws of hell that September evening, they did not. They came on through the stream of lead, losing height and speed, until they were finally able to touch-down on the scrubland of the landing site, the door gunners continuing to suppress the enemy as the loadmaster shoved various supplies off the ramp. The stretcher bearers, including Sergeant Brangan, and Captain Stacey, who was sticking close to his patient, headed for the rear of the Chinook, and delivered their loads as the pilot pulled on the collective and lifted his aircraft back into the tracer-streaked sky. 'The MERT got to work on Moonbeam as soon as the stretcher hit the floor of the aircraft. We knew he was in good hands and we were giving him his best chance of surviving', Brangan remembered. The aircraft was well on its way back to Bastion when it was noticed that Stacey was absent. He had

---

37   Jowett, *No Way Out,* p.158.
38   Jowett, *No Way Out,* p.157.

been conducting a handover with the MERT and the Chinook lifted before he had time to get off. He would have a few unscheduled hours in Bastion, before returning the following morning.

Lance Corporal Paul Muirhead, or Moonbeam as his friends had christened him, arrived at Bastion alive. He underwent surgery there to stabilise his condition before being airlifted on a medical evacuation flight to a hospital in Muscat, Oman. The loss of Ranger Anare Draiva –'D' as he was known to his comrades – left an unfillable void in the ranks of the Royal Irish soldiers. The big Fijian, from the city of Suva, had been popular with all who knew him and his death hit everyone hard. He was one of a number of men from the South Pacific island who had travelled half-way around the world to join the regiment. They were popular and effective soldiers, and many friendships had been formed. The strength of these bonds was demonstrated on the first Christmas the Fijians spent with the battalion, so far away from their home. There was no way the Northern Ireland soldiers were going to leave their mates in an empty army barracks over the festive season. The solution was simple. They 'adopted' them for the holidays and took them home to meet their families. The Fijians created quite a stir on Belfast's Shankill Road.[39]

Corporal John Harding felt the loss particularly acutely. 'D was a mortarman like me, although he was serving as a rifleman in Somme Platoon in Afghanistan. I had been his Corporal for four or five years. We all lived on the same corridor. I was really very close to him, not as a friend, but as a commander'. Even 18 years after his death, Harding still retained a sharp mental picture of the soldier. 'I can see him now in my mind's eye. He was a really handsome lad with a big smile, flashing white teeth. He was so friendly. Just a really nice lad. He could light up a room just by walking into it'.[40]

Corporal Cliff Tweed also took the news badly. Both Draiva and Muirhead had been in his section and he had been on his way to relieve them when the mortar round exploded. The first emotion he felt was anger:

> After the contact, I took the L96 sniper rifle (he was a qualified sniper), went up into one of the sangars and scanned the areas where I thought the Taliban dickers might be.[41] I was probably there for about 45 minutes before I felt a tap on my shoulder and was told to stand down.[42]

Corporal Danny Groves broke the bad news to the mortar section. He had walked across to the RAP to find out what had happened. On his way back to the mortar line, he tried to compose himself, working out what he was going to say:

> We were still engaged in a fire mission so I just said 'lads, we've got one KIA and it's D, and another SI, which is Paul'. I couldn't think of another way to say it so I just came out with it. I could tell by the looks in their eyes how shocked they were but I don't think anyone knew what to say so they just said nothing.[43]

'It was a really rough time for us', recalled Lance Corporal Rab McClurg, 'But we couldn't afford to dwell on it. We had to get on with the job at hand'. The men were upset but there was no time to mourn. 'I think Draiva's death geed us up. It made us want to fight harder and longer'.[44]

---

39 Corporal John Harding, interview with author.
40 Corporal John Harding, interview with author.
41 Dicker – Army slang for look-out. The expression originated in Northern Ireland where locals watching out for approaching Army patrols were said to be 'keeping dick'.
42 Corporal Cliff Tweed, interview with author.
43 Corporal Danny Groves, diary entry, 1 September 2006.
44 Lance Corporal Rab McClurg, interview with author.

PJ Brangan recalled the last time he had seen the pair before the tragedy:

> I was sitting outside the JOC having a brew with one of the Somme Platoon section commanders when Moonbeam and Draiva came out of their accommodation to make their way up to the roof for guard duty. Draiva had his LMG on his shoulder and Moonbeam was carrying his rifle. As they walked towards the Alamo, Moonbeam turned and raised the hand carrying the rifle in a wave. Less than an hour later, D was dead and Moonbeam was seriously wounded.[45]

Ranger Pepper was in the RAP when the casualties arrived. 'Draiva was obviously dead. Moonbeam was covered in blood but he was alive. Doc Stacey and the medics went to work to get him stabilised'.[46] Pepper remembered being angry at the time, but with the contact still going on, and the high tempo of activities, he did not have time to grieve. 'I don't think I was able to process the loss properly until I was back to the UK and we went to visit Moonbeam's mother and brother and to see his grave'.[47]

Immediately after the mortar strike, the priority had been to recover the casualties and get them to medical help as quickly as possible. After that, the focus had been on organising the CASEVAC and making sure the helicopter could get in and out. There had been no time to think about clearing up at the scene of the tragedy. Corporal Harding knew it was vital that someone took on that gruesome task:

> I went and had a look and it was a terrible sight. There was blood and gore everywhere. The entrance to the position was right beside the mortar line and I didn't want any of the soldiers, but especially D's friends in the mortar team, to see the aftermath. I went and got a shovel and a burn-bag and returned to clear up the scene. Danny (Groves) saw me and came to help. The boys didn't need to see that sort of thing.

Harding was speaking from experience. At 21 he had served in Kosovo and had helped to recover bodies of civilians who had died in the fighting there. 'I knew the effect that had on me as a young man and I didn't want the boys to have to go through the same thing'.[48]

The last Royal Irish soldier to see Draiva before he was flown out, was Ranger Paul Johnston. He had helped Sergeant Major Scrivener to prepare the body for the move. With no body-bags available, the men had to improvise:

> We placed him in yellow medical waste bags, one from his feet to his waist and the other from his head down, and taped them together. Then we put him in his sleeping bag and zip-tied it shut. Just before we put the plastic bags on, I lifted his arm, shook his hand and said "see you when I get there".[49]

The MO, Captain Stacey, flew back into the compound at 0430 the following morning (2 September). Despite the violence of the previous evening, the return trip was completely uneventful.

---

45 Sergeant P J Brangan, interview with author.
46 Ranger Davy Pepper, interview with author.
47 Ranger Davy Pepper, interview with author.
48 Corporal John Harding, interview with author.
49 Ranger Paul Johnston, interview with author.

The Taliban had decided not to engage and the helicopter landed untouched. The doctor walked down the ramp and back into the DC. The soldiers were pleased to see him.

Stacey would be the butt of some banter for a day or two. As Sergeant Brangan had noted, some of the men had not taken off their helmets and body armour since they heard he had left.[50] 'We could smell him as he came off the aircraft, he was so clean, compared to us', Brangan remembered.[51]

Friendly Fire?

The day of the MO's return was notable for two things. The first was that not only had the Taliban declined to shoot at the early-morning helicopter, they also decided to forego their usual dawn assault. This put everyone in the compound on-edge, wondering what was to follow. The second was that when the fighting did eventually come, Easy Company would suffer the largest casualty event of its time in Musa Qal'eh.

The sun was well on its journey from east to west when six enemy mortar rounds, fired from two barrels, shattered the silence. The JTAC immediately responded by calling in a fire mission from the guns of I Battery, 7RHA, targeting every known firing point, and the enemy firing ceased. Three hours later, at around 0800hrs, they came again, this time with heavy small-arms fire, but once more the shooting died away quite quickly. For Major Adam Jowett, these attacks felt like little more than attempts by the Taliban to remind the garrison it was surrounded.[52] Just before 1100hrs, however, that picture changed – and not for the better. This time, the insurgents' fire, when it came, was heavy and sustained, a serious attempt to suppress the defenders so that the Taliban fighters could reach, and maybe breach, the walls. Lieutenant Paul Martin described it as a 'very aggressive and very violent 360-degrees attack'.

The Afghan police had brought some local men into the compound, and the strength of the Taliban onslaught suggested that perhaps there was someone important among the prisoners, recalled Lieutenant Martin. 'We had become accustomed to the Taliban's battle rhythm. They usually launched strong attacks at first and last light but during the day the fighting was less intense. This was much heavier, more prolonged and out of character for that time of the day'.[53] Martin and two sections of Barrosa Platoon manned firing positions on the roof of the Alamo, while the JTAC and the MFCs went back to work, directing artillery and mortar fire onto the enemy while calling frantically for A-10s or Harriers. A French Super Etendard was overhead, but Jowett felt the Gallic approach to close air support would not be sufficient. On previous occasions, their pilots, had seemed reluctant to engage ground targets with sufficient vigour to have the desired effect.[54]

On the roof of the Alamo, Paul Martin and his men were doing their best to engage targets as they popped up among the buildings. The sheer weight of enemy fire was making this difficult and it was becoming clear that the insurgents were getting close to the eastern wall. Ranger Johnston was not the only one who feared they were about to be overrun.[55] 'The Taliban were right on top of the compound. Some of the defenders were having to stand on the shoulders of their mates to get enough height to fire down along the wall', recalled the Platoon Commander. 'I was plotting target

---

50　Jowett, *No Way Out,* p.163.
51　Sergeant PJ Brangan, interview with the author.
52　Jowett, *No Way Out,* p.172.
53　Lieutenant Paul Martin, interview with author.
54　Lieutenant Paul Martin, interview with author.
55　Ranger Paul Johnston, interview with author.

grids and calling in mortars. The FOOs were directing fire from the guns in the desert. The two sections on the roof were engaging targets, loading magazines and doing everything they could to keep the enemy from breaching the walls'.

Martin had taken up a central position on the roof, with his soldiers spread out around him, when a huge explosion rocked the Alamo. Down on the floor of the compound, Jowett, heard the blast and felt debris rain down on his helmet. He knew, without having to look, that on a roof packed with men, there would be casualties.[56] Sergeant Major Scrivener commanded the rescue party, darting through a hail of incoming bullets to lead the reserve platoon to the scene. On the roof, Ranger Johnston had felt the heat of the explosion and was momentarily blinded by the cloud of dust that it had thrown up. It seemed as if there was a moment of silence and then the screaming started as wounded men called out for help. Nearly everyone in the section seemed to have been hit:

> There was a hole in the roof and me and a guy called Ossie began to help the injured to get down. The last man we helped was Mr. Martin. He seemed to be in shock, he was slurring his words and not really making any sense. He set off towards the RAP. I think I saw him fall down at one point.

But Johnston was too busy to go to the officer's aid. 'Ossie and I seemed to be the only two who were uninjured. The Taliban fighters were getting closer and we knew we had to get the GPMG going again'.[57]

Looking back on the incident after 18 years, Paul Martin remembered being blown off his feet, losing his helmet and rifle. He had been peppered with shrapnel. There were smoking pieces of metal embedded in his body armour and he was bleeding through his eyes and ears. He could see that many of his men had lacerations to their backs, the rear of their legs, and their feet:

> The sensation I experienced was just like falling from a tree, landing on your back, and having the wind knocked out of you. But usually, when you've been winded, you get your breath back quite quickly. In this instance, the sensation of breathlessness didn't go away.
>
> I was totally disorientated. I managed to help two of the others off the rooftop. I was shouting and screaming at Corporal Quinn (one of the section commanders) telling him to keep firing. I helped one of the Fijians to get down and then went back up to check on Corporal Quinn. By that time, the smoke was clearing and I was able to see the scale of the damage.[58]

Martin took himself back down a flight of steps and realised that he was in a bad way. His left boot was filling up with blood. He had blood running down his left side, and he was struggling to breathe:

> I sat down and felt sorry for myself for a bit, and then managed to pull myself together and get to the RAP, which was not far away. Mike Stacey did a cracking job. He pushed a needle through my rib-cage to release a build-up of blood which was collapsing my lung, and fitted a chest drain.[59]

---

56   Jowett, *No Way Out,* p.173.
57   Ranger Johnson, interview with author.
58   Lieutenant Paul Martin, interview with author.
59   Lieutenant Paul Martin, interview with author.

The young officer's left lung had collapsed, his spleen was bleeding, he had a damaged arm and he had numerous other small shrapnel wounds. Many, including Stacey and Jowett, were amazed that he had managed to get to the RAP under his own steam.

It took two 1,000lb bombs, dropped from American F-18s, to persuade the Taliban to break off the fight. Having assessed the situation on the roof, Scrivener sent a radio sitrep to the Ops Room. There were nine casualties among the men of Barrosa Platoon. That meant the garrison had just lost about 15 percent of its manpower. Danny Groves recorded the details in his diary. Lieutenant Martin was T1 (shrapnel wounds to chest), Corporal Quinn, Ranger Benson, Ranger Jackson and Ranger Skates were T3.[60] The others had minor shrapnel injuries, and were champing at the bit to get back into the fight.[61] Once again, the Ops Room sent a nine-liner CASEVAC request to Bastion, but with Martin stable and none of the others in a critical condition, it was decided to wait until the contact died down before sending the MERT.

With Lieutenant Martin out of the fight, Sergeant Gilchrist, became the de facto platoon commander. 'When things calmed down, I called the guys together and we had a quick chat about the situation. We were down a whole section and I needed to do a bit of reorganisation to ensure we were still a coherent force'. Meanwhile, the medics were having a problem with one of the Barrosa wounded. Ranger Bulimaibau, another of the Fijians, was refusing, point blank, to be CASEVAC'd. 'He said he was fit to fight and he wasn't leaving', recalled Gilchrist. 'Bulimaibau was a nightmare to manage in barracks, but out on the ground he was just immense'.[62] He stayed.

Initially it had been assumed that the projectile that caused the damage to Barrosa Platoon had been an enemy mortar or RPG. As the men talked about their experience, however, some of them concluded that it had actually been a 'drop-short' from the 7RHA guns in the desert. Ranger Johnston was among those who felt this was the case:

> The Taliban were at the wall. They were close. I remember Mr Martin telling us that artillery fire was coming in. It was going to be danger-close and we needed to get down behind the low wall that ran around the roof of the Alamo. We all took cover and the boss reported 'shot out' which meant the rounds were in the air. He then gave a warning that the impact would be in five seconds. I counted down the seconds and then bang…a massive explosion.[63]

Sergeant Gilchrist had a similar view:

> We talked about the possibility that there had been a drop-short. In my opinion, there is a very real possibility that it was. But there was so much ordnance going off at the time, it was impossible to know for sure. Even if it was, it was no-one's fault. It was just one of those things that happen in war. I didn't blame anyone at the time and I haven't changed my mind since.[64]

Ranger Pepper was in another part of the compound when the strike occurred. 'I remember hearing the distinctive sound of a 105mm round coming in. As far as I am concerned, it was a drop-short. The damage seemed too severe to have been an RPG or a recoilless rifle'.[65]

---

60 Corporal Danny Groves, diary entry, 2 September 2006.
61 Jowett, *No Way Out,* p.176.
62 Sergeant Stephen Gilchrist, interview with author.
63 Ranger Paul Johnston, interview with author.
64 Sergeant Stephen Gilchrist, interview with author.
65 Ranger Davy Pepper, interview with author.

Another soldier, who was close to the scene, suggested that there had been problems with one of 7RHA's guns during an earlier shoot, when its rounds had not been landing in the right place. 'We were 100 percent certain that the Alamo incident was friendly fire', he said.[66]

In Adam Jowett's account, he claims the explosion was caused by an enemy mortar round. He explains that calling in artillery on targets to the east of the compound was fraught with difficulty. 'Not only was it danger-close but the rounds would have to travel over our heads as they came from the guns to our west in the desert. If one was to fall short, it could cause more carnage than the Taliban's own indirect fire had done'. Jowett suggests that artillery fire was called in to deal with targets to the east, but only *after* [author's emphasis] the Alamo had been hit.[67]

Although the men of Barrosa Platoon did not know it, the incident had been reported up the gunners' chain of command, and thoroughly investigated by qualified, expert artillerymen, in accordance with the requirements of the relevant policy document – in this case, Artillery Training Volume III, Field Artillery, Pamphlet No 19, Regulations for Planning, Control, Conduct and Safety for Firing Practices. The possibility of a drop-short is considered by artillerymen to be a very serious issue and there is a standing requirement to report possible incidents, irrespective of the consequences. The result of the formal After-Action Review (AAR), which was reported in writing to Task Force Helmand headquarters in Kandahar, a day later, concluded that the explosion on the Alamo on 2 September had not been caused by the guns of I Battery.

The Battery Commander (BC) of I Battery at the time, Major (later Colonel) Gary Wilkinson, understood how the Royal Irish soldiers might have reached their conclusion:

> For 24 hours, before facts were gathered and analysis conducted, there was real concern, shared by me, that the damage might have been caused by one of my guns. I can tell you, that was the lowest point of that tour for me. I had thought the battery I commanded had potentially been responsible for those casualties and while I waited for the facts, I felt that very personally.[68]

According to Major Wilkinson, the initial view of the Company Commander, Adam Jowett, in the immediate aftermath of the incident, was that it had probably been friendly fire. However, a day later, after careful study of the ground, the impact point, and the circumstances, he accepted that the most likely cause had been an ACM (Anti-Coalition Militia – the term used by the Task Force at the time to describe the Taliban) mortar.[69] What had happened over the course of a day to change Jowett's mind?

Crater analysis, conducted by the Fire Support Team in the compound at the time, had established that the weapon that exploded on the roof of the Alamo had been fired from the south-east. I Battery had been firing from the south-west. In addition, it was considered that the damage to the Alamo, and the injuries suffered by the casualties, were not consistent with the effects of a 105mm artillery round. In Wilkinson's expert opinion, if a 105mm round had been responsible, there would have been more structural damage, the impact crater would have been larger, the wounds would have been even more serious, and it is highly likely that there would have been fatalities. This latter point is supported by the fact that this type of artillery ammunition has a lethal splinter distance of about 40m. Furthermore, according to Wilkinson, the ACM mortars landing in the compound the following day were examined and had the same properties (including indicating

---

66 Royal Irish Regiment soldier, private interview with author.
67 Jowett, *No Way Out,* p.175.
68 Major Gary Wilkinson, interview with author.
69 Major Gary Wilkinson, interview with author.

that they had been fired from the south-east) as the crater from the round that had caused the casualties on 2 September. Some of the witnesses have suggested that the shell was an airburst. If it was, that would reduce even further the likelihood that it came from the 7RHA guns. The gunners certainly used airburst ammunition to engage enemy fighters in the open, well away from friendly troops. However, for danger-close fire missions only PD (Point Detonated) munitions were used – to reduce the risk of friendly casualties. This was because the lethal splinter distance for PD was about 20 percent less than for airburst.

There are some defects that could cause an artillery piece to become inaccurate. The most likely of these would be a worn barrel, which can be the result of over-use and the lack of proper maintenance. However, the Battery Commander was clear that there was nothing to indicate his guns were not in good order and no defects had been reported. The 105mm Light Guns used had been physically checked and verified as part of the investigation and the results were recorded in the AAR.[70]

Sceptics might point out that the investigation was conducted by the gunners themselves and cannot, therefore, be considered to be independent. However, it was the gunners who were the most suitably qualified and experienced people to carry out the review. In addition, the seriousness of such an incident, the fact that it had been fully investigated, and the results submitted, in writing, up the chain of command, suggests that those carrying out the investigation were reasonably sure of their findings and prepared to justify them if required.

Also, as Wilkinson explained, although it was his gunners who had the professional qualifications and experience to undertake such a review, there had been input from infantrymen at the scene, including the Company Commander, as part of both the analysis and the conclusion reached. The result of the review had been seen, and [presumably] accepted, by those in the chain of command at Battlegroup level and above:

> In my professional opinion, the facts and analysis explain the conclusion reached in 2006 that the round that caused the injuries on 2 September, 2006, did not come from the guns of I Battery, 7RHA. I base that view not only on the details that were contained in the After-Action Review, but also on my own personal experience, as a gunner with combat experience alongside infantry, with significant service in Helmand Province.[71]

Major Wilkinson had fought in Sangin on rooftops similar to the Alamo, so was fully aware how the lethality of mortar and RPG rounds could be magnified by the structures and masonry of the local buildings. Wilkinson noted that on 1 July 2006 a single 107mm Chinese Rocket killed three soldiers and wounded a number of others who were serving with A Company Group, 3 Para. The Alamo was not on the Gun Target Line (the direction from which the guns were firing). The bearings on which each of the guns had been laid had been checked against the fire direction computer data for the targets being engaged. That information was itself checked by a second computer. According to Wilkinson, and despite what the Easy Company Commander wrote in his book, I Battery's fire, although falling very close to the DC, was not passing directly over the heads of the men in the compound on this occasion. Wilkinson understood that one of the injured was only a few metres from the impact point – well inside the 40 metres lethal splinter distance had it been 105mm ammunition. In his view '…the evidence points…to it being an ACM mortar round, and probably quite an aged munition, given the lack of fatalities'.[72]

---

70 Major Gary Wilkinson, interview with author.
71 Major Gary Wilkinson, interview with author.
72 Major Gary Wilkinson, interview with author.

The fog of war is real. It obscures and conceals. It is impossible, therefore, to be 100 percent certain about the cause of the injuries to Lieutenant Martin and his soldiers. However, given the evidence set out above, the balance of probability seems to lean towards it being a Taliban mortar or RPG. Paul Martin, the man who was most seriously injured in the incident, believes it was an RPG round that did the damage.[73] Readers will, no doubt, weigh the evidence above and come to their own conclusions.

The JTAC and MFCs had been making increasing use of the guns of I Battery due to the growing shortage of 81mm mortar rounds. According to Corporal John Harding, the team went into Musa Qal'eh with only about half the number of mortar bombs that it would have expected as a normal allocation. It was the equivalent of a rifleman going into an attack with half of his magazines empty. The war stock just did not seem to exist. As a result, they had to use their 81mm mortars sparingly, almost from the start. This meant a greater reliance was placed on artillery support from the guns based out in the desert to the west. 'Eventually, we got told off for calling in too many fire missions. Apparently, we had ordered more artillery strikes than the rest of the battlegroup combined'. The MFCs felt obliged to point out that they were not using the artillery for fun. 'I had to refuse dozens of targets on a daily basis as the Taliban were attacking and trying to kill us. It was like trying to be a sniper with a shotgun. We didn't have the ammo and I would rather use the stocks we did have for targets where the juice was worth the squeeze'. Eventually, in a bid to keep the garrison supplied, the logistics chain managed to obtain a quantity of mortar ammunition from the American forces.[74]

After another heavy contact that afternoon, Battlegroup Headquarters was once again reluctant to authorise a CASEVAC flight, particularly since Paul Martin's condition remained stable. The chest drains, inserted by Captain Stacey, were continuing to do their job, but the patient really needed the services of a surgeon in a hospital, and after further consideration, the airlift was finally approved. Once more, the garrison repeated the by-now familiar ritual of preparing to receive the aircraft. Having been notified that the Chinook had left Bastion, everyone spent the next 30 minutes thinking about all the things that could go wrong. Nothing did.

The aircraft approached from the east, circled around to the north and touched down on the HLS without so much as a single Taliban bullet being fired. It carried replacements for the wounded: a new second-in-command, Captain Austen Salusbury, Welsh Guards, to take some of the weight off Adam Jowett's shoulders; a platoon commander, Captain Dean Whitten, 3 Para, in place of Paul Martin, and some much-needed ammunition for the 81mm mortars. In under a minute, it was back in the air, carrying Martin and the walking wounded out of the conflict zone and back to the relative luxury of Camp Bastion.

Although Captain Mike Stacey, working in pretty basic field conditions, had done a good job of patching up and stabilising Martin so he could be evacuated to hospital, the casualty was still in a critical condition. When he arrived at Camp Bastion, the medical team there was most concerned about a piece of shrapnel that had lodged about 1cm from his heart. There was no MRI scanner at Bastion so it was decided that he needed to be transferred to Kandahar, where there were slightly better medical facilities. Before he left, however, fellow Royal Irish Regiment officer, Captain Graham Rainey, managed to arrange for him to call his girlfriend and parents in the UK. 'Graham had been in Gereshk when news of my injury came through and he managed to get himself to Bastion so I could see at least one familiar face. I don't know how he did it, but he managed to find

---

73 Lieutenant Paul Martin, interview with author.
74 Corporal John Harding, interview with author.

a telephone-on-wheels, which he brought to my bedside so I could call home'.[75] His family were surprised to hear him speak because they had been told he had been shot in the throat.

Arriving at Kandahar, Martin was admitted to a Canadian field hospital, which had the only MRI scanner in the region. The hospital was staffed by French-Canadians whose English was no better than Martin's poor French. He spent several 'fairly sad and horrific' days there 'in a really bad place, physically and mentally'.[76] A platoon of Canadians taking part in Operation Medusa had suffered a friendly-fire incident, involving an American A-10, killing one and seriously wounding 25 others. All the surviving casualties ended up in the same hospital, on the same ward. 'There was blood and mess everywhere. Men were screaming and moaning with pain, and I got lost in a bed-space. It felt like no-one knew I was there', recalled Lieutenant Martin.[77]

A British officer serving at Kandahar was allocated to visit and keep him informed about plans to have him flown back to the UK:

> He would come and give me a daily update, but because of the lack of airframes and the Canadian medical staff trying to deal with a mass casualty event, every evening he brought bad news. Meanwhile, I was tripping on morphine, often lying in my own piss and blood, in considerable pain…and I wasn't the most seriously injured there.
>
> I shut up and lay there for four days until they were finally able to arrange for a C-17 to fly me back to the UK.[78]

Paul Martin still has pieces of shrapnel in his body from the Alamo explosion.

According to ICOM, the Taliban had known that there had been casualties at the Alamo. That meant they also knew there would be an attempt to fly them out. The fact that they had allowed the Chinook to come and go, without attempting to interfere, was the subject of some speculation that evening, although few conclusions had been drawn. The insurgents returned to their familiar routine at dawn the following morning, welcoming the new arrivals with another heavy RPG and small-arms attack. Later that day, four mortar rounds crashed into the side of the Alamo, killing one Afghan and injuring three others. The wounded were assessed as T3 and CASEVAC was requested, although it was determined that the injuries did not require immediate hospital attention. Once more the Chinook evacuation helicopter was able to fly in and out without being engaged. The reason for the Taliban's restraint became clear later that evening when ICOM intercepts concluded that the insurgents were conducting an ammunition replenishment.[79] They had clearly fired themselves to a standstill. But with their supplies topped up again, the enemy returned to the offensive early the following morning. At first light, long streams of tracer and a heavy bombardment of RPGs confirmed that they had no more ammunition worries. As the attack developed, it became clear that this was a bit different from the familiar hit-and-run assaults. The insurgents appeared to be making a concerted attempt to overrun the position. At first, they feinted from the south. MFC(B), Lance Corporal Rab McClurg, was in Sangar 4 and called down the mortars on target Xray-63, which was about 800m out. But having drawn the garrison's fire in that direction, the attackers switched to the other fighting positions. Sangar 3, to the north-east, was struck three times by RPGs, sending the sentries sprawling, unhurt, across the dusty ground. As Corporal Danny Groves recalled:

---

75 Lieutenant Paul Martin, interview with author.
76 Lieutenant Paul Martin, interview with author.
77 Lieutenant Paul Martin, interview with author.
78 Lieutenant Paul Martin, interview with author.
79 Jowett, *No Way Out*, p.193.

Every one of our X-ray numbers (recorded targets) seemed to have numerous insurgents in them. The main threat was assessed to be from Xray-66, which was about 200m to the west, in the bazaar, among some ISO containers. We hit it with 10 rounds of American HE airbursts. There was incoming tracer flying through the wall towards the mortar line but the boys never flinched.

They fired continuously, switching from one target to another, hitting each one as hard as they could. The artillery joined in the fight, engaging Xray-66 and when that failed to silence the enemy, A-10s, Harriers and a B-1 arrived and the JTAC directed airborne ordnance on to all the recorded targets as well as gun-runs on Xray-53 to the north and Xray-64, 300m due east. At one stage, Groves had four missions on his fire control computer and he engaged them one at a time until the incoming fire died down. The LEWT reported that the Taliban's radio traffic, in the aftermath, contained many references to 'brothers going to Allah'.[80]

That evening, the men in the western sangars spotted Taliban moving around in the vicinity of Xray-66. Usually, the enemy returned, unarmed, to collect their dead, and the men in the DC were content to let them go about their grisly task unmolested. But on this occasion, the insurgents were carrying weapons, and the garrison responded without hesitation. Rifles and machine guns opened up on the ghostly figures, and the mortars hit them with HE. The airwaves were alive with calls from a Taliban commander to his subordinate, berating him for allowing his men to be killed and wounded.[81]

The insurgents having sustained heavy casualties on 5 September, the next day began quietly in the DC. A few mortar rounds were aimed at the compound but these were inaccurate and caused no damage. The enemy mortar teams seemed to have developed a belt of targets and the Outpost appeared to be one of the locations they returned to time after time. This had caused some concern amongst the soldiers who were detailed for duty there.[82] The section occupying the position were usually required to remain there for 24 hours at a time. The sangars were on the roof, and on the floor below was the sleeping accommodation where the garrison would go to rest when not on guard. At 1715 the indirect fire became more precise. At least two mortar bombs landed on or near the Outpost, where men of Somme Platoon and some ANP were on duty.[83] The reserve platoon, under Sergeant Brangan, doubled to the scene while Major Jowett and his JTAC worked to counter the incoming fire, calling in fast air to hammer the enemy firing points. There had been six casualties among the soldiers and police in the Outpost – two Royal Irish and four Afghans. Ranger Whitehouse (shrapnel wound to his backside) and the Afghans were classified as T3, walking wounded, but Ranger Matanasinga had a much more serious injury. A jagged piece of red-hot flying metal from the disintegrating mortar bomb had sliced through his throat causing extensive damage and putting his life in peril. Corporal French, one of the medics, was quickly on the scene. He applied a field dressing to try to stem the bleeding before the big Fijian was man-handled down from the roof and laid on the back of the quad-bike that served as an ambulance. The move from the Outpost to the RAP took only seconds and just a few minutes after being injured, Matanasinga was being worked on by the MO.

Easy Company was dependent on a diesel generator to produce the power that charged the batteries for its radios. With the diesel supply running low, it had been decided, a few days earlier, to cease monitoring the Battlegroup radio net on a 24-hour basis, in a bid to extend battery life and

---

80   Corporal Danny Groves, diary entry, 5 September 2006.
81   Corporal Danny Groves, diary entry, 5 September 2006.
82   Sergeant PJ Brangan, interview with author.
83   Corporal Danny Groves, diary entry, 6 September 2006.

reduce diesel consumption. Instead, the signallers would switch on the radio only to report troops in contact, and to send their daily sitrep to headquarters at Bastion. When the fighting began, the second-in-command, Captain Salusbury, powered up the set to send a contact report, and prepare to request a CASEVAC helicopter. As the radio burst into life, it was obvious that Musa Qal'eh was not the only place in Helmand with a problem. There were also serious contacts at Sangin and Kajaki, and the troops in those locations were also asking for helicopters to fly out their wounded.[84] Matanasinga, Whitehead and the Afghan policemen would have to take their turn.

At Kajaki, seven soldiers of 3 Para had been wounded after triggering old Soviet-era antipersonnel mines. The events have since become the subject of a feature film, taking the name of the lake and its hydro-electric plant as its title. They were eventually airlifted out by an American Blackhawk, but by the time they reached Bastion, one of their number, Corporal Mark Wright, had died of his injuries. At Sangin, Royal Irish Regiment Colour Sergeant Richard Spence, of Ranger Platoon, was conducting an Orders Group, surrounded by his junior commanders, when a Taliban mortar landed close by. One soldier, Lance Corporal Luke McCulloch, sustained a serious head wound and was categorised as T1, requiring immediate CASEVAC. Five others, including Spence himself, were assessed as T2 or T3.

At Bastion, Commanding Officer, Lieutenant Colonel Stuart Tootal, his medical advisor, Lieutenant Colonel Peter Davies and the Battlegroup staff, again had some tough decisions to make. There was only one MERT and one helicopter on standby to fly the rescue missions. After consulting with the medics at Sangin and Musa Qal'eh, Davies advised that McCulloch should be the first priority. Matanasinga was critical but stable for the time being.

The helicopter that went to evacuate the Sangin wounded was met with a curtain of enemy tracer as it came in to land, but the crew pressed on through the firestorm to get the wheels on the ground. The casualties were loaded into the back and the big twin-rotor machine clawed its way back into the sky, through the same maelstrom of fire, and set a course for Bastion. Its engines screamed as the pilot pushed his aircraft to its operating limits in an attempt to complete the journey as rapidly as possible. In the rear, the Medical Emergency Response Team worked frantically to try to save, Lance Corporal McCulloch. Sadly, their efforts were in vain. He died on the journey back. His injuries had been just too severe.

Refuelled and rearmed the Chinook was then tasked to repeat the process at Musa Qal'eh.[85] The garrison was told to expect the aircraft at 2015hrs. That was three hours after the casualties had occurred. To make things worse, the LEWT had picked up Taliban radio transmissions that suggested they were aware that a CASEVAC mission would be coming in.[86] This may have been due to the fact that the police had been talking to each other using insecure Motorola radios.[87] Once again, the men of Easy Company made ready to receive the aircraft, aware that the Taliban were waiting. This time, however, knowing the enemy had replenished their ammunition supply, they expected that things would certainly be different – and not in a good way. The Taliban would be going all out to bring down the aircraft and score a major PR victory. Adam Jowett was feeling the heavy weight of command on his shoulders. All he could do was to be ready for the worst and hope for the best.[88]

Thirty minutes before the aircraft was due, the garrison stood-to around the compound. It was certain that the enemy would be focusing on the HLS so that was where the defenders would

---

84 Adam Jowett, *No Way Out,* p.204.
85 Hammond, *Immediate Response,* p.117.
86 Jowett, *No Way Out,* p.208.
87 Corporal Danny Groves, diary entry for 6 September 2006.
88 Jowett, *No Way Out,* p.208.

direct their attention. The remaining serviceable .50in machine gun was moved to a position on the northern wall, where the weight of its deadly fire was likely to do the most good. The MFCs and the mortar line were standing by, their barrels laid on the two most likely targets while the JTAC maintained contact with coalition aircraft tracing lazy figure-of-eight holding patterns high above, ready to call them in, if – when – required. The riflemen on the walls watched and waited, their fingers kept well away from their triggers. They had been warned not to fire unless the enemy engaged for fear of provoking a reaction. Five minutes out, the tell-tale sound of the approaching Chinook, its rotors beating their familiar tattoo, could be heard by the defenders… and the Taliban.

Up in the dark night sky, the pilot, Royal Marine Major Mark Hammond, nervously shifted his position in the right-hand seat and warned his crew that he was about to begin the decent into hell. He dropped the machine down to low-level as he neared the eastern outskirts of the town and, as the first buildings flashed by below, the sky exploded as the insurgents opened up with everything they had. 'It seemed that… everyone in the world wanted to kill us…and we hadn't even ID'd the landing site', he wrote later.[89] The side-door and ramp gunners returned fire, hosing down as many of the enemy firing points as they could locate. On the ground, the men, looking to the north-east, could see the Chinook, lumbering above the rooftops, illuminated by the light of the tracer that seemed to be reaching out for it. With a minute to run, every rifle and machine gun in the compound let loose in an attempt to suppress the enemy fire, trying to force the Taliban shooters down into cover for long enough to get the big machine on the ground. As it edged closer, it was clear that the helicopter was being hit. Jowett took a deep breath and ordered the landing to be aborted. Desperate as he was to get his wounded men out, he could not risk the Chinook being brought down. Hammond dropped the helicopter's nose to gain speed and accelerated away. As he pulled up, he could see explosions on the ground as the Taliban began, too late, to mortar the LZ.[90] Watching and willing the aircraft to get away, Jowett heard the reports of two RPGs as the missiles flew into the air, in front and behind, and saw streams of tracer following it as it gained altitude and disappeared into the darkness.[91]

For those who had witnessed the sheer weight of the Taliban onslaught that night, there could only be one conclusion. If they were going to get a helicopter safely in and out of the LZ at Musa Qal'eh, and save the life of Ranger Matanasinga, they would have to silence the insurgents' fire. And to do that, they would need to flatten their firing points. Since that could not be done safely while the aircraft was making its approach, they would need to hit the targets before it arrived – using preliminary fires. However, under the existing rules of engagement, they could not use artillery or aircraft unless they were actually under fire or there was an obvious threat to life. And the enemy would not fire until they could hear and see the helicopter. It seemed like a circular argument and someone was going to have to find a way to square the circle. Time was ticking by. The wounded had now been waiting for nearly four hours for rescue. Eventually, the lawyers at Task Force Headquarters, in Kandahar, were persuaded to sign off on an exception to the extant ROE. In view of the risk to the wounded soldiers, the garrison would be granted the use of preliminary fires.

Task Force Helmand in Kandahar assigned as much fast air as it could muster. And in addition, the garrison would have the assistance of an American AC-130 Spectre gunship – a Hercules aircraft armed with an array of heavy weaponry, including a quick-firing 105mm side-mounted cannon.[92]

---

89 Hammond, *Immediate Response,* p.121.
90 Hammond, *Immediate Response,* p.124
91 Jowett, *No Way Out,* p.212.
92 Jowett, *No Way Out,* p.215.

This represented a truly frightening combination of firepower. To save Ranger Matanasinga, the centre of Musa Qal'eh was about to be reduced to rubble.

The next attempt to get a helicopter in to the HLS was scheduled for 0130hrs the following morning, with stand-to in the compound set for 0100hrs. The same aircrew and MERT would be making the return trip, but not the airframe. The machine had been too badly mauled by Taliban fire. Bullet holes pock-marked its thin aluminium skin, but the most worrying damage was close to a linkage pin that held one of the huge rotors in place. Examining the airframe with a technician, back at the flight line at Bastion, the pilot learned how close his aircraft had come to disaster. If the round had impacted two inches nearer, he was told, the pin would have failed and the 30ft blade would have been flung away from its mounting. The resulting damage would have sent the aircraft spiralling into the ground. The big helicopter could absorb a lot of punishment, but losing a rotor blade in flight was not survivable. Of that there was no doubt.[93] Major Mark Hammond and his crew, and the medics, moved their kit to a new aircraft and started to go through their pre-departure checks.

As the time ticked by until the extraction, Jowett and his JTAC set about ensuring that the insurgents would pose no further threat. With massive firepower on tap and authorised, they pummelled every known enemy firing point, forming-up area and shelter. Fires broke out in the wreckage of buildings, adding their light to the flashes of detonating high explosives. In the sangars, the men of Somme and Barrosa platoons watched open-mouthed, in awe, at the sight of the town centre being dismantled, bit by bit, before their eyes. As one Texan A-10 pilot drawled 'It's just nothing but a sea of fire down there'.[94] Sergeant Stephen Gilchrist described the scene as being like 'Guy Fawkes night on steroids'.[95] As soon as the first bombs began to fall, the Taliban radio net burst into life with messages, reporting casualties or near misses. The LEWT and the intelligence section used the information to refine their targeting and the planes came in again and again, wave after wave, sewing death and destruction from above.

The garrison was supposed to stand-to as the rescue flight lifted from Bastion. In reality, though, most of the men were already lining the walls before that, watching the deadly fireworks display before them. With a minute to go until the Chinook's arrival, the bombing and artillery fire stopped. As the roar of explosions died away, dogs barked, blazes crackled and sparked, but no enemy fire could be heard. In the distance, the sound of the helicopter's rotors cut through the sky, just as on the previous occasion, but this time there was no answering fusillade from the insurgents. The pilot, approaching from the north-west, put his aircraft down, unmolested, right in the centre of the landing site. The stretcher, carrying Matanasinga, was lifted into the hold as the walking wounded clambered up the ramp, and, in less than 30 seconds, it was off again, climbing into the darkness and heading for Bastion, sent on its way not by lines of enemy tracer, but by cheers of relief and joy from the men on the ramparts. Ranger Panapassa Matanasinga would live.

Only after the sound of the helicopter had died away, did those insurgents who had survived, make their presence felt. But the attack was desultory and half-hearted, beaten down by the garrison in less than half-an-hour. Another assault, the following morning, was more determined and vigorous, but was again driven off. However, the jubilation sparked by the successful casevac of Matanasinga and Whitehead did not last long. Later that day the garrison learned of the deaths of Lance Corporal Luke McCulloch, and, more shockingly, of Lance Corporal Paul Muirhead, who had passed away in hospital in Oman. Having watched 'Moonbeam' get out alive, many of the Royal Irish soldiers struggled to accept that he had not survived. 'The news hit us like a steam

---

93 Hammond, *Immediate Response,* p.140.
94 Jowett, *No Way Out,* p.215
95 Sergeant Stephen Gilchrist, interview with author.

train. We were all pretty low that day', remembered Danny Groves. He had walked across to the Operations Centre and met Captain Johnson coming the other way. 'He seemed upset. I asked him what was wrong and he said Paul Muirhead had passed away. He told me to tell the others'.[96]

Understandably, the men took the news badly. Corporal John Harding spoke for many when he said he had been hopeful 'Moonbeam' was going to be OK. 'You think that if you can get the casualty out of the compound and onto an operating table at Bastion then, surely, they've got a good chance of pulling through. We had been conditioned by what had happened to Ally McKinney. He had survived so we thought Paul would pull through too'.[97]

As the bad news spread among the men, one of the soldiers expressed the feelings of all, writing on a wall of one of the buildings: 'Luke and Moonbeam. Our hearts are heavy with such a sad loss. We will all RV in Ranger land one day. Keep the beers cold. FAB.[98] Rest In Peace Brothers'.[99] With Paul Muirhead's passing, the losses sustained by the garrison to that point totalled three dead and 12 wounded. They had fought off over well over 100 attacks.

Platoon Sergeant, Stephen Gilchrist, felt the losses as keenly as anyone. But he knew he had to keep his men fixed on the job in hand:

> Obviously, the deaths had a particular effect on those soldiers who had been close friends with Draiva and Muirhead. But the guys also knew there was a task at hand. We couldn't just down tools. We had to maintain focus, stay professional. The only way out was to keep doing what we were doing.[100]

The real mourning would have to wait until they were home.

Meanwhile, back at Fort George on the outskirts of Inverness, Commanding Officer Michael McGovern, his command team, the rest of the battalion, and the families of all those deployed, were following events in Helmand as closely as they could from 5,000 miles away. As well as the soldiers fighting in Musa Qal'eh and Sangin, the regiment had officers attached to brigade headquarters. The battalion second-in-command, Major Steve Ocock, was serving as Military Assistant to the Brigade Commander. Captain Tom Forrest was Brigadier Butler's ADC, and Colonel Stewarty Douglas was the Deputy Commander in Helmand. Between them, they represented a strong regimental network and, within the restrictions of operational security, these officers worked to ensure a steady stream of information found its way back to Scotland and Northern Ireland.

Despite this, however, Michael McGovern found it extremely frustrating to be at home while his soldiers were in Afghanistan. 'It would be difficult to adequately capture how hard it was to be dislocated from such a large contingent of my officers and soldiers in a brigade in which the whole of my chain of command was also forward-based'.[101] He was determined to visit the theatre, but getting there was far from easy. Seats on aircraft were few and were being prioritised by the PJHQ movers for personnel directly involved in the operation, particularly those moving to and from Helmand for Rest and Recuperation (R&R). The brigade staff tried to be helpful, but all attempts to reach Helmand during the early part of the deployment had failed. By September, though, after the deaths of three Royal Irish Regiment soldiers, the CO decided to short-circuit the normal process and appeal directly to the Brigade Commander. 'In the end, I rang Ed Butler,

---

96   Corporal Danny Groves, interview with author.
97   Corporal John Harding, interview with author.
98   FAB = *Faugh a Ballagh*, Gaelic for Clear the Way, the motto of The Royal Irish Regiment.
99   Corporal Danny Groves, diary entry, 7 September 2006.
100 Sergeant Stephen Gilchrist, interview with author.
101 Brigadier (Retd) Michael McGovern, interview with author.

told him I needed to visit, and I was finally given clearance to go out there', he recalled.[102] But even after arriving at Camp Bastion, there were problems getting to the outstations where the Royal Irish soldiers were serving. 'The Brigade staff were adamant that we should not go to Sangin because of the risk of becoming fixed there, but that was a risk we were prepared to take. We did not manage to get to Musa Qal'eh and that remains a matter of some regret, but it wasn't unreasonable, given the conditions at the time'.[103] No one wanted to risk a helicopter unless it was an operational necessity.

Sangin was not Musa Qal'eh, but it did provide the commanding officer with a feel for conditions 'at the sharp end' in the province. 'It was the isolation of the platoon houses that really struck home', he remembered. Despite having just lost Lance Corporal Luke McCulloch to a mortar attack at the base, McGovern found the moral of the Royal Irish soldiers there to be high. 'Sometimes young soldiers don't know what they don't know, so as long as they are confident in their chain of command, and the man standing next to them, that is enough'.[104] The soldiers of Ranger Platoon had perhaps become 'a bit too Para' for the CO's liking. Some of them had acquired Para helmets and walked about with an unfamiliar air of arrogance, but he put that down to their desire to fit in with their adopted company. 'That was not totally the Royal Irish way, but I understood it, and the company commander, Paddy Blair, obviously inspired confidence'.

Standing on the Sangin rooftops late at night, the CO was 'hounded' by the history he had read about Afghanistan, and by the fact that the forward operating bases were so far apart from each other, which denied them any hope of mutual support. The other key take-aways from his visit were the impact of the allied air power and artillery fire support, and the way his young soldiers acquitted themselves under fire:

> I was impressed at the way they behaved, exactly as they had on the ranges back home, and in the training scenarios we had devised for them. People often say that operations can be a disappointment compared to the training. I would not say that about Afghanistan at that time. It was often just like we had trained and the airpower in particular was awesome in the true sense of the word.

However, he could not avoid comparing and contrasting the situation of the men in Sangin with those in Musa Qal'eh:

> Ranger Platoon were part of a Parachute Regiment company that had been formed long before they arrived in Helmand. They had been through all the pre-deployment training together. Their role had been anticipated and planned for. By contrast, Easy Company was ad hoc. It was a cobbled-together, under-resourced sub-unit that had been created because of the operational requirement to garrison the District Centre. That was quite different and, some would argue, a much more intense and greater tactical challenge than Sangin, although that is not to take anything away from the Sangin task, which was also extremely difficult.[105]

---

102 Brigadier (Retd) Michael McGovern, interview with author.
103 Brigadier (Retd) Michael McGovern, interview with author.
104 Brigadier (Retd) Michael McGovern, interview with author.
105 Brigadier (Retd) Michael McGovern, interview with author.

12

Ceasefire

8 September was a day of surprises for the men garrisoning the Musa Qal'eh DC. First, the Taliban did not conduct their routine dawn attack. Second, a short, sharp radio message was received from Battlegroup Headquarters, telling them to prepare for extraction. Corporal Danny Groves recorded in his diary:

> The OC told us that we would be moving out as early as 13 September. The Sergeant Major then explained that we might not be handing over the compound to a relieving force. Instead, there was a possibility that all the heavy equipment and vehicles would be piled up in the centre of the compound to be destroyed by coalition aircraft while we would leave on foot, carrying only light scales (weapons, ammunition, food and water).[1]

Some found the news disheartening. The troops had no particular desire to stay. But they had invested heavily in the compound, spilled blood there, and lost friends to defend it. They did not want to see the DC fall into Taliban hands. If that happened, they reasoned, all the sacrifices would have been for nought. At the same time, however, they were aware that they were running low on ammunition and other supplies and they had been told that since the Brigade RIP was about to take place (16 Air Assault Brigade was being replaced by 3 Commando Brigade), they could not count on receiving a replenishment. That meant they were now down to 15 rounds of 81mm HE per barrel – about enough to defend against a single concerted Taliban attack.

Some were beginning to doubt the wisdom of those in command, beyond the walls of the compound. As Danny Groves recorded:

> We can't help but feel that the chain of command has no real grip on this situation. They spout on about ammo shortages and the risk of flying Chinooks in here, but the bottom line is that to do our jobs we need more ammo. Perhaps when the ammunition state hits danger point, it will force Bastion's hand and they will finally organise a resupply.[2]

However, there was more bad news on the way. ICOM was picking up enemy communications that suggested the insurgents were gearing up for another attempt to take the compound. Their transmissions included references to 'the final sacrifice', 'the end of the story', and 'the final push'. On the morning of 11 September, Groves was ordered to get an accurate ammunition state for all of the sangars, add that to whatever was left in the makeshift armoury, and then redistribute it evenly across all the fighting positions. He was to get as much .50in ammunition as possible to

---

1 Corporal Danny Groves, diary entry, 8 September 2006.
2 Corporal Danny Groves, diary entry, 8 September 2006.

the Outpost. When he had finished, each sangar had about 1,000 rounds of 7.62mm link for the GPMGs and the cupboard was bare.[3]

Groves found out later that his ammunition distribution mission had been sparked by the sighting, by a Harrier aircraft, of a gathering of as many as 500 people in the desert on the southern edge of the town. The pilot was unable to see if the group was armed and without that confirmation, it was not permissible to call in an airstrike or to engage with artillery or mortars. The men on guard in the sangars spent the day on extra-high alert but the feared assault did not take place. It was Ranger Davy Pepper's twenty-first birthday, but there was no time or appetite for celebrating:

> I'm not going to lie, we all thought "this is it". We were down to minimal ammunition supplies. We were scraping about on the roof of the Outpost, picking up empty link for the LMGs so we could make new belts with loose 5.56mm rounds. The .50in could only fire single shots because of defective ammunition. We really thought this could be the end…then nothing happened.[4]

That evening, when the radio was switched on to send the daily sitrep (situation report), Battlegroup Headquarters instructed Jowett to call the CO by satellite phone.[5]

'You Stop Shooting at us, We'll Stop Shooting at you…'

On 5 September, as the men in the District Centre were responding to the mass-casualty event at the Alamo, the LEWT had picked up an unexpected exchange between two Taliban commanders. They appeared to be talking about a ceasefire. In the midst of everything that was going on at the time, the remark made little impact on the garrison commander. There was no way it could relate to the fighting in Musa Qal'eh. It was probably about some local tribal factions who were fighting amongst themselves, he had concluded.[6] He was wrong. Unknown to Jowett and his men, discussions had been taking place between Governor Daoud, the local elders and the insurgents, aimed at bringing the fighting to an end.

Even before the long-delayed extraction of Ranger Matanasinga, or the deaths of Corporal Mark Wright and Lance Corporal Luke McCullagh, the Task Force Commander, Brigadier Ed Butler, had become convinced that the policy of holding the District Centres was unsustainable. He understood the important symbolism of not allowing the compounds to fall into Taliban hands: that was why he had agreed to go there in the first place. But neither he, nor anyone else, had foreseen the scale of the Taliban's reaction or the intensity of the fighting that had been required to keep them at bay. The men had been doing a great job in very difficult circumstances, but, from a personal and professional standpoint, he could not ask them to keep on fighting when he was struggling to resupply them, and, as importantly, when he could not guarantee to get them out quickly if they were wounded:

> Stuart Tootal and I were in constant discussion about the situation in the DCs. We had a matrix with key statistics for each of the compounds – food, water, ammunition, medical

---

3 Corporal Danny Groves, diary entry, 11 September 2006.
4 Ranger Davy Pepper, interview with author.
5 Jowett, *No Way Out,* p.238.
6 Jowett, *No Way Out,* p.203.

stores, casualties – and we monitored these daily, knowing that at some point we would have to make the call to pull the plug. There wasn't an hour in which I wasn't thinking about how we could mitigate what was going on. In the end, I had to make it very clear to Governor Daoud that, unless the situation changed, we were going to have to pull out.[7]

The problem was not the soldiers. They were holding their own, despite their losses, thanks to their own steely courage and determination, and the support being provided by coalition aircraft and the guns of 7RHA. The critical issue was in relation to the helicopters they relied on for resupply and casualty evacuation. Politically, the UK could not risk having a Chinook shot down. But without the helicopters, the garrisons could not be maintained. 'The new CDS, Jock Stirrup, made it absolutely clear to me that we could not lose a Chinook', recalled Butler. In the wake of the disaster that had occurred on 2 September, when 14 Service personnel had perished after a Royal Air Force Nimrod reconnaissance aircraft had exploded in mid-air, near Kandahar, the UK's appetite for risk had plunged. The political and military leadership had concluded that if the Taliban brought down a Chinook it could spell the end of the country's involvement in Afghanistan. The media campaign had already been lost at home and public support was on the wane, Stirrup had explained. The loss of another strategic asset would be disastrous, not just for the Service people involved, but for the whole future of the operation.[8] This was the beginning of what became known as the 'Wooten Bassett effect'. The small Wiltshire town, close to RAF Lyneham, became synonymous with the deaths of British service personnel. Lyneham was the receiving airfield for repatriation flights bringing casualties back to the UK – Operation Pabbay. The townspeople of Wooten Bassett turned out in large numbers to pay their respects as the black hearses, carrying the coffins of the dead, passed through the town centre, sparking national media coverage, and a public debate about the losses that were being incurred.

There was no doubting the seriousness of the threat to the transport helicopters. Events during the latter half of August and early September had demonstrated that despite the incredible bravery of the pilots and aircrew, the likelihood of one of the aircraft being brought down by enemy fire was increasing by the day. The Taliban recognised the PR value in shooting down a coalition aircraft and were deliberately targeting them with small-arms fire and RPGs. Thankfully they did not have surface-to-air missiles in their arsenal. Butler explained:

> We had known for a while that it was too dangerous to fly in and out of the DCs in daylight, but now it was becoming clear that the risk was almost as great during the hours of darkness.
>
> We were having to make go-no-go decisions on a constant basis. There were times when critical casualties were having to wait longer than anyone would have wished. Added to that, there was a shortage of Giving Sets, which were vital to deliver intravenous fluids to keep seriously wounded casualties alive. It was clear that we would have to pull out. I was not going to have it on my conscience that I kept people in those compounds, knowing that I could not provide resupply or CASEVAC.[9]

A separate issue was adding urgency to the debate. Ambient light was set to grow dimmer during September, and it would get to the point when the pilots would be unable to fly during the hours of darkness because there would be insufficient light for their night vision goggles to function.[10]

---

7   Brigadier Ed Butler, interview with author.
8   Brigadier Ed Butler, interview with author.
9   Brigadier Ed Butler, interview with author.
10   Brigadier Ed Butler, interview with author.

These devices work by intensifying existing light. If there is no light there is nothing to intensify. The pilots would not be able to see well enough to fly safely and at that point there would be no possibility of urgent casualty evacuation.

Butler discussed his options with Lieutenant General Nick Houghton at PJHQ, and took soundings from CDS and his political bosses. They agreed that if he judged that he needed to come out of the DCs then he should do so. However, he now ran up against the immutable force that was ISAF commander, Lieutenant General David Richards. 'When I talked through my proposal with General Richards, he was quite clear that I was not to withdraw from the DCs'. This led to a 'stand-up row' between the two officers, probably to the detriment of Butler's career.[11] Richards saw withdrawal as tantamount to a strategic defeat for the British mission in Helmand and was not prepared to sanction it.[12]

The ISAF commander was caught on the horns of a dilemma. He was, rightly, concerned about how the optics of a unilateral withdrawal from Musa Qal'eh would play out both in Afghanistan and on the international stage. He feared that the Taliban would use it to claim a PR victory, and that the Afghans would regard it as a defeat for the British, lowering their stock – and his – in the eyes of Karzai and his administration. He was also concerned about how it would look to other NATO nations, who were already whispering that the Brits were big on talk and low on outcomes.[13] At the same time, however, he had been desperate to free up British combat power to support his big set-piece operation, code-named Operation Medusa (2 –17 September, 2006).[14] With the Canadians, who were leading the fighting, initially struggling against an aggressive and effective Taliban defence, he needed to find additional resources to prosecute the fight. The ISAF commander had talked up the operation as 'the first large-scale offensive in the history of NATO', seeing it as an opportunity to drive the Taliban out of the strategically important Panjwayi and Zhari districts of Kandahar Province, and to give him something tangible to show for his period in command. It was in his own interests, therefore, to support Butler to find a solution that allowed the garrison to leave Musa Qal'eh whilst ensuring that the Government of Afghanistan's flag continued to fly there, unmolested. As it turned out, by the time the Royal Irish and Parachute Regiment soldiers had been extracted from their Platoon Houses, Op Medusa was over, and they would play no part in it.

In his autobiography, Richards refers to a discussion with the UK's Chief of Joint Operations, Lieutenant General Nick Houghton, who was Butler's national boss. This took place on 5 September. Houghton apparently told the ISAF commander that the UK was thinking of unilaterally withdrawing from Musa Qal'eh and Now Zad. Richards was furious:

> I told Nick that Ed Butler needed to get properly stuck in to Helmand and find an agreed solution with the Governor, the Chief of Police and the Afghan National Army commander. He cannot simply order activity in the shape of a unilateral withdrawal that ignores the strategic and political realities of the environment in which he is operating.[15]

He had also taken the opportunity on 7 September, to brief the UK Minister for the Armed Forces, Adam Ingram, who was visiting Kabul, pointing out 'the huge risks to the UK of unilateral

---

11 Brigadier Ed Butler, interview with author.
12 Richards, *Taking Command,* p.251.
13 Richards, *Taking Command,* p.252 and p.256.
14 Brigadier Ed Butler, interview with author.
15 Richards, *Taking Command,* p.257.

withdrawal'.[16] The next day, according to his memoir, he told Butler he expected to see 'a qualitative change of approach' in Helmand and explained in detail what he needed to do to get alongside the Provincial Governor and persuade him of the merits of allowing local militias to relieve the British troops in Musa Qal'eh.[17] Butler has a different recollection of the situation. 'We – Task Force Helmand, the British Embassy and Governor Daoud – had been working on a ceasefire option for a number of weeks. It was not General Richards' idea'.[18]

Salvation arrived in the shape of Musa Qal'eh's tribal elders. Butler had managed to convince Governor Daoud that the situation at Musa Qal'eh could not continue and Daoud had opened a communication channel with the town's tribal leaders. Along with most of the rest of the population, the elders had left the town during August, but they had been keeping an eye on the situation and they were angry about what was happening there. The daily firefights and bombing runs were causing massive damage and they wanted it to stop so that the people could return, commerce could resume, and the locals could get on with harvesting their crops and planting poppy seed for the following year. They were supportive of bringing about an end to the fighting. Recognising the political imperative of not allowing the Taliban flag to fly over the DC, the elders had offered to take responsibility for security in the town and ensure that the Taliban did not occupy the compound. But the Taliban, who had sustained massive casualties and achieved no military or political advantage, needed to be convinced that if they stopped fighting and left, the British would follow suit. The gathering spotted from the air on 11 September, had been a shura in which the elders and Taliban leaders had met to thrash out a peace plan. 'Working together we had developed a plan that consisted of seven or eight points. The first step was to bring about a ceasefire. At about 2000hrs on 12 September, Daoud told me he had got a deal. The elders and the Taliban were prepared to sign up'. Butler explained to Daoud that the Taliban had to stop shooting at 2200hrs that evening as a gesture of good faith. Tootal was told to inform the garrison that they must do the same.[19] At the compound in Musa Qal'eh, Jowett made the satellite phone call to Tootal as directed. At first, he could not believe what his boss was telling him. He thought it was a joke by one of his regimental colleagues in Bastion and abruptly ended the call. However, Tootal called him back immediately and assured him that he was serious. There was going to be a ceasefire. The Taliban would stop shooting from 2200hrs that evening and he needed to do the same. And the next day he would have to leave the compound and meet his enemy face-to-face.[20]

Following his conversation with the Battlegroup Commander, Jowett called together his platoon commanders and NCOs to update them on the situation.[21] At this stage it was expected that the garrison would be withdrawing in a matter of days. There was some relief, but this was tempered with a lot of anger, disbelief and distrust. It was hard for the men to accept that, after the high-intensity fighting they had been involved in, the enemy were simply going to put down their weapons and disappear, or that the garrison would be forced to walk away from the ground that had been paid for with so much of their comrades' blood.

One soldier who did not welcome the development was Corporal John Harding:

> I felt really let down by the chain of command. I was disappointed that they were talking to the enemy. I was angry and frustrated. We had fought our guts out and won an attritional struggle against an able and committed enemy. It had been a great achievement. When you

---

16 Richards, *Taking Command,* p.258.
17 Richards, *Taking Command,* p.259.
18 Brigadier Ed Butler, interview with author.
19 Brigadier Ed Butler, interview with author.
20 Jowett, *No Way Out,* p.238.
21 Corporal Danny Groves, diary entry, 12 September 2006.

fight that hard for something, you become emotionally invested in it. We'd lost soldiers, killed and wounded. If we were just going to leave, what had all the sacrifice been for?

I felt exactly the same when I watched the coalition forces leaving Kabul in 2021 and I think a lot of other soldiers who fought in Afghanistan will have had a similar reaction.[22]

Danny Groves shared Harding's misgivings:

> There is a lot of apprehension and mistrust about the day's events', he wrote in his diary. 'Some of us can't believe that after weeks of constant fighting they [the Taliban] are prepared to just give up and walk away. As the Sergeant Major said, though, it is they who want the ceasefire, not us [this was incorrect, but it is how the Company Commander and the CSM had chosen to present the move to their soldiers]. We have to give them the benefit of the doubt. But the moment things kick off again, we'll escalate back to the old SOPs at the drop of a hat.[23]

Ranger Paul Johnston had been on guard duty in the main gate sangar and handed over to his relief before the news was announced:

> I went off to get my head down. When I woke up in the middle of the night to go back on stag, Ranger Osbourne said: 'Oh, we're on Card Alpha'. Ossie was from St Helena and I sometimes struggled to understand him. I asked him what he was talking about and he said 'We're now on Card Alpha.[24] We're not allowed to open fire unless fired upon'. I couldn't believe it.[25]

Johnston finished his period of guard duty, then went back to sleep. When he awoke in the morning, he could hear the sounds of 'normal life' going on in the bazaar beyond his sangar. 'I had a look and people were already gathering in the market area. A couple of stalls had been set up. These were the first non-combatant civilians I had seen there. I couldn't believe what I was witnessing'.[26] For Johnston, the news was both good and bad. He was relieved that there was a ceasefire, but he was not prepared to trust the Taliban. 'Guard duty at night became doubly scary. Before the ceasefire, if you heard a noise, you could open fire. Now, you just had to sit there and hope it wasn't the enemy about to over-run your position'.[27]

Lance Corporal Rab McClurg had a nuanced view of the news of a ceasefire. Coming from Northern Ireland, he understood that to find a political solution it was sometimes necessary to speak to people who were disliked and distrusted. 'To be honest, I think we (the British), and the Taliban, realised that neither side was making any progress. They were hitting us and we were hitting them. They were low on food, water, ammunition and people and so were we. Nothing was being achieved apart from both sides constantly knocking the shit out of each other'. Initially, McClurg was sceptical about the ceasefire. 'The Taliban were saying they were not going to return to fighting. I had trouble believing that at the time. But then it did start to happen…and everyone's thoughts turned to when are we going to get out of here?'

---

22 Corporal John Harding, interview with author.
23 Corporal Danny Groves, diary entry, 12 September 2006.
24 Card Alpha is a reference to the Rules of Engagement that were extant once the ceasefire came into effect. The card provides 'guidance for opening fire for service personnel authorised to carry arms and ammunition on duty' and applies during normal peacetime operations.
25 Ranger Paul Johnston, interview with author.
26 Ranger Paul Johnston, interview with author.
27 Ranger Paul Johnston, interview with author.

Like Ranger Johnston, he felt the ceasefire had come as a relief, but it made the job more difficult:

> The local populace started to return to the town. That became a concern for me. Before, there was no CIVPOP to worry about. If we saw someone in the town, we could be pretty sure they were Taliban and we could engage them without worrying about killing civilians in the process. But now, the bakers were back in the bakery. Everything was starting to open up and I began to think about how we would manage if we were attacked. We could no longer hammer the bazaar with our mortars. We couldn't use anti-structural munitions or drop 500lb bombs. If it kicked off again, how were we going to defend ourselves?[28]

Somme Platoon Sergeant, PJ Brangan and his opposite number in Barrosa Platoon, had to work hard to keep their soldiers on-task and focused:

> The ceasefire had come out of the blue. No-one was expecting it. One minute we were trying to kill each other, the next we were weapons-tight and the boss was going off to talk to the Taliban.
>
> The new challenge for Gilly and I was ensuring that soldiers who had been used to opening fire at the slightest movement, now understood and observed the new Rules of Engagement. We couldn't allow the ceasefire to be compromised by a frightened, sleep-deprived soldier mistakenly shooting at a farmer in his field, or a shopper in the bazaar.[29]

At the same time, the two Senior NCOs had to try to manage the anger and frustration that many of their soldiers were feeling. 'There was a lot of anger, but there was also hope that the fighting could be brought to an end', explained Sergeant Brangan. These emotions were intertwined with a genuine concern that the losses might have been for nothing:

> The soldiers' anger was understandable, and, I suppose, to some extent, it was justified. I thought, at the time, they had the right to express their concerns. But I don't think anyone below the OC really understood the level of political pressure that the Battlegroup and Brigade Commanders were under, and, if I'm honest, I don't think they cared. We had all got to the point where we were thinking 'just tell us what we need to do and we'll do it'.[30]

Monitoring Taliban radio traffic later that evening, the LEWT confirmed that the insurgents had issued a ceasefire order to their fighters at around 2130hrs. Despite that, it was an apprehensive Major Jowett who stepped out of the District Centre at 1000hrs the following morning (13 September) and walked slowly towards the bazaar anxiously watched by the garrison, who had lined the wall, weapons at the ready in case the arranged meeting turned out to be a ruse.

Accompanied by a single Afghan interpreter, and armed with only a pistol, securely holstered at his side, Jowett made his way to where a group of locals had gathered. Shaking hands with the senior tribal elder, who was introduced as Haji Ramatoulah, and the local Taliban commander, Mullah Ghulam Sadiq, Jowett spoke first. He told the gathering that he understood it would be possible to stop the fighting and return the town to the local people. The elder and Mullah Sadiq nodded their agreement. Then he addressed the Taliban commander, pointing out that while he

---

28 Lance Corporal Rab McClurg, interview with author.
29 Sergeant PJ Brangan, interview with author.
30 Sergeant PJ Brangan, interview with author.

was prepared to continue to fight, he had been ordered to stand down, providing the insurgents did likewise. Mullah Sadiq said he did not want to stop fighting either but, like Jowett, he too had been ordered to do so. Jowett continued: 'We can stop shooting. There will be no artillery, no bombing. I can do this because you will not come for us. Agreed?' After a pause, the Taliban nodded. Jowett again offered his hand and his adversary took it.[31]

The following day, Butler met with the elders and Taliban representatives at a shura in the desert to the west of Musa Qal'eh. The site had been secured by B Company, 3 Para, and a large camouflage net had been erected, forming a temporary pavilion, to shield the delegates from the sun. Stuart Tootal watched the elders and the Taliban arrive in a fleet of Toyota Hilux pick-up trucks. The elders wore dish-dashes and long white beards, denoting their age and seniority. The Taliban were much younger, and dressed mostly in black.[32] Major Gary Wilkinson, who had accompanied Tootal and Butler, was leaving nothing to chance. Unwilling to put his trust – or the safety of his bosses – in the hands of the insurgents, he had coalition combat aircraft circling overhead, beyond sight and sound of the ground, ready to respond if the Taliban turned hostile. He also had the guns of I Battery on standby, with defensive fire missions plotted, awaiting his call to execute. 'We were walking softly, but we had a big stick ready, out of sight, if needed'.[33]

After the opening pleasantries, Butler spoke to formally propose a ceasefire. He told the Taliban commanders: 'You stop shooting at us and we'll stop shooting at you'. He also made it clear that if the ceasefire held, after a reasonable period of time, there could be further talks about withdrawals.[34] The discussions concluded, both sides drank tea, and, as the elders and Taliban rose to leave, the deal was sealed with handshakes and nods of agreement. The fighting was over.

The initial plan to vacate the DC within a few days was short-lived. The troops were eager to leave. If there was no fighting, if a deal had been done, surely there was no need for them to stay, some reasoned? But there could be no extraction until the higher echelons of command – political and military – had confidence that the ceasefire was going to hold, and that the Taliban were going to stand by their side of the bargain. In the meantime, it was important that the men stayed sharp. Guards were maintained on all the fighting positions, and while there were no breaches of Jowett's agreement with his opposite number, it took a week or more before people began to accept that the fighting was not going to resume and started to relax. The hyper-vigilance that had characterised every waking moment for the past six weeks took longer to wear off. But as local people returned to the town in greater numbers, and with each day that passed, the soldiers felt able to breathe more easily. Five days after the last shots were fired, Danny Groves noted in his diary: 'It is strange to see people moving around the place that we have only ever known as a war zone and ghost town. We were suspicious towards the locals and they were equally unsure of us at first. Day by day, they seem to have relaxed and so have we'.[35]

Paul Johnston was highly suspicious about the ceasefire. 'At first it was just weird. We didn't believe the Taliban and we didn't think we could trust them. I kept saying to myself 'this is a trap, it's a set up'. But I began to get used to the peace and quiet and before long it became the new normal'.[36]

Although initially frustrating, the delay in leaving the compound brought some important benefits. It allowed the men time to adjust to their new reality. 'As the days went by, a lot of the

---

31 Adam Jowett, *No Way Out,* pp.252–253.
32 Tootal, *Danger Close,* p.244.
33 Major Gary Wilkinson, interview with author.
34 Brigadier Ed Butler, interview with author.
35 Corporal Danny Groves, diary entry, 17 September 2006.
36 Ranger Paul Johnston, interview with author.

anger that had existed during the fighting, and in the immediate aftermath of the ceasefire, started to go', Corporal Groves explained. 'For some of us, it required a big mind-shift to be prepared to believe in and trust people who had spent the past six weeks trying to kill us. But as time passed, people began to think maybe this is not so bad after all. It was a bit like pre-decompression'.[37]

Commanders tried to come up with ways to keep the men busy. At first, they put the troops to work to improve their defences and make good the damage that had been caused by Taliban rockets and mortars. When that was done, various competitions were organised, with the second-in-command, Captain Austen Salusbury, leading the way. The first of these was an archery tournament. In his diary, Corporal Groves recorded the run-up to the event:

> The 2ic took the competition very seriously. He began to build himself a massive cross-bow. It must have been 2m in length and 1.5m wide. He made the mistake of leaving his bow unattended and a gang of unnamed soldiers abducted his creation. A lot of fingers were pointed at the mortar team for some reason. The kidnappers then proceeded to send the 2ic a list of demands that had to be met if he wanted to see his crossbow again. These included the delivery of magazines, chocolate, Pepsi etc. Needless to say, the 2ic failed to deliver and he was informed his bow would be destroyed. That evening, as the daily brief was taking place outside the Ops Centre, we all looked up to see smoke and a number of masked men on the roof of the Alamo. They flung a large burning cross off the roof where it hung by a rope against the wall. The 2ic could only look on in horror as his pride and joy, which had been doused in diesel fuel, burned away. The OC was a little concerned about the symbolism of a burning cross in a Muslim town.[38]

Meanwhile, although the ceasefire agreement precluded helicopter resupply flights, the garrison was provided with food and other provisions via a complicated logistics process that began in Bastion. The supplies would be trucked across the desert to a transfer point on the outskirts of the town. There, they were handed over to locals who transported them, in their own vehicles, to the compound. The garrison was also able to buy vegetables, bread, goats and sheep from local traders. The animals were slaughtered and butchered inside the compound and shared out among the troops, who made their own arrangements for preparing the meat for consumption.

At such a remote location, it had been impossible to provide any of the usual welfare facilities that helped to make the soldiers' down-time slightly more tolerable, such as internet connectivity, videos and phone calls to family back at home. With the fighting apparently over, the garrison decided to take things into their own hands. They built a swimming pool, which was cobbled together using an inflatable storage container, filled with water and added chlorine. The pool was a big hit with the men and certainly helped to improve morale. But the biggest contribution to driving up the general mood within the compound occurred on 26 September, when they managed to acquire some potatoes and cooking oil from one of the local traders. A chip pan was fashioned from some chicken wire and, according to Danny Groves, the resulting chips were 'a taste sensation'.[39]

As time ticked by, there were a number of false dawns for the men waiting impatiently for the day when they could leave the DC. They had been told on several occasions that they were to be relieved, and had begun to pack their kit, only to have the moves cancelled at short notice. 'Each

---

37 Corporal Danny Groves, interview with author. The MOD recognised that soldiers who had been involved in prolonged combat needed time to adjust. They called this decompression.
38 Corporal Danny Groves, diary entry, 2 October 2006.
39 Corporal Danny Groves, diary entry, 26 September 2006.

time we heard we were leaving, morale would improve, only to be undermined when the move was cancelled', explained Ranger Johnston:

> The last time this happened the lads decided to make their feelings known. We stripped off our clothes and went dancing around the compound naked, playing Queen's "I Want To Break Free", over and over again, on an iPod and a small set of speakers. First, we went to the mortars and then to the Ops Centre. Everyone had a good laugh and felt better after that. Apparently, Sergeant Major Scrivener thought we had taken the bad news very well.[40]

Sergeant Stephen Gilchrist well understood his men's frustration:

> We'd get told we were going and then it would be called off. That happened a few times and the boys were getting fed up with it. As Platoon Sergeant it is your job to stick to the party line, whether you believe it or not. I'd go to the O Groups and they'd tell me what was supposed to happen. I'd go and talk to the lads and pass on the information. And then the move would get cancelled. We just had to get on with things, even though I personally found it difficult to accept.[41]

Extraction

After more than four weeks, the news the garrison had been waiting for finally arrived. On 14 October they learned that they would be leaving the compound three days later. But there was a catch. Because the ceasefire agreement did not allow helicopters to fly in or out, they would have to rely on a different means of transport. CSM Scrivener called in Brangan and Gilchrist to break the news. The two platoon sergeants were anxious to know when the Chinooks would be arriving, but Scrivener shook his head. 'We're not going out by helicopter', he explained. Brangan asked if they would be walking out. Again, the Sergeant Major shook his head. At this point, the two sergeants looked at each other, wondering what other possible option was available. After a pause, Scrivener explained that the garrison would be leaving in lorries, known as 'jingly trucks', being provided by the locals. To make things worse, the drivers would be Taliban and the insurgents would also be providing escorts, all the way out into the desert. 'We didn't know what to say. We'd just spent the past two months trying to kill those bastards and now they were going to be driving us out like taxi drivers? It just didn't make any sense', Brangan recalled.[42]

But the plan had been the subject of a lengthy and tense negotiation between Butler, the elders and the Taliban, and it was not going to change. The Platoon Sergeants broke the news to their soldiers and the men once more began to pack for the move. Nothing that might be of use to the Taliban could be left behind. They were also told to obliterate the Easy Company mural that been painstakingly painted on the gable wall of one of the buildings. This had contained the names of every soldier in the garrison, with the dead and wounded annotated. The soldiers were reluctant to see it destroyed. It had become a memorial to their friends and the deeds that had been done there. But they recognised that it was important to avoid allowing the names to fall into Taliban hands. It was duly painted over.

Corporal John Harding was still angry:

---

40 Ranger Paul Johnston, interview with author.
41 Sergeant Stephen Gilchrist, interview with author.
42 Sergeant PJ Brangan, interview with author.

> I didn't want to go. At one point we thought we were going to be relieved by the Royal Marines and I volunteered to stay behind. I just wanted to get stuck in to them [the Taliban] again. But the request was turned down and, in any case, we were not being relieved by the Marines, we were handing over to the local militia.[43]

On the day of departure, 17 October, the vehicles arrived as promised and the men conducted careful searches of each one, outside the compound, to ensure there were no boobytraps. The trucks were then brought inside the walls, where sandbags were placed on the floors to act as blast-absorbers in the event of a mine-strike or IED explosion. Once that was done, they loaded all the equipment and the troops climbed aboard, carrying their personal kit, weapons and ammunition, their rifles and machine guns pointing out through the bars, ready to engage if required. The vehicles were started up and they set off, out through the main gate, Jowett and the JTAC in the leading vehicle. As he drove his ailing Pinzgauer 'being held together with black masking tape and cable ties' out into the street, Lance Corporal Rab McClurg noticed several people with video cameras, filming as the convoy departed.[44]

It had been arranged that the vehicles would drive through the desert to a rendezvous point where the men would transfer into helicopters for the final leg of the journey to Camp Bastion. Adam Jowett had been concerned to ensure that the route had been proved clear of mines and IEDs. As a confidence measure, he had demanded that a member of the Taliban and one of the tribal elders travelled in each vehicle. This had been the subject of some debate before agreement was reached.[45] Even though they could see Apache helicopters circling in the distance, there were a lot of worried soldiers sitting in the back of the jingly trucks as they turned left out of the main gate and headed south to the edge of town before turning right and driving along the wadi, eventually passing to the west of the town and then heading north into the desert.

Corporal John Harding was in the front passenger seat of the first Pinzgaur. 'The gearbox was completely wrecked. It wouldn't go into gear. But Rab McClurg crawled underneath with his Gerber [multi-tool] and managed to get it to work'. Harding was laser-focused on making sure the engine did not seize:

> How that vehicle drove out I do not know. I was sitting in the passenger seat with an improvised funnel running down into the engine bay. I was pouring water into the radiator and it was coming straight out again, with steam flying everywhere. It was like something out of Thomas the Tank Engine.
>
> As we drove through the desert the Taliban, in their pick-ups, were cutting about in between the trucks. Before we left, I had been convinced that it was all going to go wrong. But once we were on the way, and I was busy working to keep the vehicle moving, I started to relax a bit. As I looked around, I could see the Apaches. The Taliban were providing an outer cordon in their pick-up trucks. But the attack helicopters were a big incentive for the insurgents to avoid doing anything stupid.

The route took the convoy a long way north before turning west. Trying to follow the route on his map, Harding struggled to understand why they went that way:

> We had to take a route that the Taliban and the elders had selected, which made absolutely no sense to me. They seemed to be following their noses and it was a really round-about journey.

---

43 Corporal John Harding, interview with author.
44 Lance Corporal Rab McClurg, interview with author.
45 Jowett, *No Way Out,* p.271.

At one stage we drove through an old Soviet minefield. I could see the metal prongs that initiated the mines sticking up out of the sand on both sides of the vehicle. There was a safe lane marked by cairns. It seemed incredibly narrow but the Taliban drivers managed to keep us clear of danger.[46]

Sergeant Gilchrist, in one of the rear vehicles, was not paying much attention to the route:

I was too busy scanning my arcs and making sure the blokes were doing the same. We didn't know what was coming, and we all felt really vulnerable. But I knew that if it all went wrong, we would need to retain our professionalism if we were to stand any chance of surviving, so that's what we did.[47]

Corporal Groves sensed that some of the younger soldiers were quite frightened. 'I'm sure it was going through their minds that this might be an elaborate trap. What we were doing – trusting the Taliban – didn't feel right to them. It was mad…and it wasn't very dignified'.[48]

Ranger Pepper could not understand why they were being extracted by the Taliban and not coalition troops:

From the minute we left the compound I had my rifle in my shoulder, ready to fire, and I kept it there until we arrived at the Chinooks in the desert. That must have been about eight hours later. We turned left out of the gate and drove down a street none of us had seen before. We were expecting to be ambushed. We were not expecting to survive.[49]

Sitting on a sandbag on the floor of one of the jingly trucks, manning his GPMG, Ranger Paul Johnston was another soldier who was feeling more than a little concerned:

I was definitely worried. Some of the lads thought we were going to be ambushed and killed. Stuck in the back of the trucks, with no cover, we would be easy targets.

I looked at the Taliban in the pick-up trucks. They all had these evil eyes. You could tell they didn't like us. Many of us didn't expect to get through the town, never mind back to Bastion. And even when we did get out of the town and into the desert, every time one of their pick-ups went past, we expected them to open fire.[50]

Corporal Cliff Tweed, travelling in the front of one of the vehicles, beside a Taliban driver, was '100 percent on edge' and kept the muzzle of his rifle pointing at the insurgent for the whole of the journey.[51]

In the last truck, PJ Brangan was having communications problems:

The radio was playing up so contact with the others was really intermittent. We were moving slowly and I could see the convoy beginning to pull away from us, although we managed to catch up eventually. The route took us up a fairly steep road through a mountain pass. The

---

46 Corporal John Harding, interview with author.
47 Sergeant Stephen Gilchrist, interview with author.
48 Corporal Danny Groves, interview with author.
49 Ranger Davy Pepper, interview with author.
50 Ranger Paul Johnston, interview with author.
51 Corporal Cliff Tweed, interview with author.

trucks slowed to walking pace and I didn't think they were going to make it, but they proved me wrong.[52]

The sight of an Apache helicopter dropping down to fly alongside the vehicles, the pilot and gunner waving and giving the thumbs-up, signalled that the end of the road journey was not far off. 'Once we were out in the desert, I began to feel a bit safer. If the Taliban were going to do something they would have done it by now. Then the Apache turned up, flying very low beside us and I thought 'oh, it's all good'', recalled Lance Corporal McClurg.[53] For Ranger Johnston, the route through the desert seemed to take all day and was 'the longest journey of my life':

> As we started to relax a bit, some of the lads brought their weapons in but one of the NCOs gripped them and told them to stay alert. We weren't out of danger. The sight of the Apache was the signal for most of us that everything was going to be alright. It made a really low, slow pass right down the length of the convoy. We were waving and the pilot and gunner waved back.[54]

Eventually, the line of vehicles reached the rendezvous point, which had been secured by Royal Marines of 3 Commando Brigade, who had already taken over from 16 Air Assault Brigade. Johnston felt the marines were shocked to see the state of the Royal Irish soldiers as they dismounted from the vehicles:

> Compared to us, the Marines looked like something from a recruiting poster. They were all smart and clean and tidy and they all seemed to be pale. They looked fit and well-fed. We were dirty, covered in desert dust, with thick beards and long hair, and our skin was darkened from weeks in the sun. Our uniforms were falling off. They were full of holes and torn after three months of fighting, and we were skinny from living on compo rations for most of the time we had been in the DC.[55]

Danny Groves agreed:

> Everybody was looking at us. We were just bags of bones. I had gone from 16 stone to 12.5 stone over the three months I had been in Musa Qal'eh. When I got home, I had lost so much weight my mum didn't recognise me. On the other hand, my girlfriend thought I had never looked better – all tanned and slim.[56]

McClurg, feeling suddenly exhausted after all the tension of the journey and hours in the driving seat, was pleased to see the back of the Pinzgauer he had been nursing along for the whole journey. 'When we arrived at the RV I turned off the engine, handed the keys to a young Royal Marine, and just walked away to talk to my mates. I didn't care if I never saw that vehicle again'.[57]

Corporal Danny Groves and Sergeant PJ Brangan went and sat on the ramp of one of the Chinooks. Brangan recollected:

---

52   Sergeant PJ Brangan, interview with author.
53   Lance Corporal Rab McClurg, interview with author.
54   Ranger Paul Johnston, interview with author.
55   Ranger Paul Johnston, interview with author.
56   Corporal Danny Groves, interview with author.
57   Lance Corporal Rab McClurg, interview with author.

Danny had a Romeo and Julieta cigar in a tube. He broke it in half and we sat there and smoked it, while the RAF aircrew looked on, wondering if they should tell us off for smoking on their aircraft. I think they had been told not to say or do anything that might aggravate us, so they just watched and said nothing.[58]

Once everyone had been accounted for, and the Taliban and elders had departed, the troops were loaded into the Chinooks for the short flight to Bastion, where they handed in what little ammunition they had left, and went off to the cookhouse in search of some fresh food. They would have liked a cold beer too, but 3 Commando Brigade had decided they would have a 'dry' tour so there was no alcohol available.

PJ Brangan was furious when a Royal Marine RQMS told the men to split their ammunition into separate piles:

We had British, American and Danish rounds and he wanted us to divide it up by nationality. After what we'd just been through, that seemed a bit unreasonable. The guys just wanted to get a shower and head to the cookhouse. There was no way we were going to start trying to sort it out. We dumped it all in one pile and left.[59]

Ranger Pepper was unimpressed that the reception party at Bastion consisted of Royal Marines rather than men from their own brigade. But he felt a bit better when the marines ushered the Musa Qal'eh men to the front of the queue for the cookhouse.[60] Some of the men were looking forward to enjoying fresh food again after spending so long eating boil-in-the-bag rations. 'We all thought we were starving so when we got to the cookhouse, we were piling our plates high with hamburgers and chips. But after three or four mouthfuls, we were full. Obviously, our eyes were bigger than our shrunken stomachs'.[61]

After surviving on 'compo' rations for months, Jonty Johnson was desperate for some 'proper chicken'. 'I asked the guy behind the servery if I could have two pieces. He said no. I took a second piece anyway. He started to get angry but someone told him to leave it and he backed down'.[62]

For some, relief from the tension of living under a constant threat of incoming mortars and rockets came with the ability to sit on the toilet for as long as they wished without having to worry if they were going to be caught with their trousers down as a firefight kicked off or a mortar landed.[63] The following morning, most of the Royal Irish Regiment soldiers who could be spared from kit-packing attended a church service for their dead comrades at the Bastion Memorial. The commemorative concrete cairn, set with local stones and topped with a cross, fashioned from 30mm brass shell cases, had been built by the Brigade's engineers. It included a plaque on which had been etched the names of the Brigade's dead, including Lance Corporal Jon Hetherington, Lance Corporal Luke McCulloch, Lance Corporal Paul Muirhead and Ranger Anare Draiva.[64]

---

58 Sergeant PJ Brangan, interview with author.
59 Sergeant PJ Brangan, interview with author.
60 Ranger Davy Pepper, interview with author.
61 Corporal Danny Groves, interview with author.
62 Ranger Paul Johnston, interview with author.
63 Sergeant PJ Brangan, interview with author.
64 As the casualties mounted among British forces in Afghanistan, the small original memorial had to be replaced twice by larger structures that were able to accommodate the growing list of the dead. The original cairn and cross was taken back to the UK and is now in the 16 Air Assault Brigade Garden of Remembrance in Colchester. The final Bastion Memorial was recreated at the National Arboretum in 2015, after the British withdrawal from Afghanistan.

It was an emotional time. Some of the men talked about their thoughts and experiences with the padre, and took photographs, before heading back to their accommodation to complete packing and prepare to depart.

After the usual admin – accounting for equipment and bundling weapons for the journey home – the Royal Irish soldiers boarded a Hercules transport aircraft for Kabul and from there they flew to Cyprus, where they had 36 hours of 'decompression'. This was designed to provide them with an opportunity to unwind and let off steam among friends before they arrived in the UK. The details of this short stop-over are probably best left unreported. The final leg of their journey to the UK was interrupted at Stansted Airport in Essex, where some Parachute Regiment soldiers disembarked for the short road journey to their base at Colchester. The remainder flew on to Aberdeen where they were delighted to see Lieutenant Paul Martin, by then well-recovered from his shrapnel wounds, waiting for them as they passed through passport control. Ranger Pepper was pleasantly surprised to see him. 'Given how badly he had been wounded, I didn't expect to see him anytime soon. But there he was, in uniform, looking well-recovered'.[65]

---

65   Ranger Davy Pepper, interview with author.

Part 5

What you don't know going in is that when you come out you will be scarred for life. Whether you were in for a week, a month, or a year – even if you come home without a scratch – you are never, ever going to be the same.

PFC Edward 'Babe' Heffron,
Easy Company,
506th Parachute Infantry Regiment,
US Army,
Second World War.[1]

---

1 William Guarnere and Edward Heffron (with Robyn Post), *Brothers in Battle, Best of Friends* (New York: Berkley Publishing Group, 2008), p.xxiii.

13

The Aftermath…

Military operations can be brutal and violent endeavours. Death, mutilation, the destruction of land and property, are the inevitable consequences of clashes of opposing forces on the battlefield – a domain that today includes not only the familiar dimensions of land and air, but also cyberspace.

The Psychological Effects of War

The physical effects of war are usually obvious. As the conflict in Ukraine has demonstrated, traditional and social media channels can beam the sights and sounds into our living rooms, often in real-time. What are not so obvious, however, are the psychological impacts that combat can have on those who are required to do battle on behalf of their nation, although these effects have been recognised for almost as long as human societies have resorted to violence as a means of settling disputes. One of the earliest reports of chronic mental symptoms among fighters – a case of hysterical blindness – is recorded in Herodotus's account of the battle of Marathon, in 440BC.[1] Herodotus did not give the disorder a name, but two millennia later, during the French Revolutionary Wars of 1800–1815, army physicians noticed that soldiers collapsed into a long-lasting daze after near misses by artillery shells. This led to the idea of *vents du boulet* or 'wind of the cannonball' syndrome. With the coming of the industrial revolution, doctors became puzzled by the psychological symptoms shown by survivors of early railway disasters. Some felt these were the result of microscopic lesions of the spine or brain while others argued that emotional shock was the cause. German physician, Hermann Oppenheim coined the term *'traumatic neurosis'* in 1884 in a book that described a number of cases caused by railway or workplace accidents.[2]

Psychiatric battle casualties were identified almost from the beginning of the First World War. German psychiatrist, Robert Gaupp, wrote in 1917 that the massive artillery bombardments of 1914 had filled hospital wards with 'unscathed soldiers and officers, presenting with mental disturbances'. By that time, psychiatric patients were the largest category of war-damaged German troops. The main causes were thought to be 'the fright and anxiety brought about by the explosion of enemy shells and mines, and seeing maimed or dead comrades…' The resulting symptoms were sudden muteness, deafness, general tremor, inability to stand or walk, episodes of loss of consciousness and convulsions.[3] In the British military, soldiers exhibiting these symptoms were initially

---

1 Henry Cary (trans), *The Histories of Herodotus, Book VI* (New York: D Appleton and Co, 1904), p.357.
2 Quoted in Crocq, Marc-Antoine, MD and Crocq, Louis, MD, 'From shell shock and war neurosis to post-traumatic stress disorder: a history of psychotraumatology', *Dialogues in Clinical Neuroscience,* Vol 2, No 1-2000, pp.45–55.
3 Quoted in Crocq, Marc-Antoine, MD and Crocq, Louis, MD, 'From shell shock and war neurosis to post-traumatic stress disorder: a history of psychotraumatology', *Dialogues in Clinical Neuroscience,* Vol 2, No

diagnosed as cases of shell shock. The term reflected the thinking of the day, that the symptoms were the result of the concussive effect of prolonged exposure to heavy artillery bombardments. Although this theory was quickly discredited, the idea of brain damage, leading to symptoms not unlike some of those associated with Post Traumatic Stress Disorder or PTSD, thought to be caused by repeated exposure to the damaging concussive effects of explosions, has made a reappearance in medical and psychiatric journals as Traumatic Brain Injury, following the conflicts in Iraq and Afghanistan.[4]

Long after the First World War, some of the combatants were still struggling with nightmares, depicting their experiences in battle. One young officer, identified only as Captain B, said: 'The chief trouble now is dreams – not exactly dreams, either, but right in the middle of an ordinary conversation the face of a Bosche that I have bayoneted comes sharply into view, or I see the man whose head one of our boys took off by a blow on the back of his neck with a bolo knife, and the blood spurted high in the air before the body fell'.[5] These are vivid descriptions of what would today be termed flashbacks. By the Second World War, these conditions were being labelled 'war neurosis' and later 'combat fatigue', 'combat stress', or, in some cases, just plain 'exhaustion'.[6] The term Post Traumatic Stress Disorder, a diagnostic category, did not appear until the 1980s, when it was applied to a syndrome that had been identified in veterans of the Vietnam War. The charity, PTSD UK, defines this as 'a mental disorder that may develop after exposure to exceptionally threatening or horrifying events'. It can occur after a single traumatic experience or from prolonged exposure to trauma, and is not confined to those involved in combat operations, or, indeed to the military. There is also a sub-category, known as complex PTSD, or C – PTSD, which is usually a result of repeated or sustained traumas.[7]

Although each person's experience of the disorder is unique to them, common symptoms seem to be grouped into four types:

> Re-experiencing – these can include flashbacks; recurring memories or nightmares related to a traumatic event; distressing, intrusive thoughts or images; and physical sensations like sweating, trembling, pain or feeling sick.
>
> Avoidance – staying away from places, events of objects that are reminders of the trauma; feeling they need to stay busy; using alcohol or drugs to avoid memories; feeling emotionally numb; being unable to remember details of the traumatic event.
>
> Alertness and Reactivity – being jumpy and easily startled; feeling tense, on-guard or 'on-edge' (also known as hyper-vigilance); difficulty concentrating on simple, everyday tasks; difficulty falling asleep or staying asleep; panic attacks; feeling irritable and having angry or aggressive outbursts; self-destructive or reckless behaviours; aversion to or difficulty in tolerating sound.

    1-2000, pp.45–55.

4   Rona RJ, Jones M, Fear N.T., et al, 'Mild traumatic brain injury in UK military personnel returning from Afghanistan and Iraq: cohort and cross-sectional analyses'. *Journal of Head Trauma Rehabilitation*, 2012 Jan-Feb; 27(1):33-44. <doi: 10.1097/HTR.0b013e318212f814. PMID: 22241066>, accessed 22 February 2024.

5   Quoted in Bourke, Joanna. 'Effeminacy, Ethnicity and the End of Trauma: The Sufferings of 'Shell-Shocked' Men in Great Britain and Ireland, 1914-39'. *Journal of Contemporary History*, vol. 35, no. 1, 2000, pp.57–69. JSTOR, <http://www.jstor.org/stable/261181>, accessed 22 February 2024.

6   Boone, Katherine N, 'The Paradox of PTSD'. *The Wilson Quarterly (1976-)*, vol. 35, no. 4, 2011, pp.18–22. JSTOR, <http://www.jstor.org/stable/41484367>, accessed 22 February 2024.

7   UK PTSD, <https://www.ptsduk.org/what-is-ptsd/causes-of-ptsd/>, accessed 22 February 2024.

Feeling and Mood – Trouble remembering key features of the trauma; unable to trust anyone; distorted thoughts about the trauma that cause feelings of blame and guilt; overwhelming negative emotions, including fear, sadness, anger, guilt or shame; loss of interest in previous activities; feeling nowhere is safe; and difficulty feeling positive emotions, such as happiness or satisfaction.

The MOD's Approach to Post-operational Stress Management

In 2006, the Ministry of Defence's view was – and still is – that the prevention and management of operational stress should be regarded as a chain of command, rather than a medical, responsibility, and that good leadership and training were vital to countering the associated ill-effects.[8] Reaching back to the experiences of troops involved in combat operations during the Falklands Conflict in 1982, the Gulf War of 1991, and in the Balkans in the later 1990s, by 2005 the Ministry of Defence had developed a four-stage process, entitled Post-Operational Stress Management or POSM. This was set out in a policy document, published in September of that year.[9] This document did not define Operational Stress, but an updated version, issued as Land Forces Standing Order 3029, in June, 2011, described it as 'any individual or group reaction to stressors relating to the operational context, which, if not managed, may result in impaired performance and possible effects on health'.[10]

The first element of POSM was decompression.[11] Although this later became mandatory for those who had served a month or more in an operational theatre, in 2006 the decision to decompress was 'a command discretionary, risk-based one, to be made at Brigade Level (sic)'. In practice, it was often missed out by individual reinforcements whose end of tour dates were not always synchronised with the units in which they were serving.[12] It was to be delivered in a formal, structured and monitored environment, away from the area of operations, and immediately before recovery to the home base. The idea was to give the returning soldiers an opportunity, in a light and relaxed atmosphere, to spend some time thinking and talking about their experiences on operations, in the company of others who had shared, and understood, what they had been through. The Royal Irish Regiment soldiers, returning from Musa Qal'eh, went through a decompression process in Cyprus on their way home.[13] In reality, most used it as an opportunity to let off steam, aided by the inhibitions-lowering effects of liberal quantities of alcohol, and few took much notice of the advice being offered by mental health professionals. 'Most of us took their leaflets, crumpled them up, threw them in the bin, and went to look for beer,' said one.[14]

Stage 2 was called normalisation. This was to be conducted at the unit's home barracks, the duration – two to five days – being at the Commanding Officer's discretion, and followed by mandatory Post-Operational Tour Leave (POTL) of up to 10 weeks. This was not to be modified for anyone unless exceptional circumstances had been approved by HQ Land Forces. It was

---

8   Land Forces Standing Order 3209, 'Post Operational Stress Management (second revise)', dated June 2011.
9   Army document, D/DFS(A)/33/64/2/PS4(A), Army Post Operational Stress Management Policy, dated 20 Sep 05, obtained by author through a Freedom of Information Act request.
10 Land Forces Standing Order 3209, 'Post Operational Stress Management (second revise)', dated June 2011.
11 In a later iteration of the policy, an earlier element, Stage 0, was added, to include briefings to soldiers and their families before operational deployments.
12 The author, a reservist, spent eight weeks as an Individual Reinforcement in Afghanistan in 2006, and was never offered decompression.
13 Land Forces Standing Order 3209, 'Post Operational Stress Management (second revise)', dated June 2011.
14 Private interview.

acknowledged that a day spent taking part in beach activities, followed by a night of drinking and letting their hair down, was unlikely to be sufficient to prepare the men to go back into a society – and an army – largely ignorant of what they had been through. Although the Musa Qal'eh cohort was desperate to go on leave and see families and friends, it was considered prudent to keep the men together for a further period of about a week. The purpose of this was to ensure they could conduct important post-tour administration in slow time while maintaining regular contact with each other; talk about their thoughts and feelings; and provide help for them to understand what was a normal part of returning from operations and, just as importantly, what was not.

The third element was In-service Support. This was intended to begin when the service person returned to their unit after Post Operational Tour Leave and to extend for the remainder of their military career. It included further briefings, which would eventually be delivered either by a health professional or by a unit officer or senior NCO who had been trained to conduct Trauma Risk Management (TRiM). TRiM was originally intended to be a way of reducing PTSD, using unit personnel rather than outside medics. Later research showed that while it was not effective in that regard, it did prove useful in helping to drive up the number of personnel who were prepared to seek help.[15] Routine chain of command interviews were to follow, and if any concerns were raised the service person was to be signposted to the unit Medical Officer, Padre or a TRiM practitioner.

The fourth and final stage was Immediate Aftercare. Responsibility for the delivery of medical care passed from the military to the NHS when the individual Serviceperson was discharged or retired. The 2005 policy document explained that the Army had very limited means to directly support retired soldiers in the short and longer-term. Ex-Service organisations and other Government departments, such as the Department of Health, were expected to play the key roles.[16] In the first 12 months after retirement, the Army's main responsibility lay in signposting individuals to organisations that could help. These included Combat Stress, SSAFA, The Army Welfare Service, the 13 reginal Reserve Forces and Cadets Associations and the wider body of charitable organisations and governmental departments.[17] In other words, the Army and the Ministry of Defence was handing off the mental health care of veterans to a range of charity and Government entities.

The 2011 version states that Mental Health Social Workers in the Service Departments of Community Mental Health would provide follow-up contact with these individuals for 12 months post-discharge to ensure a smooth transition into the hands of the NHS. All soldiers retiring or being discharged were to be informed that their main avenue for dealing with Service-attributable mental health or stress-related difficulties was their GP and the National Health Service. The Defence Medical Services did not have 'the capacity or prerogative to provide referral, diagnosis or treatment for mental health difficulties'.[18]

---

15   Prof Sir Simon Wessely, evidence to HCDC, 27 March 2018, Q26, <https://data.parliament.uk/writtenevidence/committeeevidence.svc/evidencedocument/defence-committee/armed-forces-and-veterans-mental-health/oral/80886.html>, accessed 21 February 2024, and *King's Centre for Military Health Research: A fifteen-year report*, September 2010, p.32, <https://assets.publishing.service.gov.uk/media/5a7905d7ed915d07d35b440c/15YearReportfinal.pdf> accessed 21 February 2024.

16   D/DFS(A)/33/64/2/PS4(A), 'Army Post Operational Stress Management Policy', dated 20 Sep 05, obtained by author through a Freedom of Information Act request.

17   D/DFS(A)/33/64/2/PS4(A), 'Army Post Operational Stress Management Policy', dated 20 Sep 05, obtained by author through a Freedom of Information Act request.

18   D/DFS(A)/33/64/2/PS4(A), 'Army Post Operational Stress Management Policy', dated 20 Sep 05, obtained by author through a Freedom of Information Act request.

14

Welcome Home

From Aberdeen airport, the men of Easy Company were transported by road to their home barracks at Fort George near Inverness, where they arrived in the early morning, met by a delegation from the battalion, including the Regimental Sergeant Major and the CSMs. This initial greeting was warm despite the hour. Those who had not deployed wanted to ensure their comrades were properly welcomed back. But for some of the returning soldiers, their erstwhile colleagues seemed a little distant. It transpired that the battalion had been warned to give space to the returnees, to allow them time to come to terms with being back home.

For Lance Corporal Rab McClurg, this had seemed strange because he had expected a quick return to pre-deployment normality – and it did not feel like that at the time.[1] Ranger Paul Johnston felt the welcome had been less than wholehearted. 'I got off the coach and started to lift off the weapons bundles. A Sergeant Major came over and said "make sure you shave off those sideburns by tomorrow". He was having a bit of a laugh and a joke, but I didn't think it was very funny at the time'.[2] PJ Brangan described the following days as 'RSOI in reverse'. RSOI stands for Reception, Staging and Onward Integration and relates to the process that troops go through when they arrive in a theatre of operations. It usually involves spending a lot of time in a room, being talked at by a series of subject matter experts, who cover a wide range of topics including intelligence updates, threat assessments, counter-intelligence policies, reaction to alarms, welfare, and theatre-specific medical issues. 'There was an obviously planned series of lectures and talks. The one that stands out for me was about coming to terms with what we'd seen and done, how that might affect us, how to recognise PTSD, and how to get help if we needed it'.[3] Ranger Pepper remembered going out, with the other returnees, to a pub in Inverness, called Johnny Foxes, where a large volume of alcohol was consumed. They also travelled south, to the Midlands, to call on Lance Corporal Muirhead's family and visit his grave. From there, they went to the Queen Elizabeth Medical Centre in Birmingham to see Corporal Ally McKinney:

> At the time, we all felt a bit angry about being held back from leave. This had created pressure on our families as well as on us. As a young Ranger, after seeing what I had seen, I just wanted to go home. But I was pleased to have had the opportunity to go to Birmingham and to see Moonbeam's grave and talk with his mum.[4]

Not all of the returning troops had the benefit of the extra week of 'normalisation'. Ranger Johnston had been booked on a Junior NCO cadre and spent only a day in barracks before travelling home

---

1 Lance Corporal Rab McClurg, interview with author.
2 Ranger Paul Johnston, interview with author.
3 Sergeant PJ Brangan, interview with author.
4 Ranger Davy Pepper, interview with author.

so he could complete his post-operational tour leave before reporting for the course. He went straight out drinking and got into trouble. It was, perhaps, an indication of what was to follow later. 'In retrospect, I don't think I should have been allowed to go home so quickly', he admitted.[5]

For many of the soldiers who had been to Afghanistan, it seemed as if there was now a two-tier battalion – those who had experienced Musa Qal'eh and those who had not. For Lance Corporal Rab McClurg, this manifested itself in different ways. 'Some of the guys who had not deployed seemed to think they had missed out, or wished they had been there. There was a bit of a divide for a while'.[6] Ranger Pepper also felt a clear gap had opened up between them and the remainder of the unit. 'In the background there was a bit of distance between us and those who had not experienced Helmand. That lasted for a few months. I found it strange that no-one seemed to want to ask us what it had been like there'.[7]

Paul Johnston noted a similar trait in the wider Army, as he attended his Junior NCO course:

> I was doing things the way I had done them in Afghanistan and the training team were giving me grief for it. But they hadn't been to Helmand. They had no idea what it was like to fight there against the Taliban. For about a year after we got back, I felt the Army looked down on us because of what we had seen and done. It seemed to me that they were teaching the wrong stuff and that they weren't interested in learning from us and what we had found out from fighting the Taliban.[8]

It is easy to see how this attitude could be frustrating for soldiers who felt they had something to contribute, based on their recent experiences. But perhaps the Army's attitude was understandable in the circumstances. British doctrine and tactics – how the Army thinks about warfare and how it puts that thinking into practice – were based on what had been learned from previous conflicts. In a sense, Johnston and the others who had fought at Musa Qal'eh, were ahead of the Army's learning curve, and it was inevitable that it would take some time for the formal lessons-learned process to catch up with them and for those lessons to feed through to tactics, techniques, procedures, and training. For a period after their return, the men of Barrosa and Somme platoons were known within the battalion as 'the Musa Qal'eh Boys'.

At Fort George, as he worked to reintroduce the Helmand veterans back into battalion life, Commanding Officer, Lieutenant Colonel Michael McGovern, had only the Army's policy document, together with his own humanity, compassion and common sense, to help him with that difficult task. In his view, reintegration was made more difficult because only a small proportion of the battalion had experienced Musa Qal'eh. Usually, a unit goes on operations together and comes back together. Looking back, the Commanding Officer now recognises that he and his men were faced with a unique set of circumstances. A few platoons and individual officers had experienced things that those who had remained at home could not comprehend. Mixing them back into a battalion in which most of the personnel had been at home since the Iraq tour, was always going to be a challenge.[9]

When the men returned after leave, they found themselves spread across the unit, often separated from those with whom they had served in Afghanistan. The Commanding Officer, aware that the whole unit would be deploying to Helmand in March 2008, wanted his battalion to

---

5   Ranger Paul Johnston, interview with author.
6   Lance Corporal Rab McClurg.
7   Ranger Davy Pepper, interview with author.
8   Ranger Paul Johnston, interview with author.
9   Lieutenant Colonel Michael McGovern, interview with author.

benefit from the experiences of the Musa Qal'eh cohort as it entered its pre-deployment training cycle. For some, however, this approach deprived them of the 'crutch' of being with comrades who could relate to what they had seen and done, and for whom no explanations were necessary:

> It would be easy, in hindsight, to conclude that we should have kept the Musa Qal'eh men together but these were composite platoons that had been created specifically for the Helmand mission, drawn from across the battalion, made up from the very best that we had. I don't remember even considering keeping them together. To have done so would have resulted in a small number of platoons that were very strong, at the expense of the rest of the unit. I was thinking about it from the point of view that these men were considered legends. They had acquitted themselves superbly in Helmand. They were the Warrant Officers and RSMs of the future and the idea was to spread them out within the battalion. What I wasn't thinking about was the long-term vulnerabilities.[10]

Although Lieutenant Colonel McGovern had been to Helmand and had witnessed the intensity of combat at first hand, alongside Ranger Platoon, in Sangin, he is honest enough to admit that he did not realise, at that stage, how different Afghanistan would be, or how it would affect the young men over time:

> My focus was: "let's get these men out across the battalion and let's be ready for war when we have to deploy again" as was already scheduled.
>
> I moved on in August, 2007 and at that time I did not have any idea of the scale of the problem or that people were struggling. In those days, we weren't going to ask people "how are you, is everything alright?" We were waiting for the companies to identify individuals who were having problems and then try to deal with these on an individual basis. We did not realise how big a challenge that would be.
>
> You never really know, with young soldiers, who are going to be the thrivers and who are the ones who are just trying to survive day by day. Afterwards, I saw an article in a Sunday newspaper about the number of suicides in the Army, post Afghanistan, and I remember crying as I read it. We should have done better by them. But it wasn't as if someone said "here's what you should be doing" and we disregarded it.
>
> As commanders, we love the soldiers who serve under us and now, as I hear about the struggles of men like Ranger Armstrong and others, I genuinely wish we had done more for them. I sent those men out there and I will have to live with that for the rest of my days.[11]

The Commanding Officer agreed that some of the returnees might have felt the rest of the battalion remained at a respectful distance for a time:

> We were trying hard to avoid these newly-returned Afghanistan warriors from coming up against routine battalion life after what they had been through. Our lives were pretty strict so I wanted to avoid a scenario in which a Musa Qal'eh veteran found himself being pulled up by a well-meaning Senior NCO for wearing his sideburns a little too long or acting a bit jilty.[12] We were trying to recognise their phenomenal individual service and reintegrate them,

---

10 Lieutenant Colonel Michael McGovern, interview with author.
11 Lieutenant Colonel Michael McGovern, interview with author.
12 Jilty is a Northern Irish expression that means 'very good' but in this case it is being used to suggest arrogance.

primarily by not being too hard on them. At the same time, however, I have no doubt there was a certain amount of jealousy among those soldiers who had not been to Helmand because of what they had seen and done.[13]

'Mad, Bad, Sad' – Myth and Reality

There is a persistent myth, common across the UK, and perpetuated, to some extent, by well-meaning but often hysterical tabloid news media outlets, and some charities, that the veterans of Iraq and Afghanistan are all 'mad, bad or sad'. The House of Commons Defence Select Committee (HCDC) reported in 2018 that the public perception of the extent of mental health problems among people who had served in both war zones, was much higher than the research data suggested.[14] A senior academic, Professor Sir Simon Wessely, of King's College, London, told the Committee that all large studies on the topic showed there was a widespread belief 'that most people who served in Iraq and Afghanistan have come back physically, emotionally or psychologically damaged'.[15] Research published the previous year suggested that 82 percent believed mental health problems were one of the three most common issues faced by people leaving the Armed Forces. Seventy-eight percent thought mental health problems were either somewhat or much more likely to happen to someone who had been in the armed forces compared to people in general.[16]

The reality was, and is, not so clear-cut. Giving evidence to the same Committee, on 26 June 2018, Professor Nicola Fear, Professor of Epidemiology at King's, explained that research conducted in 2003–04 found a prevalence of PTSD of four percent among service personnel. A later phase of the same research, in 2014–16, revealed that the figure had increased to six percent overall.[17] These are relatively small numbers and not much different from what is found in the general population. But the cohort on which they are based included those who deployed to conflict areas in all roles – not just those who were involved in combat. When the data were further broken down, however, they revealed that those with a direct involvement in combat roles – i.e. those who actually engaged the enemy or were engaged by them – unsurprisingly reported higher incidences of the disorder, rising to up to 9 percent.[18]

This third iteration of the study, published in 2018, also showed that of the three main mental health problems measured, PTSD, Common Mental Disorders (CMD), and alcohol misuse, the latter two – 21.9 percent for CMD and 10 percent for alcohol misuse – continued to be the most

---

13 Lieutenant Colonel Michael McGovern, interview with author.
14 HCDC Report, 'Mental Health and the Armed Forces, Part One: The Scale of mental health issues', 25 July 2018, p.35, <https://publications.parliament.uk/pa/cm201719/cmselect/cmdfence/813/813.pdf>, accessed 12 June 2024.
15 Prof Sir Simon Wessely, HCDC evidence session, 27 March 2018, Q35, <https://data.parliament.uk/writtenevidence/committeeevidence.svc/evidencedocument/defence-committee/armed-forces-and-veterans-mental-health/oral/80886.html>, accessed 12 June 2024.
16 Lord Ashcroft KCMG PC, The Veterans' Transition Review, October 2017, *Perceptions of service leavers and veterans*, pp.20–21, <https://www.veteranstransition.co.uk/wp-content/uploads/2024/02/vtr3_followup_2017.pdf>, accessed 7 July 2024.
17 Professor Nicola Fear, HCDC evidence session, 27 March 2018, Q3, <https://data.parliament.uk/writtenevidence/committeeevidence.svc/evidencedocument/defence-committee/armed-forces-and-veterans-mental-health/oral/80886.html>, accessed 7 July 2024.
18 Professor Sir Simon Wesseley, HCDC evidence session, 27 March 2018, Q14, <https://data.parliament.uk/writtenevidence/committeeevidence.svc/evidencedocument/defence-committee/armed-forces-and-veterans-mental-health/oral/80886.html>, accessed 7 July 2024.

common problems reported by serving personnel, although those who had left the Services related higher levels of probable PTSD.[19] This may have been due to late-onset of the disorder, and a greater willingness to report the symptoms and seek help when military careers were not threatened, or both.

The MOD's own figures for PTSD – based on serving personnel who self-declared and sought treatment – were much lower. The UK Armed Forces Mental Health Annual Summary, looking at trends between 2007/08 and 2021/22, suggested that the rate of PTSD among UK Armed Forces was around 0.1 percent or 1 in 1,000 in 2021/22.[20] Given the basis on which these Defence statistics were collected, this is unsurprising. In addition, there is evidence that in the early days of Afghanistan, there was significant under-reporting by servicemen and women. Many chose not to acknowledge problems or seek help due to fears of the negative impact of a mental illness diagnosis on their future careers, and the stigma associated with such a finding in the eyes of their peers, and of society more widely.[21]

Research into suicide rates among armed forces veterans shows a similar correlation with those of the wider population. A study conducted in 2023 by the University of Chester, and published in the respected British Medical Journal, concluded that although there was a paucity of academic inquiry on the subject, there appeared to be 'no significant difference in rates of suicide in the UK veteran community compared with the civilian population'. The work did find, however, that veterans who took longer to seek help for mental difficulties reported more suicidal thoughts and mood disorders and were found to be at an increased risk of suicide.[22]

Despite the wide variations between Defence statistics and those of academic studies, the numbers appear to paint a picture of relatively low levels of PTSD among military personnel – not much different from those seen in the general population. The same applies for suicide rates. If reliable, these figures paint a positive picture and may demonstrate the remarkable resilience of those who wear – or who have worn – the King's uniform. However, these statistics are of no consolation to those personnel, serving or retired, who were at Musa Qal'eh in 2006 and now find themselves engaged in daily struggles with their demons. Nor are they of any comfort to the families of those soldiers who found that the mental pain of the recurring battles with their thoughts and feelings, the nightmares and flashbacks, was just too difficult to continue to bear.

As the research suggests, many of the men – and they were all men – who had fought through the exceptionally threatening and horrifying events of the Siege of Musa Qal'eh, found little difficulty in readjusting to being back in the UK. After a period of post-operational tour leave they returned, relatively seamlessly, it appeared, to the routine of battalion life and the familiar requirements of the training and readiness cycle. For some, however, the months that followed their arrival back at Fort George were far from comfortable or straightforward. Not everyone was making a painless

---

19 Stevelink SAM, Jones M, Hull L, et al. 'Mental health outcomes at the end of the British involvement in the Iraq and Afghanistan conflicts: a cohort study'. *The British Journal of Psychiatry*. 2018;213(6):690-697. <doi:10.1192/bjp.2018.175>, accessed 12 June 2024.

20 'UK Armed Forces Mental Health: Annual Summary & Trends Over Time 2007-08 to 2021-22', 23 June 2022, <https://assets.publishing.service.gov.uk/media/62b03e138fa8f5357984239b/MH_Annual_Report_2021-22.pdf>, accessed 22 February 2024.

21 HCDC Report, 'Mental Health and the Armed Forces, Part One: The Scale of mental health issues', 25 July 2018, p.28, <https://publications.parliament.uk/pa/cm201719/cmselect/cmdfence/813/813.pdf>, accessed 12 June 2024.

22 R. Randles, et al. 'Prevalence and risk factors of suicide and suicidal ideation in veterans who served in the British Armed Forces: a systematic review', *BMJ Mil Health* 2023;0:1–7, doi:10.1136/military-2023-002413, <https://militaryhealth.bmj.com/content/early/2023/06/15/military-2023-002413>, accessed 22 February 2024.

transition from war to peace. This manifested itself in various ways. It was noticeable that some were drinking too much and too often. Eventually this began to have an impact on their work. Others appeared fidgety, on-edge, easily-startled and quick to anger. Some noticed that they felt restless or anxious or were suffering from insomnia. Others found they had difficulty concentrating, constantly worried that something bad was going to happen, or were continuously on the look-out for threats – traits that one or two had also noticed while they were in Helmand. A few had unjustified feelings of guilt in relation to some of the events that had occurred. For the majority, these problems would grow less acute as the weeks went by, and, eventually, disappear altogether. For others, however, there would be no long-term relief.

Some of the issues had begun to appear during the siege itself. Although Sergeant Gilchrist felt his men were 'just unbelievably brave', there were times when this mask of courage slipped and the true vulnerabilities of some soldiers peeked through. Corporal Cliff Tweed found himself having to manage one or two of the younger men who were reluctant to patrol outside the walls of the compound.[23] Lieutenant Martin, conducting his commander's checks in the evenings, occasionally came across soldiers in tears after a hard day of fighting:

> For many of the younger Rangers, this was their first experience of combat. There was, understandably, a lot of fear and boys had to become men very quickly. They were seeing their mates killed and maimed and they were having to go back and man blood-stained sangars, where the casualties had occurred. That wasn't easy for anyone. I would occasionally find a soldier crying his eyes out on the floor of a sangar.
>
> Things you experience and then put away when you are busy, come back in the quiet hours. I had soldiers coming to me and saying they couldn't keep going because of the nightmares they were experiencing, brought on by what they had seen and done.
>
> You can tell a soldier not to look when he's at the corner of a stretcher carrying the remains of his mate, but they are going to look… and they can't unsee those sights. It was a pretty horrific experience for some of those young soldiers and it gave rise to a lot of issues and concerns and troubles – some at the time and some later.[24]

But, as Sergeant Gilchrist put it:

> Whenever push came to shove, when lives depended on it, those guys were on the ball. The two platoons rubbed each other up the wrong way once or twice, but it was not hard to maintain discipline. Even in the face of casualties, they stuck to the task, putting their grief to one side and getting on with the job.[25]

It was obvious, though, as the days went by, that men were becoming increasingly tense, jumpy and irritable. Things that, back in barracks, would have been little more than a minor irritation, began to take on a much greater significance for some. One example of this was an issue with a chest freezer, used to keep the bottled water supplies chilled. The freezer had a heavy lid which, if slammed shut, sounded remarkably similar to the report of a distant mortar being fired. 'Every time someone slammed that lid, it did my head in', said one.[26] Sergeant Gilchrist recalled the problems this caused:

---

23   Corporal Cliff Tweed, interview with author.
24   Lieutenant Paul Martin, interview with author.
25   Sergeant Stephen Gilchrist, interview with author.
26   Private interview.

> Occasionally, one of the lads would forget to close the lid gently and it would fall with an almighty crash. If you were nearby, it really did sound a bit like a mortar being fired. Everyone would stand-to, thinking we were about to be attacked.
>
> It was bad enough having to respond to all the genuine attacks, without reacting to false alarms as well. Tempers became frayed and it got to the point where we had to sit the boys down and talk through the matter before it became an issue.[27]

Despite these incidents, it was thought, at the time, that most of the soldiers were coping reasonably well with the impact of prolonged exposure to the rigours of siege warfare. It was only when they tried to return to normality that some began to realise that they had been mentally scarred by their experiences. As one of the returners explained: 'There were definitely some soldiers who reacted worse than others …and I was eventually one of them'. He had been fine while he was in Musa Qal'eh, too busy to dwell on what he was going through. However, not long after he got home, he began to notice that something was amiss. He was able to access some help from the military system, and, for a time, he felt better. But matters took a turn for the worse on St Patrick's Day, 2007. 'I had quite a lot to drink on the night before the Paddy's Day parade. On the day itself, there was a fly-past by fast jets and that seemed to trigger a reaction. A friend came to see me later and he said "you're not right, are you?" I wasn't'.[28]

On his return from POTL, this soldier had been sent to London to work with the National Army Museum, helping them to put together an exhibition on the Helmand campaign:

> It was good fun at the time, but looking back now, I think it was a mistake. I probably could have done with stepping away from Helmand but at the National Army Museum I was reliving it all, day after day. I felt as if Op Herrick IV stopped for everyone else, but it continued for me. I think that had an adverse effect as far as I was concerned.

By now, the battalion was aware that he was having problems, but it was reluctant to move too quickly. The regimental authorities understood that once the matter became 'official' it would kick-start a chain of events that could not be reversed. 'Eventually, I had to go and see a doctor. As soon as I talked about what I'd been involved in, the die was cast. It wasn't a case of 'let's think about this'. They went straight to a diagnosis and from there the Army started the discharge process'. The thought of losing the career he loved added to his woes:

> It hit my confidence. I wanted to go back to the battalion but I couldn't. I was devastated. I had committed myself to a full army career. In my mind I had thought I would be a Sergeant Major. But now, as well as all the stuff going on in my head about Musa Qal'eh, I was also having to try to deal with an uncertain future. It was a perfect storm.
>
> Looking back now, I realise I have been lucky. I've got a good job. I've got myself back on my feet. I can talk about my experiences and it doesn't bother me anymore because I think I've been able to process it all. But it was a slow road back. It took a good seven or eight years to get to the point where I was really feeling ok again.[29]

A happy-go-lucky attitude helped Lance Corporal Rab McClurg to put the Musa Qal'eh experiences behind him. 'I was always quite flippant. To a degree, my approach was to tell myself "It

---

27   Sergeant Stephen Gilchrist, interview with author.
28   Private interview.
29   Private interview.

happened – now let's move on".' For McClurg, it was a future tour of Helmand that had the greatest effect on him:

> During Herrick IV I didn't know any better. I was young. It was exciting and interesting. But on Herrick VIII, I knew what to expect. I understood what high-intensity combat was like. We were out on the ground, patrolling, rather than being in defence within a compound. We were dealing with short and long-range contacts and the constant threat of IEDs. I found that situation more difficult to handle. I think everyone who has been through these experiences will have issues of one kind or another. I have certainly felt the need to have a chat with medical people over the years since.[30]

Ranger Paul Johnston noticed, in the weeks after he returned, that he did not want to be alone:

> I just needed to be with other people. I couldn't handle being on my own. One of the things that continued to bother me was the sight of Anare Draiva as I helped to put him into his sleeping bag after he'd been killed. But eventually I was able, I thought, to put the experiences out of my mind and crack on.[31]

Johnston would promote to Lance Corporal and complete two further deployments to Afghanistan, but it would be a number of years before the full impact of his time in Helmand came to the fore. Having left the regular Army after his third Herrick tour, Johnston signed on as a reservist with the regiment's 2nd Battalion, based in Northern Ireland, and undertook a period of Full Time Reserve Service, guarding the regimental depot at Ballymena. After his marriage failed, he began to experience bouts of what he believed was depression. 'I put it down to my marriage breakdown and I went to speak to a therapist. However, when I began to describe my symptoms all the other stuff related to Afghanistan came flooding out and it was obvious there was something else wrong. Eventually, I was diagnosed with complex PTSD and medically discharged from the Army'. Before he became ill, Johnston could not understand why people committed suicide. 'I used to think that however bad things got I would never feel like that. But two years ago, when things were really dark, I finally understood. People commit suicide because they don't want to go on feeling the way I was feeling at that time'.[32]

The same was true for one of the other soldiers. 'I knew people were struggling. I used to talk about Musa Qal'eh with my friends, usually only when I'd had a drink or two. But I wasn't personally having any problems that I could recognise and so I didn't give it much thought'.

However, after returning to Afghanistan a few years later, things were much worse. 'I had been involved in three roadside bomb strikes. I was definitely using up some of my nine lives'. After the last IED event, this soldier began to develop a fear of enclosed spaces. He was having to force himself to get into vehicles. 'If I'm honest, I knew there was something going on, but I kind of ignored it. Later on, after some personal upheaval in my life, I found myself in a really dark place, even contemplating suicide'.[33] After a crisis, he eventually checked himself into a mental institution and underwent therapy. 'I have got better, although I still travel with a dark passenger who raises his head now and again. But the therapy I went through gave me a coping

---

30   Lance Corporal Rab McClurg, interview with author.
31   Ranger Paul Johnston, interview with author.
32   Ranger Paul Johnston, interview with author.
33   Private interview.

mechanism. It taught me not to bottle things up, and instead to talk about the issues that were causing the problems'.[34]

Another soldier who was injured in Afghanistan in 2008, and went back again in 2011, 2016 and 2019, found that he was misusing alcohol as a coping mechanism:

> After Musa Qal'eh I wasn't too bad, although I was drinking more than before – not really bingeing but going out more and more often. I wasn't getting into trouble but I was definitely drinking too much. One of my mates served in Ranger Platoon and even today, 18 years later, we still talk about our time in Helmand when we meet.

But it was later tours that seemed to have a greater impact. 'I think about Afghanistan a lot. It's hard to avoid it, with social media and television documentaries. But I try not to dwell on it'.[35]

Ricky's Story

Despite all the problems recounted above, these soldiers are among the more fortunate of the Musa Qal'eh cohort. Some of their comrades have taken their own lives and some of those who have survived continue to suffer from trauma-related problems that include depression, alcohol misuse, anger-management issues, flashbacks and panic-attacks and suicidal thoughts.

One of these is Ranger Ricky Armstrong. He was just 21 years old when he lost part of his ear to a Taliban bullet as he stood next to Corporal Ally McKinney on the Outpost. The physical injury was not serious and soon healed, but the mental trauma will be with him for as long as he lives. 'The sniper fired a three-round burst. The first bullet hit me, spun me around and knocked me unconscious for a few seconds. The second hit Ally in the head and the third went into a post next to us', he recalled.[36] He came-to to find the men on the Outpost engaged in a fierce firefight with incoming rounds flying over his head and slamming into the wall in front of him. He picked up his GPMG and began to return fire:

> I didn't realise I had been injured until one of the guys started to grab me. Then I noticed that blood was pouring from my ear. Ally was lying a few feet from me, making a noise like a dying animal. I could also hear the crackle of the incoming and outgoing fire. One of the medics gave me an injection of morphine. I wasn't in much pain so I don't understand why he did that. The next thing I remember was being in the helicopter on the way back to Bastion. At the hospital they put a couple of steri-strips on the wound and sent me off on my own to the accommodation tent. I remember being worried because I had no weapon.[37]

Armstrong spent about 10 days at Bastion, during which he was left on his own most of the time. With most of his Royal Irish comrades already out on the ground, there was not a single familiar face with whom he could discuss what had happened. 'After a firefight like that, I felt it was just wrong that they had left me completely on my own'. No one came to talk to him. It was as if no one cared about the experience he had just been through.[38] Eventually, he was offered a choice: he

---

34 Private interview.
35 Private interview.
36 Ranger Ricky Armstrong, interview with author.
37 Ranger Ricky Armstrong, interview with author.
38 Ranger Ricky Armstrong, interview with author.

could go home or he could go back to Musa Qal'eh. He chose the latter. Having been fostered as a child, Armstrong regarded the men of Somme Platoon and the mortar section as his family. 'I didn't think I could just pack up and go home. I had volunteered for the deployment. I had gone there with a group of people I knew, who were all my friends. If they were back in Musa Qal'eh fighting for their lives, I felt it was right that I was back there with them'.[39]

Ricky, like many of his fellow soldiers, had planned a long-term future in the Army and he had to know if he was going to be able to get back into the fight. 'Going home wasn't an option. My confidence had been shaken and I needed to face my fears. I felt alright when I arrived back in the compound, although the boys all thought I was mad to return when I didn't need to'.[40] But while he put a brave face on it, deep down he was worried about how he would react when the bullets started flying. 'I was thinking am I still any good? Have I lost the edge? Do I still have what it takes to get on with what I needed to do?'[41]

His commanders probably shared some of those fears. They too needed to know if he was going to be an asset or a liability. 'Captain Johnston and Sergeant Brangan took me out of the DC on patrol and gave me an opportunity to demonstrate that I was ok. I think they were trying to ease me back into the job and helping to build my self-confidence. I totally appreciated that because it definitely helped me at that time'.[42]

Ricky knew that his fellow soldiers were pleased to see him back. But at the same time, he imagined that people were looking at his damaged ear and he wondered if they were thinking Ally McKinney should have been there instead of him. 'Ally was a very experienced and well-respected soldier and I was just another Ranger. I worried that I might be bringing them bad luck'.[43] It took the young Ranger a long time to understand that he was experiencing the symptoms of survivors' guilt.

Armstrong was able to function effectively as an infantry soldier for the rest of his time in Musa Qal'eh, although he admits to having been 'shit scared' during the extraction from the compound. But his disfigured ear was only the physical manifestation of the damage he had sustained during the siege. The most significant wounds were in his mind and these became apparent as soon as he arrived back at Inverness:

> The rest of the battalion – those who had not been to Afghanistan – did not seem to care much about what we'd been through. It was like: "Oh, you've been to war – so what?" When I asked for help, I was told to go out and have a drink.
>
> To make matters worse, we had to go down to Birmingham to visit Ally McKinney. Ally shook everyone else's hand except for mine and that made me worse. It was my birthday. But instead of celebrating, I sat at the back of the coach on the way back to Inverness, drinking from a bottle of vodka. By the time we got back, I was in bits.[44]

Ricky again asked for help and got the same response: 'Go out and have a drink and forget about it'. 'That was no help at all. I now understand what they were trying to do. They thought I would

---

39 Ranger Ricky Armstrong, interview with author.
40 Ranger Ricky Armstrong, interview with author.
41 Ranger Ricky Armstrong, interview with author.
42 Ranger Ricky Armstrong, interview with author.
43 Ranger Ricky Armstrong, interview with author.
44 Ranger Ricky Armstrong, interview with author.

just get over it. No-one really understood the intensity of that tour and the effect it had on some of us'.[45]

With his mental health deteriorating and with no help forthcoming, Armstrong and his fellow-mortarman, Ranger Jason Mooney, who was experiencing the same problems, could no longer bear to be in barracks, alongside people they thought did not care about them. They decided to go Absent Without Leave (AWOL). 'We went back to Northern Ireland and for a long time we heard nothing from the Army'.[46]

That absence of contact reinforced the idea in Armstrong's mind that his Army family had forsaken him. 'Until Afghanistan, Jason and I had been good soldiers. Why did they not come and look for us? Why did they not call to ask if we were ok? It would have cost very little for someone to get on a plane from Inverness to Belfast and come and talk to us. But no-one did'.[47] He never returned to the battalion. After about a year, the Army sent him to see a doctor in Belfast. He was told he did not have PTSD and that if he failed to return to his unit he would be administratively discharged. That process was completed in 2010. Ricky found himself even more isolated from his friends and fellow soldiers and his problems became more acute.

Instead of drawing a line under his problems, Ricky believes the Army's approach was responsible for exacerbating his mental health challenges. 'You lose all your friends. You lose the connection with your mates. You lose everything. And on top of that you have to deal with the stigma of people believing you've been thrown out of the Army with a black mark against your name'.[48] His personal kit that had been left behind in Inverness was not returned. But of much greater concern to him was that he had left his medals behind at Fort George and that he never received a medal to which he was entitled, the Operational Service Medal for Afghanistan. This contributed to his feelings of worthlessness.

Ranger Armstrong continues to express a strong loyalty towards the Army and to his former colleagues. But he believes administrative action was the wrong way to deal with his situation. A medical discharge would have been more appropriate. As well as removing the perceived 'black mark' that administrative action suggests, his release on medical grounds might have helped to ensure that he could get access to the health care he so desperately needed. Under the Army's Post Operational Stress Management policy, once a mental health problem had been identified, he would have been eligible to receive treatment within the military system. It would probably not have prevented his discharge, but the transition from military to civilian care might have been actively managed. But because he had not been diagnosed with a mental health issue, and had been treated as an absconder, that never happened. By walking away from the Army, he had never completed the 'normalisation' process and thus an opportunity for an early identification of his mental health problems had been lost. Instead, for Armstrong, it would take a tragedy to unlock the door to treatment.

On 17 April 2022, Ricky's close friend and fellow Musa Qal'eh veteran, Jason Mooney, took his own life. Jason had been an exceptional Mortar Detachment Commander in Afghanistan but just could not come to terms with what he had seen and done. 'I went to his home and when the family described how he had died I didn't want to go on. I just wanted to be with him. I completely broke down and tried to kill myself. The police came and took me to the Ross Thompson Unit at Causeway Hospital in Coleraine'.[49] By attempting suicide, Ricky's cry for help was answered and

---

45 Ranger Ricky Armstrong, interview with author.
46 Ranger Ricky Armstrong, interview with author.
47 Ranger Ricky Armstrong, interview with author.
48 Ranger Ricky Armstrong, interview with author.
49 Ranger Ricky Armstrong, interview with author.

he was able to access the mental health system, diagnosed with complex PTSD. But that did not immediately lead to an improvement in his situation. As an inpatient at the Ross Thompson Unit, he found himself being given 36 tablets each day, not, he believed, as treatment for his condition, but to keep him sedated enough to allow medical staff to feel safe around him. 'I am a big fella, and I am sure the sight of me could be intimidating for some people', he agreed.[50] But the clinical approach adopted in his case seems *prima facie* evidence that the medical system in Northern Ireland was simply not prepared for dealing with the complex needs of military veterans. The doctors and nurses seemed more concerned with their own personal safety than with providing care that might make a difference to Armstrong's condition. They appeared, at least to Armstrong, to focus on what they could see, rather than trying to deal with the root causes of his problems.

Colonel (Retd) Stewarty Douglas, who, at the time, was working closely with the NI Regimental Associations in the veterans' space, visited Armstrong in hospital and found a young man in crisis. And he understood the medical staff's caution in relation to their patient:

> I walked in to a tiny interview room within the secure unit and found a hulking great Viking with a thick beard and tattoos. The first thing he said to me was 'I could pull that light fitting off the wall and kill you with it'. I felt I was in a room with a hand grenade and the pin was half-out.[51]

After the initial shock, and as they talked, however, Colonel Douglas recognised that he was standing in front of an intelligent and articulate man who had reached the end of his tether:

> He was in a bad way. He was in tears and he insisted that he wanted to end it all. It wasn't a matter of if, but of when. In his mind, no matter what the doctors and nurses did, they wouldn't be able to stop him from killing himself. He was a threat to himself, but I sensed that he wasn't going to do harm to me or anyone else.[52]

Royal Irish Regimental Secretary, Lieutenant Colonel (Retd) Andy Hart, who also visited Armstrong not long after he was admitted to hospital, queried the patient's treatment with medical staff. He felt there was little therapeutic value in maintaining him in a state of medicated sedation without a parallel programme of counselling therapy. Following an altercation with a fellow-patient, the medics had described Armstrong as 'a trained killer'.[53] He was certainly a trained infantry soldier, who had been taught to apply controlled violence within the laws of armed conflict. That did not make him a 'trained killer' in the pejorative sense implied by the comments of the health professionals quoted above and this attitude suggests a lack of understanding and, perhaps empathy, among civilian medical staff at that time.

Colonel Douglas continued to visit over the following weeks and Ricky appeared to be making progress in terms of his mental health. However, there seemed to be little continuity in terms of his treatment:

> He was eventually discharged from the unit and told to go home, even though he had nowhere that he felt that he could go to. He ended up sleeping on a sofa in a friend's house for that first night after discharge. That seemed to undo any progress that might have been made in

---

50   Ranger Ricky Armstrong, interview with author.
51   Col (Retd) Stewarty Douglas, interview with author.
52   Col (Retd) Stewarty Douglas, interview with author.
53   Lieutenant Colonel (Retd) Andy Hart, interview with author.

hospital. I met him outside Coleraine the next morning. He quickly broke down in tears and told me this was his "last day". He said "I'll be dead by tonight". I believe that was his lowest point.[54]

As they talked, however, Ricky began to recover his composure and to understand that he still had something to live for. He eventually returned to his home, while the Regiment helped his partner and children to find a place to live nearby. The two former soldiers have formed a bond, a lasting friendship, and continue to keep in touch.

After two years of battling with bureaucracy, the MOD finally reissued Ricky Armstrong's medals and they were presented to him by the Colonel of the Regiment, Major General (Retd) Colin Weir, at a ceremony at Regimental Headquarters in Belfast. Ranger Armstrong still has some bad days. He knows he will never be free of the symptoms of PTSD. But he has moved on, at least for now, from regarding suicide as the solution to his problems. Ranger Jason Mooney's reissued medals were also presented to his mother at a private ceremony.

---

54   Colonel (Retd) Stewarty Douglas, interview with author.

15

Things Can Only Get Better – but when?

For Musa Qal'eh veterans, in the years immediately following their 2006 deployment, gaining access to mental health services has been likened to a post-code lottery. The Government that had been so quick to send them into the Helmand cauldron failed to act with the same alacrity when it came to ensuring all could access the medical help they needed when they returned.

Providing they felt able to report their problems – and many did not – those who were still serving when the symptoms were identified and diagnosed were able to avail themselves of care provided by the NHS and various charities, under contract to the MOD. But for those who had left the armed forces and transitioned back into civilian life without a diagnosis, access to help was heavily dependent on geography...and politics. In some parts of the United Kingdom – notably England, Wales and Scotland – most veterans have been able to benefit from mental health services, tailored to their specific needs. However, in Northern Ireland (and in the Republic of Ireland), where many of the Royal Irish Regiment soldiers returned to settle, no such bespoke statutory services existed at that time, or have been instituted since. The province's health service was not geared up to deal with this new generation of veterans, and what one soldier described as the 'outbreak of PTSD' that followed the campaigns in Iraq and Afghanistan.[1]

Recognising that many military personnel who had lived and served in Northern Ireland during Operation Banner (The Troubles), required help with their mental and physical scars, in 2007, upon the disbandment of the Royal Irish (Home Service) battalions, the MOD established and funded the Ulster Defence Regiment/Royal Irish Regiment (Home Service) Aftercare Service.[2] This organisation, which was paid for and administered by the Army from the headquarters of 38th (Irish) Brigade, at Thiepval Barracks in Lisburn, was charged with providing 'welfare, medical, vocational and benevolence' support for ex-UDR/Royal Irish (Home Service) soldiers. However, as the Royal Irish Regimental Association pointed out in a submission to the Northern Ireland Affairs Select Committee of the House of Commons, in 2013, this was of no benefit to the veterans of Musa Qal'eh. According to the Regiment's memorandum to the Committee, General

---

1 Ranger Paul Johnston, interview with author.
2 The Ulster Defence Regiment was established in 1970 as a replacement for the Ulster Special Constabulary. Its job was to provide a locally-raised military capability that would supplement the Royal Ulster Constabulary in the fight against Irish Republican and Loyalist terrorism. Its main roles included guarding key points, patrolling, surveillance and manning vehicle checkpoints. It consisted of 11 infantry battalions and personnel were initially recruited on a part-time basis, although a full-time cadre was added later. In 1992, the UDR merged with the Royal Irish Rangers to form The Royal Irish Regiment with the UDR battalions becoming the new regiment's Home Service units.

Service personnel had 'no right of access to the service'.[3] It was not funded to support soldiers from the regular Army, only those who had served in the UDR and its successor, the Royal Irish (Home Service) units.

Nearly 20 years on from Tony Blair's military adventures in Iraq and Afghanistan, although the situation has improved, Northern Ireland veterans are still not receiving parity of treatment with those on the mainland. This is largely due to the unique political circumstances prevailing there, and Whitehall's apparent unwillingness to rock the Stormont boat. The extent of the mental healthcare divide between Northern Ireland and the mainland was spelled out in evidence to the House of Commons Defence Select Committee in 2018 by Professor Cherie Armour then of the Institute of Mental Health Services at Ulster University and more recently Director of the Research Centre for Stress Trauma and Related Conditions (STARC) at Queen's University, Belfast:

> There is a different level of provision for veterans in Northern Ireland, compared with other parts of the UK… Veterans can access the National Health Service and any statutory services in the same way that other members of the population can, but there are no bespoke statutory services provided to veterans in Northern Ireland and there is certainly no priority treatment given to them…[4]

This lack of state-sponsored provision meant that veterans living in the province were forced to rely more heavily on the services of the charity and community sectors than is the case for their comrades in the rest of the UK. But that too was a lottery. Professor Armour reported that only 19, or 0.4 percent of the charity and community sector organisations, were providing support for veterans in Northern Ireland. By way of comparison, at that time there were 1,818 charity providers in England and Wales and 461 in Scotland.[5] Even accounting for different population densities, it seems there was a wealth of additional voluntary and community service organisations in other parts of the UK, compared with Northern Ireland.

That does not mean that the situation in the rest of the UK was perfect. An independent review of Government welfare services for veterans, conducted in 2023, made 35 recommendations for improvements and concluded:

> The HMG-delivered veterans welfare services are a complex system that is often trying to be all things to all people without a real sense of direction or purpose. It is not well-cohered nor well-communicated and as a result is incredibly hard to navigate.[6]

---

3   Royal Irish Regimental Association submission to the House of Commons Northern Ireland Affairs Select Committee, February 2013, <https://publications.parliament.uk/pa/cm201314/cmselect/cmniaf/51/51we08.htm>, accessed 30 May 2024.
4   Professor Cherie Armour, Ulster University, evidence to HCDC, 24 April 2018, Q71,<https://committees.parliament.uk/oralevidence/7857/pdf/>, accessed 30 May 2024.
5   Professor Cherie Armour, Ulster University, evidence to HCDC, 24 April 2018, Q71,<https://committees.parliament.uk/oralevidence/7857/pdf/>, accessed 30 May 2024.
6   Report of the Independent Review of UK Government Welfare Services for Veterans, published on 17 July 2023, p.62. <https://www.gov.uk/government/publications/the-independent-review-of-uk-government-welfare-services-for-veterans>, accessed 31 May 2024.

The Armed Forces Covenant – a Toothless Tiger?

The Armed Forces Covenant is a promise by the nation that those who are or have been in the Armed Forces should be treated 'with fairness and respect in the communities, economy and society they serve with their lives'.[7] It is enshrined in law within the Armed Forces Act 2006, and forms part of the bargain between the country and those who go to war on its behalf. The Serviceperson writes a cheque to pay a price, up to and including their life, in defence of their homeland. In return, the nation promises to treat them with respect and dignity and to look after them and their families if they come home from war, or any other military activity, wounded, injured or sick. This agreement is underpinned by two principles: that those who serve should face no disadvantage compared to other citizens in the provision of public and commercial services; and that special consideration is appropriate in some cases, especially for those who have given most, such as the injured.

The Covenant was established in its current form in 2011, and since then, thousands of organisations – businesses, local authorities, NHS Hospital Trusts, educational establishments and charities – have signed and pledged their support. Shamefully, despite the principles the Covenant espouses, veterans in Northern Ireland have been treated differently, and less favourably, than those in the rest of the country for which they had been fighting.

Answering a parliamentary question in the House of Lords about whether military veterans living in Northern Ireland could access all the provisions of the Covenant available in other parts of the UK, Defence Minister, Baroness Goldie, stated in October 2023 that:

> The Armed Forces Covenant applies equally across the UK, including Northern Ireland. Good progress is being made in delivery of the Covenant in Northern Ireland, though its unique historical and political circumstances mean that delivery… has to be approached in a different way to the rest of the UK.[8]

This answer, while technically correct, represents a considerable flexing of the reality surrounding how the Covenant was being implemented in the province at that time. Nearly two decades after the events of 2006, and despite anecdotal and statistical evidence that points to significant mental health problems among those who made it home, the principles of the Armed Forces Covenant were not being adhered to in Northern Ireland as far as mental health care for veterans was concerned. There were no bespoke statutory services for veterans in the Six Counties, as there were in England, Scotland and Wales. As Professor Armour put it: 'We still don't have parity with the levels of provision you would see in England, Scotland and Wales because there is still this non-implementation of the Armed Forces Covenant'.[9]

The civil servants who support the Northern Ireland power-sharing executive and its various departments – and some of their political masters – claim that by providing such services they would be in breach of Section 75 of the Northern Ireland Act, 1998. In common with the rest of the UK, health is a devolved matter in Northern Ireland. Although the National Health Service exists as an umbrella organisation, most decisions about health care are devolved from Whitehall to the four National Health Services. In the Six Counties, health policy and service delivery are overseen by the Department of Health, which is part of the Stormont power-sharing executive.

---

7   Armed Forces Covenant, <https://www.armedforcescovenant.gov.uk/about-the-covenant/>, accessed 27 April 2024.
8   Hansard, House of Lords Debate, 26 October <https://questions-statements.parliament.uk/written-questions/detail/2023-10-24/HL10799>, accessed 15 May 2024.
9   Prof Cherie Armour, interview with author.

The Northern Ireland Act 1998 was brought into being by Tony Blair's Labour Government in the UK Parliament to give legal force to the Good Friday Agreement, the deal that was intended to end the three decades of conflict known as 'The Troubles'. Section 75 of the Act is concerned with equality of opportunity. It places a statutory duty on public authorities, in carrying out their functions relating to Northern Ireland, to have 'due regard to the need to promote equality of opportunity between persons of different religious belief, political opinion, racial group, age, marital status or sexual orientation'.[10] In the province, Section 75 has been interpreted – by some – as prohibiting anything that might be considered to result in any single group within Northern Ireland society being given priority over another. As Professor Armour explained, some political parties in Northern Ireland argue that veterans of the armed forces, resident in the province, come predominantly from one section of the community and thus cannot be treated differently from any other part of society.[11] The Royal Irish Regimental Association made a similar point when it gave evidence to the Northern Ireland Affairs Select Committee. 'Unfortunately, officials in various (NI) Government Departments, who would be able to help ex-service personnel, have refused to do so as they would be in breach of Sect 75 of the Act'.[12]

In the other Home Nations, the NHS faces a similar – but not identical – dilemma. The NHS is required by law to treat all patients on the basis of clinical need. In theory, that means it should not provide priority treatment for veterans based on their status as former members of the Armed Forces. However, in stark contrast to the Northern Ireland approach, the health authorities in England, Scotland and Wales, avoid this constitutional speed-bump by pointing to the principle of treating the patient's illness by providing 'bespoke pathways to care'. In effect, the NHS is taking a practical approach by saying it recognises that in order to effectively treat someone it needs to understand their background. For a veteran, their time in service is fundamental to who they are as a person and the illness from which they may be suffering. In these circumstances, it is entirely appropriate to have a pathway to care that meets the specific needs of veterans. But not, it seems, in Northern Ireland.

Former NI Veterans' Commissioner, Danny Kinahan, found himself coming up against the Section 75 issue on an almost daily basis, and despite Baroness Goldie's statement in the House of Lords, there seemed to be no easy solution:

> The Armed Forces Covenant doesn't really happen in Northern Ireland – at least not the way the Office of Veterans' Affairs wants it to work – it's a bit of a mess.
>
> If I wrote to the Department of Health, they would tell me I couldn't do anything for veterans due to Section 75. If someone wanted to be difficult, they could say they had passed the 'due regard' test [in the Armed Forces Act] by stating they had considered the needs of veterans and decided to do nothing.
>
> Stormont policy makers believe that as long as they can prove they have thought about the needs of veterans they don't actually have to do anything specific to help them. When I asked who, in the Executive, was going to be responsible for interpreting the requirements of the Covenant Duty, I was told it was the First Minister's Office.[13]

---

10 Northern Ireland Act, 1998, <https://www.legislation.gov.uk/ukpga/1998/47/section/75>, accessed 24 April 2024.
11 Professor Cherie Armour, interview with author.
12 Royal Irish Regimental Association submission to the House of Commons Northern Ireland Affairs Select Committee, February 2013, <https://publications.parliament.uk/pa/cm201314/cmselect/cmniaf/51/51we08.htm>, accessed 30 May 2024.
13 Danny Kinahan, former NI Veterans' Commissioner, interview with author prior to his resignation.

The UK Government's official position on 'due regard' in relation to the Covenant Duty was set out in the Armed Forces Covenant and Veterans Annual Report, 2023, which stated: 'The Duty of due regard to the covenant applies across the UK, including Northern Ireland, and is carefully phrased to ensure that it in no way conflicts with the requirements of Section 75 of the Northern Ireland Act 1997 [sic]'.[14] Despite this, Stormont has continued to maintain that the Covenant requirements are directly incompatible with the equality clauses in the Northern Ireland Act. Faced with this situation, Kinahan resorted to guerrilla tactics, working 'below the radar' to sidestep the system and help a small number of veterans to 'jump the queue' by sending them to the mainland – against the advice of the NI Civil Service.[15] But this has only benefitted a very few of those most in need.

According to MOD sources, however, Section 75 is a 'red herring', a convenient excuse for some of those in power in the province to avoid having to explain the real reasons for their resistance to the Covenant and all it stands for. Perhaps understandably, from their perspective, few nationalists are prepared to openly countenance any specific support for former members of what they once called 'the forces of occupation'. At the same time, however, UK politicians have been content to accept the status quo, even if it means veterans get a raw deal, rather than doing or saying anything that might embarrass the nationalists.

In view of Stormont's intransigence, MOD officials sought legal advice to establish if Section 75 was a real barrier to the full implementation of the Armed Forces Covenant in the province. The clear, unequivocal response was that it was not.[16] This is because the requirements of the AFC to prioritise support for those service personnel and their families who have given most, including those who have been injured, is written into the Armed Forces Act. Since Defence is a reserved power, the NI Assembly does not have the authority to ignore the requirements of the Act. And yet they do. The nationalists use Section 75 as cover to do nothing and UK ministers have been unwilling to call them out. As a result, at the time of writing, initiatives that have made a real, positive difference in other parts of the UK, are not available in Northern Ireland. These include, for example, Op Courage, which provides a bespoke mental health pathway for veterans, and Op Restore, which is delivering physical health and wellbeing support.

Other Barriers to Care

But even if the Covenant was being implemented in full and bespoke mental health care services existed, there are other barriers that make it more difficult for Northern Ireland-based ex-servicemen and women to get the help they need. According to Professor Armour, veterans of the fighting in Iraq and Afghanistan are probably doing 'less well than their equivalents on the mainland'. 'My hypothesis would be that compared to those on the mainland, it would take veterans in Northern Ireland longer to seek help. This is partly because the sources of support available are not so readily accessible'.[17] But there are other factors that exacerbate the situation. 'They also have their own barriers to help-seeking, which are caused by fear, safety and security

---

14 The Armed Forces Covenant and Veterans Annual Report 2023, MOD and OVA, presented to Parliament pursuant to Section 343A of the Armed Forces Act 2006 (amended), <https://www.gov.uk/government/publications/armed-forces-covenant-and-veterans-annual-report-2023>, accessed 15 May 2024.
15 Danny Kinahan, interview with author.
16 Private interview.
17 Professor Cherie Armour, QUB, interview with author.

and stigma, and additional problems arising from the political culture in the province. This means veterans often suffer in silence'.[18]

At the end of the first decade of the twenty-first century, as the mental health impacts of the military operations in Afghanistan were becoming apparent, the only way a Northern Ireland-based Musa Qal'eh veteran experiencing mental health problems could access statutory medical support was by obtaining a GP referral for psychiatric evaluation, and then joining the long waiting list for NHS treatment. Northern Ireland already had the highest rate of poor mental health in the UK so this meant that even if an individual was demonstrating immediate suicidal tendencies, he or she would be joining the end of a very long queue.[19] Before they could get that initial referral, however, many former soldiers had to overcome significant personal security concerns about revealing their service history. Throughout their time in uniform, soldiers were constantly reminded, as part of their personal security and counter-intelligence training, to avoid doing or saying anything that could identify them as being connected with the military. In these circumstances, Northern Ireland veterans are often reluctant to discuss their service background with their GPs... or anyone else that they do not know and trust.

Viewed from the UK mainland, or anywhere that is not Northern Ireland, this secrecy and mistrust may seem incomprehensible or even unreasonable. But for military veterans in the province, it was, and continues to be, the reality of their daily lives. Although the Republican terrorist campaign was supposed to have come to an end with the signing of the Good Friday Agreement, on 22 May 1998, not every Republican group was prepared to buy-in to the peace plan. At the time of writing (2024), the threat level in the province, stemming from local – as opposed to international – terrorism, stood at 'substantial', having been recently reduced from 'severe'.[20] The threat level is set by the UK's Joint Terrorist Analysis Centre and the Security Service (MI5). 'Substantial' means a terrorist attack is likely. Severe means one is highly likely. Despite the veneer of normality on the streets of cities like Belfast, Armagh and Londonderry, dissident Republican groups remain active, and continue to target members of the Security Forces. Although the number of attacks is now miniscule compared with the height of the so-called 'armed struggle' between 1970 and 1990, they have not stopped. Detective Chief Inspector John Caldwell of the Police Service of Northern Ireland (PSNI) was left fighting for his life after being shot multiple times at a sports centre in Omagh in February 2023. Responsibility for the attack was claimed by the so-called 'New IRA'.[21]

Professor Armour is clear that veterans' concerns about their personal security are real and understandable as far as the individuals are concerned. 'Psychologically, we understand that if someone genuinely believes they are under threat, whether that perception is subjective or objective doesn't matter. If they genuinely believe the threat exists, that belief will impact on their

---

18 Professor Cherie Armour, QUB, interview with author and Cherie Armour et al, 'Hitting The Wall: The impact of barriers to care and cumulative trauma exposure on PTSD among Northern Ireland Veterans', *Journal of Military Veteran and Family Health*, <https://jmvfh.utpjournals.press/action/showCitFormats?doi=10.3138%2Fjmvfh-2022-0078>, accessed 13 June 2024.

19 Mental Health Foundation, <https://www.mentalhealth.org.uk/explore-mental-health/publications/mental-health-foundation-northern-ireland-manifesto-2022>, accessed 24 February 2024. The waiting times varied depending on in which part of the province the veteran lived.

20 The Security Service (MI5), <https://www.mi5.gov.uk/threats-and-advice/terrorism-threat-levels#:~:text=Current%20Northern%20Ireland%2Drelated%20Terrorism,related%20terrorism%20in%20Northern%20Ireland>, accessed 5 May 2024.

21 *Belfast Telegraph*, 2 April 2024, <https://www.belfasttelegraph.co.uk/news/northern-ireland/new-ira-urged-to-pursue-peaceful-path-after-statements-vowing-to-continue-armed-campaign/a438602497.html>, accessed 2 May 2024.

psychological well-being, and their decision-making'.[22] Michael Donaldson, a qualified mental health nurse, and an Army Reservist with operational service in Iraq, who works with Ireland-based mental health charity, Inspire Wellbeing, explained how these security concerns could affect access to care:

> If a veteran, experiencing flashbacks or suicidal thoughts, goes to a GP for help, one of the first questions they are going to be asked is why they are feeling that way? Is there something from their past that might be responsible? In my experience, if the client feels unable to say why he is feeling suicidal, the GP is unlikely to be able to provide much help.[23]

A second barrier was waiting times. In the event that the patient was able to convince the GP that there was a problem, it could take many months to get an appointment with a psychiatrist, and even longer to begin treatment for the condition. Many gave up trying to get medical help and opted to suffer in silence, in some cases until it was too late.[24] Others self-medicated, resorting to alcohol, the misuse of prescription drugs or illegal narcotics, although in Northern Ireland, drink is the most likely 'medicine' of choice.

Another obstacle has been highlighted by Ricky Armstrong and Paul Johnston. Even when they managed to break down the barriers and had found a sympathetic GP who was willing to take them seriously, it was clear that few people in the healthcare system in Northern Ireland had any real appreciation or understanding of their background or the experiences they had endured. This made it more difficult for them to have the sort of frank, open conversations necessary to benefit from treatments such as Cognitive Behavioural Therapy (CBT) and Eye Movement Desensitisation and Reprocessing (EMDR). There is no doubt that veterans can be a tough client group to work with. They speak their own language and see themselves as being different from other sections of society by virtue of their training, values and standards. Rightly or wrongly, they consider themselves to be a step up from most of their civilian counterparts. They are disparaging about those who have not shared their experiences. As a result, they sometimes find it difficult to engage with people from outside their circle of military comrades. This attitude can cause frictions when it comes to getting help. In Stewarty Douglas's words, they can be 'a closed shop'. 'If you haven't been where they've been and done what they've done, they don't trust you and they don't want to know you'.[25]

As Michael Donaldson points out, however, trust is an essential element of treatment for PTSD. 'If the client doesn't trust the therapist, they will not open up about the causes of their mental health problems. If we can't get the bad stuff out, we can't begin the healing process'.[26] CBT and EMDR are both talking therapies. They rely on the therapist and the patient working together to unpack the experiences that are causing the symptoms. 'When you experience events, your brain processes them and stores them away, putting round pegs in round holes. But when you see something traumatic, your brain goes into protection mode. It may not process the event at all, or it may deal with it by trying to put a square peg in a round hole'.

Donaldson likes to use a military analogy to explain this to clients:

---

22   Professor Cherie Armour, interview with author.
23   Michael Donaldson, interview with author.
24   Michael Donaldson, interview with author.
25   Col (Retd) Stewarty Douglas, interview with author.
26   Michael Donaldson, interview with author

> It's a bit like packing your Bergan at speed after a contact. Sometimes you get it right and the load sits comfortably. Other times, you just ram stuff in so when you are tabbing off with your section you discover one of the straps is twisted, a mess tin is digging into your side, a rifle magazine is poking into your back or a radio battery is banging against your shoulder.[27]

It is this non-processing or mis-placing of the memory that leads to flashbacks and causes emotional pain. Therapy aims to persuade the mind to reprocess the experience and store it in the right place so it can be managed:

> Unless you can persuade the patient to unpack their experiences – and that can involve getting them to relive some pretty painful memories – it is never going to be possible to repack them in a way that allows the patient to better manage the mental anguish. Therapy gives the client the opportunity to take off the Bergan, empty out the contents in a safe and secure environment, and then repack it properly. The weight hasn't changed but it is better packed and less uncomfortable.[28]

But as Ricky Armstrong explained: 'It's hard to talk about these things, even with your mates. It's even harder to talk about them with people you don't know and who haven't been through the same experiences, who have no understanding of what you have faced'.[29] In many cases, through a lack of knowledge, clinicians could appear to be unempathetic or disbelieving and this further undermined trust.

It was problems such as this that encouraged Michael Donaldson to found Connect to Protect (CTP). Donaldson was aware that the issue was not necessarily a willingness to help but about understanding the unique needs of veterans. Too many fell through the cracks. CTP grew out of that frustration, but also out of hope: a belief that education, awareness and honest conversations could make a real difference.

---

27 Michael Donaldson, interview with author.
28 Michael Donaldson, interview with author.
29 Ranger Ricky Armstrong, interview with author.

16

The Wheels of State Turn Slowly

Despite the problems outlined above, there are signs that veterans' access to mental healthcare in Northern Ireland is beginning to move in the right direction, although perhaps too slowly for some. The Northern Ireland Veterans Support Committee (NIVSC) was established in 2012, sitting within the Reserve Forces and Cadets Association (RFCA), to engage with statutory and other bodies to support delivery of welfare services. The success of the NIVSC, backed up by a recommendation in an academic report written by Professor Armour and others, was followed by the creation of the Northern Ireland Veterans' Support Office (NIVSO) in 2018.[1] This was initially a joint endeavour funded by COBSEO, a confederation of Service charities, and the Armed Forces Covenant Trust, again supported by the RFCA. Its role was to act as an influencing and convening body, bringing together key stakeholders to try to break down some of the log jams that were holding up the delivery of care. The MOD took over the funding of NIVSO in 2022.

A Mental Health Forum was also set up including the statutory health providers, the 11 Local Authority Veterans' Champions, the charity sector and the Veterans' Commissioner, which has been instrumental in enabling some veterans to access care on the UK mainland. After repeated calls for the UDR/R Irish (Home Service) Aftercare Service to be expanded to include all veterans, this was finally achieved in April 2023. At the same time, the Northern Ireland Veterans Welfare Service (VWS) was created, providing a one-stop-shop that signposts ex-service personnel to a range of support services and providers, taking on the role previously being delivered by the NIVSO. Four field teams, based in Coleraine, Portadown, Enniskillen and Holywood, work with veterans across the province. In a bid to overcome some of the trust issues, the caseworkers are all security-cleared. Some are ex-forces.

The VWS sits under Veterans UK as part of the MOD's Defence Business Services (DBS) department, which is responsible for delivering a range of HR, payroll, Armed Forces Pensions and Compensation, Finance, and Information Services nation-wide. It operates on a tri-service basis and is funded to help all veterans, navy, army or air force, regardless of when or where they served. The Aftercare Service is provided under two contracts, with the mental health element being delivered by Inspire Wellbeing. These arrangements are intended to be enduring, and there are plans to broaden the scope of the mental health contract to include psychiatric assessment and medical review. Between 2007 and 2023, it is estimated that Inspire Wellbeing handled up to 150 referrals per year for psychiatric help. Each referral could involve an initial assessment and 8–10 therapy sessions, depending on the individuals' needs as identified by clinicians. The care is not rationed and additional sessions can be authorised if required.[2]

---

1 Professor Cherie Armour et al, 'Supporting and Serving Military Veterans in Northern Ireland', Northern Ireland Veterans' Health and Wellbeing Study, Forces in Mind Trust, <https://www.fim-trust.org/wp-content/uploads/supporting-serving-military-veterans-northern-ireland.pdf>, accessed 13 June 2024.
2 Private interview.

The appointment, in 2020, of a Veterans' Commissioner for Northern Ireland has also helped to move things forward. The first person to hold this post, Danny Kinahan, himself a former army officer, recognised the problems to be confronted but admitted he had faced an uphill struggle in trying to improve the situation. Speaking before his resignation, he said:

> My job is to look at all the structures and things that are in place [to support the veterans] and make sure they work for them. That involves lobbying at Westminster and Stormont and with local authorities.
>
> When I took up the post I was starting with a blank sheet of paper. I had no database to identify my client group and I was working within a political system where no-one wanted to take responsibility for identifying veterans. I believed there was a veterans' population of between 450,000 and 500,000, including families – but I couldn't prove it.[3]

The MOD's own statistics only count veterans who are in receipt of a pension or Armed Forces Compensation Scheme payments. In 2015, the MOD figures suggested there were 8,585 veterans in the province. By 2023 that number had increased to 9,445 or two percent of the UK total. But as Professor Armour has pointed out, these figures are unrepresentative.[4] Although there is some robust research on this cohort, focused on Northern Ireland, there is no data set that can quantify the number of veterans in the province, nor the number in sub-cohorts, such as those who served in Afghanistan. The 10-yearly census does not require people to declare their veteran status, and pension data is not reliable as some ex-service personnel do not draw their Armed Forces pensions to avoid being identified as a veteran.[5]

The 2021 UK census introduced a question about veteran status in an attempt to improve national data. However, the question was not included in the Northern Ireland version, partly because it was believed veterans would not wish to answer it, and partly to avoid a political row.[6] Without data that can be used to demonstrate the scale of the problem, it can be difficult to make the case for resources or even to prove that a problem exists. It also makes it hard to demonstrate if things are improving or worsening. Evidence-based policy-making becomes impossible. Despite all these obstacles, Kinahan believes some things are getting better:

> I tried to focus on areas where I could make a difference. One of these was the availability of information about the help that already exists. In reality, there is now lots of support available to veterans, but many simply didn't know about it and some were falling down the gaps between the various bits of provision. They'd go to a therapy provider and complete a course of sessions but, in some cases, there was no follow-up. Or they had exhausted the help available from one provider so they went off and found another. It was a disjointed patchwork but we had begun to identify where the holes were and to get the providers to talk to each other.[7]

---

3   Former NI Veterans' Commissioner, Danny Kinahan, interview with author.
4   Professor Cherie Armour, interview with author.
5   Professor Cherie Armour, interview with author.
6   Independent Review of UK Government Welfare Services for Veterans, p.5, <https://assets.publishing.service.gov.uk/media/64b148dc07d4b8000d3472e3/Independent_Review_of_UK_Government_Welfare_Services_for_Veterans.pdf>, accessed 12 June 2024.
7   Former NI Veterans' Commissioner, interview with author.

He has also worked to ensure that every organisation, statutory, charity or voluntary, that might be in contact with veterans, has at least one person who is trained in mental health and knows where to point people to get help:

> Wherever a veteran may go to look for help, there should be someone who knows enough to be able to pick them up and point them in the right direction. If veterans seek support, they will be able to find it. We have also got some really good Regimental Associations who are leaning-in to the problem and making a real difference.[8]

Veterans Champions in each of the 11 Local Authorities were all elected representatives but Kinahan was trying to adapt the system to include nominated council officers with responsibility for veterans' affairs. At the same time, he was working to encourage participation by the other political parties:

> At present only Unionist councillors are taking on the role. But veterans are not just Unionists. They come from all sections of society. I wanted to find a way to depoliticise veterans in Northern Ireland. 'I know there are SDLP and Alliance Councillors who would be willing to help and I wanted to encourage them to get involved.'[9]

Sadly, Danny Kinahan resigned from his position as Veterans' Commissioner after the General Election in 2024 and the arrival of the new Labour Government. His decision came following an 'open and frank' discussion with the Northern Ireland Secretary, Hilary Benn. In a statement Kinahan said he had concluded that he could no longer provide the independent voice that veterans needed – a signal, perhaps, that the new Government had sought to silence his increasingly vocal attempts to persuade national and local politicians to put the province on the same level as the rest of the UK in the delivery of mental health support for former soldiers. He continued: 'Veterans in Northern Ireland do not enjoy the same protection as their counterparts in Great Britain. They have particular needs and concerns which need to be addressed by the UK Government, which I have made very clear in our discussions'.[10]

Meanwhile, the small improvements that have been delivered have not come a moment too soon. In the four months from January to April 2024, the numbers seeking help through VWS were two-thirds of those for the whole of the previous year.[11] This up-tick can be explained, in part, by improved communications with veterans and extending the qualifying criteria for the Aftercare Service. But it may also herald a more worrying trend. As veterans age, they may become more susceptible to mental health issues and those retiring may be more inclined to report their symptoms when they are no longer concerned about their employment or their military pensions. 'We could be seeing the bow-wave of a much greater problem coming around the corner', a MOD source admitted.[12]

Time will tell… In the meantime, it is to be hoped that the new Veterans' Commissioner, former Royal Irish Regiment reservist, David Johnstone, will be able to break down the barriers that still exist. It will be for him, and the politicians at Stormont and at Westminster, to ensure

---

8   Former NI Veterans' Commissioner, interview with author.
9   Former NI Veterans' Commissioner, interview with author.
10 Statement by Danny Kinahan, NI Veterans' Commissioner, 5 September 2024, <https://www.bbc.co.uk/news/articles/c5y5327mjxzo>, accessed 6 September 2024.
11 Private interview.
12 Private interview.

that former service personnel in the province, who suffer with mental health issues, are treated on the same basis, and have access to the same level of care and support, as their comrades across the Irish Sea.

The last words go to the man who had the responsibility of sending the soldiers of Somme and Barrosa platoons to Helmand, their Commanding Officer, Michael McGovern:

> I don't think we are perfect today, but we have made huge progress compared to 2006. We owe it to the families of those who were there at that time, those who are still serving today, and also to those who are about to join the regiment, that we have learned from these experiences. Some would argue that we have re-learned because we had already learned these lessons following the Falklands conflict, although I believe many of those veterans have suffered from mental health issues much later in life.

Although it is possible to identify young soldiers who are struggling, the former CO believes the Army also needs to think about those whose problems are not so readily apparent. This, he is certain, reinforces the importance of the regiment as a support network:

> Soldiers who develop coping strategies while they continue to serve and are among friends who have shared their experiences, can find it much more difficult to manage their mental health problems when they are cut off from their comrades. In my experience, people feel most supported when they are part of a regimental network, most importantly when they can be with people who understand what they have been through so they don't need to explain or describe their experiences and feelings. The problem is that sooner or later they will leave the army and they will be dealing with people who, through no fault of their own, just won't understand. The antidote to that is an effective regimental safety net, such as that being provided by the Royal Irish Regiment.[13]

Faugh a Ballagh!

---

13   Brigadier (Retd) Michael McGovern, interview with author.

Bibliography

Books referenced

Bishop, Patrick, *3 Para* (London: Harper Perennial, 2008)
Blair, Tony, *Tony Blair, A Journey* (London: Arrow Books, 2010)
Bush, George W, *Decision Points* (London: Virgin Books, 2010)
Brown, Gordon, *Gordon Brown: My Life, Our Times* (London: The Bodley Head, 2017)
Carey, Henry (transl), *The Histories of Herodotus* (New York: D Appleton and Co, 1904)
Churchill, Winston S, *My Early Life: A Roving Commission* (London: Eland, 1930)
Clarke, Michael (Ed), *The Afghan Papers – Committing Britain to War in Helmand 2005-6* (Abingdon: Routledge, 2011)
Clausewitz, Carl von, (edited and translated by Sir Michael Howard and Peter Paret), *On War* (Princeton, NJ: Princeton University Press, 1984)
Clinton, Bill, *My Life* (London: Hutchinson, 2004)
Coughlin, Con, *American Ally – Tony Blair and the War on Terror* (London: Politico's Publishing, 2006)
Cowper-Coles, Sherard, *Cables From Kabul* (London: Harper Press, 2011)
Dannatt, General Sir Richard, *Leading From the Front – The Autobiography* (London: Transworld Publishers, 2010)
Elliott, Christopher L., *High Command – British Military Leadership in the Iraq and Afghanistan Wars* (London: C Hurst and Co, 2015)
Fairweather, Jack, *The Good War – Why We Couldn't Win the War or the Peace in Afghanistan* (London: Jonathan Cape, 2014)
Farrell, Theo, *Unwinnable – Britain's War in Afghanistan 2001-2014* (London: Vintage, 2017)
Fergusson, James, *Taliban* (London: Transworld Publishers, 2010)
Giustozzi, Antonio, *Koran, Kalashnikov, and Laptop: The Neo-Taliban Insurgency in Afghanistan* (London: Hurst, 2007)
Hammond, Mark, *Immediate Response* (London: Penguin Books, 2018)
Hefron, Edward and Guarnere, William, *Brothers in Battle, Best of Friends* (New York: Berkley Publishing Group, 2008)
Jackson, General Sir Mike, *Soldier* (London: Transworld Publishers, 2007)
Johannesen, Lars Ulslev, *The Tigers and the Taliban* (Copenhagen: Story House and ISIS Audio LLC A/S, 2013)
Jowett, Major Adam, *No Way Out* (London: Pan Books, 2019)
Killcullen, David, *The Accidental Guerilla – Fighting Small Wars in the Midst of a Big One* (London: C Hurst and Co, 2009)
Ledwidge, Frank, *Losing Small Wars – British Military Failure in Iraq and Afghanistan* (New Haven and London, Yale University Press 2012)
Maley, William, *Rescuing Afghanistan* (London: Hurst, 2006)
Mayer, Christopher, *DC Confidential* (London: Weidenfeld and Nicholson, 2005)

Peters, Gretchen, *Seeds of Terror – How Drugs, Thugs and Crime Are Reshaping the Afghan War* (Oxford: One World Publications, 2009)
Rashid, Ahmad, *Descent into Chaos* (London: Allen Lane, 2008)
Rashid, Ahmad, *Taliban* (London: Pan Macmillan, 2001)
Rawnsley, Andrew, *Servants of the People, The Inside Story of New Labour* (London: Hamish Hamilton, 2000)
Richards, General David, *Taking Command* (London: Headline Publishing Group, 2014)
Sanchez, Lieutenant General Ricardo S. (with Donald T Phillips), *Wiser In Battle, A Soldier's Story* (New York: Harper Collins, 2008)
Sun Tzu, *The Art of War* (Oxford: Oxford University Press, 1971)
Thatcher, Margaret, *Margaret Thatcher, The Downing Street Years* (London: Harper Collins, 1993)
Tootal, Colonel Stuart, *Danger Close – Commanding 3 Para in Afghanistan* (London: John Murray, 2009)
Woodward, Bob, *Plan of Attack* (London: Simon and Schuster UK Ltd, 2004)
Zaeef, Abdul Salam, *My Life With The Taliban* (London: Hurst and Co, 2011)

Other books consulted

Army Directorate of Land Warfare, *Operation Herrick Campaign Study* (Warminster: Directorate of Land Warfare, 2015)
Docherty, Leo, *Desert of Death – A Soldier's Journey From Iraq to Afghanistan* (London: Faber and Faber, 2007)
Fergusson, James, *A Million Bullets – The Real Story of the British Army in Afghanistan* (London: Transworld Publishers, 2008)
Grey, Stephen, *Operation Snake Bite* (London: Penguin Books, 2010)
Hagans, Dominic, *Wounded Rangers – Under Enemy Fire in Afghanistan* (Cirencester: Mereo, 2013)
Hoon, Geoffrey, *See How They Run* (London: Unicorn Publishing, 2022)
Rayment, Sean, *Into the Killing Zone: The Real Story from the Frontline in Afghanistan* (London: Constable, 2008)
Reynolds, Lieutenant Colonel David (collated by), *The Battle for Helmand – The Paras in Southern Afghanistan* (Plymouth: DRA Publishing, 2007)

Journal Articles

Barnett, Rubin R., 'Road to Ruin: Afghanistan's Booming Opium Industry', *The Centre for American Progress*, 7 October, 2004, p.2, <https://cdn.americanprogress.org/wp-content/uploads/kf/ROADTORUIN.PDF>
Beadle, Nick, 'Afghanistan and the Context of Iraq', in Clarke, M. (2012) (ed), *The Afghan Papers: Committing Britain to War in Helmand, 2005–06*, Routledge. <https://doi.org/10.4324/9780203096284>
Boone, Katherine N., 'The Paradox of PTSD.' *The Wilson Quarterly (1976-)*, vol. 35, no. 4, 2011, pp.18–22. *JSTOR*, <http://www.jstor.org/stable/41484367>
Bourke, Joanna. 'Effeminacy, Ethnicity and the End of Trauma: The Sufferings of 'Shell-Shocked' Men in Great Britain and Ireland, 1914-39.' *Journal of Contemporary History*, vol. 35, no. 1, 2000, pp.57–69. *JSTOR*, <http://www.jstor.org/stable/261181>

Butler, Brigadier Ed, 'Setting Ourselves Up For a Fall in Afghanistan', *RUSI Journal* Vol 160, Issue 1, 2015, pp.46–57.

Crocq, Marc-Antoine, MD and Crocq, Louis, MD, 'From shell shock and war neurosis to posttraumatic stress disorder: a history of psychotraumatology', *Dialogues in Clinical Neuroscience*, 2(1), pp.47–55. <https://www.ncbi.nlm.nih.gov/pmc/articles/PMC3181586/>

Farrell, G. and Thorne, J., 'Where have all the flowers gone?: evaluation of the Taliban crackdown against opium poppy cultivation in Afghanistan', p.81. *International Journal of Drug Policy*, 16 (2005) pp.81–89, <https://www.researchgate.net/publication/28576871_Where_have_all_the_flowers_gone_Evaluation_of_the_Taliban_crackdown_against_poppy_cultivation_in_Afghanistan>

Felbab-Brown, Vanda, 'Pipe Dreams: The Taliban and drugs from the 1990s into the new regime', *Small Wars Journal*, 15 September, 2021. <https://smallwarsjournal.com/jrnl/art/pipe-dreams-taliban-and-drugs-1990s-its-new-regime>

Fry, General Sir Rob and Bowen, Desmond, 'UK National Strategy and Helmand', in Michael Clark (ed), *The Afghan Papers: Committing Britain to War in Helmand, 2005-06*, Routledge. <https://doi.org/10.4324/9780203096284>

Hoehn, Andrew R and Harting, Sarah, 'A Greater Role for Nato in Afghanistan', in *Risking Nato: Testing the Limits of the Alliance in Afghanistan*, Rand Corporation, <www.jstor.org/stable/10.7249/mg974.af.11>

Hoehn, Andrew R and Harting, Sarah, 'Risking NATO: Testing the Limits of the Alliance in Afghanistan', *Rand Corporation, 2010*, pp.5–12, <www.jstor.org/stable/10.7249/mg974.af.9>

Kavanagh, Matt, 'Ministerial Decision-Making in the Run-Up to the Helmand Deployment', *The RUSI Journal*, 2012,157:2, pp.48–54.

Malkasian, Carter and Meyerle, Jerry, 'Ambush in Now Zad, Helmand, June 2006', research paper on Insurgent Tactics in Southern Afghanistan 2005-2008, sponsored by the US Marine Corps Intelligence Agency, August, 2009. <https://nsarchive2.gwu.edu/NSAEBB/NSAEBB370/docs/Document%205.pdf>

Randles R., et al. 'Prevalence and risk factors of suicide and suicidal ideation in veterans who served in the British Armed Forces: a systematic review', *BMJ Military Health* 2023, 0, pp.1–7, doi:10.1136/military-2023-002413, <https://militaryhealth.bmj.com/content/early/2023/06/15/military-2023-002413>

Rona R.J., Jones M., Fear N.T., et al, 'Mild traumatic brain injury in UK military personnel returning from Afghanistan and Iraq: cohort and cross-sectional analyses', *Journal of Head Trauma Rehabilitation*, 2012 Jan-Feb; 27(1), pp.33–44. doi: 10.1097/HTR.0b013e318212f814. PMID: 22241066.

Saideman, Stephen M., and Auerswald, David P., 'Comparing Caveats: Understanding the Sources of National Restrictions upon NATO's Mission in Afghanistan.' *International Studies Quarterly*, vol. 56, no. 1, 2012, pp.67–84. JSTOR, <http://www.jstor.org/stable/41409823>

Stevelink, S.A.M., Jones, M., Hull, L., et al. 'Mental health outcomes at the end of the British involvement in the Iraq and Afghanistan conflicts: a cohort study'. *The British Journal of Psychiatry*. 2018;213(6):690-697. doi:10.1192/bjp.2018.175.

Other works consulted

Donnelly, Thomas and Schmitt, Gary J., 'Musa Qala: Adapting to the Realities of Modern Counterinsurgency', *Small Wars Journal*, 2008, <https://smallwarsjournal.com/blog/journal/docs-temp/96-donnelly.pdf>

Gordon, Stuart, 'Winning Hearts and Minds? Examining the Relationship between Aid and Security in Afghanistan's Helmand Province', Feinstein International Centre, Tufts University, Medford, MA, April 2011, <https://fic.tufts.edu/publication-item/winning-hearts-and-minds/>

Gray, Joshua, 'The Challenges of British Counterinsurgency in Helmand – Why Did It Go Wrong?', *E-International Relations*, <https://www.e-ir.info/2014/11/17/the-challenges-of-british-counterinsurgency-in-helmand-why-did-it-go-so-wrong/>

Hoehn, Andrew R. and Harting, Sarah, 'The Nato That Once Was' in 'Risking Nato: Testing The Limits of the Alliance in Afghanistan', *Rand Corporation*, 2010, pp.5–12, <https://www.rand.org/content/dam/rand/pubs/monographs/2010/RAND_MG974.pdf>

Isby, David C., 'The High Stakes Battle for the Future of Musa Qala', *CTC Sentinel*, Vol 1, Issue 8, July 2008, Combating Terrorism Centre, West Point, <https://ctc.westpoint.edu/the-high-stakes-battle-for-the-future-of-musa-qala/>

Moon, Younghoun, 'The Future of Nato – The Purpose of the Alliance After the Cold War', *Harvard International Review*, Vol 34, No 3 (Winter 2013), pp.19–21, <https://www.proquest.com/docview/1470800205?sourcetype=Scholarly%20Journals>

Palmer, D.A.R. (2019) in 'A Strategic Odyssey: Constancy of Purpose and Strategy-making in Nato, 1949-2019', pp.73–90, *Nato Defence College*, JSTOR, <www.jstor.org/stable/resrep19967.11>

Peters, Gretchen, 'How Opium Profits the Taliban', *Peaceworks, journal of the United States Institute of Peace*, No. 62, August, 2009, <https://www.usip.org/sites/default/files/resources/taliban_opium_1.pdf >

Rona, R.J., Jones, M., Fear, N.T., et al, 'Mild traumatic brain injury in UK military personnel returning from Afghanistan and Iraq: cohort and cross-sectional analyses', *Journal of Head Trauma Rehabilitation,* 2012 Jan-Feb;27(1), pp.33–44. doi: 10.1097/HTR.0b013e318212f814. PMID: 22241066.

Webber, M., 'Nato: Crisis? What Crisis?', *Great Decisions*, 2013, pp.31–44, JSTOR, <www.jstor.org/stable/43682510>

Newspaper Articles

Ali, Yasmeen Aftab, 'Understanding Pashtunwali', *The Nation,* 6 August, 2013, <https://www.nation.com.pk/06-Aug-2013/understanding-pashtunwali>

Arkin, William, 'The General Unease With Wesley Clark', *Los Angeles Times,* 7 December, 2003, <https://www.latimes.com/archives/la-xpm-2003-dec-07-op-arkin7-story.html>

Baldauf, Scott and Khan, Ashraf, 'New Guns, New Drive for Taliban', *Christian Science Monitor*, 26 September, 2005, <https://www.csmonitor.com/2005/0926/p01s03-wosc.html>

Chandrasekaran, Rajiv, 'Afghanistan, how the US army battled it out with the British', the *Guardian,* 3 July, 2012, <https://www.theguardian.com/world/2012/jul/03/us-army-battles-british-afghanistan>

Cornwell, Rupert, 'Rumsfeld 'mends fences' by lumping Germany with Cuba and Libya in an axis of bad boys', *The Independent,* 8 February 2003, <https://www.independent.co.uk/news/world/politics/rumsfeld-mends-fences-by-lumping-germany-with-cuba-and-libya-in-an-axis-of-bad-boys-118343.html>

Crick, Bernard, 'Blair should beware the boiling up of little irritations', the *Guardian*, 29 September, 2003, <https://www.theguardian.com/politics/2003/sep/29/labour.uk>

Erlanger, Steven, 'For NATO, Little is Sure Now but Growth', *The New York Times*, 19 May 2002, <https://www.nytimes.com/2002/05/19/world/for-nato-little-is-sure-now-but-growth.html?searchResultPosition=1>

Gall, Carlotta, 'Taliban Continue to Sow Fear', *The New York Times*, 1 March 2006, <https://www.nytimes.com/2006/03/01/world/asia/taliban-continue-to-sow-fear.html?searchResultPosition=1>

Gordon, Michael R., 'NATO Chief Says Alliance Needs Security Role in Afghanistan', *The New York Times*, 21 February, 2003, <https://www.nytimes.com/search?dropmab=false&endDate=2003-05-05&query=NATO%20Chief%20Says%20Alliance%20Needs%20Security%20Role%20in%20Afghanistan&sort=best&startDate=2003-01-02>

Harding, Luke, 'World's opium source destroyed', *The Observer*, 1 April, 2001, <https://www.theguardian.com/world/2001/apr/01/internationalcrime.drugstrade>

Haynes, Deborah, Loyd, Anthony, Kiley, Sam, Coughlin, Tom, 'Officers' mess: military chiefs blamed for blundering into Helmand with 'eyes shut and fingers crossed'', *The Times*, 9 June, 2010, <https://www.thetimes.com/article/officers-mess-military-chiefs-blamed-for-blundering-into-helmand-with-eyes-shut-and-fingers-crossed-gs9sdn8zn35>

James, Barry, 'Iraq Debate Intensifies Within European Union and NATO', *The New York Times*, 13 February, 2003, <https://www.nytimes.com/2003/02/13/international/europe/iraq-debate-intensifies-within-european-union-and-nato.html>

Kaiser, Robert G. and Richburg, Keith B., 'NATO Looking Ahead to a Mission Makeover', *The Washington Post*, 5 November 2002, <https://www.washingtonpost.com/archive/politics/2002/11/05/nato-looking-ahead-to-a-mission-makeover/84f6164d-22c2-4bc8-9f5d-2a7fa92793db/>

Khan, Ishmail and Gall, Carlotta, 'Taliban Leader Promises More Afghan War', *The New York Times*, 5 January, 2007, <https://www.nytimes.com/2007/01/05/world/asia/05taliban.html?searchResultPosition=1>

Kissinger, Henry, 'Role Reversal and Alliance Realities', *The Washington Post*, 10 February, 2003, <https://www.washingtonpost.com/archive/opinions/2003/02/10/role-reversal-and-alliance-realities/eb4531b4-43aa-493d-b28e-c4a375c6b4df/>

Lamb, Christina, 'Have you ever used a pistol?', *Sunday Times*, 2 July, 2006, <https://www.thetimes.com/article/have-you-ever-used-a-pistol-5btnlkwfkkm>

Loyd, Anthony and Luddin, Tahir, 'After the fighting and dying, the Taliban return as British depart', *The Times*, 30 October, 2006, <https://www.thetimes.com/search?source=search-page&q=%22After+the+fighting+and+dying%22>

McElroy, Damien, 'Afghan governor turned 3000 men over to Taliban', *The Daily Telegraph*, 20 November, 2009, <https://www.telegraph.co.uk/news/worldnews/asia/afghanistan/6615329/Afghan-governor-turned-3000-men-over-to-Taliban.html>

McGurk, Tim, 'The Taliban on the Run', *Time Magazine*, 28 March, 2005, <https://time.com/archive/6671860/the-taliban-on-the-run/>

Norton-Taylor, Richard, 'Iraq dossier drawn up to make the case for war – intelligence Officer', the *Guardian*, 12 May, 2011, <https://www.theguardian.com/world/2011/may/12/iraq-dossier-case-for-war>

Rawnsley, Andrew, 'How Kosovo Strained Blair's Special Relationship', the *Guardian*, 17 September, 2000, <https://www.theguardian.com/politics/2000/sep/17/labour.labour1997to99>

Stacey, Kiran, 'The complex and corporate rise of the Tony Blair Institute', the *Guardian*, 17 September, 2023, <https://www.theguardian.com/politics/2023/sep/17/tony-blair-institute-rise>, accessed 22 February, 2025

'75 killed in mosque blast', the *Guardian*, 29 August, 2003, <https://www.theguardian.com/world/2003/aug/29/iraq.usa>

'Afghanistan: A Chronology Of Suicide Attacks Since 2001', *Radio Free Europe*, 17 January, 2006, <https://www.rferl.org/a/1064789.html>

'Bush Doesn't See NATO Sending in Troops for Iraq', *The New York Times*, 11 June, 2004, <https://www.nytimes.com/2004/06/11/world/reach-war-summit-politics-bush-doesn-t-see-NATO-sending-troops-for-iraq.html?searchResultPosition=59>

'Full Text of Tony Blair's Foreword to the dossier on Iraq', the *Guardian*, 24 September, 2002, <https://www.theguardian.com/world/2002/sep/24/iraq.speeches>

'Military Fights largest Afghanistan battle since March', *Tampa Bay Times*, 29 January, 2003, <https://www.tampabay.com/archive/2003/01/29/military-fights-largest-afghanistan-battle-since-march/>

'Miracle Escape of the new Rorke's Drift Paras', *the Daily Mail*, 6 August, 2016, <https://www.dailymail.co.uk/news/article-3727024/Cut-Surrounded-Outnumbered-Just-88-British-soldiers-resigned-defeat-fighting-500-Taliban-54-days-against-odds-Miracle-escape-Rorke-s-Drift-Paras.html>

'NATO Chief Says Alliance Needs Security Role in Afghanistan', *The New York Times*, 21 February 2003, <https://www.nytimes.com/2003/02/21/world/threats-responses-afghan-security-nato-chief-says-alliance-needs-role.html?searchResultPosition=1>

'New IRA urged to pursue 'peaceful path' after statements vowing to continue armed campaign', *Belfast Telegraph*, 2 April, 2024, <https://www.belfasttelegraph.co.uk/news/northern-ireland/new-ira-urged-to-pursue-peaceful-path-after-statements-vowing-to-continue-armed-campaign/a438602497.html>

'Split Shows EU Divisions Over Iraq', *The Irish Times*, 11 February, 2003, <https://www.irishtimes.com/news/split-shows-eu-divisions-over-iraq-1.348464>

'Taliban Raids Widen in Parts of Afghanistan', *New York Times*, 1 September, 2003, <https://www.nytimes.com/2003/09/01/world/taliban-raids-widen-in-parts-of-afghanistan.html>

'Taliban Sniper Shot Me in the Head', *Sunday Life*, 27 July, 2008, <https://www.belfasttelegraph.co.uk/sunday-life/news/taliban-sniper-shot-me-in-the-head-but-i-wouldnt-miss-my-brothers-wedding/28443596.html>

'The Afghan Papers – a secret history of the war', *The Washington Post*, 9 December, 2019, <https://www.washingtonpost.com/graphics/2019/investigations/afghanistan-papers/afghanistan-war-corruption-government/>

'They Went Into Helmand With Eyes Shut and Fingers Crossed', *The Times*, 9 June, 2010. <https://www.thetimes.co.uk/article/they-went-into-helmand-with-eyes-shut-and-fingers-crossed-jvbhc2mr07p>

'Transcript of Rumsfeld's Pentagon Press Conference', *The Washington Post*, 18 October 2001, <https://www.washingtonpost.com/wp-rv/nation/specials/attacked/transcripts/rumsfeld_text101801.html>

Documents Obtained under Freedom of Information Act

MOD document, FOI/2025/04329, Letter from Defence People Secretariat regarding Operational Honours List published in December, 2006, dated 31 March, 2025.

Army document, D/DFS(A)/33/64/2/PS4(A), Army Post Operational Stress Management Policy, dated 20 Sep 05.

Foreign Commonwealth and Development Office document, FOI2023/03265, The UK Joint Plan for Helmand, dated 12 January, 2024.

Podcasts

Scrivener, Major Jo, 'An Unbelievable Military Story', H-Hour Podcast, Hugh Keir (5 February, 2025), <https://open.substack.com/pub/hughkeir/p/livestream-recording-254-full-interview?r=2h98zl&utm_medium=ios>

News Websites

'12,000 more UK Troops for Kosovo', *BBC News*, 26 May, 1999, <http://news.bbc.co.uk/1/hi/uk_politics/353495.stm>

'Baghdad falls to US forces', *Sky History, 4 April, 2019,* <https://www.history.com/this-day-in-history/baghdad-falls-iraq-war>

'Commentary: NATO Caveats', *UPI*, 10 July, 2009, <https://www.upi.com/Emerging_Threats/2009/07/10/Commentary-NATO-caveats/UPI-47311247244125/>

'Iraqi ambush of Americans made a mockery of 'Mission Accomplished', *Reuters*, 16 March, 2023, <https://www.reuters.com/world/middle-east/iraqi-ambush-americans-made-mockery-mission-accomplished-2023-03-16/#:~:text=%22Falluja%20is%20the%20cemetery%20of,Michael%20Teague%20and%20Scott%20Helvenston>

'Million March Against Iraq War', *BBC News*, 16 February, 2003, <http://news.bbc.co.uk/1/hi/uk/2765041.stm>

'Rumsfeld: Major Combat Over in Afghanistan', *CNN*, 1 May, 2003, <https://edition.cnn.com/2003/WORLD/asiapcf/central/05/01/afghan.combat/>

'US: Rumsfeld's 'Old' And 'New' Europe Touches on Uneasy Divide', Radio Free Europe, 24 January, 2003, <https://www.rferl.org/a/1102012.html>

Parliamentary Papers
Questions, Statements and Debates

Blair, Tony (Prime Minister), Prime Minister's Questions, 26 May, 1999, *Hansard*, <https://hansard.parliament.uk/Commons/1999-05-26/debates/3eaf839e-1b51-4fb2-94c5-f8b812a1acab/CommonsChamber>

Blair, Tony (Prime Minister), Statement to the House of Commons, 8 October, 2001, *Hansard*, Column 814, <https://publications.parliament.uk/pa/cm200102/cmhansrd/vo011008/debtext/11008-01.htm>

Blair, Tony (Prime Minister), Statement to the House of Commons, 3 February, 2003, *Hansard*, Column 22, <https://publications.parliament.uk/pa/cm200203/cmhansrd/vo030203/debtext/30203-05.htm#30203-05_spmin4>

Browne, Des (Defence Secretary), Statement to the House of Commons, 'Afghanistan (Troop Levels)', 10 July, 2006, *Hansard*, Column 1132-1133. <https://hansard.parliament.uk/commons/2006-07-10/debates/06071010000002/Afghanistan(TroopsLevels)>

Hoon, Geoff (Defence Secretary), 'Statement on Iraq', *Hansard*, 8 September, 2004, Column 4, <https://hansard.parliament.uk/Commons/2003-09-08/debates/ab05aa2a-0b9e-4d9f-b201-02015f23e7d1/Iraq>

Jenkin, Bernard (Shadow Defence Secretary), *Hansard*, 8 September, 2004, Column 5, <https://hansard.parliament.uk/Commons/2003-09-08/debates/ab05aa2a-0b9e-4d9f-b201-02015f23e7d1/Iraq>

Mackay Andrew (MP Bracknell), *Hansard*, 8 September, 2004, Column 4, <https://hansard.parliament.uk/Commons/2003-09-08/debates/ab05aa2a-0b9e-4d9f-b201-02015f23e7d1/Iraq>

Reid, Dr. John (Defence Secretary), Statement to the House of Commons on Afghanistan, *Hansard*, 26 January, 2006, Column 1529, <https://publications.parliament.uk/pa/cm200506/cmhansrd/vo060126/debtext/60126-10.htm>

Reid, Dr. John (Defence Secretary), Statement on Afghanistan, 26 January, 2006, *Hansard*, Col 1530-1532, <https://publications.parliament.uk/pa/cm200506/cmhansrd/vo060126/debtext/60126-10.htm#60126-10_spmin0>.

Watson, Tom (Parliamentary Under-Secretary of State for Defence), Defence Debate, 4 July, 2006, *Hansard*, Column 517, <https://hansard.parliament.uk/commons/2006-07-03/debates/06070310000002/BritishForces(Afghanistan)>

'Debate on Iraq', House of Commons 18 March, 2003, *Hansard*, Column 760, <https://hansard.parliament.uk/Commons/2003-03-18/debates/ddc70cf1-f37d-4936-bc03-d5a5ecb02d40/Iraq>

Evidence to Parliamentary Committees

Browne, Des (Defence Secretary), evidence to HCDC, 8 May, 2007, <https://publications.parliament.uk/pa/cm200607/cmselect/cmdfence/408/408.pdf>

Browne, Lord (former Defence Secretary), evidence to HCDC, 29 March, 2011, EV120, Q562, <https://publications.parliament.uk/pa/cm201012/cmselect/cmdfence/554/554.pdf>.

Butler, Brigadier Ed (former Commander, 16 Air Assault Brigade), evidence to HCDC, 15 March, 2011, <https://publications.parliament.uk/pa/cm201012/cmselect/cmdfence/554/554.pdf>.

Butler, Brigadier Ed (former Commander, 16 Air Assault Brigade), evidence to HCDC, 16 December, 2014, EV19, Q41, <https://committees.parliament.uk/oralevidence/4405/pdf/>

Cook, Robin, MP, Evidence to Commons Select Committee on Foreign Affairs, 17 June, 2003, Q10, <https://publications.parliament.uk/pa/cm200203/cmselect/cmfaff/813/30617a02.htm>

Fry, Lieutenant General Sir Rob (former Deputy Chief of Defence Staff (Commitments)), Evidence to HCDC, 8 February, 2011, <https://publications.parliament.uk/pa/cm201012/cmselect/cmdfence/554/554.pdf>.

Fry, Lieutenant General Sir Rob (former Deputy Chief of Defence Staff (Commitments), evidence to HCDC 16 December, 2014, p.26, Q58. <https://committees.parliament.uk/oralevidence/4405/pdf>

HCDC Report, *Mental Health and the Armed Forces, Part One: The Scale of mental health issues*, 25 July, 2018, <https://publications.parliament.uk/pa/cm201719/cmselect/cmdfence/813/813.pdf>

HCDC Report, 'UK Operations In Afghanistan', Thirteenth Report of Sessions 2006-07, <https://publications.parliament.uk/pa/cm200607/cmselect/cmdfence/408/408.pdf>.

Houghton, General Sir Nick (Vice Chief of Defence Staff), evidence to the HCDC, 11 May, 2011, EV147, Q679, <https://publications.parliament.uk/pa/cm201012/cmselect/cmdfence/554/554.pdf>.

House of Commons Defence Select Committee, 'Operations in Afghanistan, Fourth Report of Session 2010-12', <https://publications.parliament.uk/pa/cm201012/cmselect/cmdfence/554/554.pdf>

House of Commons Defence Select Committee Report, *The UK Deployment to Afghanistan, 6 April, 2006*, <https://publications.parliament.uk/pa/cm200506/cmselect/cmdfence/558/558.pdf>.

House of Lords Select Committee, on International Relations and Defence, The UK and Afghanistan, transcript of evidence, 21 October, 2020, <https://committees.parliament.uk/oralevidence/1102/pdf/>

Howard, Martin (MOD Director General Operational Policy), evidence to HCDC, 17 January, 2006, EV3, Q10, <https://publications.parliament.uk/pa/cm200506/cmselect/cmdfence/558/558.pdf>.

Jackson, General Sir Mike (former Chief of the General Staff), evidence to HCDC, 15 March, 2011, EV112, Q511, <https://publications.parliament.uk/pa/cm201012/cmselect/cmdfence/554/554.pdf>.

Ninth Report of the Commons Select Committee on Foreign Affairs, 3 July, 2003, <https://publications.parliament.uk/pa/cm200203/cmselect/cmfaff/813/81308.htm/>

Northern Ireland Act, 1998, <https://www.legislation.gov.uk/ukpga/1998/47/section/75>

Parliamentary Question, Armed Forces Covenant: Northern Ireland, *Hansard*, House of Lords, 26 October, 2023, <https://questions-statements.parliament.uk/written-questions/detail/2023-10-24/HL10799>

Peach, Air Marshal Sir Stuart (Chief of Joint Operations), evidence to HCDC, 10 November, 2010, EV35, Q135, <https://publications.parliament.uk/pa/cm201012/cmselect/cmdfence/554/554.pdf>.

Peach, Air Chief Marshal Sir Stuart (Chief of Joint Operations), evidence to HCDC, 10 November, 2010, <https://publications.parliament.uk/pa/cm201012/cmselect/cmdfence/554/554.pdf>.

Reid, Lord (former Defence Secretary), evidence to HCDC, 8 February, 2011, EV91, Q415, <https://publications.parliament.uk/pa/cm201012/cmselect/cmdfence/554/554.pdf>.

Richards, General Sir David (Chief of Defence Staff), evidence to HCDC, 11 May, 2011, EV145, Q676, <https://publications.parliament.uk/pa/cm201012/cmselect/cmdfence/554/554.pdf>.

Royal Irish Regimental Association submission to the House of Commons Northern Ireland Affairs Select Committee, February, 2013, <https://publications.parliament.uk/pa/cm201314/cmselect/cmniaf/51/51we08.htm>

Sedwill, Lord (former National Security Advisor), evidence to House of Lords Select Committee on International Relations and Defence Inquiry, *The UK and Afghanistan*, 21 October, 2020, <https://committees.parliament.uk/oralevidence/1102/pdf/>

Stirrup, Air Chief Marshal Sir Jock (Chief of Defence Staff), evidence to HCDC, 4 May, 2011, EV130, Q604, <https://publications.parliament.uk/pa/cm201012/cmselect/cmdfence/554/554.pdf>.

Wall, General Sir Peter (Deputy Chief of Joint Operations), evidence to HCDC, 11 May 2011, <https://publications.parliament.uk/pa/cm201012/cmselect/cmdfence/554/554.pdf>.

Wall, General Sir Peter (Chief of the General Staff), evidence to HCDC, 11 May, 2011, EV145, Q676, <https://publications.parliament.uk/pa/cm201012/cmselect/cmdfence/554/554.pdf>

Wessely, Professor Sir Simon (Kings College, London), evidence to HCDC, 27 March, 2018, Q26 <https://committees.parliament.uk/oralevidence/7789/pdf/>

Iraq Inquiry documents
Quoted in the Report

AD Iraq to APS/SofS Minute, 2 September 2003, 'Post-Najaf; Meeting with the Prime Minister, Vol VII, p.263, <https://assets.publishing.service.gov.uk/media/5a7f968fe5274a2e8ab4d16a/The_Report_of_the_Iraq_Inquiry_-_Volume_VII.pdf>

Tony Blair, Vol VII, p.350, <https://assets.publishing.service.gov.uk/media/5a7f968fe5274a2e8ab4d16a/The_Report_of_the_Iraq_Inquiry_-_Volume_VII.pdf>

Blair – Bush Discussion, Record of Briefing, Vol VII, <https://assets.publishing.service.gov.uk/media/5a7f968fe5274a2e8ab4d16a/The_Report_of_the_Iraq_Inquiry_-_Volume_VII.pdf>

Bowen – Baker Letter, 13 May 2004, 'Iraq: Security', Vol VII, p.372. <https://assets.publishing.service.gov.uk/media/5a7f968fe5274a2e8ab4d16a/The_Report_of_the_Iraq_Inquiry_-_Volume_VII.pdf>

Chiefs of Staff Committee Discussion, 11 June, 2003, Vol VII, p.222, <https://assets.publishing.service.gov.uk/media/5a7f968fe5274a2e8ab4d16a/The_Report_of_the_Iraq_Inquiry_-_Volume_VII.pdf>

DCDS(C) – PSO/CDS Minute, 12 May, 2004, 'Strategic Failure in Iraq – Consequences and Risks', Vol VII, p.371, <https://assets.publishing.service.gov.uk/media/5a7f968fe5274a2e8ab4d16a/The_Report_of_the_Iraq_Inquiry_-_Volume_VII.pdf>

Executive Summary, <https://webarchive.nationalarchives.gov.uk/ukgwa/20171123122743/http://www.iraqinquiry.org.uk/the-report/>

Hoon – McColl Discussion, 14 June 2004, p.387, <https://assets.publishing.service.gov.uk/media/5a7f968fe5274a2e8ab4d16a/The_Report_of_the_Iraq_Inquiry_-_Volume_VII.pdf>

Hoon – Rice Discussion, Vol VII, p.2230, <https://assets.publishing.service.gov.uk/media/5a7f968fe5274a2e8ab4d16a/The_Report_of_the_Iraq_Inquiry_-_Volume_VII.pdf>

Hoon – Rumsfeld Bi-lateral, Vol VII, p.200, <https://assets.publishing.service.gov.uk/media/5a7f968fe5274a2e8ab4d16a/The_Report_of_the_Iraq_Inquiry_-_Volume_VII.pdf>

Howard – PS/SofS(MOD) Minute, 'HQ ARRC Deployment Options', 18 June, 2004, Vol VII, p.390, https://assets.publishing.service.gov.uk/media/5a7f968fe5274a2e8ab4d16a/The_Report_of_the_Iraq_Inquiry_-_Volume_VII.pdf>

Naworynsky – Owen Letter, 'Meeting between the Secretary of State for Defence and Senior British Military Representative – Iraq', 17 June, 2004, Vol VII, p.387, <https://assets.publishing.service.gov.uk/media/5a7f968fe5274a2e8ab4d16a/The_Report_of_the_Iraq_Inquiry_-_Volume_VII.pdf>

Naworynsky – Rycroft Letter, 25 May 2004, 'Iraq: options for a UK military contribution to the wider South', Vol VII, p.378, <https://assets.publishing.service.gov.uk/media/5a7f968fe5274a2e8ab4d16a/The_Report_of_the_Iraq_Inquiry_-_Volume_VII.pdf>

PJHQ Assessment of situation in UK AOR, Vol VII, p.224, <https://assets.publishing.service.gov.uk/media/5a7f968fe5274a2e8ab4d16a/The_Report_of_the_Iraq_Inquiry_-_Volume_VII.pdf>

Rycroft – Baker Letter, 'Iraq: US Approaches for additional UK forces', Iraq Inquiry Report, Vol VII, pp.360–361, <https://assets.publishing.service.gov.uk/media/5a7f968fe5274a2e8ab4d16a/The_Report_of_the_Iraq_Inquiry_-_Volume_VII.pdf>

Rycroft – Baker Letter, 'Iraq: Prime Minister's meeting 3 June', dated 3 June, 2004, Iraq Inquiry Report, Vol VII, p.384, <https://assets.publishing.service.gov.uk/media/5a7f968fe5274a2e8ab4d16a/The_Report_of_the_Iraq_Inquiry_-_Volume_VII.pdf>

Rycroft – Baker Letter, 'Iraq: Prime Minister's Meeting', 15 June, Report of the Iraq Inquiry, Vol VII, p.388, <https://assets.publishing.service.gov.uk/media/5a7f968fe5274a2e8ab4d16a/The_Report_of_the_Iraq_Inquiry_-_Volume_VII.pdf>

Sawers, Sir John, UK Special Representative to Baghdad, Vol 7, section 9.2, p.226, <https://webarchive.nationalarchives.gov.uk/ukgwa/20171123122743/http://www.iraqinquiry.org.uk/the-report/>

Sawers to FCO London Telegram, 3 July 2003, 'Personal: Iraq: Follow up to the Bush/Blair VTC', including Manuscript Comments Manning and Blair, Vol VII, p.237. <https://assets.publishing.service.gov.uk/media/5a7f968fe5274a2e8ab4d16a/The_Report_of_the_Iraq_Inquiry_-_Volume_VII.pdf>

Sheinwald – Blair Minute, 2 May, 2004, 'US Request for More British Troops', <https://assets.publishing.service.gov.uk/media/5a7f968fe5274a2e8ab4d16a/The_Report_of_the_Iraq_Inquiry_-_Volume_VII.pdf>

Tebbit – Hoon Minute, 28 May, 2004, 'Iraq: UK military presence' Vol VII, p.380, <https://assets.publishing.service.gov.uk/media/5a7f968fe5274a2e8ab4d16a/The_Report_of_the_Iraq_Inquiry_-_Volume_VII.pdf>

Thompson to Ehrman and Private Secretary (FCO) Minute, 20 November 2003, 'Possible Deployment of the ARRC to Afghanistan/Iraq', Vol VII, <https://assets.publishing.service.gov.uk/media/5a7f968fe5274a2e8ab4d16a/The_Report_of_the_Iraq_Inquiry_-_Volume_VII.pdf>

Watkins – Manning Letter, Section 9.2, p.209, <https://webarchive.nationalarchives.gov.uk/ukgwa/20171123122743/http://www.iraqinquiry.org.uk/the-report/>

Williams – Rycroft Letter, 4 September, 2003, Vol VII, p.268, <https://assets.publishing.service.gov.uk/media/5a7f968fe5274a2e8ab4d16a/The_Report_of_the_Iraq_Inquiry_-_Volume_VII.pdf>

Personal Evidence

Blair, Blair, 29 January, 2010, <https://webarchive.nationalarchives.gov.uk/ukgwa/20171123123302/http://www.iraqinquiry.org.uk/the-evidence/witness-transcripts/>

Dannat, General Lord, 28 July, 2010, <https://webarchive.nationalarchives.gov.uk/ukgwa/20171123123302/http://www.iraqinquiry.org.uk/the-evidence/witness-transcripts/>

Fry, Lieutenant General Sir Rob, 16 December, 2009, <https://webarchive.nationalarchives.gov.uk/ukgwa/20171123123302/http://www.iraqinquiry.org.uk/the-evidence/witness-transcripts/>

Hoon, Geoff, 19 January, 2010, <https://webarchive.nationalarchives.gov.uk/ukgwa/20171123123302/http://www.iraqinquiry.org.uk/the-evidence/witness-transcripts/>

Jackson, General Sir Mike, 28 July, 2010, <https://webarchive.nationalarchives.gov.uk/ukgwa/20160512093902/http://www.iraqinquiry.org.uk/transcripts/oralevidence-bydate/100728.aspx#pm>

Reid, Dr John, 3 February, 2010, <https://webarchive.nationalarchives.gov.uk/ukgwa/20171123123054/http://www.iraqinquiry.org.uk/the-evidence/witnesses/r/rt-hon-dr-john-reid/>

Reith, General Sir John, 15 January, 2010, <https://webarchive.nationalarchives.gov.uk/ukgwa/20171123123302/http://www.iraqinquiry.org.uk/the-evidence/witness-transcripts/>

Sheinwald, Sir Nigel, 16 December, 2009, <https://webarchive.nationalarchives.gov.uk/ukgwa/20140204101857/http://www.iraqinquiry.org.uk/transcripts/oralevidence-bydate/091216.aspx#pm2>

Sheriff, Lieutenant General Sir Richard, 11 January 2010, <https://webarchive.nationalarchives.gov.uk/ukgwa/20160512094010/http://www.iraqinquiry.org.uk/transcripts/oralevidence-bydate/100111.aspx>

Torpy, Air Marshal Sir Glenn, 18 January, 2011, <https://webarchive.nationalarchives.gov.uk/ukgwa/20171123123053/http://www.iraqinquiry.org.uk/the-evidence/witnesses/t/air-chief-marshal-sir-glenn-torpy/>

Walker of Aldringham, Field Marshal Lord, 1 February, 2010, <https://webarchive.nationalarchives.gov.uk/ukgwa/20160512094012/http://www.iraqinquiry.org.uk/transcripts/oralevidence-bydate/100201.aspx#pm>

Other Evidence

CDS Directive, <https://assets.publishing.service.gov.uk/media/5a7f968fe5274a2e8ab4d16a/The_Report_of_the_Iraq_Inquiry_-_Volume_VII.pdf>

Greenstock – FCO Telegram, 011657ZJan04, <https://webarchive.nationalarchives.gov.uk/ukgwa/20171123123237/http://www.iraqinquiry.org.uk//media/225184/2004-01-01-telegram-337-iraqrep-to-fco-iraq-six-final-months-of-occupation.pdf>

Hoon – Blair Letter, '2004: Managing UK Defence Capability', 12 January, 2004, <https://webarchive.nationalarchives.gov.uk/ukgwa/20170203171757/http://www.iraqinquiry.org.uk/search/?query=&searchRefine=0&fm=0&fy=0&tm=0&ty=0&da=&dr=&dc=1&ft=1&sortByDate=true&page=22>

Sawers – PS/Foreign Secretary Minute 27 November 2003, 'Deployment of the ARRC', evidence to Iraq Inquiry, <https://assets.publishing.service.gov.uk/media/5a7f968fe5274a2e8ab4d16a/The_Report_of_the_Iraq_Inquiry_-_Volume_VII.pdf>

Straw – Blair Letter, '2004: Managing UK Defence Capacity', dated 20 January, 2004, Evidence to Iraq Inquiry, <https://webarchive.nationalarchives.gov.uk/ukgwa/20171123122901/http://www.iraqinquiry.org.uk/media/212193/2004-01-20-minute-straw-to-blair-2004-managing-uk-defence-capacity.pdf>

Watkins – Manning Letter, *'Iraq: Possible Role for the ARRC'*, Evidence to Iraq Inquiry, <https://webarchive.nationalarchives.gov.uk/ukgwa/20171123123237/http://www.iraqinquiry.org.uk//media/244376/2003-04-17-letter-watkins-to-manning-iraq-possibl-e-role-for-the-arrc.pdf>

NATO documents

AWACS – NATO's Eyes in the Skies, <https://www.NATO.int/cps/en/NATOhq/topics_48904.htm#:~:text=AWACS%20surveillance%20aircraft%20played%20an,take%20place%20across%20the%20Alliance>

Founding Treaty of the North Atlantic Treaty Organisation (NATO), <https://www.NATO.int/cps/en/NATOhq/topics_67656.htm#:~:text=The%20foundations%20of%20the%20North,Atlantic%20Treaty%20Organization%20%E2%80%93%20or%20NAT>

Jaap De Hoop Scheffer, NATO Secretary General, joint press conference with Hamid Karzai, 11 May, 2005, <https://www.NATO.int/cps/en/NATOhq/opinions_21766.htm?selectedLocale=en>

Jens Stoltenberg, Secretary General, NATO, Speech at Riga, 30 November, 2021, <https://www.NATO.int/cps/en/NATOhq/opinions_189089.htm?selectedLocale=en>

Lord Robertson, Secretary General of NATO, NATO HQ Press Conference transcript, dated 6 June, 2002, <https://www.nato.int/docu/speech/2002/s020606f.htm>.

Lord Robertson, Opening Statement at Informal North Atlantic Council Defence Ministers Meeting, Warsaw, 24 September, 2002, <https://www.nato.int/cps/en/natohq/opinions_19723.htm?selectedLocale=en>

Lord Robertson, speech, NATO Summit, Prague, 20 November, 2002, <https://www.NATO.int/docu/speech/2002/s021120a.htm>

NATO's Assistance to Iraq, <https://www.NATO.int/cps/en/NATOhq/topics_51978.htm?selectedLocale=en>

NATO Istanbul Summit Communique, 28 June, 2004, <https://www.nato.int/cps/en/natohq/official_texts_21026.htm?selectedLocale=en>

NATO, 'SACEUR Operational Plan for the International Security Assistance Force (ISAF) in Afghanistan (unclassified version)', OPLAN 10302 (Revise 1), Secretary General, North Atlantic Treaty Organisation, 8 December, 2005.

NATO Secretary General Addresses Parliamentary Assembly, 26 May 2003, <https://www.NATO.int/docu/speech/2003/index.html>

NATO Support to Turkey – Background and Timeline, <https://www.NATO.int/cps/en/NATOhq/topics_92555.htm>

The NATO Alliance's Strategic Concept (1999), <https://www.NATO.int/cps/en/NATOhq/official_texts_27433.htm>

Transcript of Press Conference with Pres Vaclav Havel and President George W Bush, NATO Summit, Prague, 20 November, 2002. <https://www.nato.int/cps/en/natolive/opinions_19684.htm>

Other Sources

Armed Forces Covenant, https://www.armedforcescovenant.gov.uk/about-the-covenant/, accessed 12 March, 2024.

Armed Forces Covenant and Veterans Annual Report 2023, MOD and OVA, presented to Parliament pursuant to Section 343A of the Armed Forces Act 2006 (amended), <https://www.gov.uk/government/publications/armed-forces-covenant-and-veterans-annual-report-2023>.

Armour, Professor Cherie et al, 'Hitting The Wall: The impact of barriers to care and cumulative trauma exposure on PTSD among Northern Ireland Veterans', *Journal of Military Veteran and Family Health*, <https://jmvfh.utpjournals.press/action/showCitFormats?doi=10.3138%2Fjmvfh-2022-0078>

Armour, Professor Cherie et al, 'Supporting and Serving Military Veterans in Northern Ireland, Northern Ireland Veterans' Health and Wellbeing Study, Forces in Mind Trust, <https://www.fim-trust.org/wp-content/uploads/supporting-serving-military-veterans-northern-ireland.pdf>

Army, Land Forces Standing Order 3209, Post Operational Stress Management (second revise), dated June, 2011, <https://assets.publishing.service.gov.uk/media/5a80cb4740f0b62305b8d2f0/20150612-LFSO_3209_V2_Jun_11.pdf>.

Ashcroft, Lord, 'Veterans' Transition Review, Third Follow-up Report, Perceptions of service leavers and veterans', October 2017, <https://www.veteranstransition.co.uk/wp-content/uploads/2024/02/vtr3_followup_2017.pdf>

Bush, President George W., Speech to EU Leaders, Brussels, 22 February, 2005, <https://georgewbush-whitehouse.archives.gov/news/releases/2005/02/20050222-8.html>

Butler Review, <https://www.butlerreview.org.uk/report/report.pdf>

CIA Assessment, The National Security Archive, Volume I: Terrorism and US Policy, <https://nsarchive2.gwu.edu/NSAEBB/NSAEBB55/index1.html#I>

Clark, Professor Michael, former Director General of RUSI, *Afghanistan and the UK's Illusion of Strategy*, <https://rusi.org/explore-our-research/publications/commentary/afghanistan-and-uks-illusion-strategy>

Defence, Ministry of, *British Fatalities, Operations in Iraq*, <https://www.gov.uk/government/fields-of-operation/Iraq>

Defence, Ministry of, Statistics, 'UK Armed Forces Mental Health: Annual Summary & Trends Over Time 2007-08 to 2021-22', 23 June, 2022, https://assets.publishing.service.gov.uk/media/62b03e138fa8f5357984239b/MH_Annual_Report_2021-22.pdf

Eida, Captain Alex, Death of, <https://www.gov.uk/government/fatalities/captain-alex-eida-2nd-lieutenant-ralph-johnson-and-lance-corporal-ross-nicholls-killed-in-afghanistan#:~:text=The%20soldiers%20were%20killed%20following,grenades%20and%20heavy%20machine%20guns>

FBI archive, <https://archives.fbi.gov/archives/news/testimony/al-qaeda-international>

Groves, Corporal Danny, Section Commander, 1 Royal Irish Regiment Mortar Platoon, Easy Company, 3 PARA Battlegroup, Musa Qal'eh, 2006. Personal Diary

Human Rights Watch, November, 1998, Volume 10, No. 7, <https://www.hrw.org/legacy/reports98/afghan/Afrepor0.htm>

Kipling, Rudyard, *The Young British Soldier,* Kipling Society, <https://www.kiplingsociety.co.uk/poem/poems_youngbrit.htm>

Labour Party Election Manifesto 1997, <http://www.labour-party.org.uk/manifestos/1997/1997-labour-manifesto.shtml>

Mental Health Foundation, 'Tackling the root causes of poor mental health', <https://www.mentalhealth.org.uk/explore-mental-health/publications/mental-health-foundation-northern-ireland-manifesto-2022>

Modern War Institute West Point, *Lessons from the First Battle of Fallujah: An Urban Warfare Project Case Study,* <https://mwi.westpoint.edu/lessons-from-the-first-battle-of-fallujah-an-urban-warfare-project-case-study/>

National Statistics, *UK Defence Statistics 2007,* <https://webarchive.nationalarchives.gov.uk/ukgwa/20140116144924mp_/http://www.dasa.mod.uk/publications/UK-defence-statistics-compendium/2007/2007.pdf>

Obama, President Barack, Speech to Officer Cadets, West Point, 2 December, 2009, <https://edition.cnn.com/2009/POLITICS/12/01/obama.afghanistan.speech.transcript/index.html>

Omar, Mohammad, CIA biography, National Security Archive, <https://nsarchive2.gwu.edu/NSAEBB/NSAEBB55/ciaomar.pdf>

Phinney, Major Todd, USAF, *Operation Infinite Reach – Airpower versus Terrorism,* Air University Press, 2007, <https://media.defense.gov/2017/Dec/27/2001861438/-1/-1/0/T_0009_PHINNEY_AIRPOWER_VERSUS_TERRORISM.PDF>

Report of the Independent Review of UK Government Welfare Services for Veterans, 17 July, 2023, <https://www.gov.uk/government/publications/the-independent-review-of-uk-government-welfare-services-for-veterans>

Report of Standing Committee on National Defence, *Canadian Forces in Afghanistan,* June, 2007, <https://www.ourcommons.ca/Content/Committee/391/NDDN/Reports/RP3034719/nddnrp01/nddnrp01-e.pdf>

Rice, Condoleezza, Secretary of State, National Commission on Terrorist Attacks Upon The United States, Ninth Public Hearing, 8 April, 2004, <https://www.9-11commission.gov/archive/hearing9/9-11Commission_Hearing_2004-04-08.htm>

Terrorism Threat Levels, The Security Service (MI5), <https://www.mi5.gov.uk/threats-and-advice/terrorism-threat-levels#:~:text=Current%20Northern%20Ireland%2Drelated%20Terrorism,related%20terrorism%20in%20Northern%20Ireland>

The Joint UK Plan for Helmand: Final Report (redacted) pdf, dated 12 December, 2005, provided to the author by the Foreign, Commonwealth and Development Office on 12 January, 2024 in response to an FOI Act Request.

The US Army in the Iraq War – Vol 1: Invasion-Insurgency-Civil War, <https://apps.dtic.mil/sti/pdfs/AD1066345.pdf>

UK PTSD, Definition of Post-Traumatic Stress Disorder, <https://www.ptsduk.org/what-is-ptsd/causes-of-ptsd/>

US Embassy, Kabul to State Department, Telegram 001284, subject: PRT/Lashkar Gah – UK Officials Discuss Transition with Provincial Council and Mullahs' Council, dated 24 March, 2006, <https://wikileaks.jcvignoli.com/cable_06KABUL1284?hl=Gordon%20Messenger>

UNODC, *Afghanistan Opium Survey, 2003*, <https://www.unodc.org/documents/crop-monitoring/Afghanistan/Afghanistan_survey_2003_full_report.pdf>

UN Security Council Resolution 1386, 20 December, 2001, <https://documents-dds-ny.un.org/doc/UNDOC/GEN/N01/708/55/PDF/N0170855.pdf?OpenElement>

UN Security Council Resolution 1510, dated 13 October, 2003, <http://unscr.com/en/resolutions/doc/1510>

US State Department – US Embassy, Islamabad, Telegram, 23 August, 1998, National Security Archive, George Washington University, <https://nsarchive2.gwu.edu/NSAEBB/NSAEBB134/Doc%202.pdf>.

Who's Who in Afghanistan, <https://www.afghan-bios.info/index.php?option=com_afghanbios&id=1298&task=view&total=3195&start=2127&Itemid=2>

World Bank, *GDP per capita – Afghanistan*, <https://data.worldbank.org/indicator/NY.GDP.PCAP.CD?end=2021&locations=AF&start=1994>

Interviews conducted and/or individuals consulted by the Author

Armstrong, Ranger Ricky, Somme Platoon, 1st Battalion, Royal Irish Regiment
Armour, Professor Cherie, Psychological Trauma and Mental Health in the School of Psychology at Queens University Belfast
Bowen, Desmond, former Policy Director, UK MOD
Butler, Brigadier Ed, former Commander, Task Force Helmand and UK National Component Commander, Afghanistan, 2006, 16 March, 2023
Brangan, Sergeant P J, Platoon Sergeant, Somme Platoon, 1st Battalion, Royal Irish Regiment
Donaldson, Michael, Mental Health Therapist, Inspire Wellbeing, Belfast
Douglas, Colonel (Retd) Stewart, Deputy Commander, 16 Air Assault Brigade, Helmand, 2006
Freakley, Lieutenant General Benjamin, US Army (Retd), former Commanding General, Task Force 76, Afghanistan, 2006
Fry, Lieutenant General Sir Rob, former Deputy Chief of Defence Staff (Commitments), Ministry of Defence
Gilchrist, Sergeant Stephen, Platoon Sergeant, Barrosa Platoon, 1st Battalion, Royal Irish Regiment
Groves, Corporal Danny, Mortar Section Commander, Somme Platoon, 1st Battalion, Royal Irish Regiment, 2006

Hammond, Colonel (Retd) David, former Commanding Officer, 7th (Parachute) Regiment, Royal Horse Artillery
Harding, Corporal John, Mortar Fire Controller, 1st Battalion, Royal Irish Regiment
Hart, Lieutenant Colonel (Retd) Andy, Regimental Secretary, Royal Irish Regiment
Howard, Martin, former Director General Operational Policy, UK MOD
Johannesen, A/Major (Retd) Lars Ulslev, Officer Commanding, 1st Light Reconnaissance Squadron, Danish Guards Hussars
Johnston, Ranger Paul, Barrosa Platoon, 1st Battalion, Royal Irish Regiment.
Kinahan, Mr Danny, former Veterans' Commissioner for Northern Ireland.
Laity, Mark, former NATO Spokesman, Afghanistan.
Martin, Lieutenant (now Lieutenant Colonel) Paul, Platoon Commander, Barrosa Platoon, 1st Battalion, Royal Irish Regiment.
Messenger, General Sir Gordon, former Vice Chief of the Defence Staff, Ministry of Defence and previously Head of Preliminary Operations for Op Herrick, 2005/06.
McGovern, Brigadier (Retd) Michael, former Commanding Officer, 1st Battalion, The Royal Irish Regiment.
Pepper, Ranger David, Barrosa Platoon, 1st Battalion, Royal Irish Regiment
Tweed, Corporal Cliff, Section Commander, Somme Platoon, 1st Battalion, Royal Irish Regiment
Walker of Aldringham, Field Marshal Lord, Chief of Defence Staff, 2004 – 2006.
Wilkinson, Colonel (Retd) Gary, Battery Commander, I Battery (Bull's Tp), 7th (Parachute) Regiment, Royal Horse Artillery, 2006.

In addition, the author conducted interviews with a number of individuals who wished to remain anonymous for various reasons.

Index

PEOPLE

Abizaid, General John, 44, 58
Airey, Lieutenant Pete, 159
Akhundzada, Sher Mohammad, xv, 86, 87, 88, 99, 105
Al Marashi, Ibrahim, 40
Al-Zarqawi, Abu Musab, 42
Aldred, Margaret, 75
Albone, Tim, 101
Amiery, Dawood, 109
Anderton, Bombardier Ray, 183
Armour, Professor Cherie, 239, 240, 241, 242, 243, 244, 246, 247
Armstrong, Ranger Ricky, xvii, 136, 139, 171, 172, 173, 227, 233, 234, 235, 236, 237

Bartlett, Sergeant Paul, 106, 110
Beadle, Nick, 67
Benson, Ranger, 193
Bin Laden, Osama, 23, 122, 123, 124
Blair, Major Paul 'Paddy", 107, 108, 203, 149, 155, 203
Blair, Tony, xviii, xix, 23, 24, 25, 26, 27, 29, 30, 31, 33, 37, 38, 39, 40, 41, 43, 44, 45, 46, 47, 49, 50, 51, 52, 53, 54, 55, 56, 57, 58, 59, 61, 63, 65, 78, 80, 81, 94, 95, 112, 147, 150, 154, 239, 241
Bowen, Desmond, 59, 63, 66, 88, 89, 113, 115
Boyce, Admiral Sir Michael, 43, 44, 45
Brangan, Sergeant PJ, 142, 157, 158, 168, 170, 171, 173, 187, 188, 190, 191, 198, 210, 213, 215, 216, 217, 225, 234
Bremer, Paul, 42, 46
Brown, Gordon, 37, 41, 63, 80, 81
Browne, Des, 67, 68, 80, 81, 105, 109, 110, 113, 114, 115, 155
Bulimaibau, Ranger, 193
Burke, Major Sean, 149
Bush, George Jnr, xviii, xix, 25, 26, 27, 29, 32, 33, 34, 35, 36, 37, 39, 40, 41, 42, 45, 58, 124
Bush, George Snr, 28
Butler, Brigadier Ed, 73, 74, 77, 79, 80, 88, 89, 91, 92, 93, 94, 99, 100, 101, 102, 106, 110, 111, 112, 113, 114, 115, 149, 155, 160, 161, 202, 205, 206, 207, 208, 211, 213

Campbell, Alistair, 31, 40
Cheney, Dick, 29, 124
Chirac, Jacques, 25, 29, 33, 58
Clarke, Michael, 63
Clark, General Wesley, 31
Clausewitz, Carl von, vi, 69
Cleary, Private Jared, 178
Clinton, President Bill, xviii, 24, 25, 30, 31
Cook, Robin, 38, 40
Crombie, Susan, 96
Cutts, Private Andrew Barrie, 144, 168, 169

D'Alema, Massimo, 29
Dannatt, The Lord Richard, 54, 57, 59, 61, 79, 80, 81
Daoud, Engineer Muhammad, xix, 87, 89, 90, 91, 98, 99, 100, 101, 102, 106, 111, 112, 113, 114, 115, 116, 205, 206, 208
Davis, Lieutenant Col Peter, 188
De Mello, Sergio, 48
Denham, John, 38
Doherty, Col Darren, xvi
Donaldson, Michael, 244
Douglas, Col Stewarty, xvi, 202, 236, 244
Draiva, Ranger Anare, 139, 141, 144, 147, 187, 188, 189, 190, 202, 217, 232
Dunlop, Ranger Adam, v, 136

Eikenberry, Lieutenant General Karl, 93
Elliott, Major General Christopher, 80
Etherington, Mark, 78, 112

Fear, Professor Nicola, 228
Fehley, Captain Tom, 166
Felton, Lieutenant Colonel Richard, 187
Forrest, Captain Tom, 202
Fox, Dr Liam, 27
Franks, General Tommy, 43, 44, 45
Fraser, Brigadier-General David, 74, 94
Freakley, Lieutenant General Ben, 74, 76, 93, 102, 104
French, Corporal, 178, 198

INDEX

Fry, Lieutenant General Sir Rob, 38, 42, 50, 51, 55, 63, 64, 65, 66, 67, 68, 74, 79, 80, 81, 82, 114

Gilchrist, Sergeant Stephen, 137, 140, 141, 142, 158, 165, 180, 181, 185, 193, 201, 202, 213, 215, 230
Goldie, Baroness, 240, 241
Gorbachev, Mikhail, 25, 120
Greenstock, Sir Jeremy, 51
Groves, Corporal Danny, xvi, 111, 134, 135, 136, 137, 138, 139, 140, 141, 155, 157, 166, 167, 169, 170, 172, 173, 174, 177, 180, 181, 184, 186, 189, 190, 193, 197, 198, 201, 204, 205, 208, 211, 212, 215, 216

Hammond RM, Major Mark, 153, 200, 201
Harding, Corporal John, 135, 136, 155, 156, 158, 166, 167, 168, 169, 170, 171, 173, 174, 175, 183, 189, 190, 196, 202, 208, 209, 213, 214
Hart, Lieutenant Colonel Andy, xvi, 236
Hashmi, Lance Corporal Jabron, 109, 110
Hetherington, Lance Corporal Jon, 144, 147, 185, 186, 217
Hollingshead, Lt Paul, 103
Hoon, Geoff, 37, 38, 44, 45, 46, 49, 52, 53, 55, 56, 58, 61, 78
Houghton, General Sir Nick, 115, 207
Howard, Martin, 37, 58, 66, 72
Hunt of Kingsheath, The Lord, 38
Hussein, Saddam, 33, 39, 40, 52, 157

Ingram, Adam, 78, 207

Jackson, General Sir Mike, 39, 42, 50, 63, 66, 78, 79, 94, 113, 116
Jackson, Private Damien, 110
Jackson, Ranger, 193
Jenkin MP, Bernard, 50
Johannesen, Major Lars Ulslev, 160, 161, 162, 163, 164, 167, 172, 173, 175, 176
Johnson, Captain Mark, 170, 173, 202
Johnston, Ranger Paul, 141, 157, 178, 179, 180, 181, 182, 186, 187, 190, 191, 192, 193, 209, 210, 211, 213, 215, 216, 217, 225, 226, 232, 234, 244
Jones, General James, 36
Jowett, Major Adam, vii, 152, 178, 181, 183, 184, 185, 188, 191, 192, 193, 194, 196, 198, 199, 200, 201, 205, 208, 210, 211, 214

Karzai, Hamid, 35, 62, 86, 87, 88, 95, 98, 101, 111, 112, 115, 124, 128, 147, 207
Kay, Nick, 96
Keir, Corporal Hugh, 149, 178

Kavanagh, Matt, 81
Kennett, Brigadier Andrew, 78
Khan, Dad Mohammad, 99, 105, 106
Kimmitt, Brigadier Mark, 53
Kinahan, Danny, 241, 242, 247, 248
Kissinger, Henry, 34
Knaggs, Colonel Charlie, 94, 102
Kruyer, Sergeant Freddie, 178

Laity, Mark, 108, 112
Lamb, Christina, 107, 108, 109, 110
Laurie, Major General Michael, 40
Ledwidge, Frank, 82, 87

Mackay MP, Andrew, 49
Mackay, Major General Andrew, 71, 82
Major, Sir John, 25
Maley, William, 60
Manning, Sir David, 45, 46, 47
Martin, Lieutenant Paul, xvii, 138, 156, 157, 158, 165, 166, 168, 169, 178, 179, 180, 181, 184, 191, 192, 193, 196, 197, 218, 230
Matanasinga, Ranger Panapassa, 198, 199, 200, 201, 205
McClurg, Lance Corporal Rab, 135, 136, 156, 157, 166, 167, 168, 169, 170, 171, 173, 174, 175, 183, 189, 197, 209, 214, 216, 225, 226, 231, 232
McColl, General Sir John, 57, 58
McCulloch, Lance Corporal Luke, 149, 199, 201, 203, 217
McGovern, Lieutenant Colonel Michael, 149, 150, 154, 155, 156, 157, 202, 203, 226, 227, 228, 249
McKinney, Corporal Ally, 170, 171, 172, 173, 178, 202, 225, 233, 234
McNeil, General Dan, 88
Messenger, General Gordon, xvii, 74, 75, 76, 78, 82, 87, 95, 96, 126
Milosevic, Slobodan, 30
Mooney, Ranger Jason, 136, 140, 235, 237
Muirhead, Lance Corporal Paul, 138, 139, 144, 147, 187, 188, 189, 201, 202, 217

Newell, WOII Andy, 162, 163

Oakden, Edward, 51
Ocock, Major Steve, 202
Olson, Major General Eric, 77
Omar, Mullah, 86, 97, 112, 120, 121, 125, 124, 126, 127, 129
Osbourne, Ranger Ossie, 192, 209

Page, Lieutenant General Jacko, 46
Patton, Captain David, 106, 110, 144

Peach, Air Chief Marshal Sir Stuart, 72, 73
Pepper, Ranger Davy, 143, 152, 157, 158, 165, 182, 184, 190, 193, 205, 215, 217, 218, 225, 226
Phillipson, Captain Jim, 104, 105, 110
Pigott, Lieutenant General Tony, 46
Pike, Major Will, 107

Whitehouse, Ranger, 198
Whitten, Captain Dean, 196
Wight-Boycott, Major Nick, 164, 168
Wilkinson, Major Gary, 194, 195, 211

Williams, Corporal Ade, 183
Wolfowitz, Paul, 29
Wornham, Staff Sergeant Ian, 178
Worsley, Lieutenant Colonel Henry, 96
Wright, Corporal Mark, 199, 205

Yeltsin, President Boris, 25, 30

Zaeef, Abdul Salam, 120, 121
Zemin, Jiang, 25

PLACES

Afghanistan
Badghis, 62, 130
Baghlan, 61, 130
Bagram, 93
Bahram Chah, 76, 84
Balkh, xiii, 130
Camp Bastion, 75, 81, 82, 84, 88, 89, 90, 91, 92, 99, 101, 102, 103, 105, 106, 107, 110, 113, 131, 140, 143, 144, 154, 158, 160, 161, 163, 164, 165, 166, 168, 169, 172, 176, 178, 179, 180, 187, 188, 189, 193, 196, 199, 201, 202, 203, 208, 212, 214, 215, 217, 233
Chagcharan, 62, 130
Dai Kundi, xiv
Dishu, 84, 131
Farah, 62, 77, 84, 121, 130
Feyzabad, 61, 130
FOB Price, 74, 75, 100, 107, 108
FOB Robinson, 99, 100, 101, 102, 104, 106
Garmsir, 84, 155
Gereshk, 74, 81, 84, 89, 90, 91, 92, 100, 111, 113, 115, 131, 160, 165, 166, 184, 196
Ghazni, 127, 130
Ghor, 62, 84
Helmand, xvi, xviii, xix, xx, 23, 27, 37, 61, 62, 65, 66, 67, 71, 72, 73, 74, 75, 76, 77, 78, 79, 80, 82, 83, 84, 85, 86, 87, 88, 89, 90, 91, 92, 93, 94, 95, 96, 97, 98, 99, 100, 101, 102, 104, 105, 107, 108, 109, 111, 112, 114, 120, 125, 126, 127, 130, 131, 135, 140, 147, 150, 151, 153, 155, 156, 157, 158, 160, 166, 173, 175, 178, 179, 194, 195, 199, 200, 202, 203, 207, 208, 226, 227, 228, 230, 231, 232, 233, 238, 249
Herat, 62, 65, 121, 130
Kabul, vi, 35, 36, 61, 63, 65, 67, 79, 83, 86, 87, 90, 93, 96, 98, 99, 106, 108, 109, 112, 114, 119, 120, 121, 123, 124, 125, 127, 128, 130, 147, 149, 151, 158, 160, 207, 209, 218

Kandahar, 62, 63, 65, 66, 67, 77, 80, 84, 88, 93, 95, 96, 100, 102, 104, 120, 121, 122, 123, 124, 125, 127, 130, 176, 178, 188, 194, 196, 197, 200, 206, 207
Khost, 123, 127
Kunduz, 61, 130
Mazar e Sharif, 61, 119
Musa Qal'eh, i, v, vii, xvi, xvii, xviii, xix, xx, 90, 101, 102, 105, 110, 116, 131, 132, 133, 147, 148, 149, 150, 151, 153, 155, 159, 160, 162, 163, 164, 165, 172, 173, 174, 176, 178, 179, 182, 185, 196, 199, 201, 202, 203, 204, 207, 208, 217, 224, 226, 227, 229, 231, 232, 233, 234, 235, 238, 243
Nad Ali, 84
Nahr-e-Saraj, 84
Neshin, 84, 131
Nimroz, 84, 121
Now Zad, xix, 76, 84, 90, 102, 103, 110, 111, 112, 116, 131, 147, 151, 160, 164, 207
Paktia, 127, 130
Paktika, 127, 130
Panjwayi, 121, 207
Qal'eh-e-Naw, 62
Reg-e-Khan, 84, 131
Sangin, xix, 84, 90, 95, 99, 100, 102, 104, 105, 106, 107, 108, 109, 110, 111, 112, 113, 114, 116, 131, 144, 147, 149, 151, 155, 159, 160, 195, 199, 202, 203, 227
Spin Boldak, 77, 121, 127
Uruzgan, 62, 65, 66, 68, 77, 84, 89, 102, 104, 120, 127, 128, 130
Zhari, 207
Zumbelay, 107, 110

Canada, 66, 67, 74
  Ottawa, 66, 67

China, 60, 62, 130

European Mainland
Albania, 23
Belgium, 33, 61
Brussels, 25, 26, 31, 36, 66, 93, 94, 95
    Mons, 61
Bosnia-Herzegovina, 29, 35, 44, 46
Czech Republic, 33, 35
    Prague, 33, 36, 64
Denmark, 35, 160, 177
    Copenhagen, 175, 176
Federal Republic of Yugoslavia, 23
France, 24, 29, 33, 34
    Nice, 61
    Paris, 26, 29, 33
Germany, vi, 24, 29, 33, 34, 59, 156, 158
    Berlin, 26, 28, 33
    Rheindahlen, 59
Hungary, 35
Italy, 24, 29, 35
Kosovo, xiv, 24, 25, 26, 29, 30, 31, 44, 46, 50, 154, 155, 175, 185, 190
    Pristina, 31
Latvia, 29
    Riga, 29
Macedonia, 30, 157
Netherlands, 61, 66, 93
    Brunssum, 61, 93
    The Hague, 66
Poland, 35
Portugal, 35
Serbia, 23
Spain, 35

Iraq, vi, xvii, xix, 26, 27, 33, 34, 35, 36, 37, 38, 39, 40, 41, 42, 43, 44, 45, 47, 48, 50, 51, 52, 53, 54, 55, 56, 57, 58, 59, 60, 61, 62, 63, 71, 75, 78, 79, 80, 81, 82, 89, 91, 129, 147, 154, 155, 156, 157, 158, 174, 175, 185, 222, 226, 228, 238, 239, 242, 244
Abu Al Kasib, 75
Al Amarah, 48, 56, 156
Al Faw, 75
Al Muthanna, 47
Ali Al Sharqi, 48
Baghdad, 41, 42, 43, 45, 46, 48, 52, 53, 154, 156, 157
Basra, xix, 26, 43, 46, 47, 48, 49, 53, 154, 156, 157
Dhi Qar, 47
Fallujah, 51, 52, 53, 54
Karbala, 53
Kut, 53
Majar al-Kabir, 43, 44
Maysan, 43, 47, 48

Najaf, 48, 53, 54, 55
Qadisiyah, 54, 55
Ramadi, 52
Tikrit, 52

Iran, 42, 44, 62, 85, 96, 121, 130

Jamaica, vi, 156, 157, 158
    Port Antonio, 156

Pakistan, 62, 76, 84, 96, 111, 121, 123, 124, 125, 126, 127, 172, 174
    Baluchistan, 65, 84
    Quetta, 73, 127
    Waziristan, 65

Russia/Soviet Union, 28, 29, 30, 33, 60, 119, 120, 121

Saudi Arabia, 122

Sierra Leone, xix, 26, 44, 154, 155, 185

United Kingdom
Ayr, 28
Belfast, 172, 185, 189, 235, 237, 239, 243
Birmingham, 172, 225, 234
Colchester, 88, 218
Coleraine, 106, 235, 237
Enniskillen, 246
Epsom, 172
Fort George, 23, 156, 202, 225, 226, 229, 235
Holywood, 246
Inverness, 23, 202, 225, 234, 235
Lisburn, 2, 156
London, xix, 27, 38, 46, 47, 51, 57, 66, 74, 75, 93, 95, 108, 114, 149, 228, 231
Londonderry, 106, 243
Lydd Camp, 158
Omagh, 243
PJHQ Northwood, 39, 43, 46, 71, 72, 74, 75, 76, 77, 78, 79, 80, 81, 82, 89, 91, 92, 93, 99, 100, 106, 113, 114, 115, 116, 202, 207, 266
Portadown, 246
Queen Elizabeth Medical Centre, 172, 225
Royal Wooten Bassett, 206
Stansted, 218
Stormont, 239, 240, 241, 242, 247, 248
Turnberry, 28
Wales, 79, 84, 185, 238, 239, 240, 241
Westminster, 247, 248
Whitehall, 27, 39, 54, 63, 73, 76, 80, 88, 93, 100, 105, 107, 113, 114, 240

United States
Chicago, 24, 30
Manhattan, 23
New York, 25, 27, 35, 36
Pentagon, xviii, 26, 29, 35, 42, 54
Tampa, 93
Washington DC, xviii, 24, 28, 29, 30, 31, 33, 34, 35, 37, 53, 59, 88, 123

FORMATIONS/UNITS

16 Air Assault Brigade, vi, vii, xix, 27, 46, 74, 75, 78, 82, 86, 88, 89, 91, 93, 95, 99, 104, 149, 150, 154, 159, 204, 216
Pathfinders, 101, 159, 160, 161, 162, 163, 164, 165, 168, 169
1st (US) Marine Division, 53
173rd (US) Airborne Brigade, 74
22nd Special Air Service Regiment (22SAS), 74
23rd Special Air Service Regiment (23 SAS), 75
3rd Commando Brigade, 75, 109, 150, 204, 216, 217
5th Special Forces Group Operational Detachment Alpha, 74
74th Long Range Surveillance Detachment, 74
ANA, 65, 99, 100, 101, 102, 104, 116, 128, 207
ANP, 101, 106, 116, 151, 152, 159, 161, 177, 181, 198
Anti-Coalition Militia (ACM), 77, 194, 195
ARRC, 45, 47, 50, 51, 52, 53, 54, 55, 56, 57, 58, 59, 60, 62, 63, 66, 71, 79
CJFLCC, 57
CJTF7, 45, 47, 50, 53, 55
CJTF76, 93, 104
Combined Security Transition Command – Afghanistan (CSTC-A), 93
Danish Guards Hussars 1st Light Reconnaissance Squadron, 160
Defence Intelligence Service (DIS), 73
Defence Medical Services, 224
Gurkha Company, 102
Household Cavalry Regiment (HCR), 82, 163, 164, 165, 166
Intelligence Corps, xix, 109, 178
Jaish al Mahdi (JAM), 42
JFC Brunssum, 93
JFHQ, 75
Light Infantry, 2nd Battalion, 49
Medical Evacuation Response Team (MERT), 165, 172, 187, 188, 189, 193, 199, 201
MI5, 243
MI6, 73, 87, 88, 97
MNC-I, 57
MND(CS), 53, 55, 57
MND(SE), 47, 53, 54, 55, 56, 57, 154

MNF-I, 57
Operational Mentoring and Liaison Team (OMLT), 104
Parachute Regiment, vi, vii, xix, 82, 113, 149, 150, 152, 154, 155, 159, 178, 203, 207, 218
Provincial Reconstruction Team (PRT), 61, 62, 67, 74, 75, 76, 81, 87, 90, 92, 96, 100, 110
Regional Command (South) (RC(S)), 74, 91, 93
Royal Air Force, 61, 79, 82, 154, 158, 206, 217
  27 Squadron, 82
  RAF Regiment, xix, 183
Royal Army Medical Corps, 178
  16th Close Support Medical Regiment, 82
Royal Artillery, xix
  7th (Parachute) Royal Horse Artillery, 82, 102, 104, 164, 167, 174, 183, 193, 195
  I Battery (Bull's Troop), 159, 183, 191, 195, 206
  G Troop, 159
  32 Regiment, 82
  18 Battery, 104
Royal Corps of Signals, xix, 144, 185
Royal Electrical and Mechanical Engineers, 7 Battalion, 82
Royal Fusiliers, 177
Royal Green Jacket, 1st Battalion, 49
Royal Irish Regiment, vi, vii, xvi, xviii, xix, 23, 83, 107, 109, 136, 144, 147, 148, 149, 154, 155, 156, 163, 185, 196, 199, 202, 217, 223, 238, 248, 249
Royal Logistics Corps, 144, 168
  13 Air Assault Regiment, 82
  29 Regiment, 82
Royal Miliary Police, 43, 48
Royal Navy, 76
Special Boat Service (SBS), 106
Special Reconnaissance Regiment (SRR), 106, 144
Task Force 333, 87
Task Force Helmand (TFH), 90, 93, 94, 99, 100, 102, 194, 200, 208
UDR/Royal Irish (Home Service) Battalions, 238, 239, 246
US Central Command (CENTCOM), 44, 45, 54, 58, 93
US Fifth Corps (V Corps), 57

ORGANISATIONS

Al Qaeda (AQ), 27, 51, 63, 73, 78, 96, 122, 123, 124, 127
Al Qaeda in Iraq (AQI), 42
Blackwater Private Military Company, 52, 53
Coalition Provisional Authority (CPA), 42, 43, 46, 48, 49, 51, 54
Defence Intelligence Service (DIS), 73
Defence Medical Services, 224
International Security Assistance Force (ISAF), 35, 36, 60, 61, 62, 63, 64, 82, 93, 95, 108, 112, 115, 125, 207
Joint Intelligence Committee (JIC), 39, 51, 73
NATO, xviii, 23, 24, 27, 28, 29, 30, 31, 32, 33, 34, 35, 36, 37, 38, 45, 47, 50, 51, 52, 53, 58, 59, 61, 62, 63, 64, 65, 66, 67, 68, 71, 75, 93, 94, 95, 102, 107, 108, 112, 115, 129, 147, 160, 177, 207

North Atlantic Council (NAC), 6, 28, 31, 35, 61
   SACEUR, 31, 36, 61, 65
   Secretary General, 29, 31, 32, 48, 59, 64, 95
Northern Ireland Veterans' Support Committee (NIVSC), 246
Northern Ireland Veterans' Support Office (NIVSO), 246
Northern Ireland Veterans' Welfare Service (NIVWS), 246
Post Conflict Reconstruction Unit (PCRU). 78
Reserve Forces' and Cadets' Association, 224, 246
Stop The War Coalition, 38
United Nations (UN), 24, 28, 29, 32, 33, 35, 36, 38, 40, 47, 48, 51, 67, 119, 123, 125, 161
UN Assistance Mission Iraq (UNAMI), 48.